I0801021

SMITH+GILL

performance + assembly

the experience of space

ORO Editions
Publishers of Architecture, Art, and Design
Gordon Goff: Publisher

www.oroeditions.com
info@oroeditions.com

Published by ORO Editions

Copyright © 2024 Adrian Smith + Gordon Gill Architecture

FOLLOW ONLINE
smithgill.com
smithgill.blog
Facebook @smithgillarch
Instagram @asggarch
Twitter @smithgillarch

All rights reserved. No part of this book may be reproduced, stored in a retrieval system, or transmitted in any form or by any means, including electronic, mechanical, photocopying of microfilming, recording, or otherwise (except that copying permitted by Sections 107 and 108 of the US Copyright Law and except by reviewers for the public press) without written permission from the publisher.

You must not circulate this book in any other binding or cover and you must impose this same condition on any acquirer.

Cover image © Adrian Smith + Gordon Gill Architecture
Project Manager: Jake Anderson

10 9 8 7 6 5 4 3 2 1 First Edition

ISBN: 978-1-954081-36-9

Prepress and Print work by ORO Editions Inc.
Printed in China

ORO Editions makes a continuous effort to minimize the overall carbon footprint of its publications. As part of this goal, ORO, in association with Global ReLeaf, arranges to plant trees to replace those used in the manufacturing of the paper produced for its books. Global ReLeaf is an international campaign run by American Forests, one of the world's oldest nonprofit conservation organizations. Global ReLeaf is American Forests' education and action program that helps individuals, organizations, agencies, and corporations improve the local and global environment by planting and caring for trees.

CONTENTS

FOREWORD

PERFORMANCE + CULTURE

Andy Hayles, Managing Partner, Charcoalblue

Charcoalblue, a theater, acoustics, and digital experience design consultancy with design studios in London, Chicago, New York, San Francisco, and Melbourne, has enjoyed a number of adventures with the amazing team at Adrian Smith + Gordon Gill Architecture (AS+GG/SmithGill) over the years. Some of those adventures were formative in the growth of our own practice and many lessons have been shared and learned over the years. I remember piling into a minivan to tour UK theaters in-the-round with Gordon Gill from AS+GG and Tracey Letts and Anna Shapiro from Steppenwolf Theatre and standing on a freezing cold Navy Pier in Chicago watching theater towers being offloaded from Montreal. AS+GG has always been in the thick of it.

Performance + Assembly's glitzy renderings and confident swagger of the architectural envisioning might imply a somewhat "white glove," or "ivory tower" approach but nothing could be further from the truth. AS+GG is a team that buries into the heart of a project. They search for cultural meaning, environmental sustainability, and ethical responsibility in everything that they design. This team seeks high function for their client partners while simultaneously creating aesthetic wonder.

Steppenwolf Theatre Company is an international trailblazer for ensemble work. As a performer or artist, it is an honor to be invited to become a member. And once you have become one, you are in the ensemble for life and invited to contribute on their stages for the life of the company. Perhaps AS+GG's involvement as a supporter of Steppenwolf for many years has caused their ethos of ensemble to become part of the heart of their practice. You only have to look at the team member credits in this book to see how involved each AS+GG ensemble member has been in each project; and indeed, how the leadership team comes together for every client. AS+GG Partner Gordon Gill is "first among equals" in terms of leadership on many of these cultural projects where accountability, collaboration, leadership, and democratic participation are hallmarks of his approach.

One such project, The Yard at Chicago Shakespeare Theater, was inspired by a low-cost, 1,000 seat temporary theater that Charcoalblue designed for the Royal Shakespeare Company in the United Kingdom in 2005. Our Chicago client alighted on the idea of applying the lessons of temporary theater typology to a affordable permanent facility. Alongside Charcoalblue, AS+GG rolled their sleeves up and created tremendous value through economy and utility. They pitched the theater lobby as a testbed for innovative heat-rejection glazing, saving not only on the capital cost of installation but also reducing the cost and environmental burden of cooling the lobby for the life of the building.

While Chicago Shakespeare's journey was a cost-effective sprint, the Steppenwolf Theatre adventure was a half-marathon test of stamina, commitment, and design expertise to bring a tricky infill project in on a similarly tight budget. Collaboration with four artistic directors and three executive directors over the lifespan of the design and delivery of the project did not lead to dilution but refinement, as successive members of the Steppenwolf Ensemble collaborated and honed the design that is the true legacy vision of much-loved and missed Artistic Director, Martha Lavey.

The result, like Chicago Shakespeare's Yard, is an icon for a neighborhood and a new calling card for in-the-round production for the whole of the United States. Inspired by the Manchester Royal Exchange building in the UK – the auditorium not only wraps the actors with their audience but in turn is wrapped; cocooned even – by AS+GG's warm, inviting lobbies and education spaces. The links through to the existing theater lobbies and the collisional spaces in between creating moments for Lavey's "town-square" vision brought to life. Ten years in the making, to which every square inch is testament.

This unique pair of adventures informed our collaborations in Astana's Energy Hall and Congress Center, projects also wonderfully featured in this book, and we hope, will do so on many future adventures together. We are so proud of being collaborators and contributors to AS+GG's ensemble, so admiring of their partner engineer's ingenuity and grit in the pursuit of sustainable solutions and most of all grateful for their friendship and example to us of how to deliver a vision with modesty, drive, and sincerity. An extraordinary book by an extraordinary practice, with extraordinary leaders.

PROLOGUE

THE EXPERIENCE OF SPACE

Gordon Gill, FAIA, Parter, AS+GG

Performance and assembly structures are among some of the most complex building typologies that architects design. Theaters, museums, concert venues, churches, and conference spaces require rigorous technical requirements and specific programmatic components that are designed and assembled in precise ways.

In this book, *Performance + Assembly: The Experience of Space*, Adrian Smith + Gordon Gill Architecture (AS+GG) expands the list to incorporate structures that are less traditional, including supertall building observatories, outdoor public spaces of various types, and multi-dimensional venues. Through design research, we have found that as we introduce more types of performance and assembly spaces into traditional building typologies the overall range of cultural influence across all programs increase.

Performance + Assembly: The Experience of Space, examines how architects can help develop cultural building typologies that express their functions at a physical level, as well as the experiential and sensorial levels, layered with principles of environmental and sustainable design. The book features AS+GG's projects that explore questions related to how buildings can be used to enhance the experience of the user beyond a set of programmatic requirements. We explore how architecture and design can help advance the site, the program, the technologies, and the way cultural buildings operate.

At a sensory and experiential level, the book explores how architecture can speak to the human spirit to create a place between the art and the audience. We illustrate ways in which different projects are conceived to serve a specific set of functions; how preliminary functional requirements evolve through the design process to arrive at building solutions that are innovative and that serve the client, the public, and the profession. The projects in this book illustrate how performance and assembly buildings can do more than house an activity as a container; how they can be part of the performance itself. We explore how the building becomes the art and, through design, how the building connects the public to the art so that the building shapes itself into the subject. Through our work, which is often experimental, we aim to advance the science behind the art.

Performance + Assembly: The Experience of Space also discusses how structures can be mediators and regulators of the activities in the public realm. Connectivity, through design, allows us to expand the role of buildings to a level that generates wonder and contributes to the human experience by pushing beyond known technological boundaries, establishing architecture as a player rather than a bystander. We study the role of performance and assembly structures in public spaces and their potential to contribute to the urban experience through their relationships with the public.

The case studies within are grouped by their general use of space and then explored further through the lens of Site, Program, Form, Space, and Analysis. The content investigates ways in which architecture addresses issues other than the physical facilities including: the environment, education, public and urban space, social responsibility, emotional experiences, connectivity, and innovation, among others. This sequence ranges from conventional venues where observation and focused audience is the purpose of the buildings, to state-of-the-art facilities for learning and interaction, to avant-garde ideas and research projects that focus on immersive experiences and the use of new and emerging technologies.

We offer this book as an instrumental tool for thought and reflection on a building typology that has the potential to positively influence our communities and to expand our ideas on what Architecture can do to help improve our world.

CHAPTER 1

OBSERVE

Performance Spaces

In the 21st Century, our society places a high value on unique experiences. Theaters, operas, concert halls, and other venues seek to keep the modern audience engaged by implementing the latest practices and technologies that can elevate the performing arts and the community's experience. Functionally, adaptability, resilience, and flexibility have become key design concepts.

As performance venues are increasingly multipurpose, it is important to design them to host a range of events from different theatrical and musical performance types to community gatherings and fundraising galas; each may require a variety of configurations. Aesthetically and formally, the exterior of a performance building is important and should represent the surrounding community, as well as the character of the spaces inside.

Typologically, as places of assembly and convergence, performance venues hold a special importance to the public, therefore they must be designed to create a sense of place that is unique to each specific location. Our approach to designing performance venues allows unique opportunities for the integration of the public with the architecture in ways that other building types do not. The design should align with the locale in terms of environmental, socioeconomic, and cultural aspects. The buildings should be highly sustainable and give back to the community in both function and implementation.

Istanbul Cultural Center - Shattuck-St. Mary's School Performing Arts Hall - Astana Energy Hall - Congress Center - Willow Creek North Shore - The Yard at Chicago Shakespeare Theater - Steppenwolf Theatre Campus Expansion

ISTANBUL CULTURAL CENTER

Istanbul, Turkey

The 57,200-square-meter Istanbul Cultural Center consists of an integrated group of state-of-the-art cultural buildings that share back-of-house and public spaces. The new center allows Istanbul residents and visitors to have maximum accessibility to world-class cultural venues with an array of open and enclosed public spaces.

The project was designed as a catalyst for the district's economic development. The center reinvigorates the public square and adjacent green space, increasing land value and stimulating the property development market. Building the center would create new construction and supply chain jobs, as well as permanent employment opportunities.

The Istanbul Cultural Center seeks to restore the site of the former Atatürk Culture Center (AKM) in Taksim Square, near Gezi Park, at the center of the city. The vision replaces the former opera house, designed by architect Hayati Tabanlıoğlu in 1969. The building has been deemed a hazard for normal use after earthquake damage. The seminal building has remained vacant for years, rendering a prime area of real estate in the center of Istanbul unusable.

Function: Performing Arts Center | **Status:** Conceptual, 2015 | **Client:** Confidential | **Awards:** AIA Chicago, Unbuilt FORWARD Award, 2018; The Chicago Athenaeum, International Architecture Award, 2016; Architizer A+ Awards, Typology Categories, Cultural: Unbuilt, Special Mention, 2016; Architectural Review, MIPIM Future Project Award, Cultural Regeneration, Commendation, 2016; WAN Future Projects, Civic Award, Winner, 2015

DESIGN CONCEPT | SITE

Situated at the apex of Çamlıca Hill and fronted by Taksim Square to the west, the site is nestled between residential low-rise buildings on three sides, offering a unique opportunity for the adjacent public space. A cascading topography falling toward the Bosporus Straight enables a distinct strategy for multi-tiered architecture that maintains contextual sensitivity with the skyline, while simultaneously presenting unparalleled views of the Çatalca and Kocaeli Peninsulas.

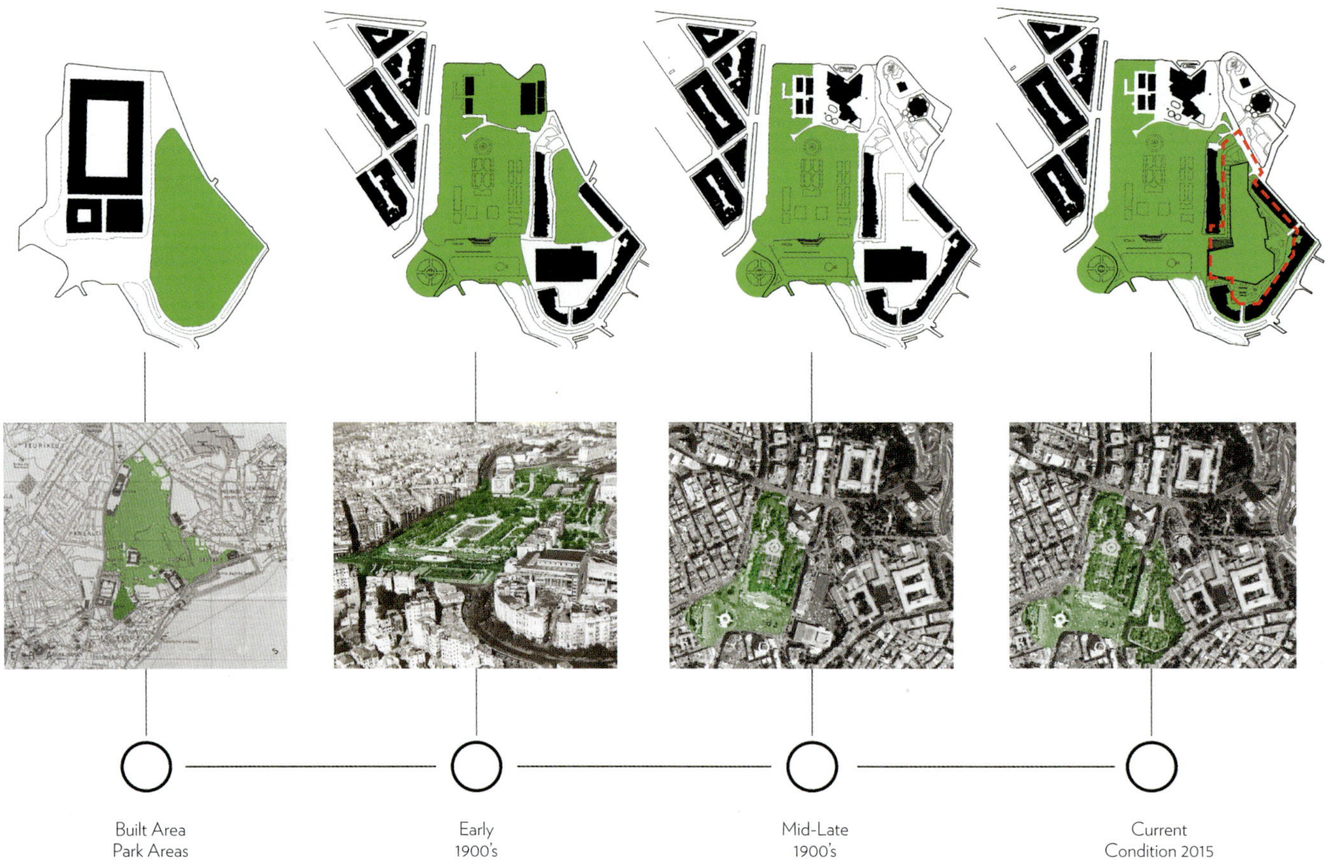

Aerial View

DESIGN CONCEPT | SITE

Taksim Square is connected to Istanbul through several public transit lines. It is an optimal location for a public venue of metropolitan and regional importance because it is easily accessible to most residents and visitors.

- 1,310,000 people access Taksim Square access rapid transit lines within 25 minutes or less.
- 1,700,000 additional people access Taksim Square access rapid transits within 35 minutes or less.

Commuter Transit

BRT
Metro
Tram
Railway
Funicular

5 Minute Walk

10 Minute Walk

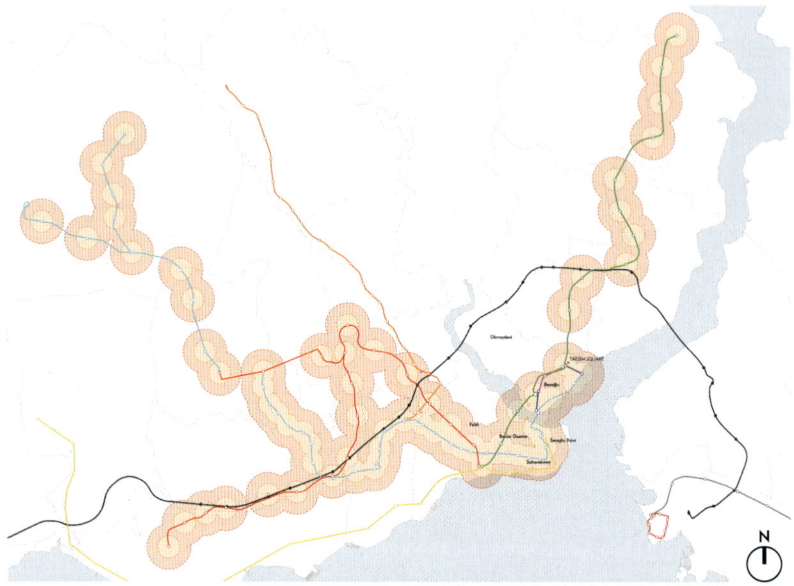

The Walk | Aerial View (Right)

DESIGN CONCEPT | SITE

The cultural center was designed as a "beacon" point for Istanbul. Spread across the pinnacle of the city, the observation tower rises from the skyline of the Beyoglu District, as seen from the Bosporus, and acts as a locator to help orientate visitors. The site's vertical circulation connects the building's ground floor lobby to the roofscape, providing an observation deck with sweeping views of the city and adding an attraction for visitors to Taksim Square.

The building folds open as Taksim Square and Gezi Park blend to reveal the front door entrance, flanked by the observation tower. The continuous facade geometry guides users inside and around the building, allowing them to actively engage in cultural events. At a height of 23-35 meters above the plaza level, viewing platforms are publicly accessible with unmatched views of the sea, Hagia Sophia, the Blue Mosque, Prince Island, and the coastline.

The site design was guided by several principles. It was important to first address the axial relationship with the plaza and the building's relationships to the adjacent park. It was also key to incorporate the plaza and the park into the cultural center's site, as well as create a focal point of city reference and an iconic presence for the plaza.

> *"The challenge of the integration of functions works well, it's imaginative, and the vision is well balanced in terms of it having civic qualities, yet it has public access. - Andrew Costa, Partner, Ryder Architecture, WAN Awards Juror, Future Project Civic Building Winner, 2015"*

Beacon Elevations

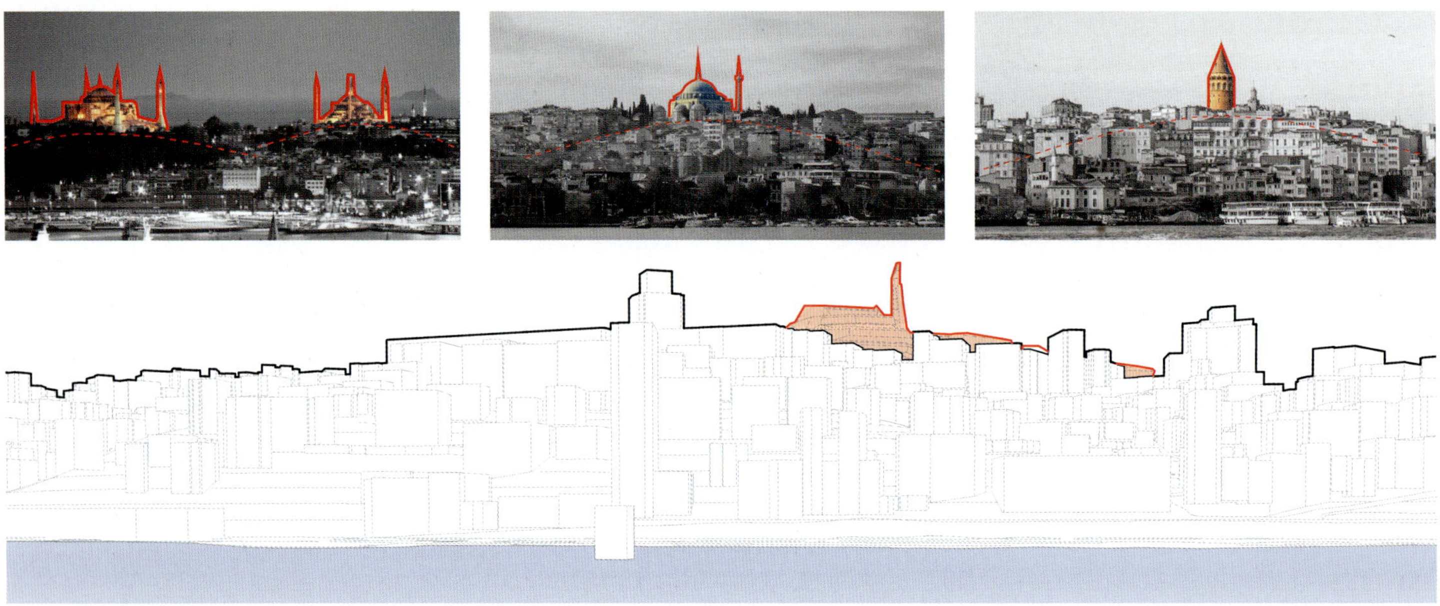

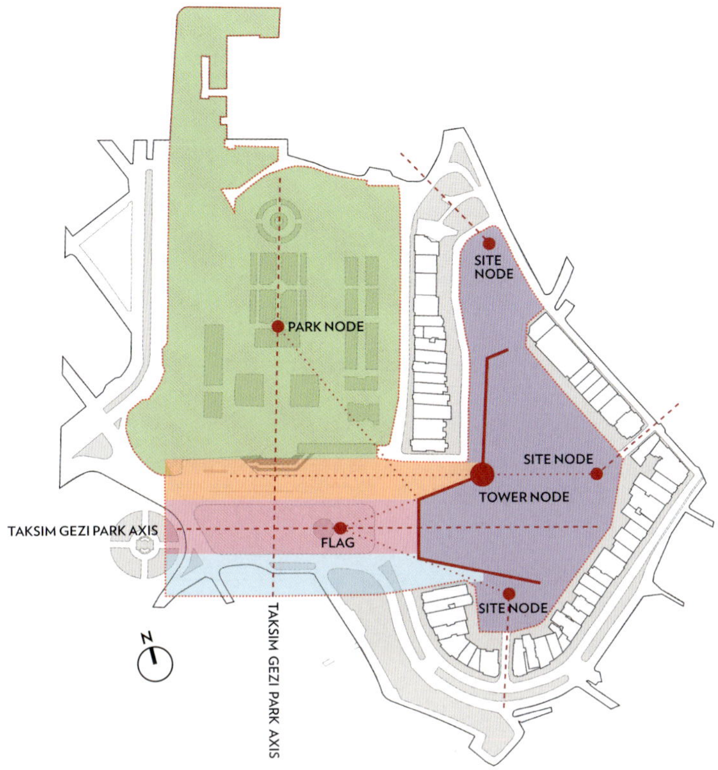

Focal Point Plans

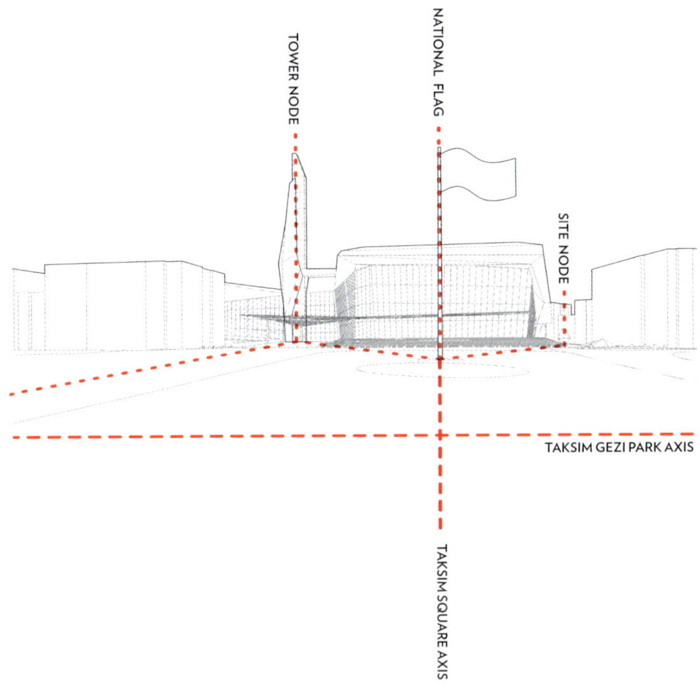

Site Conditions, 2015

DESIGN CONCEPT | SITE

Iconic Tower

- Provides a clearly identifiable marker with a vertical architectural element.
- Links the plaza and the city.
- Provides an iconic figure.
- Creates a sense of place.

Sloping Space

- Provides a roof system that doubles as a landscaped park.
- Draws people toward the building with a gentle slope.
- Provides key nodes of variety and interest.

Folding Facades

- Engages the public with a glass facade during cultural events.
- Invites and guides users inside and around the building with the facade geometry.
- Uses solid and transparent materials to provide intuitive path directions for entry points.

Public Space Studies

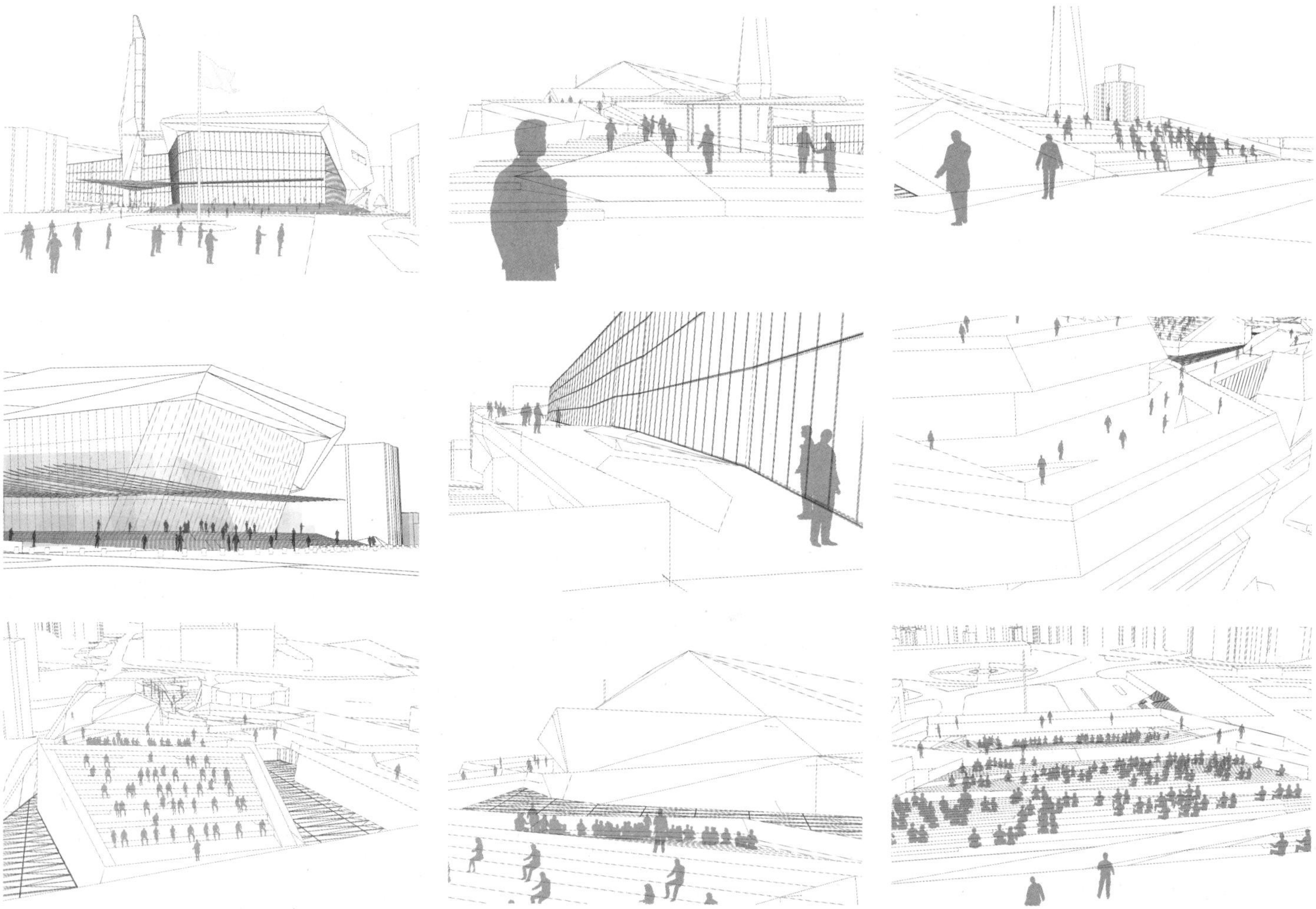

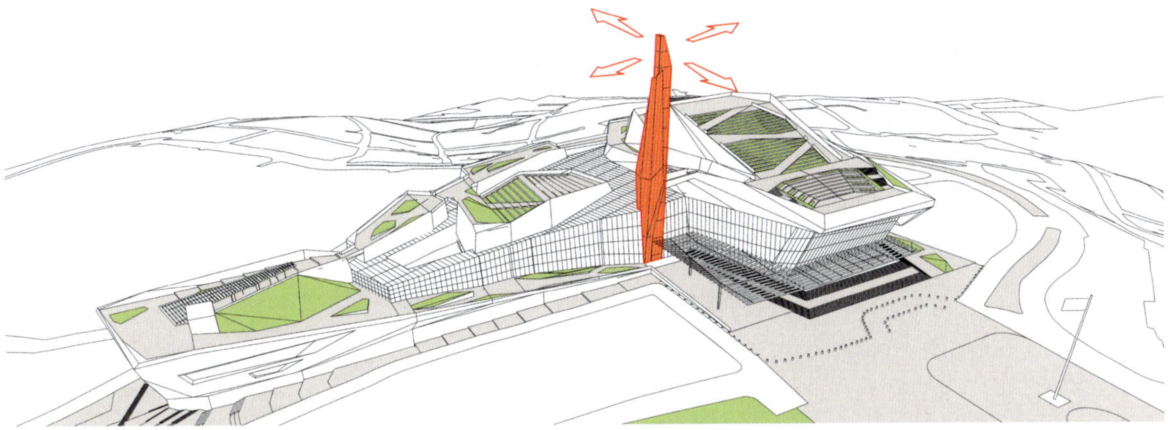

Iconic Tower

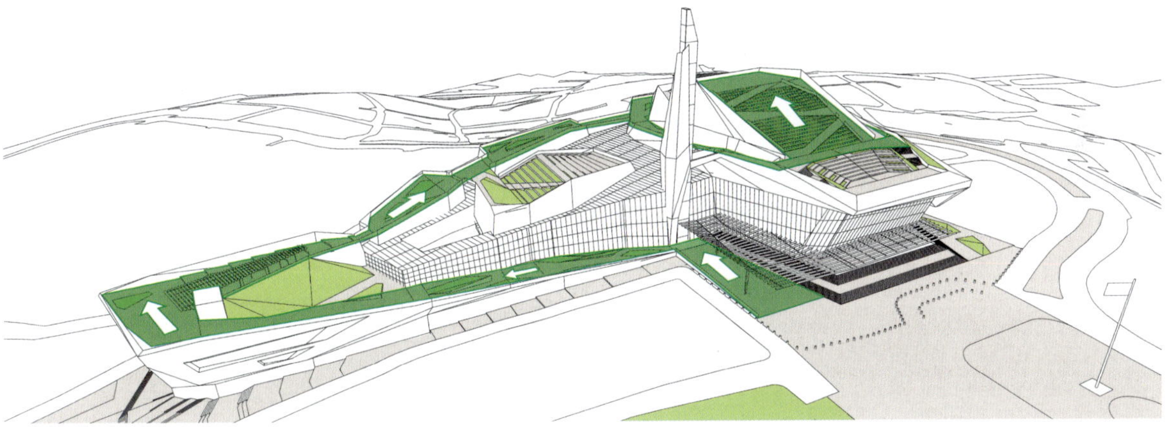

Sloping Space

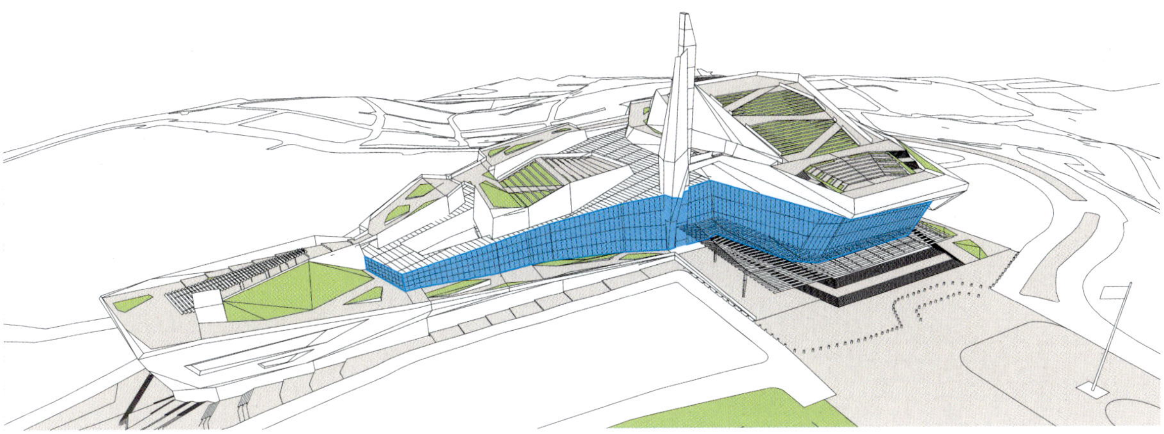

Public Domain

DESIGN CONCEPT | SITE

Current site conditions only provide views from privately accessed sections, therefore expanding the public realm was key to the client's vision of the site. By extending the park toward the inside of the block and elevating the park to meet the building, the site gives access back to the community.

100% of the current site area is being planned as publicly available space, including an additional park and plaza of approximately 27,929 square-meters. The site exceeds the existing view strategy by integrating viewing platforms and terraces into the building's design and providing amenities such as restaurants, tea houses, and cafes at high points.

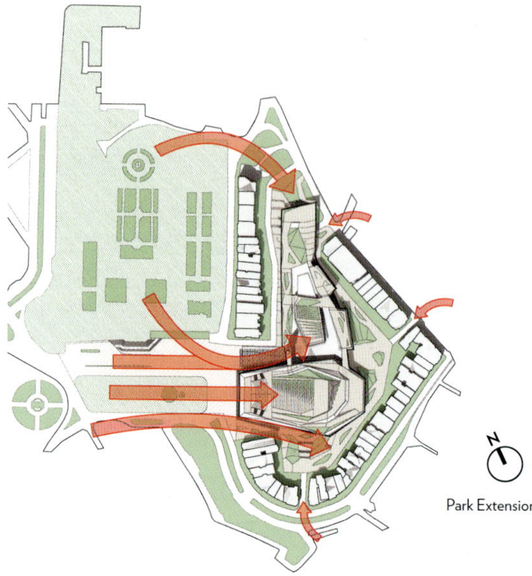

Park Extension Plan

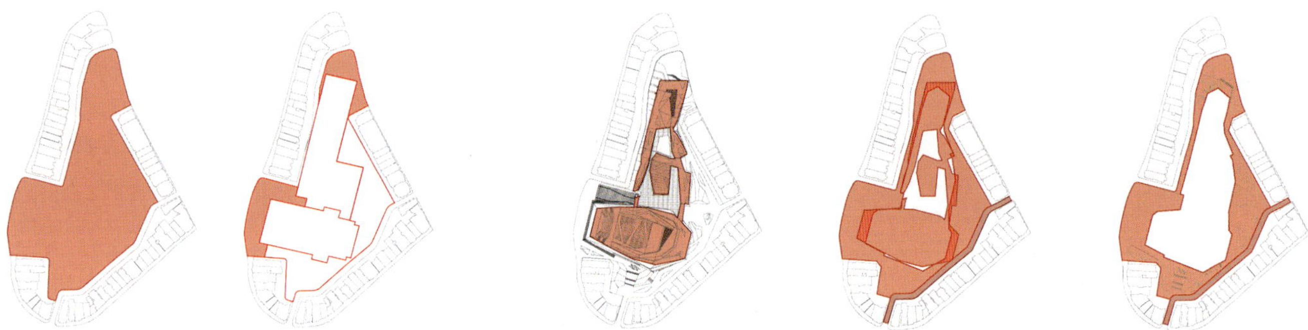

Public Space Benchmark
27,092 sm - 100%

Public Space Current
4,782 sm - 17.7%

Public Space Roofscape
Proposed 11,760 sm - 43.4%

Public Space Ground Level
Proposed 15,730 sm - 58.1%

Public Space Overall
Proposed 27,929 sm - 101.5%

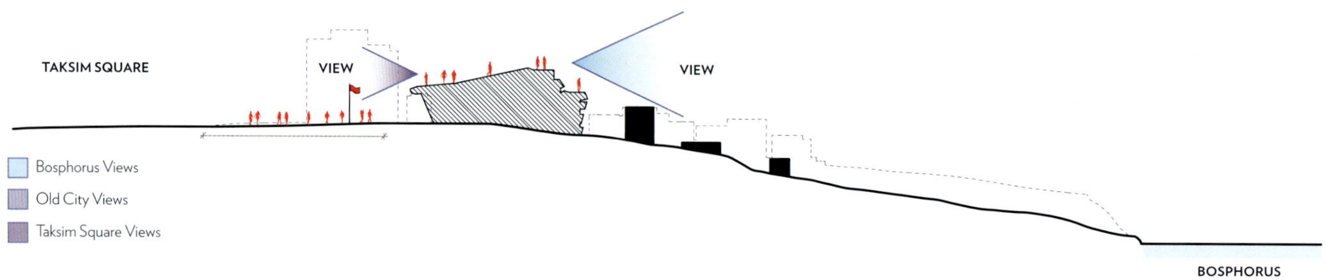

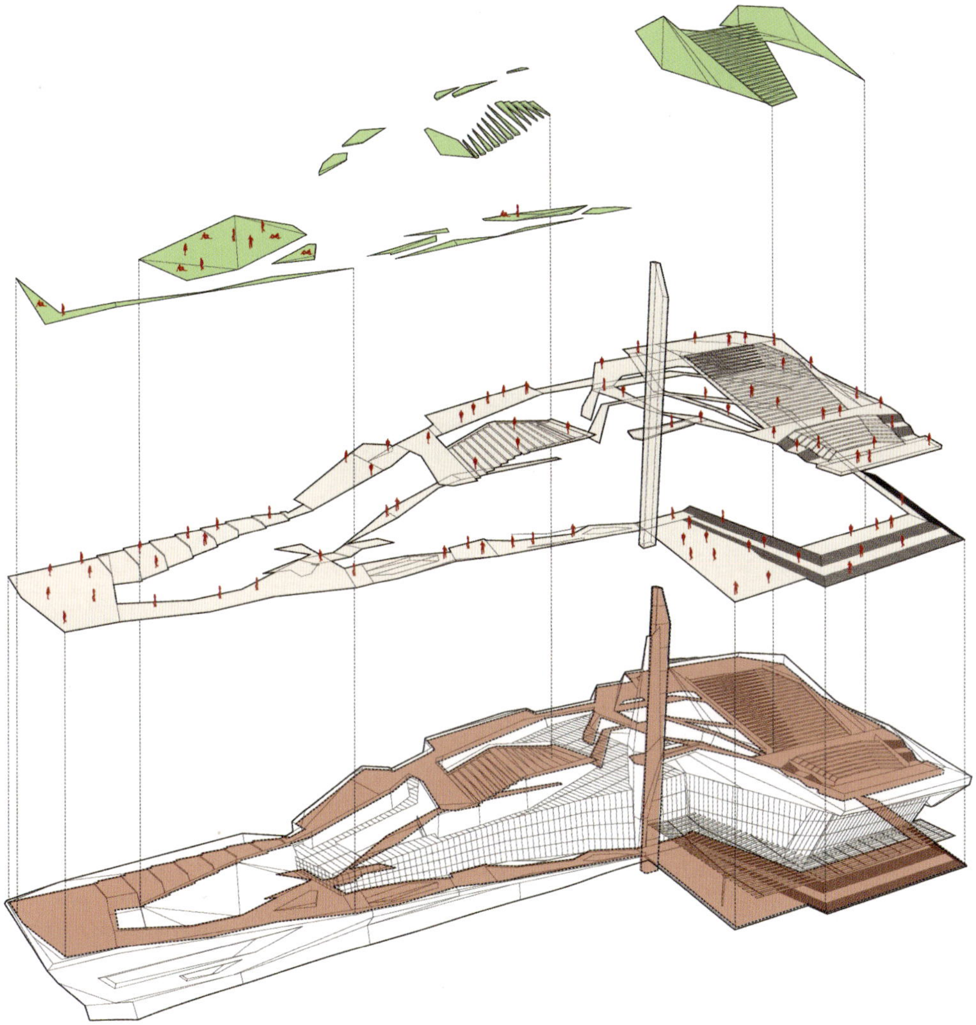

The Park

The natural component of the site contains a rich mixture of gardens, lawns, and water features.

The Plaza

The solid component of the site features places for visitors to rest, to enjoy public art, and to access the building in various locations. The observation tower serves as a connector with an all-access elevator.

Performance Venues

The four main performance spaces include the opera house with 1800 seats, a concert hall with 750 seats, a chamber theater with 220 seats, and a projection theater with 220 seats.

Interior Public Areas

Interior spaces accessible to the public include an art gallery, an informal open stage, and the pre-function areas for the main performance venues.

The Walk

This public linear park is accessible day and night. It ascends up the building, engaging visitors through a series of plazas and garden that are enhanced with public art and unmatched views.

DESIGN CONCEPT | PROGRAM

1 Grand Entry
2 Grand Stairs
3 Art Gallery/Public Square
4 Courtyard
5 Opera Pre-Function Main Floor
6 Opera Pre-Function First Balcony
7 Opera Pre-Function Second Balcony
8 Concert Hall Pre-Function
9 Cinema and Chamber Theater Pre-Function
10 Informal Performance Space
11 Opera Main Sitting Floor
12 Opera First Balcony
13 Opera Second Balcony
14 Concert Hall Main Floor
15 Concert Hall Balcony
16 Cinema
17 Chamber Theater
18 Opera Stage and Supporting Spaces
19 Retail
20 Atrium
21 Artist Studios
22 Rehearsal
23 Flex Rehearsal
24 Chorus Room
25 Admin Offices
26 Study and Changing Rooms
27 Dance Studio
28 Green Room
29 Restaurant
30 Bar
31 Back of House
32 Technical/Mechanical
33 Loading Dock
34 Warehouse
35 Storage
36 Workshops
37 Orchestra Pit
38 Orchestra Rehearsal
39 Stage Setup
40 Parking

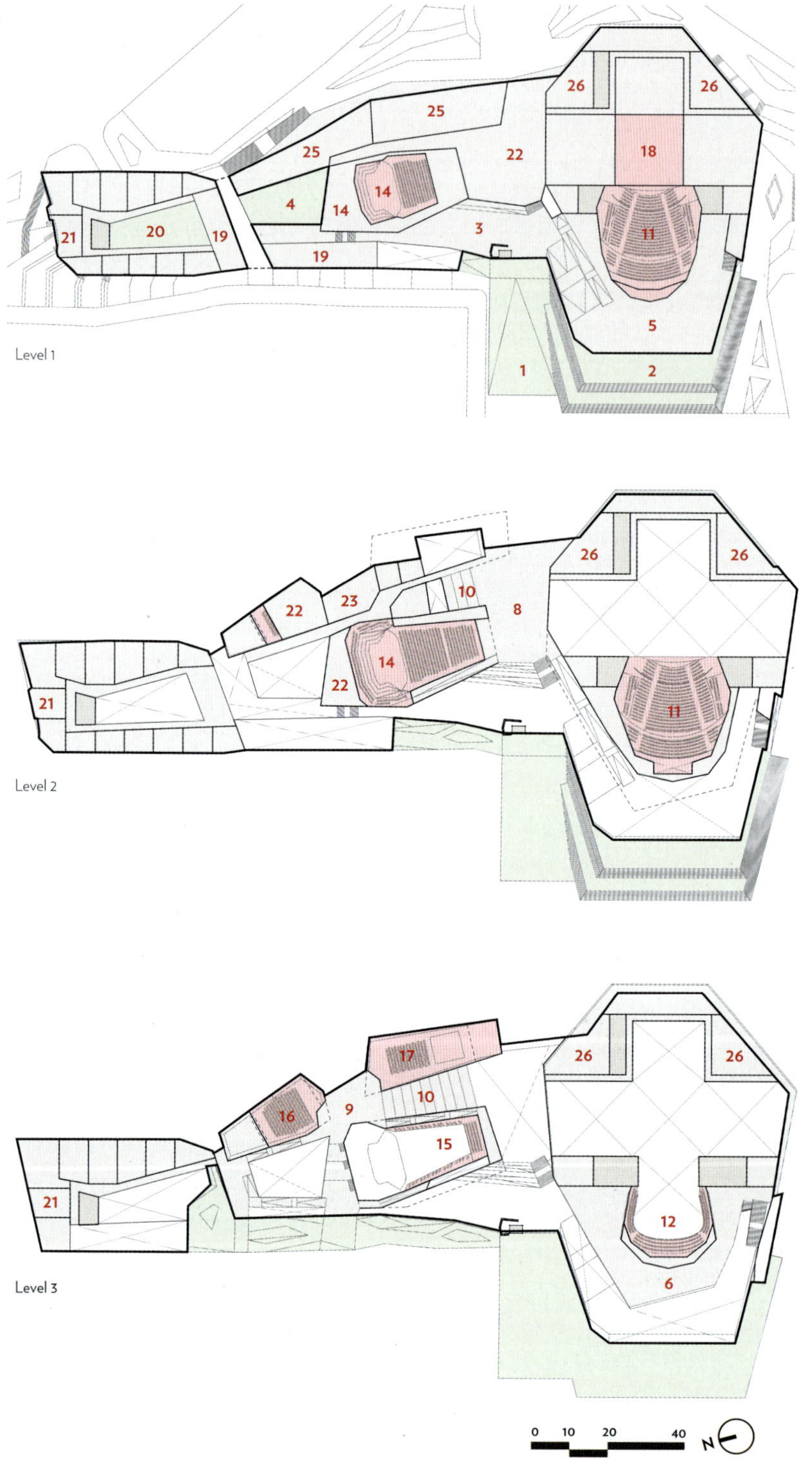

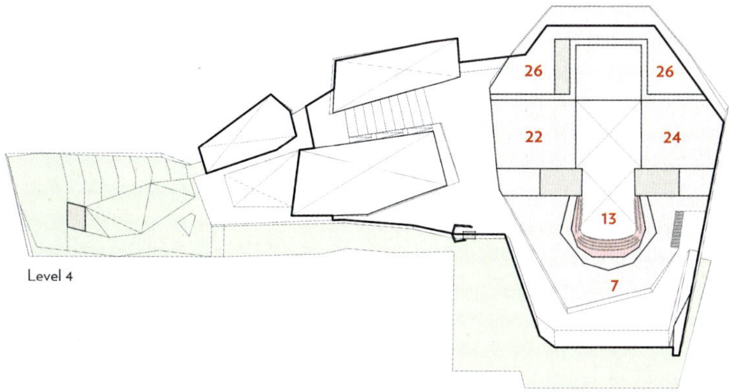

Level 4

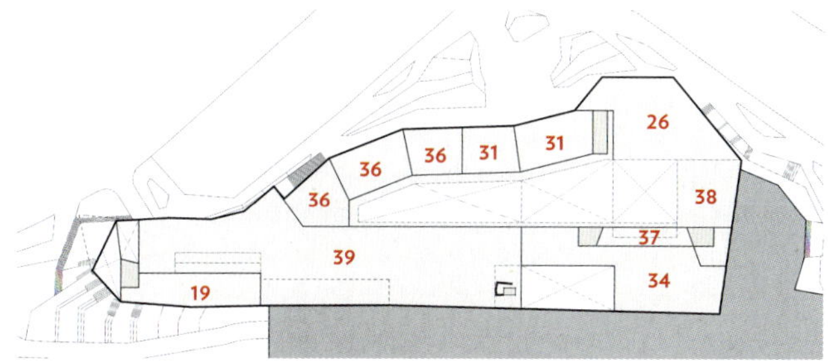

Lower Level 1

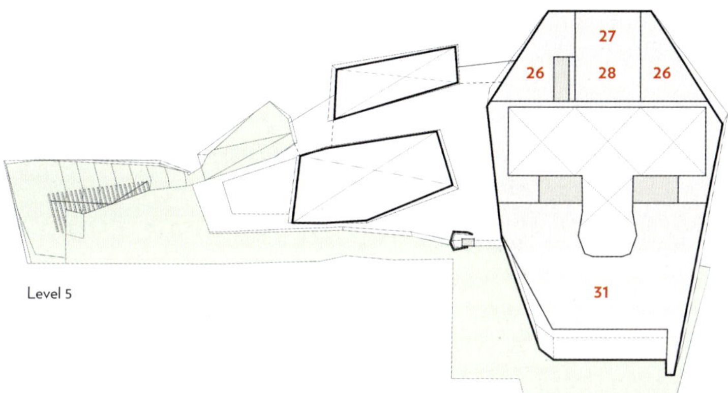

Level 5

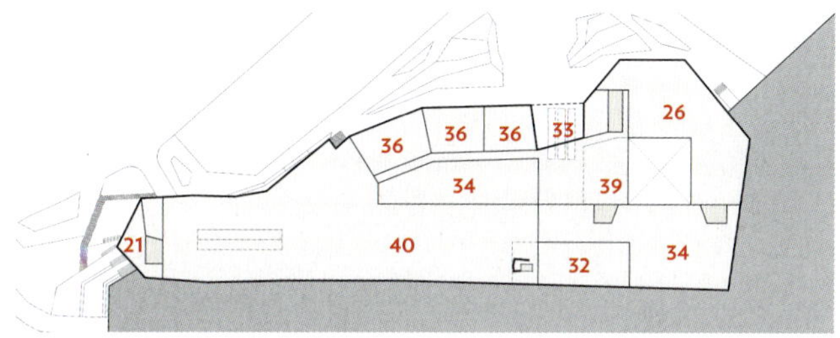

Lower Level 2

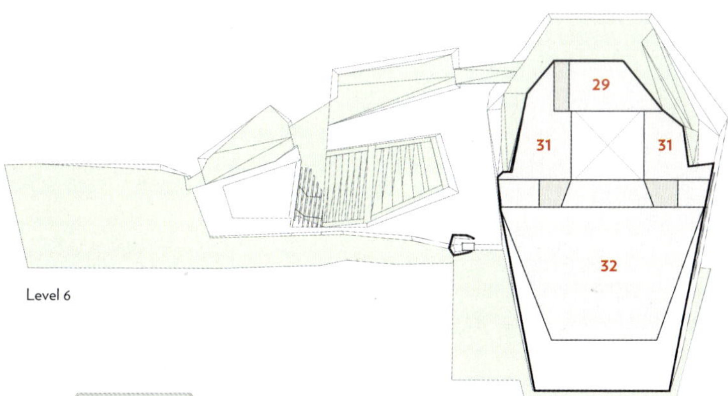

Level 6

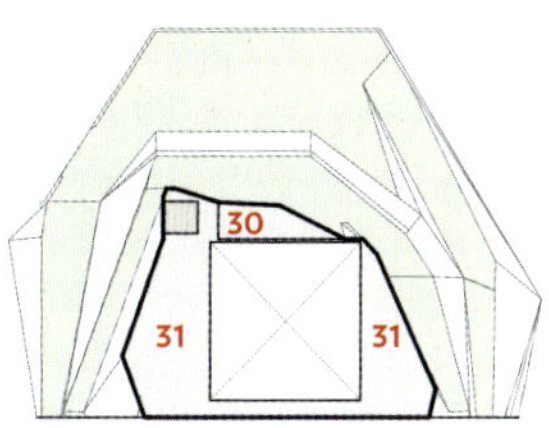

Level 7

The performance spaces program includes a 3700 sm opera hall with 1800 seats, a 1000 sm concert hall with 750 seats, a smaller 380 sm chamber theater with 220 seats, and a cinema hall that is 330 sm with 220 seats.

Prefunction spaces provide ample space for audiences to mingle before and after performances and include the 760 sm main entry lobby, 2700 sm of opera prefunction spaces over three floors, and foyers for the concert hall, chamber hall, and cinema hall cover 1700 sm over two floors. Exhibition areas include a 2000 sm art gallery.

Auxiliary and back of house spaces span several floors and include changing rooms, rehearsal spaces, dance and actors studios, workshop spaces, offices, artists dormitories, and retail spaces. Level 6 and 7 are programed for restaurant and bar functions. Below grade includes additional back of house spaces, storage areas, and parking.

DESIGN CONCEPT | FORM

The complexity of the program required a rigorous study of the adjacent properties to determine the final form. It was crucial to meet the technical requirement of the four performance venues while creating "in between" spaces for pre-function and other social activities, as well providing easy access to technical support spaces.

Multiple iterations of spaces were tested to evaluate the resulting synergies, all with the goal of attaining the broader vision of a building to be inhabited on multiple levels and with various points of access to the park/roof system.

The resulting configuration leverages the sizes of the different venues to create a sequence of volumes that gradually ascends, while aiding access and creating a rich network of semi-public areas that offer a variety of uses for the public and the flexibility needed for the building program.

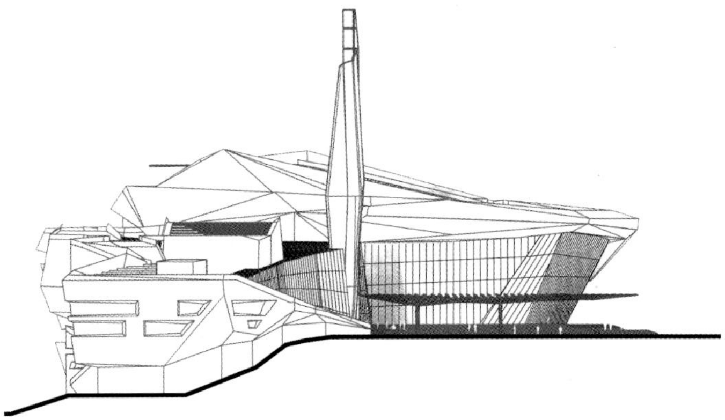

North Elevation

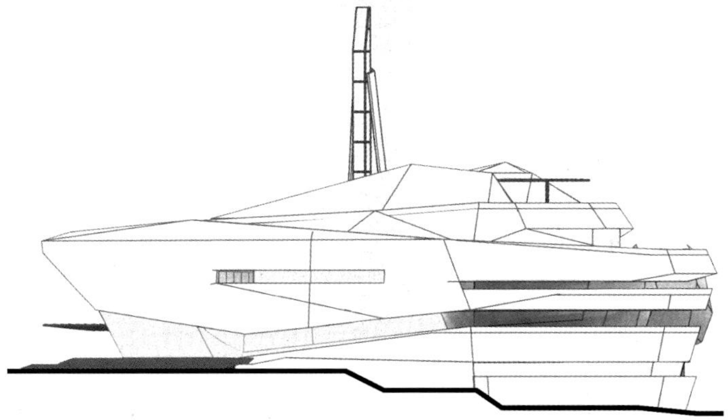

South Elevation

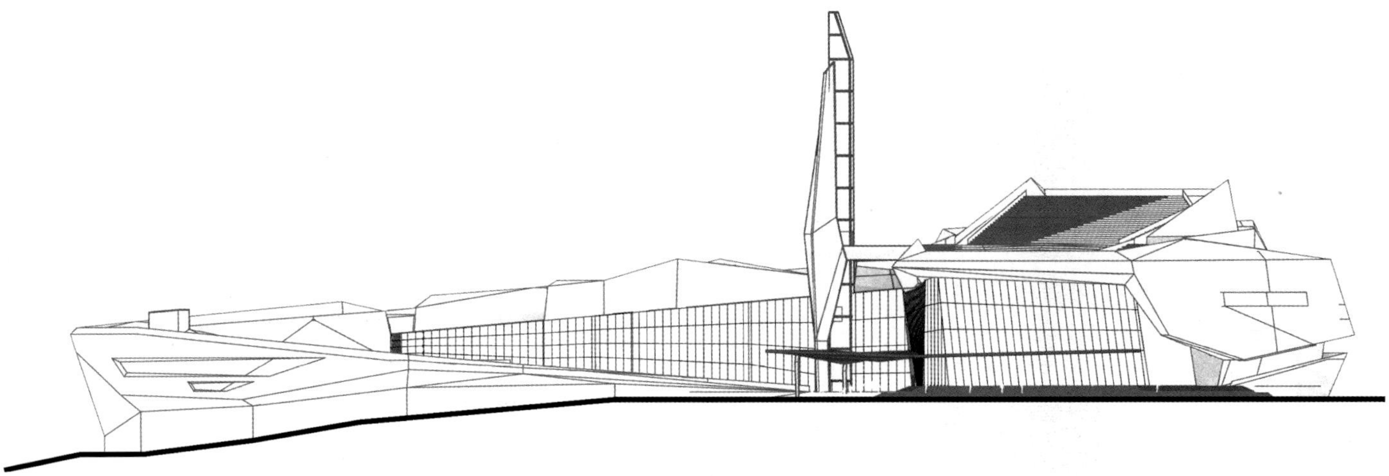

West Elevation

Design Studies

DESIGN CONCEPT | FORM

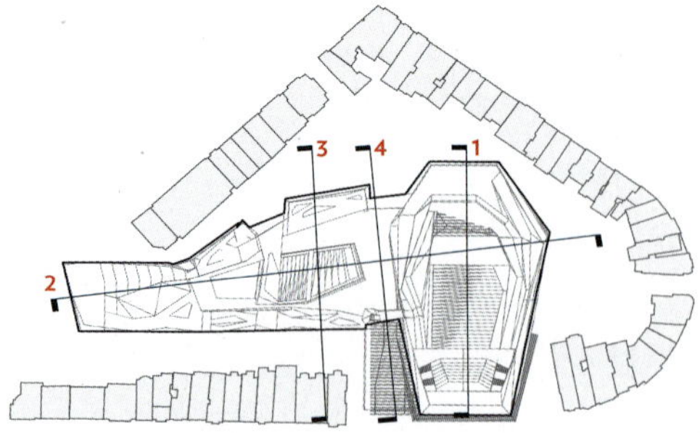

Section

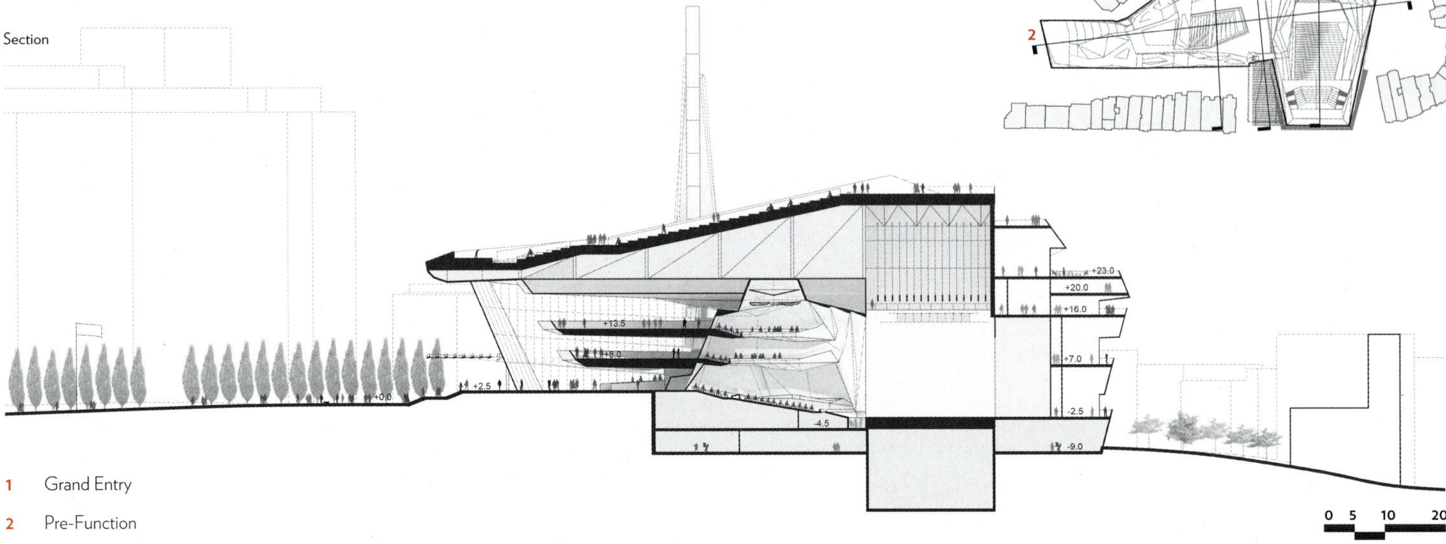

1 Grand Entry

2 Pre-Function

3 Art Gallery/Public Square

4 Courtyard

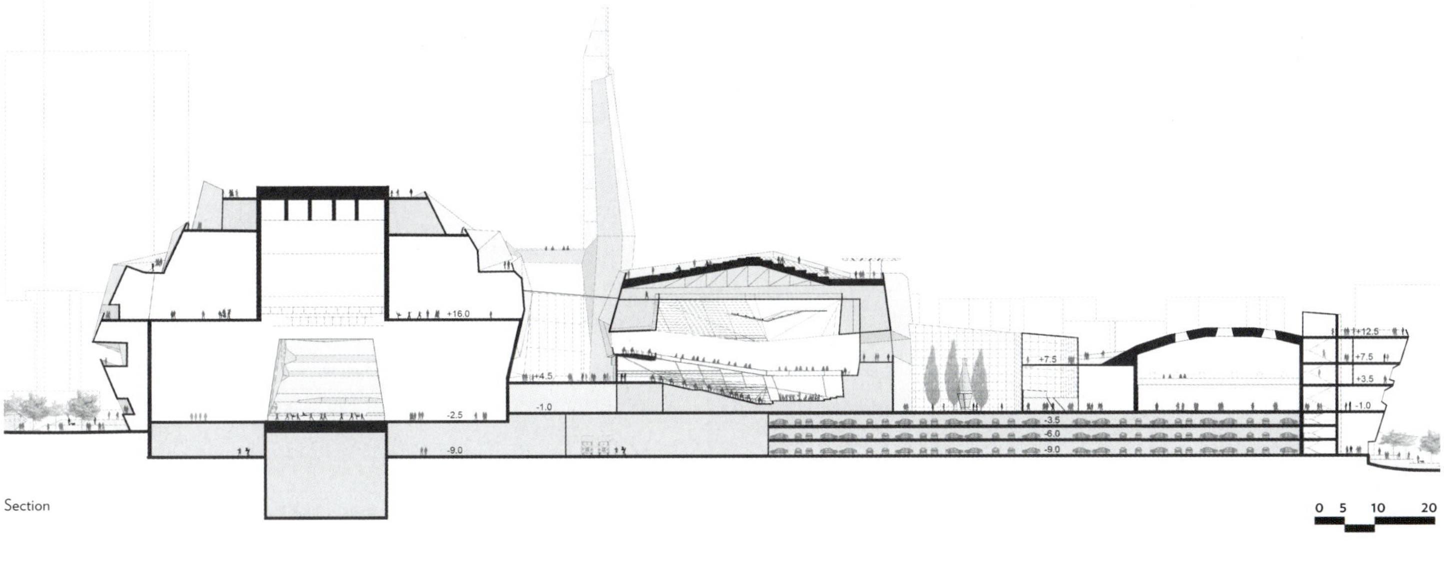

Section

DESIGN CONCEPT | SPACE

The cultural center's main entrance is accessed directly from the square by a gradually sloping walkway that brings visitors through a series of plazas, sculpture gardens, and landscaped roofscapes. Visitors are greeted by an iconic open observation platform that has unmatched views of the sea, Taksim Square, and the park. By positioning public cultural buildings on a fully accessible landscaped walkway, this new area restores the public park and The Walk, which historically occupied the site.

Pre-Function | Main Entrance (Above)

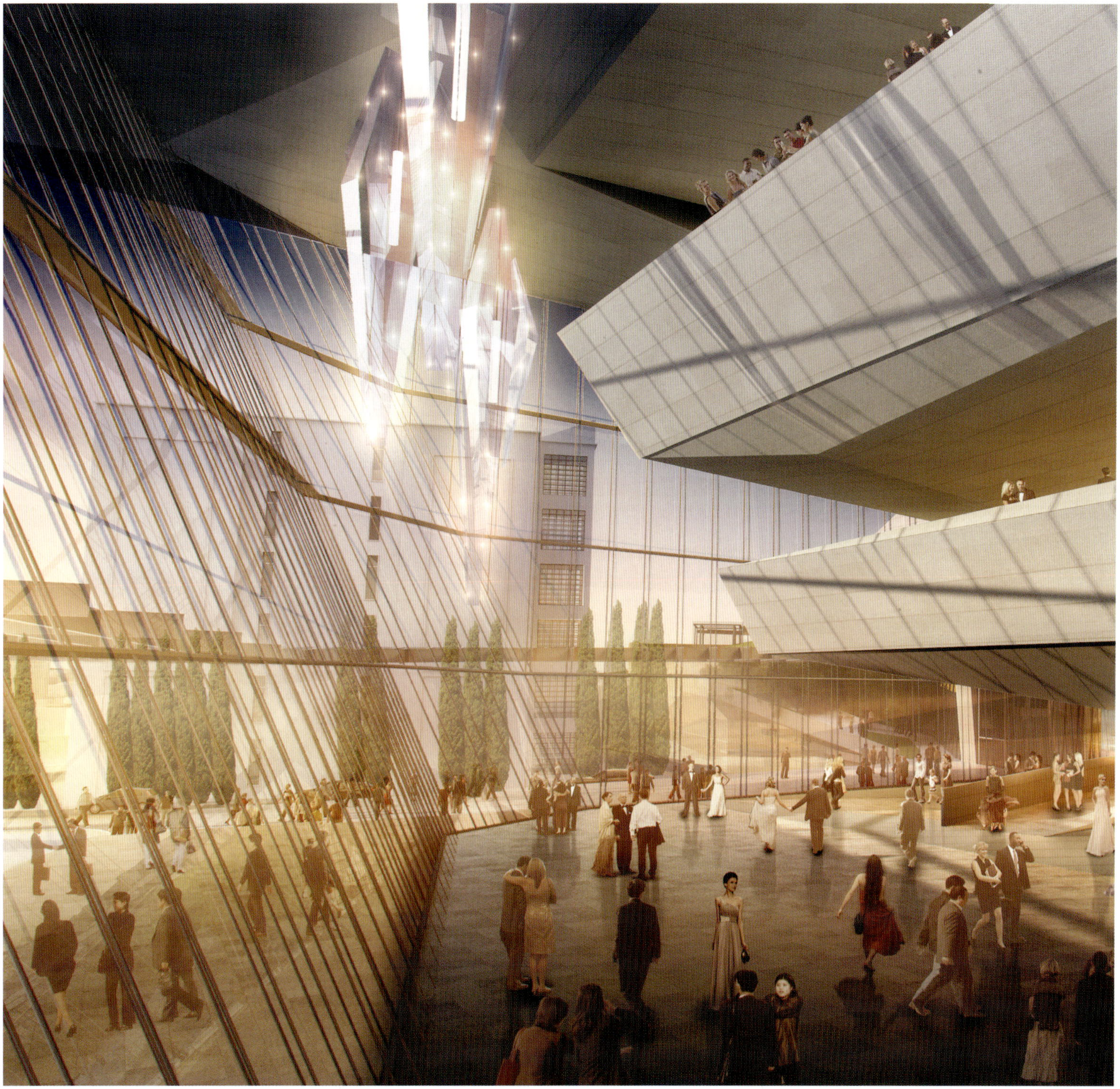

Pre-Function

DESIGN CONCEPT | MATERIALS

The design sources locally manufactured materials. It was important to the design, as well as the performance of the building, to use a natural stone that represents the permanence and strength of Istanbul as an historical, international city. Straight lined stone buildings connect to each other with glass skylights and walls, adding a striking modern element that contrasts well with the natural surroundings on the site.

The design strategy also includes the incorporation of waste segregation and recyclables storage facilities to reduce the overall environmental footprint of the building.

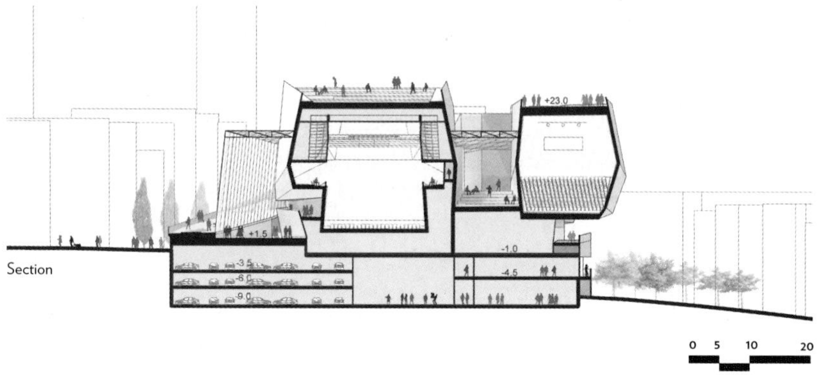

Section

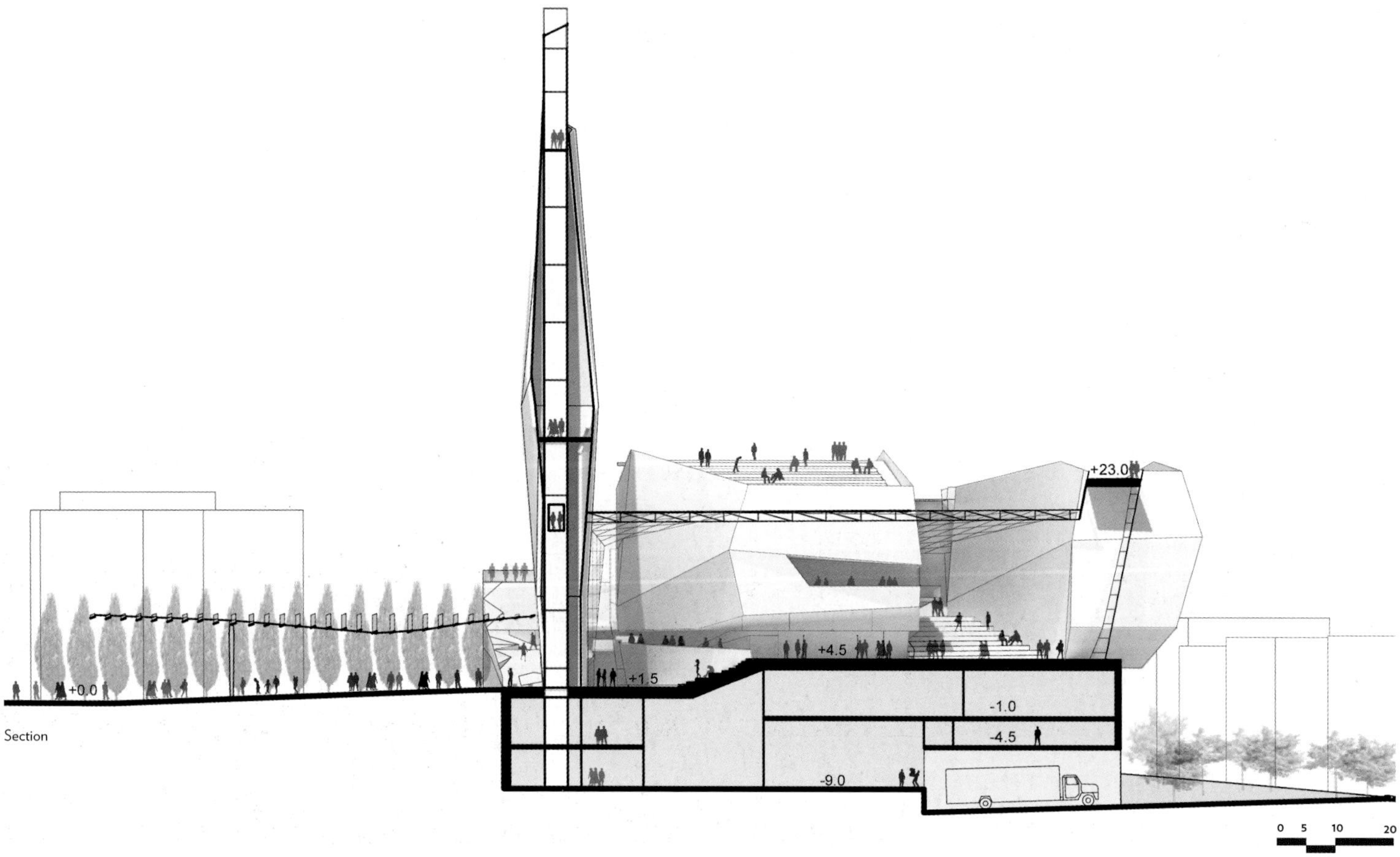

Section

RESEARCH + DEVELOPMENT | ANALYSIS

Although specific building performance metrics were not determined, many sustainable strategies were implemented in the design to ensure that, if built, Istanbul Cultural Center would be one of the highest performing cultural buildings in the world. These strategies include the use of a stone thermal mass, high-performance glazing, operable windows, solar hot water tubes that also provide shade for the top floors, a geothermal energy system that collects energy through ground source heat pumps, high-performance smart lighting, and vacancy sensors to keep lighting loads minimal. Other strategies include smart self-shading controls, outdoor green spaces to minimize the heat island effect, aggressive rainwater harvesting and greywater reuse applications, and low-flow sanitary fittings.

Sustainable Design Strategies

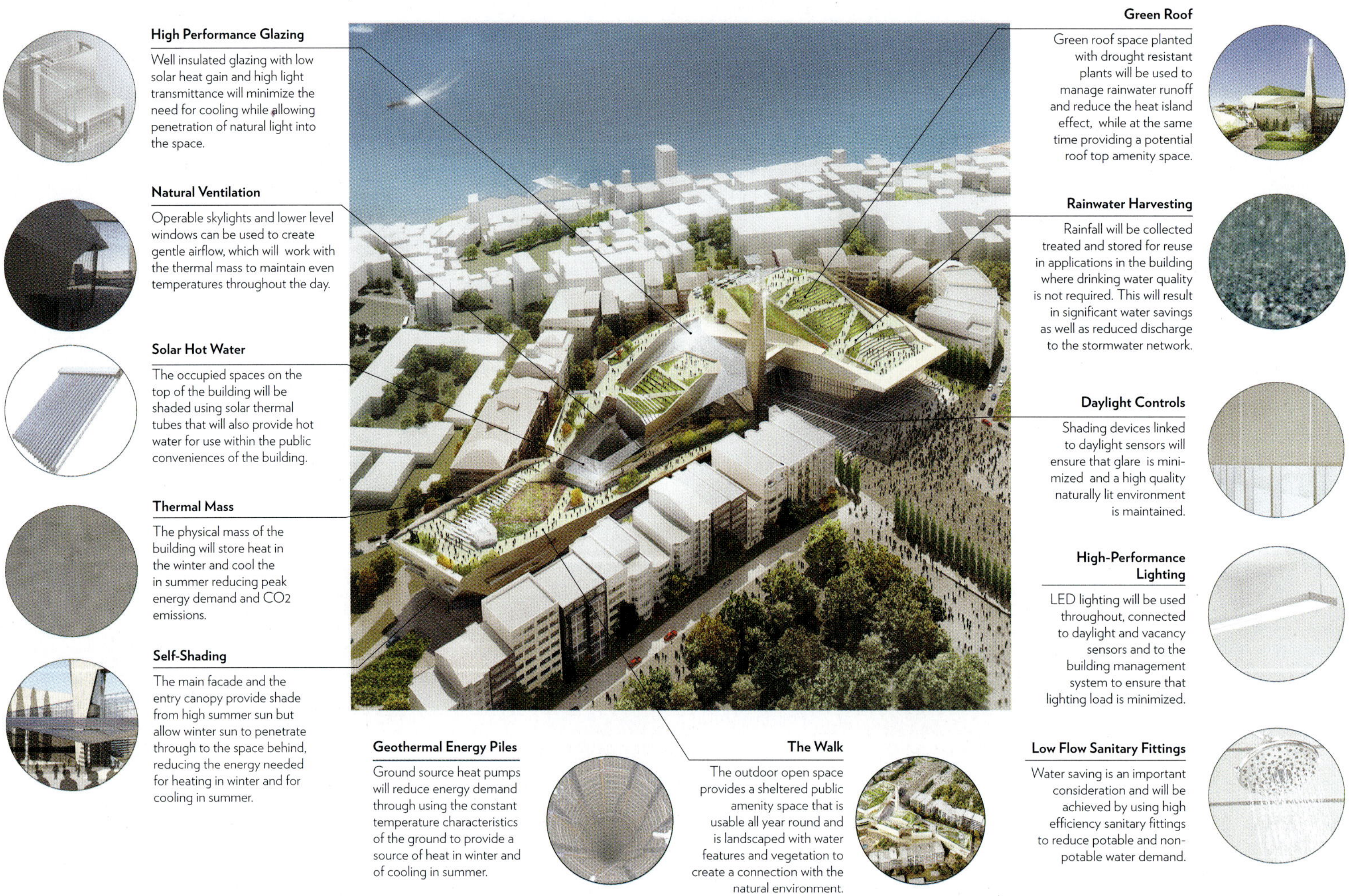

SHATTUCK-ST. MARY'S PERFORMING ARTS HALL

Faribault, Minnesota, USA

The design of the new performance hall at Shattuck-St. Mary's Boarding and Day School embraces the school's dynamic and diverse community, which is committed to excellence, integrity, and innovation. The school, well known for its excellence in bioscience, engineering, and its athletic program, sought a new cultural center to offer a more diverse set of tools and facilities for its students.

Shattuck-St. Mary's intent was to strengthen the artistic outlets and art programs that enhance the creative process. The new venue fits artfully into the existing campus built almost exclusively from local limestone. The design features flexible spaces and systems for a variety of activities such as theater productions, music performances, fund raising, school celebrations, and dining.

Shattuck St. Mary's School, in Faribault, Minnesota, was established in 1858 as an Episcopal Mission and Seminary. It evolved into a recognized school known for its "Centers of Excellence" programs in engineering, bioscience, pre-conservatory music, and vocal performance, as well as hockey, soccer, figure skating, and golf. Situated on land that is rich in natural limestone deposits, many of the buildings are built with stone quarried on-site by local artisans. The characteristic Gothic/ Romanesque architecture has staged St Mary's to become one of United States' Nationally Registered Historic Places (NRHP).

Function: Performing Arts Center | **Status:** Conceptual, 2017 | **Client:** Shattuck-St. Mary's School

SHATTUCK
ST MARYS
PERFORMANCE
HALL

DESIGN CONCEPT | SITE

The newly established performing arts drop-off area is located on the lower level of the program and provides access to studios, workshops, and production rooms, as well as a student lounge and food services. Each space opens to a landscaped outdoor terrace area. The upper level of the building houses the main theater and pre-function spaces.

A garden, nestled in an intimate outdoor courtyard separates Kingham Hall and the new center, helps increase outdoor connectivity between the programs. Juliet windows on the commons floor let students interact and watch small scale performances in the commons and garden areas.

> *In one single magnificent structure, we will create a home for artists, musicians, and actors to come together to discover, pursue, and further their passion for the arts.*
> *- Nick Stoneman, President, Shattuck-St. Mary's School, 2003-2019*

Site Plan

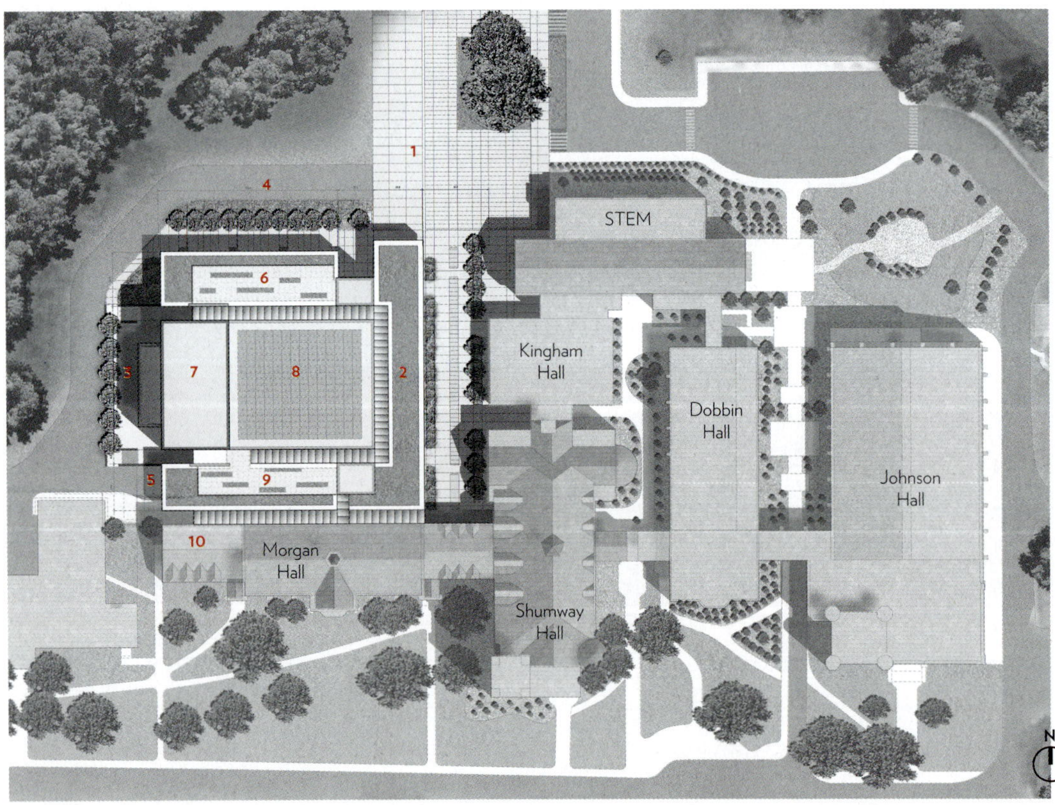

1 Plaza / Drop-Off
2 Garden East
3 Garden West
4 Linear Walkway / Windbreak
5 Loading Dock
6 Roof Sculpture Garden
7 Fly Roof
8 Theater Roof Photovoltaics
9 Roof Garden Mechanical
10 Loading Dock

SHATTUCK
ST MARYS
PERFORMANCE
HALL

DESIGN CONCEPT | PROGRAM

The new performance hall expands the school's visual arts department, providing the opportunity to produce higher quality theatrical performances and a variety of other events. The new program includes a 700+ seat flexible theater, comprehensive backstage facilities, and extensive vocal, dance, instrumental, and visual arts classrooms.

1 Dance Studio 1
2 Dance Studio 2
3 Ceramics Studio
4 Mechanical / Storage
5 Trap / Storage
6 Stage Lift
7 Prop / Costume Workshop
8 Dressing Rooms
9 Practice Rooms / Recording Studio
10 School Store
11 Student Lounge
12 Gallery
13 Snack Bar / BOH
14 Food Service
15 Loading Dock
16 Terrace
17 Painting / Drawing Studio
18 Photography Studio
19 Choral Room
20 Arts / Faculty Center
21 Faculty Office
22 Exterior Balcony
23 Pre-Function / Commons
24 Performance Hall
25 Orchestra Pit
26 Stage Lift
27 Stage
28 Back Stage
29 Food Service
30 Kitchen BOH
31 Servery
32 Connecting Bridge
33 Green Roof
34 Roof Terrace
35 Skylight
36 Balcony
37 Control Room

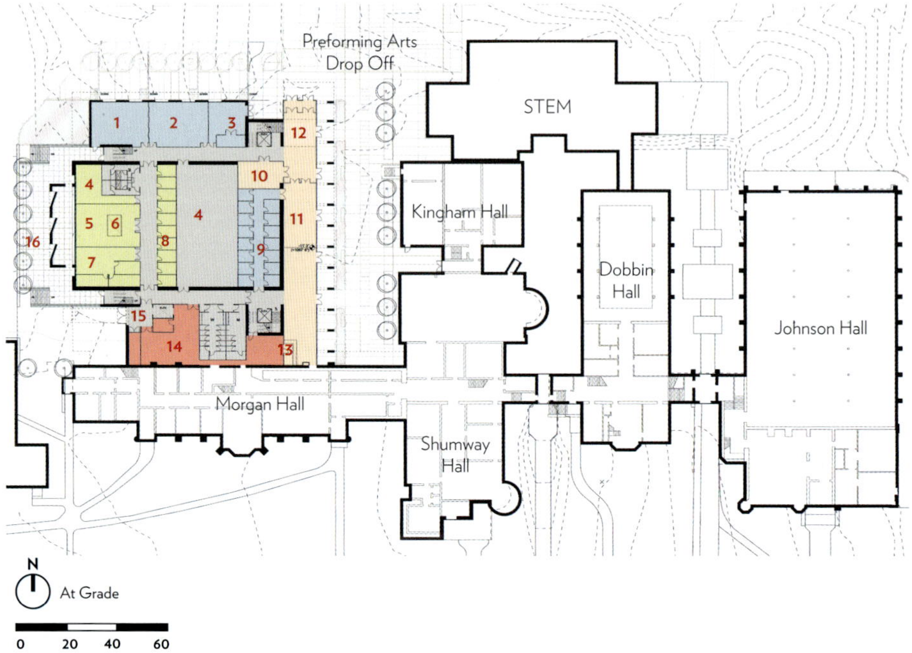

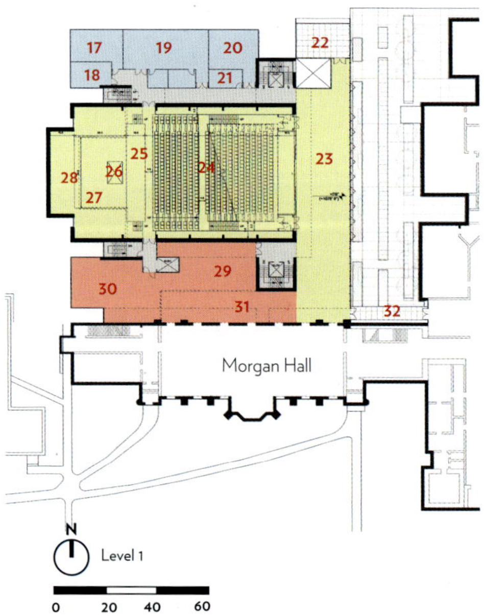

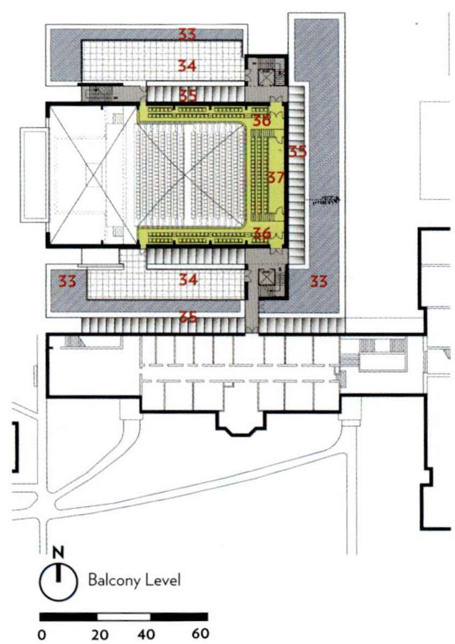

Section A Performance Hall

1 East Garden
2 Lounge
3 Commons/ Pre-Function
4 Control Room
5 Technical Floor/ Grid
6 Performance Hall/ Auditorium
7 Mechanical/ Practice Rooms
8 Fly Tower
9 Stage
10 Theater Storage/ BOH
11 Back Stage
12 Terrace

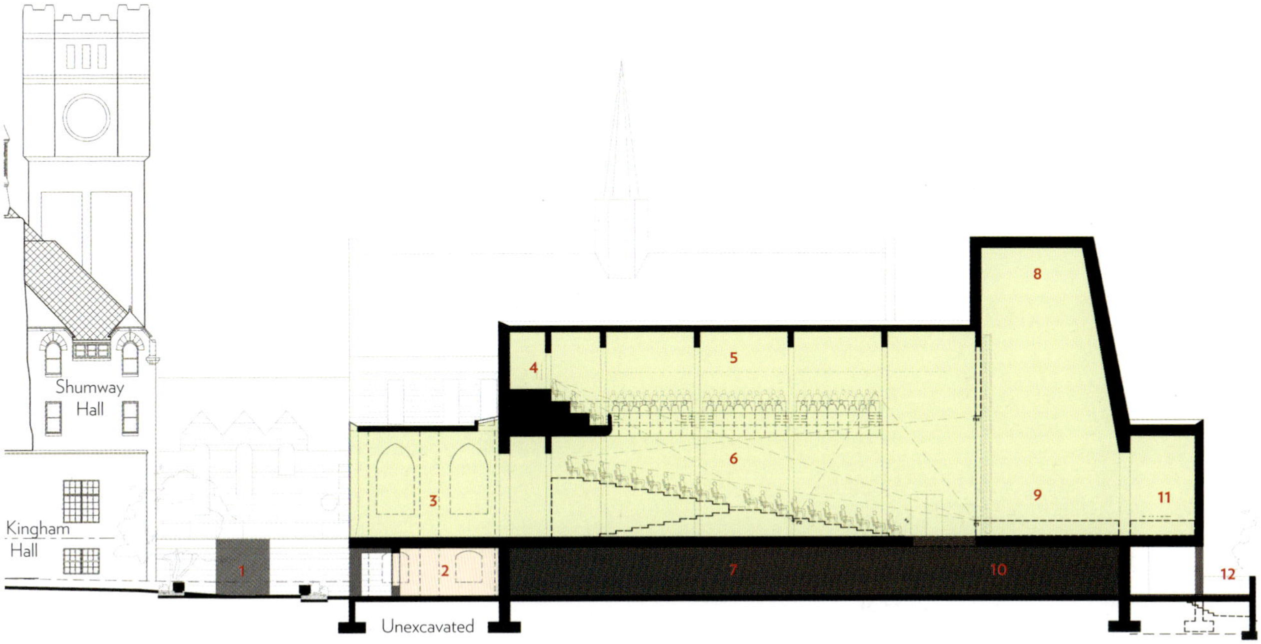

Section B Transverse

1 Choral
2 Dance
3 Lighting Grid/ Control Room
4 Theater Storage/ BOH
5 Elevator Tower
6 Kitchen
7 Loading
8 Servery
9 Kitchen Support/ Storage

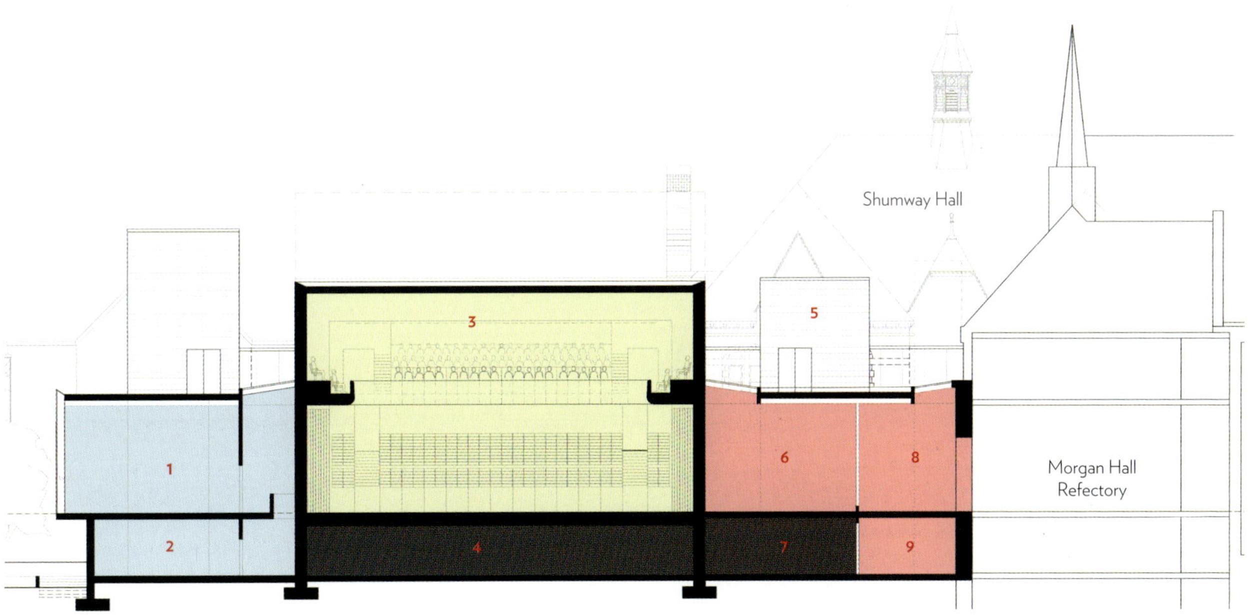

DESIGN CONCEPT | FORM

The new theater's interior accommodates various functions with unique flexible seating that is dynamic and versatile, offering several different arrangements. The main floor seating is retractable and easily stored within the side walls. When in use, the seating can be configured as a thrust stage, a theater in the round, an end stage (or raked stage), and a banquet configuration, which includes an overflow breakaway wall that flows into the commons area. As a primarily academic environment, it was important that the design have maximum flexibility so the space can be used in a range of different events.

Balcony Rendering | Theater Configurations (Right)

Theater Configurations

End Stage (Raked) 8,830 sf
Level 1 + Balcony - 670 Seats
Level 1 - 490 Seats (All)
Level 1 - 265 Seats (Front Half)

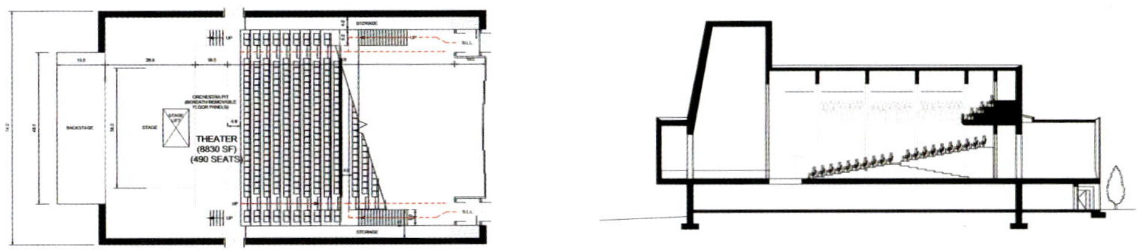

End Stage (Flat)
Level 1 + Balcony - 875 Seats
Level 1 - 715 Seats (All)
Level 1 - 604 Seats (Front Two-Thirds)
Level 1 - 265 Seats (Front Third)

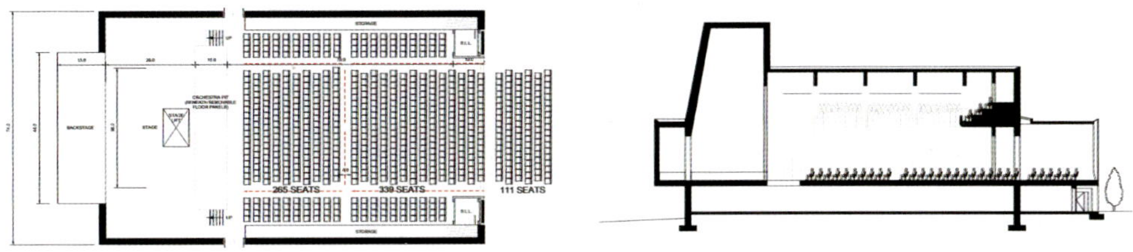

Theater In The Round
Level 1 + Balcony - 462 Seats
Level 1 - 302 Seats

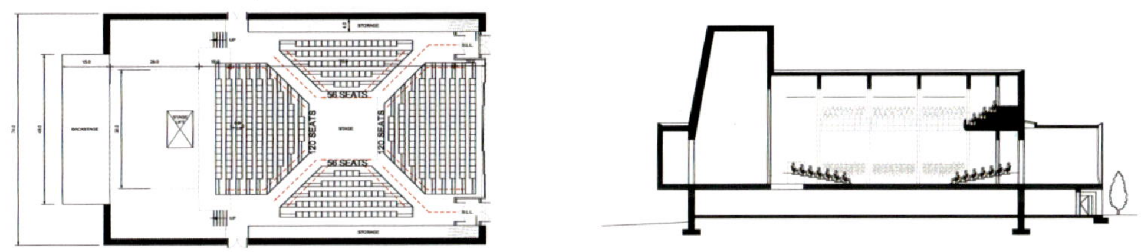

Thrust Stage
Level 1 + Balcony - 446 Seats
Level 1 - 286 Seats

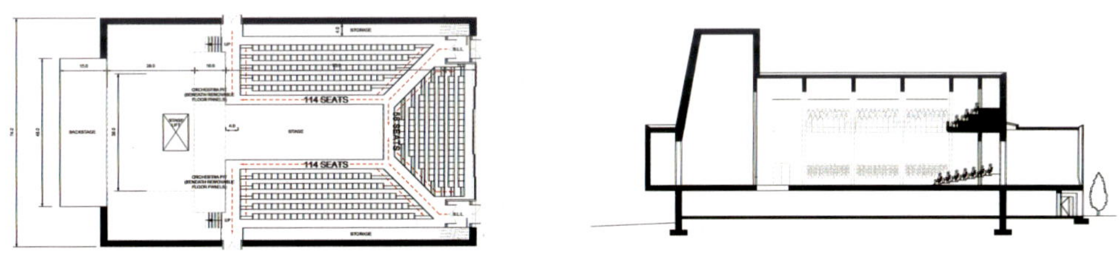

Banquet Configuration
Within Theater - 540 Seats
Including Commons - 640 Seats

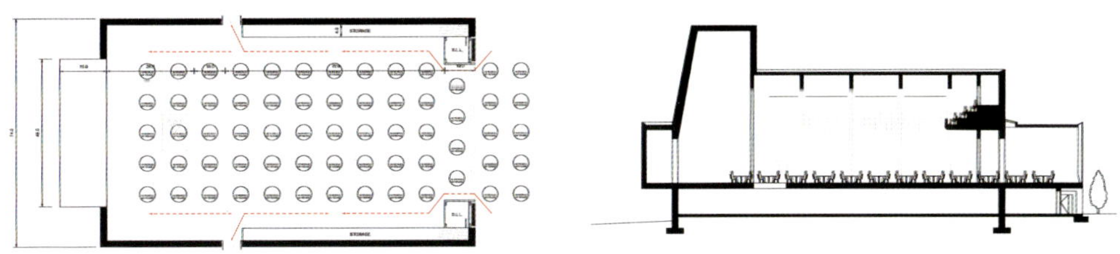

DESIGN CONCEPT | SPACE

The theater sits centered and elevated above the building's full program. A second-floor balcony wraps around the theater's stage and first floor seating. The volume beneath the stage is reserved for dressing rooms, a costume shop, a prop room, storage areas, and a state-of-the-art construction area with space to design, build, and paint sets.

A vertical 60-foot "Fly Tower" allows set changes to happen from above, further increasing the flexibility of the stage space during a performance and adding additional storage for sets.

The unique design of the wing incorporates the distinct needs of several types of programming it hosts including space with appropriate flooring for dancers, northern light exposure for painters and sculptors, protected kiln and workshop spaces for potters and woodworkers, and the high-level acoustical design needed for musicians.

A brightly lit corridor functions as the Student Lounge and the pre-function space to the classrooms and adjacent Gallery. Located at the entrance to the Performing and Visual Arts Center, the Gallery offers the school's visual artists a prominent space to show their work.

Classroom Renderings | Performance Hall Rendering (Right)

RESEARCH + DEVELOPMENT | ANALYSIS

The performance hall is separated from the building's other functions by continuous glass skylights. The skylights help define the circulation while allowing natural light to flood the interior spaces between the gallery, visual arts, and performance wings. Sunlight washes the exterior stone articulation of the mass, expressing the tectonic quality and language of the local sandstone buildings.

A direct sunlight solar analysis was completed from Summer through Winter solstice to understand the comfort levels and correct time adjustments when implementing sun-sensitive electrochromic glass. Environmental sensors tint the glass during early morning periods to reduce heat gain.

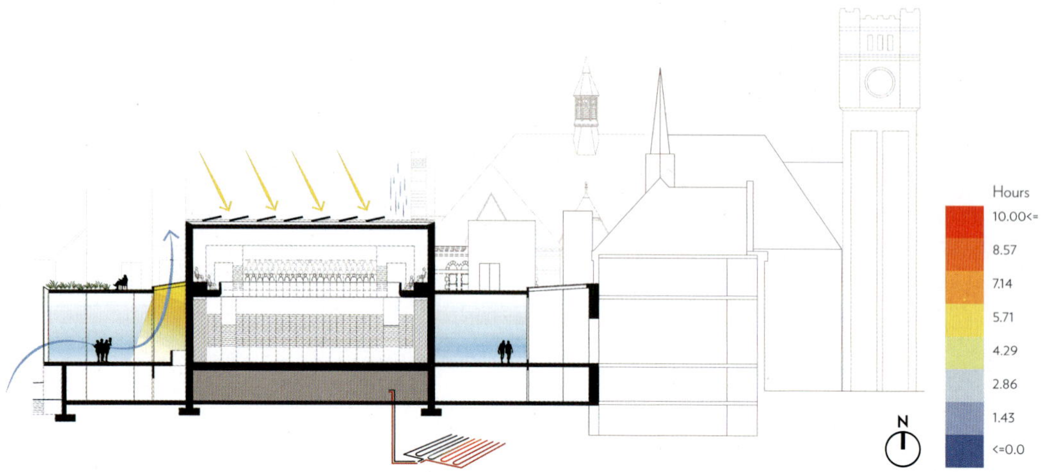

Solar + Wind Performance Analysis

East Garden Solar Analysis

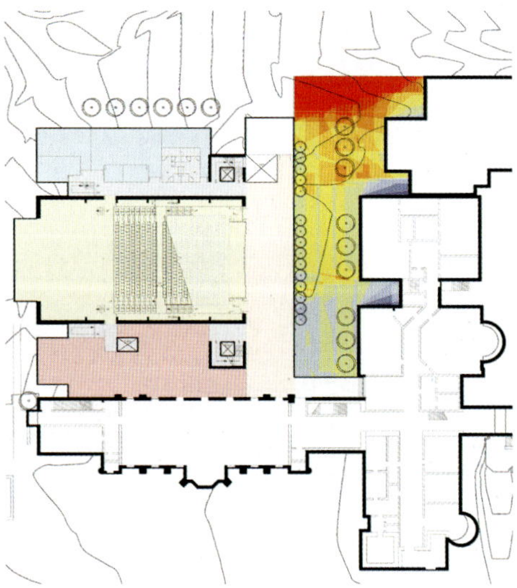

Direct Sunlight Hours on Summer Solstice
June 21, 01:00 - 24:00

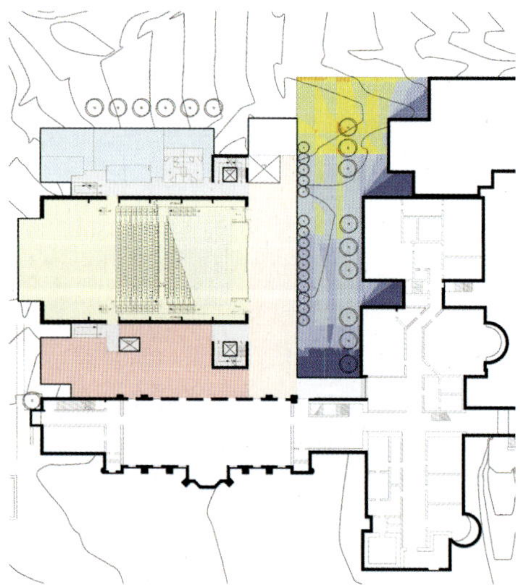

Direct Sunlight Hours on Autumn Equinox
September 23, 01:00 - 24:00

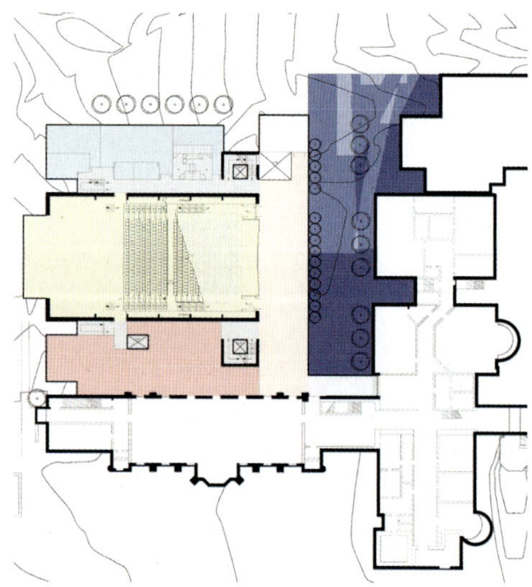

Direct Sunlight Hours on Winter Solstice
December 22, 01:00 - 24:00

Gallery | Garden Pre-function

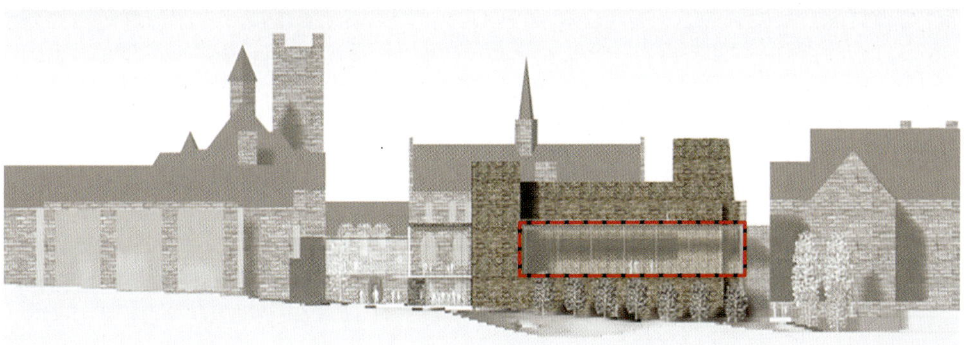

Limestone + Electrochromic Facade

The performance hall's exterior facade is respectful to the historic Morgan Hall Refectory to the south and Kingham Hall to the east. Its easterly glazed face features electrochromic glass, adding a sleek juxtaposition to the stone facades of the surrounding buildings. The glass is light sensitive and adjusts the window's level of opacity depending on the level of sunlight, much like transition lenses used in eyeglasses.

Faribault, MN
44.33 N, 93.32 W

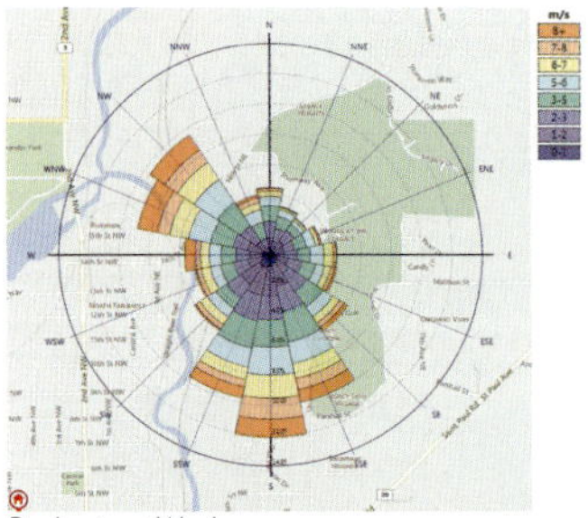

Predominant Winds
Annual

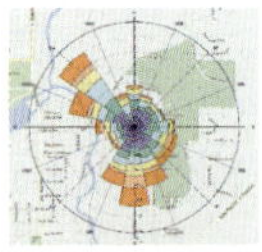

Predominant Winds
Spring

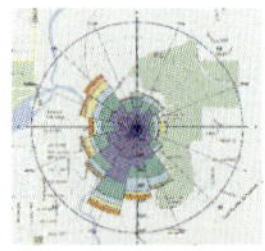

Predominant Winds
Summer

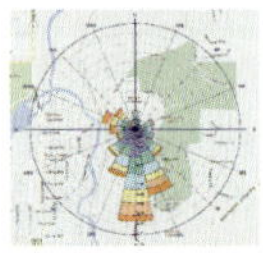

Predominant Winds
Autumn

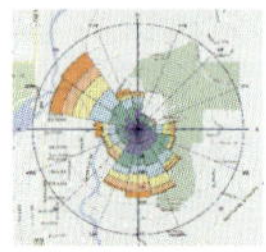

Predominant Winds
Winter

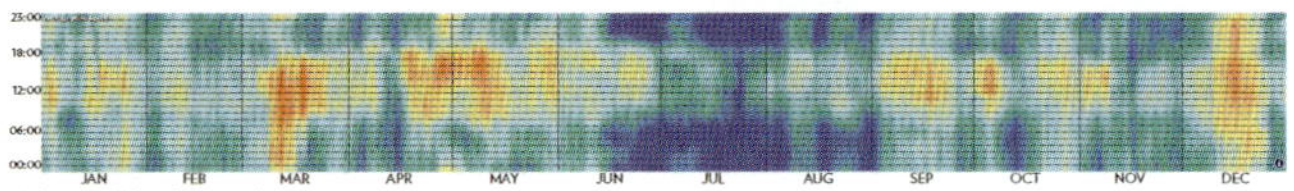

Hourly Wind Speeds
Annual

The addition was subject to rigorous sustainability goals including maintaining the building's cultural heritage through preservation of historic elements, achieving natural ventilation through passive convection, high-performance glazing to manage solar heat loss and gain, and improving indoor environmental quality through the use of Low-VOC and recycled content.

A green roof was also included to support water management and enhance biodiversity and next-generation insulation improves the wall and roof conditions to further minimize gains. The design achieves renewable energy production through the use of photovoltaic panels, while heating and cooling is supplemented through ground source heat pumps to reduce CO2 emissions.

East Garden Spring CFD Analysis

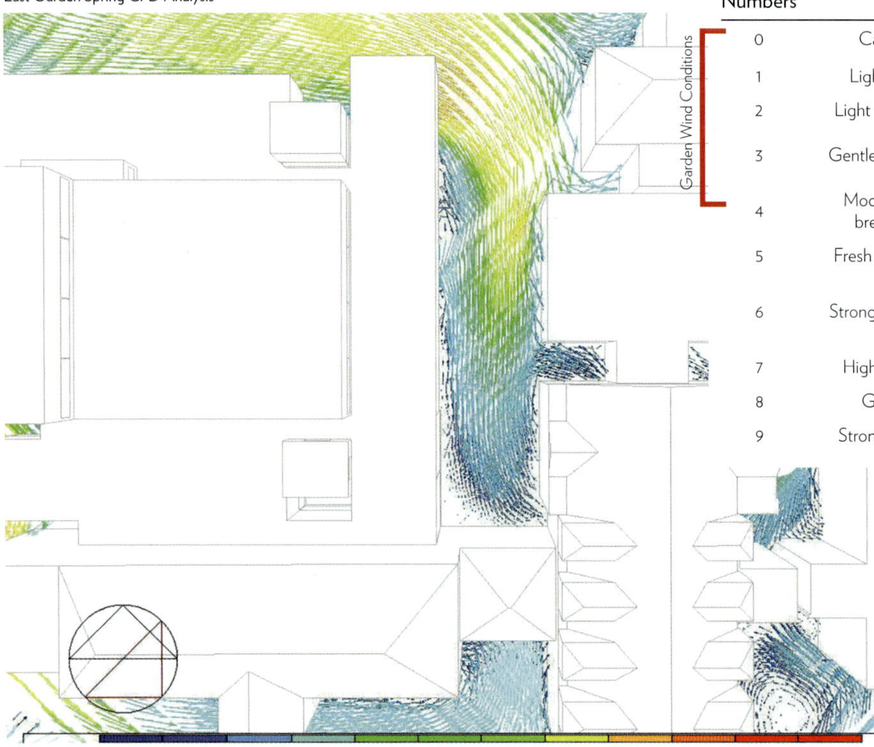

Velocity 0 1.6 3.2 4.9 6.5 8.0 9.7 11.3 13.0 14.6 16.2 17.9 mph

Garden Wind Conditions (Beaufort Numbers 0–4)

Beaufort Numbers	Description	Wind Speed at 1.75 height (mph)	Effects
0	Calm	<1	Smoke rises vertically
1	Light air	1-3	No noticeable wind
2	Light breeze	4-7	Wind felt on face
3	Gentle breeze	8-12	Hair disturbed, clothing flaps, newspaper difficult to read
4	Moderate breeze	13-17	Raises dust and loose paper, hair disarranged
5	Fresh breeze	18-24	Force of wind felt on body
6	Strong breeze	25-30	Umbrellas used with difficulty, hair blown straight, difficult to walk steadily
7	High wind	31-38	Inconvenience felt when walking
8	Gale	39-46	Extremely difficult to walk in wind
9	Strong gale	41-47	Branches break from trees

East Garden

ASTANA ENERGY HALL

Astana, Kazakhstan

Energy Hall is a building within a building: a 6,500 square-meter, 1,000 seat multi-functional Proscenium Theater set within an exterior glass envelope. The project was the main performance space for Expo 2017 in Kazakhstan.

The theater utilizes a fixed-seating system and is used for a range of performances including musical performances, physical performances, and film exhibitions. The building program includes an auditorium and working stage with wings, technical galleries, and a rear stage, as well as public areas performance support spaces.

The building's unique feature is a pre-function public space between the glass envelope and the theatrical active volume skin of the building. This area is an active space that can be used outside of regular operating hours. The theatrical skin is an active, animated, and programmable membrane that produces digital theater at any time, regardless of the performance schedule.

Astana Energy Hall is located in the arts district of the Expo 2017's post-expo, legacy community. The site has recently transformed into an office and research district known as the Astana International Financial Centre (AIFC), which features a cultural core. The theater anchors this entertainment district with frequent programs and performances that contribute to the culture of the city and surrounding regions.

Function: Performance Hall | **Status:** Built, 2017 | **Client:** Astana Expo 2017 | **Awards:** AIA National Tap/CCA Innovation Awards, Stellar Design, Astana Expo City, 2016

DESIGN CONCEPT | SITE

Positioned adjacent to Expo 2017's spherical centerpiece the Kazakhstan Pavilion—now known as Nur Alem Museum of Future Energy—Astana Energy Hall is the vibrant heart of the post-exposition's cultural core. One struggle that theaters often face is how to maintain a dynamic facade when there are no performances. If a building is inactive, and uninteresting, the pedestrian experience is affected. Energy Hall's innovative, active wall solves this issue by providing a visual experience for pedestrians, connecting them directly to the building and encouraging them to come back for future performances.

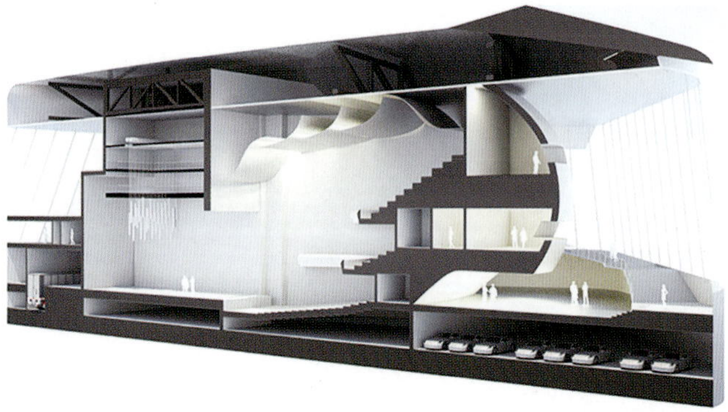

Section

Entrance with Active Facade | "Theater within a Theater" Rendering (Right)

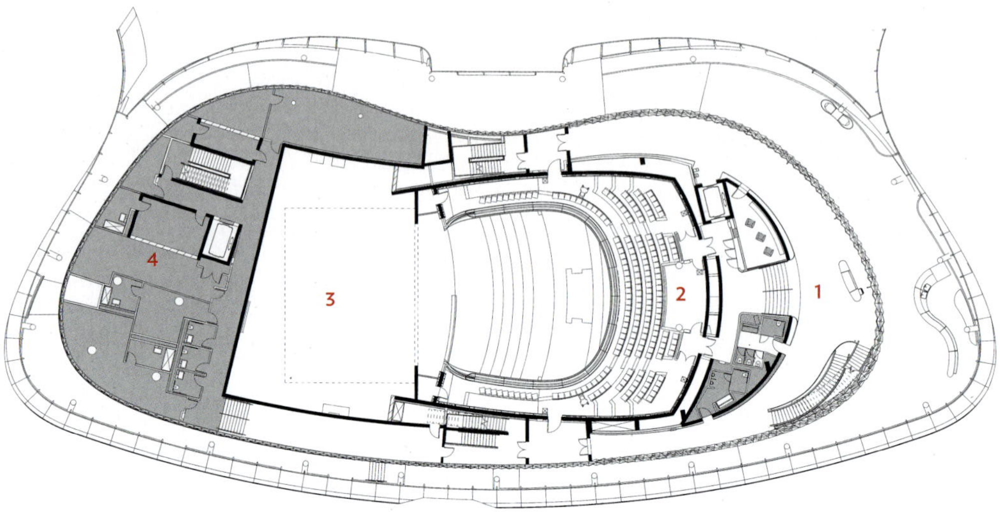

Level 1 Plan

1 Pre-Function
2 Auditorium
3 Stage
4 Back of House

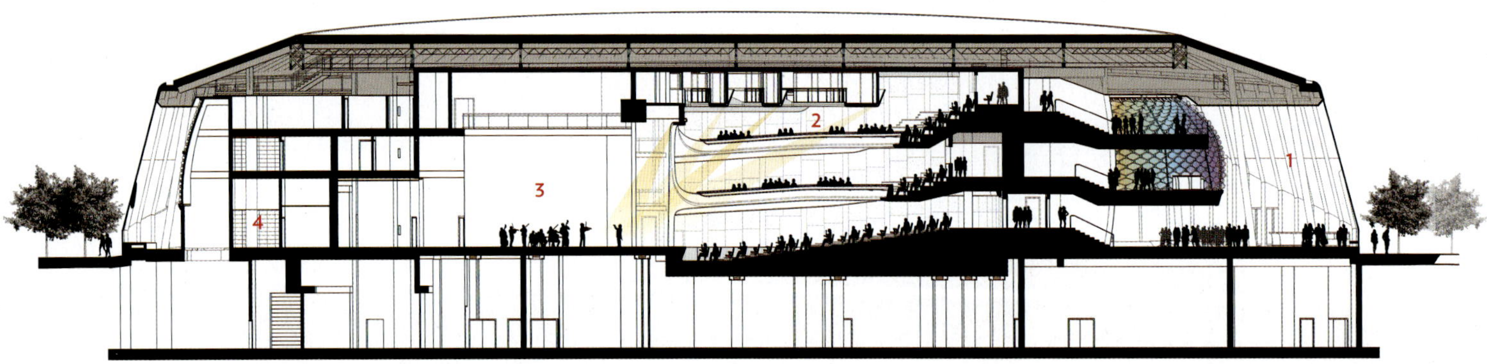

Section

1 Pre-Function
2 Auditorium
3 Stage
4 Back of House

DESIGN CONCEPT | FORM

The form of the building is dictated by the program but also by the innovative materials that were designed for the project. The exterior wall is comprised of unitized thermally broken painted aluminum and are fixed with vision panels of high-performance triple glazing and solid frit insulated glass spandrel panels. The window wall oriented to the interior also has vision panels of high-performance double-glazing and solid frit insulated glass spandrel panels.

The interior circulation "shell" wall consists of screen-printed glass of varying opacity, as well as integrated lighting and LED screens that are integrated into the panelization of the wall. The interior spaces in the pre-function and main lobby feature flooring that is composed of locally sourced granite and arranged in a custom paving pattern.

The theater shell wall in the pre-function area consists of composite curved prefinished panels that enclose the performance space and related functions. The ceiling features perforated mesh metal panels in a custom pattern to integrate the lighting.

Section | "Theater within a Theater" (Right)

DESIGN CONCEPT | SPACE

Energy Hall's main auditorium has seating spread over four levels: a shallow stalls level, a circle level, and two balcony levels with an approximately 13 meters wide and 14 meters deep stage. The audience is proportioned for the benefit of the performers with half the audience seated above and half seated in the shallow stalls level, below the eye line, creating a balanced space. The smooth form of the balconies defines the shape of the room. Two balconies were chosen instead of one because it made the scale of the otherwise large room feel smaller and more intimate.

During Expo 2017, Energy Hall was multi-functional, hosting multiple, diverse events each day. In legacy mode, the theater maintains a busy schedule with live performance events including folklore and traditional dance, cultural events, theatrical performances, acrobatic performances, and film festivals. It has also become a premiere venue for various musical performances including small concerts of composers, opera singers, and quartets, as well as curated thematic events such as the recent "Jazz Energy," featuring local talent.

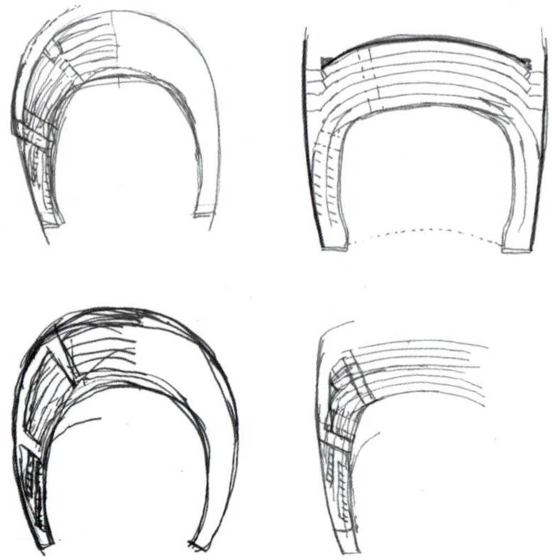

Balcony Evolution Sketches

Stair to Theater with Active Interior Facade | Theater Interior (Right)

Energy Hall's enclosure, the theater shell wall, is a digital art canvas. Ideas explored during its design included ways to make the wall interactive by integrating color, light, movement, and sound. During a prototyping period, the components of the wall were analyzed and further developed by the architects. Original studies included tests on the geometry of its underlying grid, the potential scale of its components, and studies of the geometry of each component "cell." The goal was to find the balance between a system full of complexity and geometrical articulation, and one that could be feasible to fabricate, install, and operate.

Various densities, sizes, and configurations were studied. The built concept was based on a six-sided glass LED lit cell that was stretched horizontally to allow a better flow of the overall system on the lobby space. This double-sided cell can activate a larger public area on one side and smaller spaces, such as stairs and balcony zones, on the other side. Each cell has a metal frame that connect to the mounting grid system that softly wraps around, following the form of the auditorium. The digital canvas breathes with the space, energizes its surroundings and becomes the main expression of the theater all year round. Because it is programmable, it can be curated for different events through the year.

Panelization Diagrams

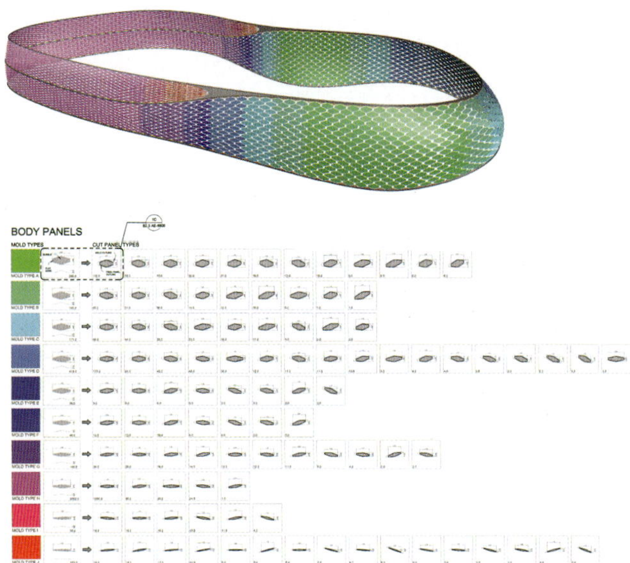

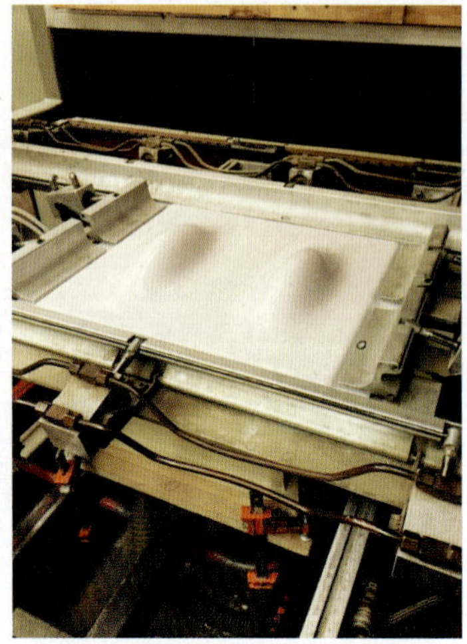

Facade Prototyping

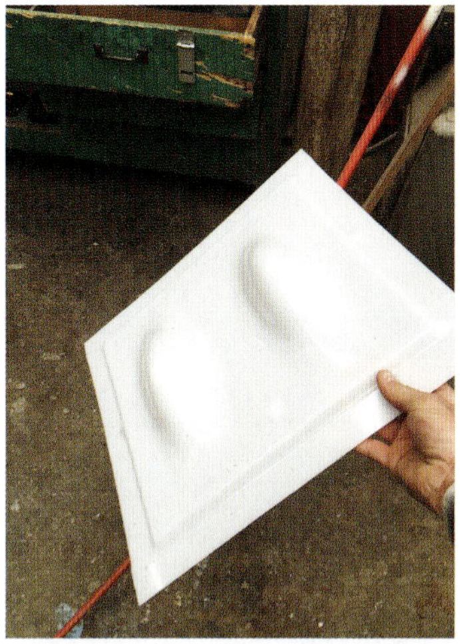

Wall Panelization Studies

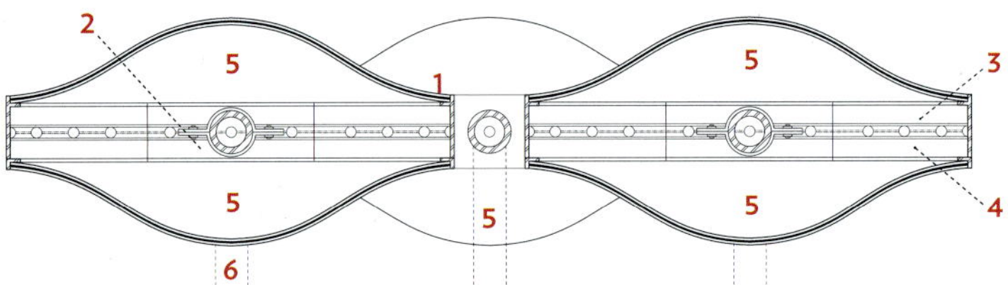

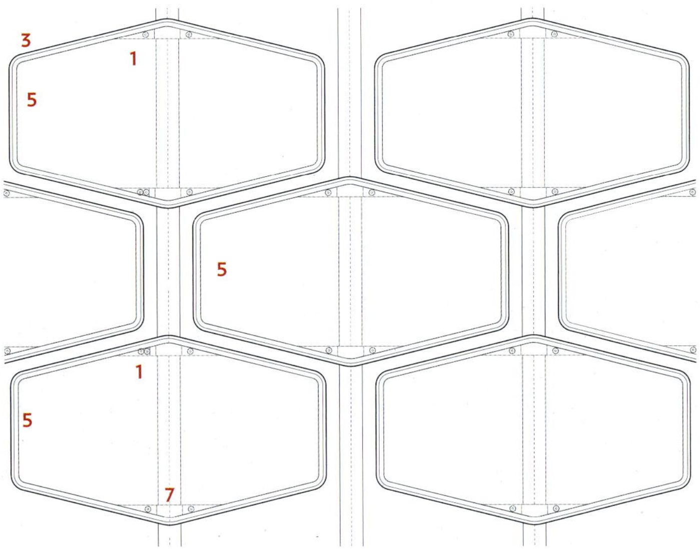

1 Structural Steel

2 Power Conduit

3 Panel Frame

4 LED Diodes

5 Six-Sided LED Glass Panel

6 Member attached at top

7 Bottom connection for vertical movement

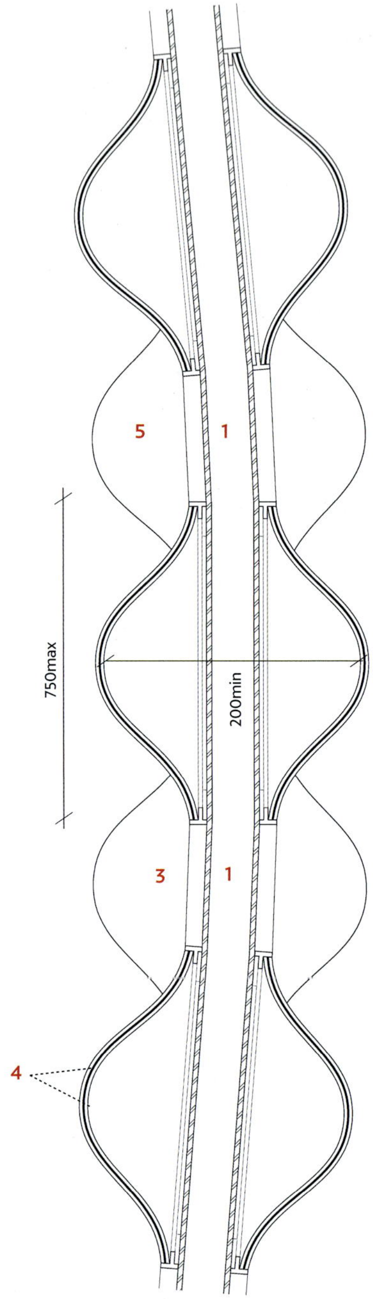

Energy Hall is a highly sustainable building with high-performance facades utilizing triple-glazed glass. All exterior walls have automated solar control shades that are tied to the building's energy management system. The roof covering is an insulated low-slope roofing system that features a building-integrated mono-crystalline photovoltaic cell roof panel system.

Other systems featured in the roofing are a stainless-steel gutter system, a roof access panel, and a fixed louver mechanical intake. Additional energy reduction strategies include hyper-insulated radiant floors, a hyper-insulated roof cavity, the use of reclaimed water for toilet flushing, and responsive lighting controls to maximize daylighting.

Ceiling lighting is also energy-conscious and is illuminated with high-performance, LED fixtures.

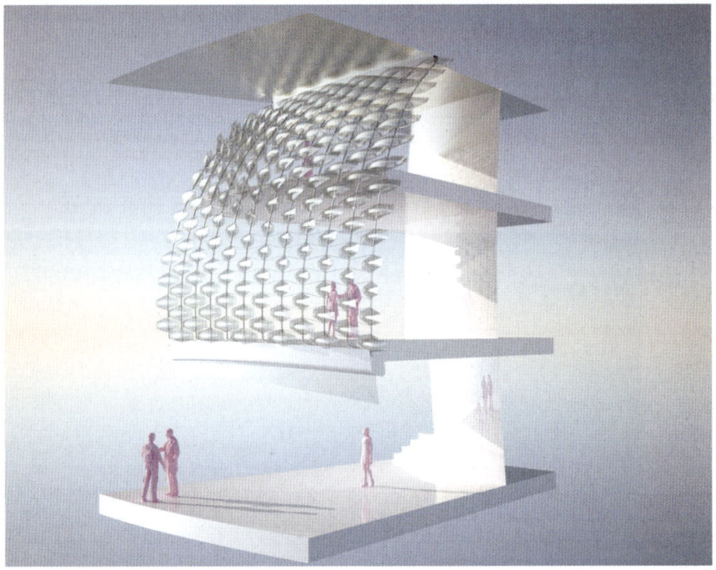

Exterior Wall Study

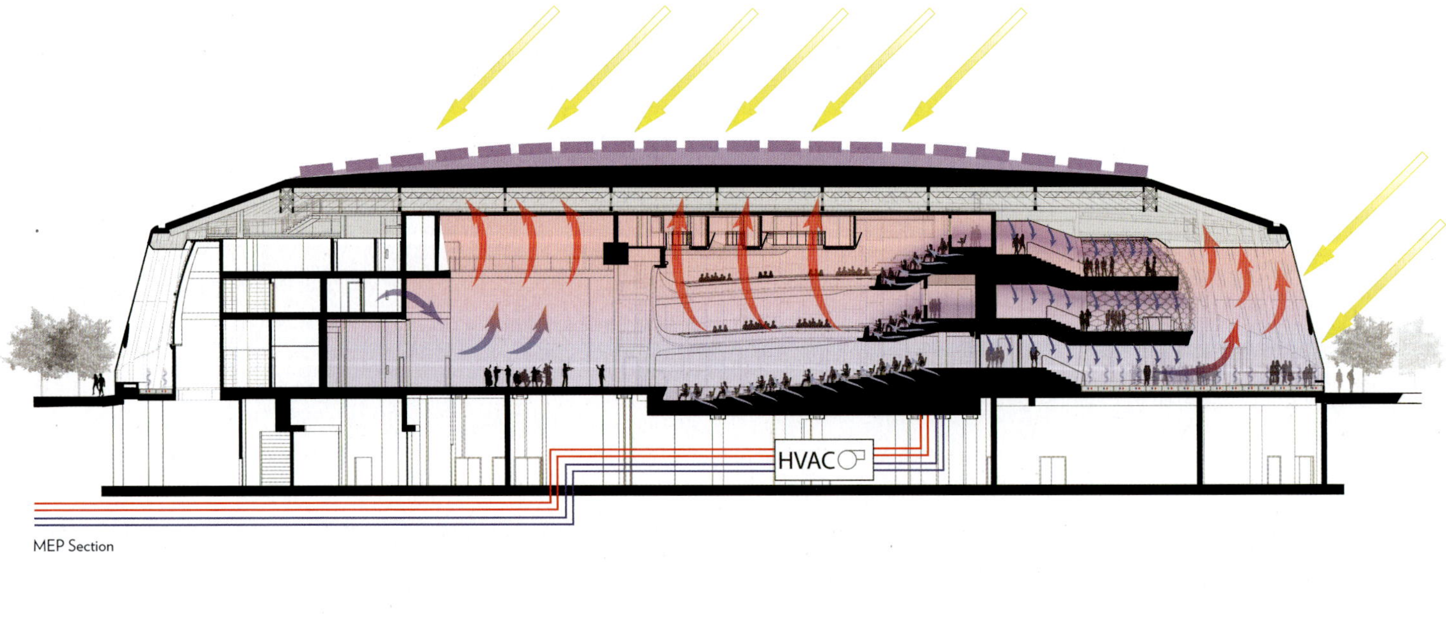

MEP Section

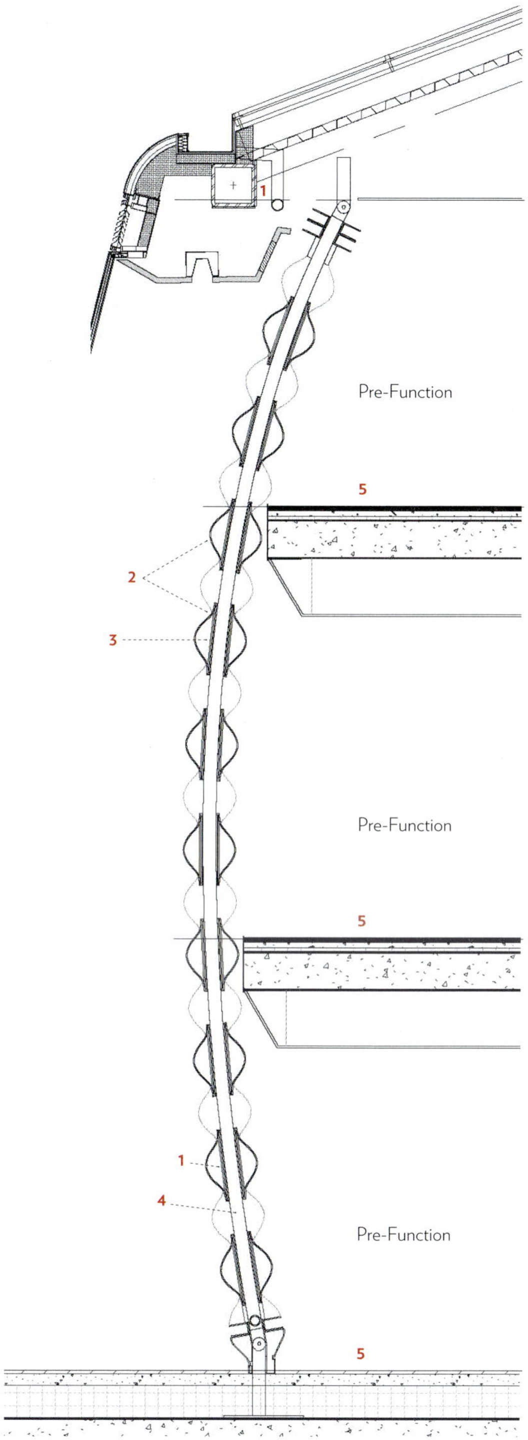

1 Extruded Frame

2 Six-Sided LED Glass Panel

3 Support Steel + Frame

4 Extruded Base

5 Floor Tile

Interior Facade Drawing

CONGRESS CENTER

Astana, Kazakhstan

Astana Congress Center was inspired by the fluid movements of the Golden Eagle or a "bürkit" that is canonized on the national flag of Kazakhstan. The structure's tapered edges and sleek sweeping form minimize the scale and surface area of the building, thereby reducing construction costs.

Completed in 2017, the center hosted many significant events during Expo 2017 and is now a hub for events in Astana International Financial Centre (AIFC), the post-expo legacy development. The project features a state-of-the-art 3,000-person auditorium, exhibition spaces, sponsor presentation areas, secure VIP and VVIP areas, associated press rooms, supporting offices, and a dedicated parking garage.

Astana Congress Center borders several mid-rise residential buildings and the greater AIFC development, Expo 2017's post-expo, legacy community. The program addresses the adjacent milieu through a contextual interface predicated on accessibility and transparency. As an integrated constituent within the neighborhood, the building provides a fundamental public amenity with performance spaces, exhibition halls, and other community amenities that foster coalescence.

Function: Auditorium + Conference Center | **Status:** Built, 2017 | **Client:** Astana Expo 2017 | **Awards:** AIA National Tap/CCA Innovation Awards, Stellar Design, Astana Expo City, 2016

DESIGN CONCEPT | SITE

Astana Congress Center's iconic design takes advantage of its national significance, functioning as an anchor for AIFC's cultural axis. The building is fully integrated into a public park with its main entrance oriented toward the expo site with full views of the spherical shaped Nur Alem, the country's premiere science museum that served as the central pavilion for Expo 2017.

The main arrival is accessed by the southeast plaza where visitors enter through a two-story atrium with required security checkpoints. Significant security measures were implemented to support the world leaders that attended the 2017 exposition and remain in the legacy condition. The entry is also accessible through two parking shuttles from the lower level to further support VVIP needs.

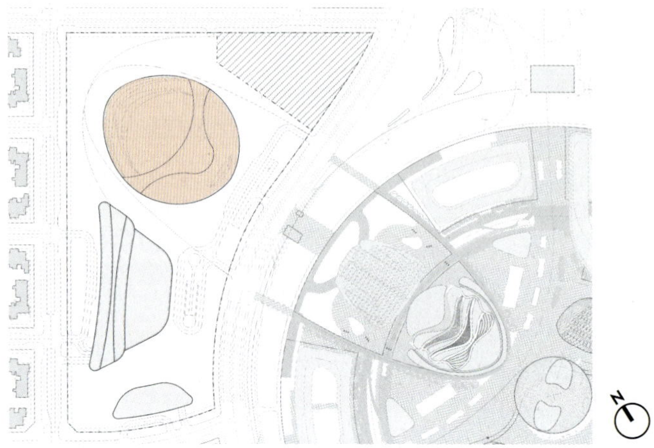

Site Plan

Program Section

1 Lyceum
2 Auditorium
3 Atrium
4 Lobby
5 Executive/VVIP

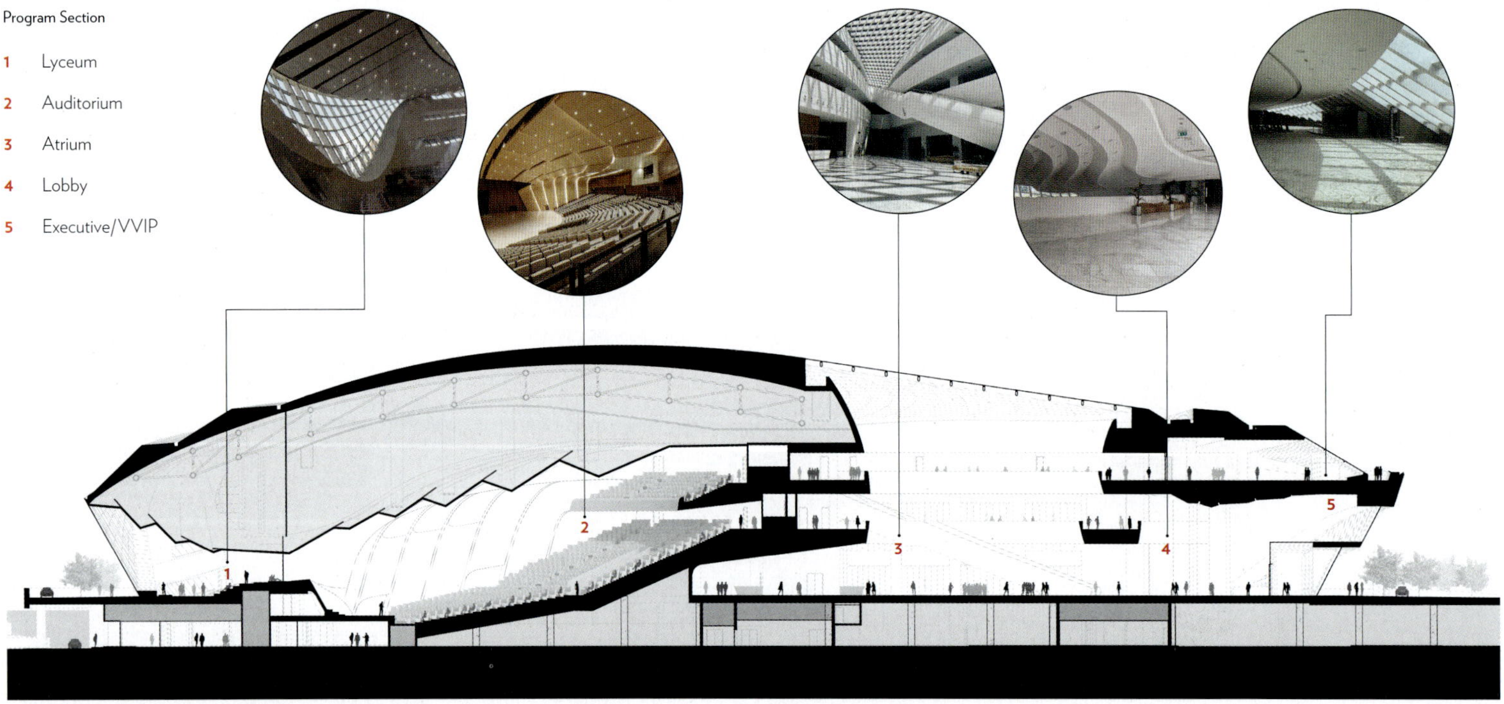

Northwest Facade

DESIGN CONCEPT | PROGRAM

A central atrium serves as the building's inner nodal point, with each floor wrapping the space. The main floor encircles and opens toward the central atrium, which is lined with exhibition and classroom spaces. A 3,000-seat, multi-functional auditorium is the primary element on the main floor. The theater is adaptable for events ranging from oratory speeches by world dignitaries to musical concerts and theatrical plays.

Several support functions surround the auditorium including green rooms, AV rooms, translation booths, and staging areas. These spaces can be partitioned and serviced with back-of-house access used for conferences, classrooms, and workshops. Also on the first floor is a separate lyceum space to support public and impromptu gatherings on a smaller scale.

The second-floor transitions to semi-public spaces including press rooms, support offices, and informal gathering spaces. The third floor contains the executive and VVIP program with dedicated personnel rooms and office spaces for associated operations.

Atrium | Auditorium (Right)

Conference Room

Press Room

Levels 1-3

1 Auditorium
2 Central Atrium
3 Press
4 Exhibition
5 Main Entry
6 VVIP

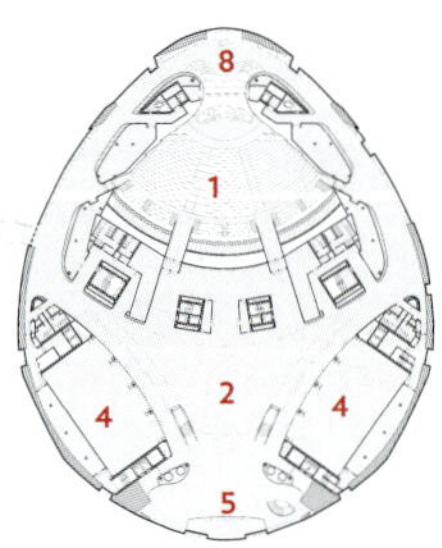

Level 1

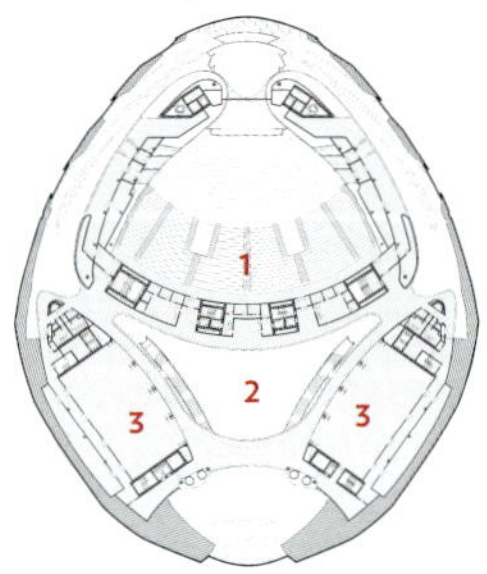

Level 2

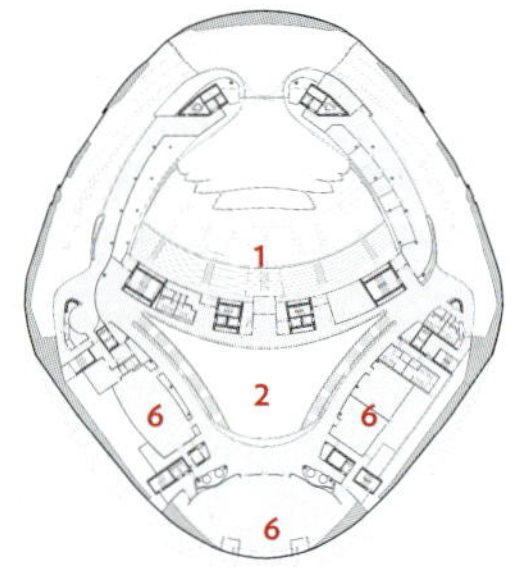

Level 3

DESIGN CONCEPT | FORM

The building's form was inspired by the Golden Eagle that adorns Kazakhstan's national flag. The eagle, or bürkit in Kazakh, is an integral symbol that is rooted in the rich history and culture of the country's eagle hunting tradition, also known as Sayat.

The building's silhouette expresses an eagle's wings in flight wrapping the program in a protective shield, while facades of varying scales and angles encompass the perimeter. The form, like the eagle, is in constant motion.

Sweeping angled facades provide interest and function, doubling as filigree—for light play into the interior spaces—and control for increasing internal heat gain during the winter and reducing heat gain during the summer.

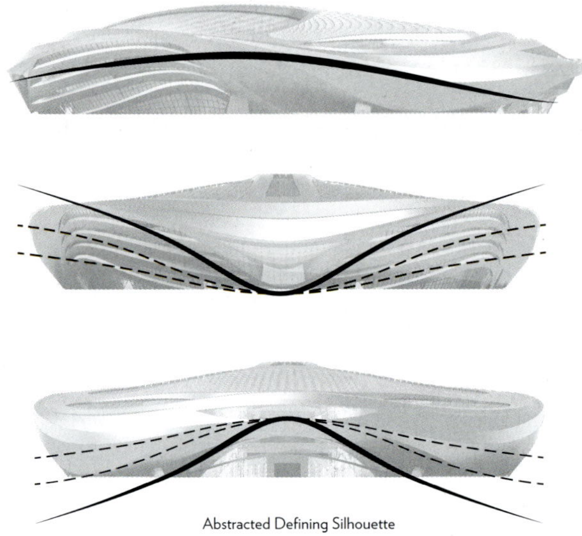

Abstracted Defining Silhouette

Congress Center Massing Model

Burkit Flight Movement Abstraction

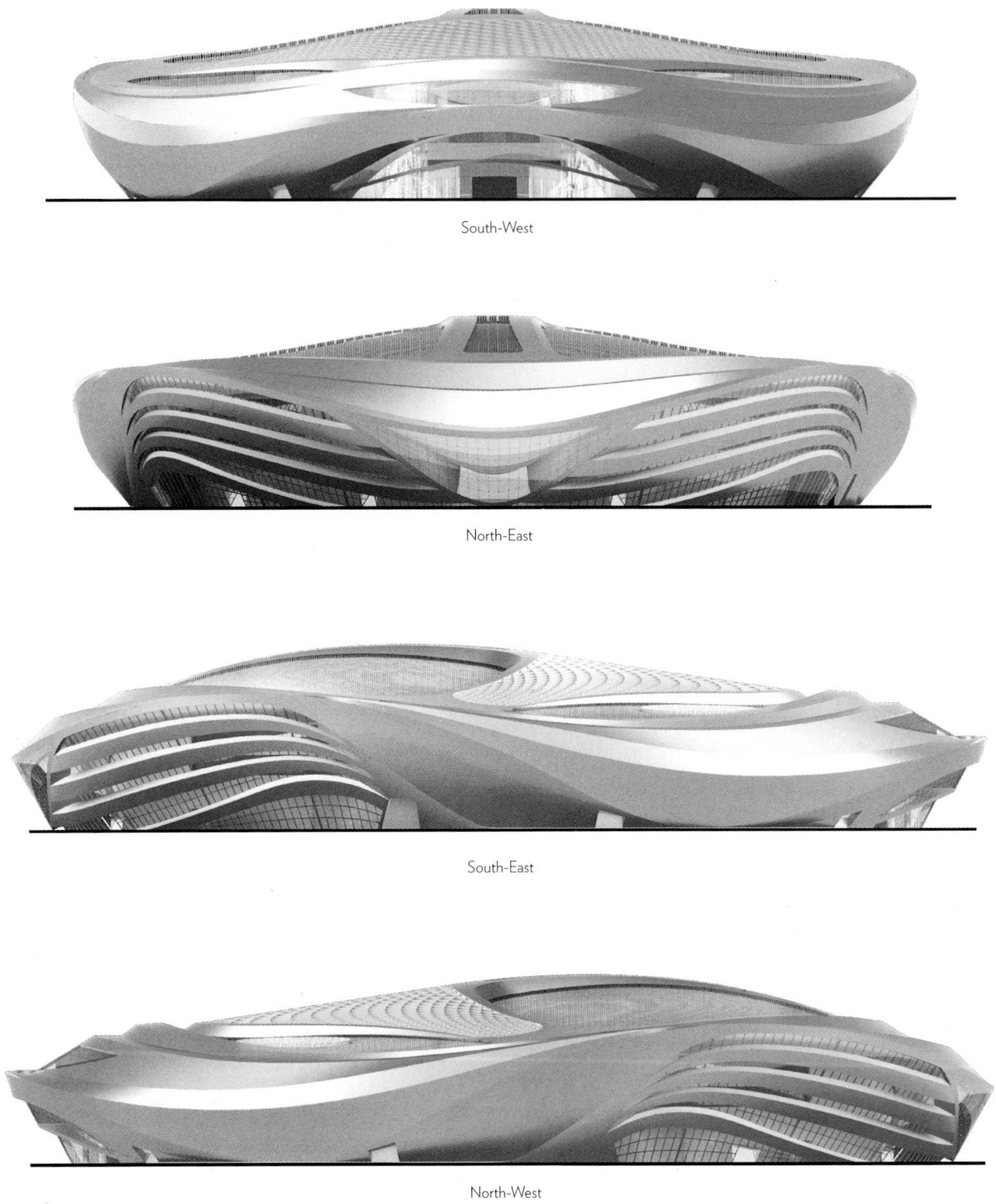

Overall Elevations | Aerial View Rendering (Right)

DESIGN CONCEPT | SPACE

The public circulation areas are accentuated with white marble floors, white walls and ceilings, and a white clad atrium. This monochromatic palette embraces the light and shadow exposed through the skylights as a dynamic aspect of the design. The fluid circulation naturally helps visitors navigate the various programmatic functions. Visual continuity enhances the circulation with uninterrupted views toward adjacent programmed spaces at multiple levels. Gallery spaces line the perimeter of the auditorium and connect the central atrium and Lyceum, serving as primary entrances to the auditorium. Twin grand staircases link the three floors on each side of the atrium.

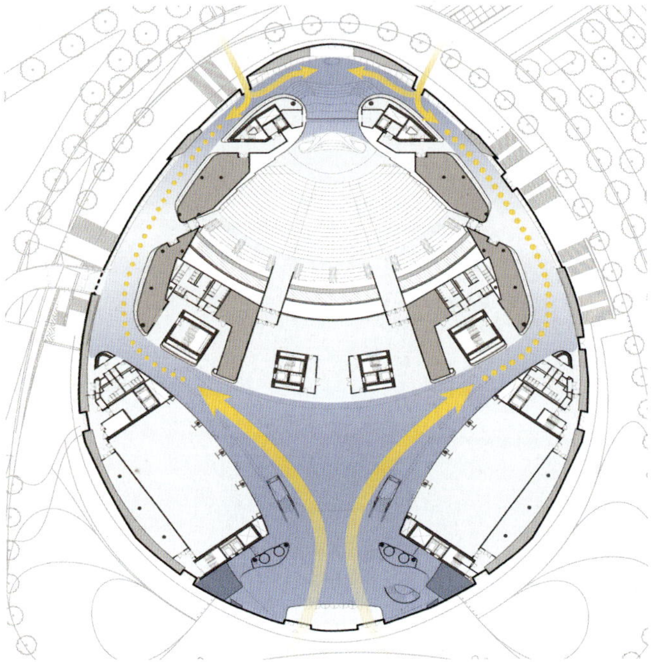

Permeable Procession Plan

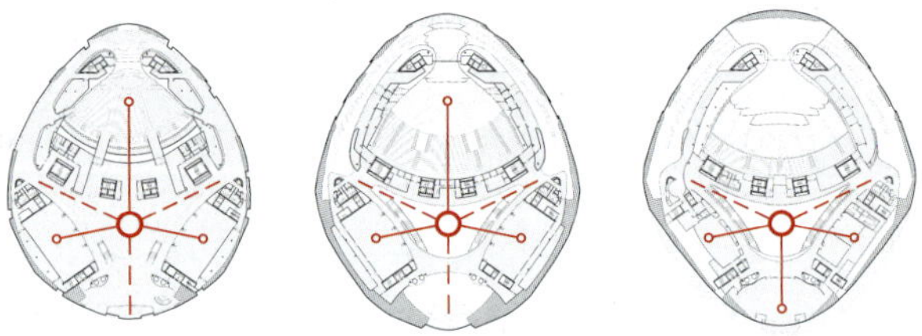

Trefoil Anchors

Grand Staircase

The procession into the performance spaces transitions to a warmer material palette of acoustical plaster and slotted wood acoustical panels that envelopes the interior of the auditorium and ancillary assembly spaces. Custom lighting accents the architectural pleating and provides localized light for performances. The auditorium's finished ceiling design is one of the key components of the room that unites the architectural language of the seating and stage areas, while also coordinating the many technical components including technical galleries, and front of house rigging positions.

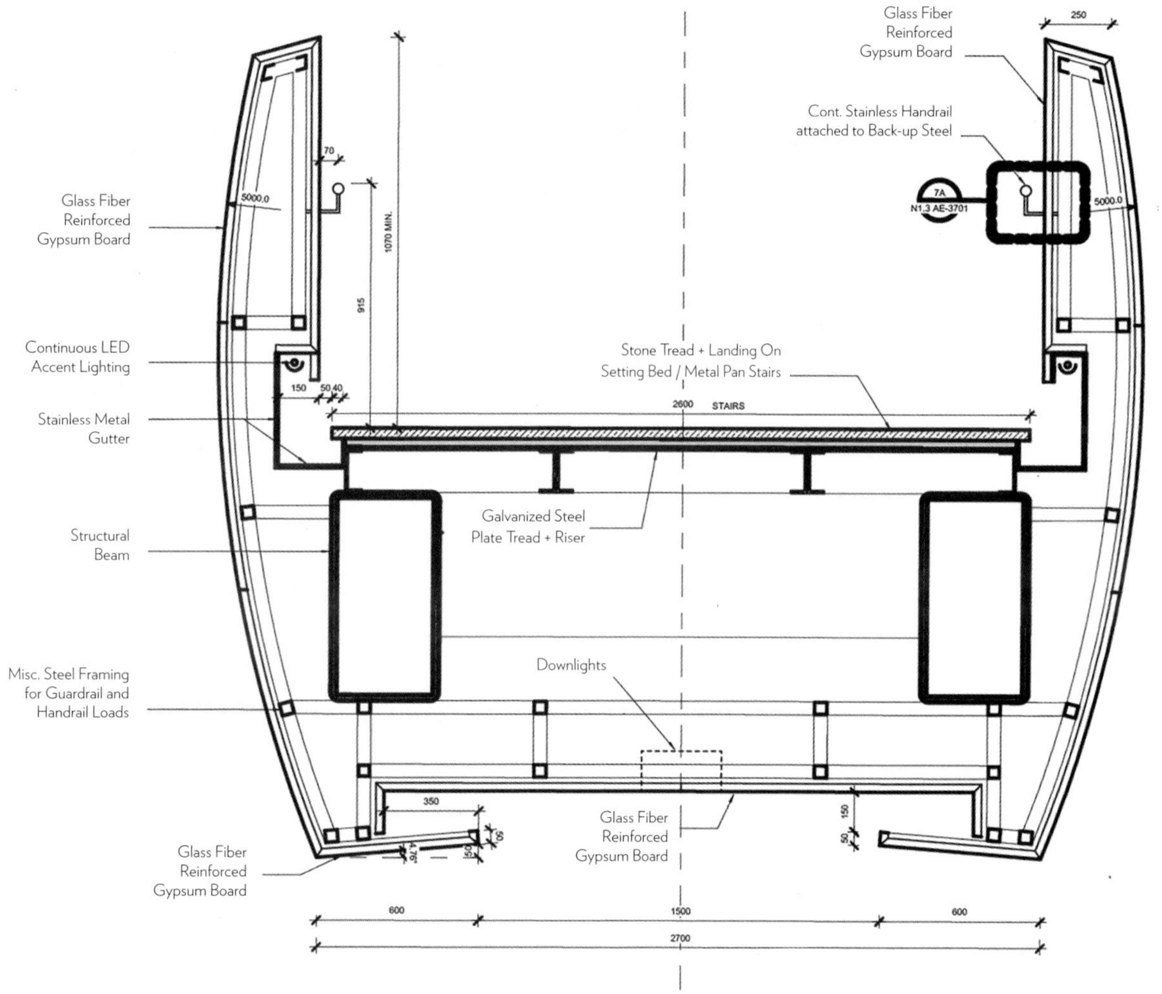

Grand Staircase Detail Section

DESIGN CONCEPT | SPACE

The central atrium skylight measures nearly 100 meters long and 40 meters wide. A diagrid structural steel grid shell with members 600mm deep provides a shallow and efficient means to span the space.

As the grid shell structure gains its strength by means of curvature inherent within the system, this presented the next challenge in terms of planarity of glazing. The long span distances and shallow curvature of the grid shell enabled a subdivision strategy using cold-bending techniques and avoided costly hot-bent glazing.

Working within the manufacturer's guidelines for maximum distances that can be cold bent over a prescribed diagonal panel length, the subdivision analysis provided instant feedback as to whether a panel was within tolerance.

Construction, 2016

Self-Similar Panel Clusters

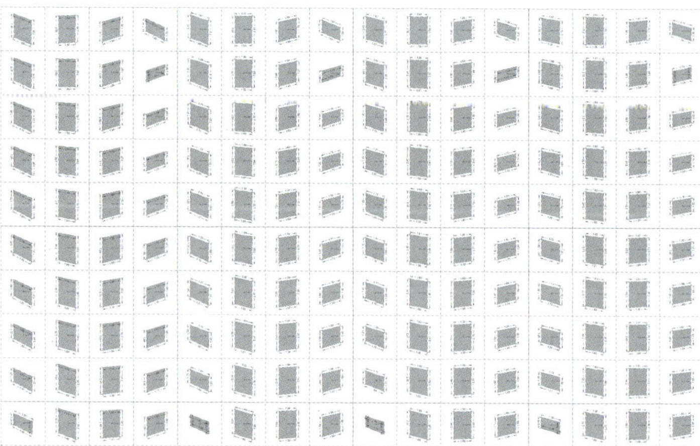

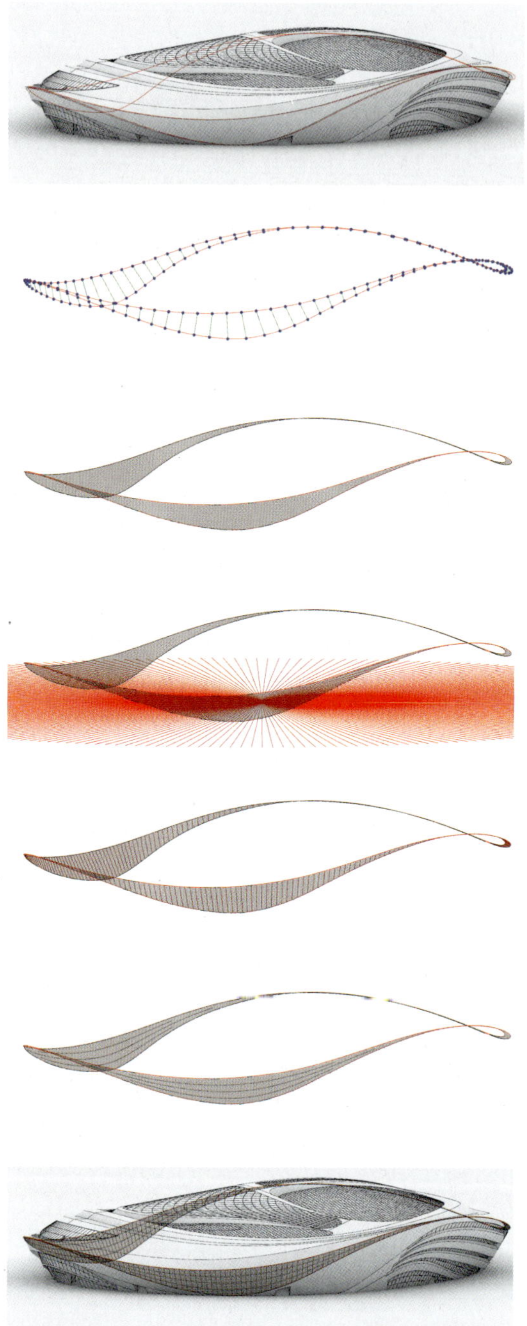

Panelization Process

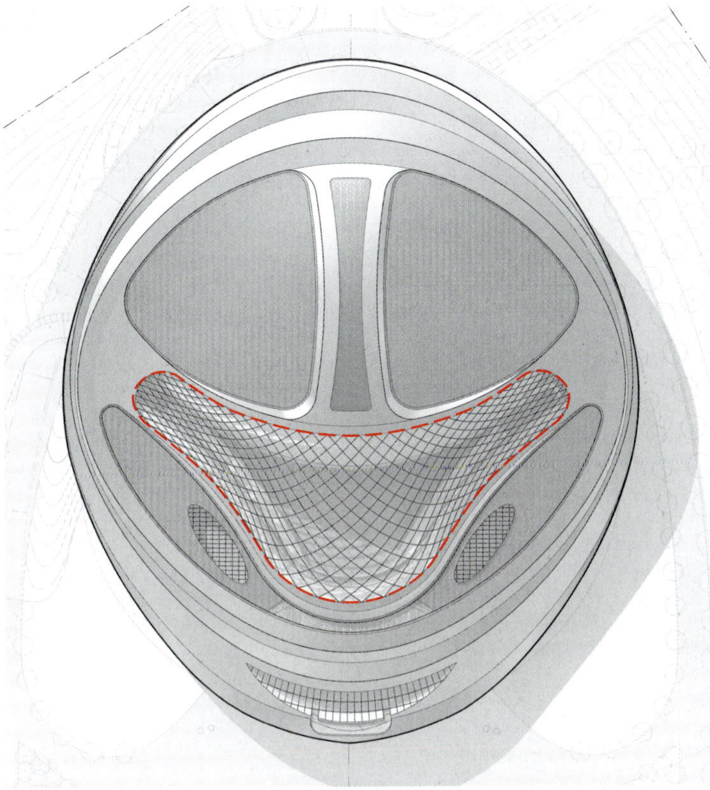

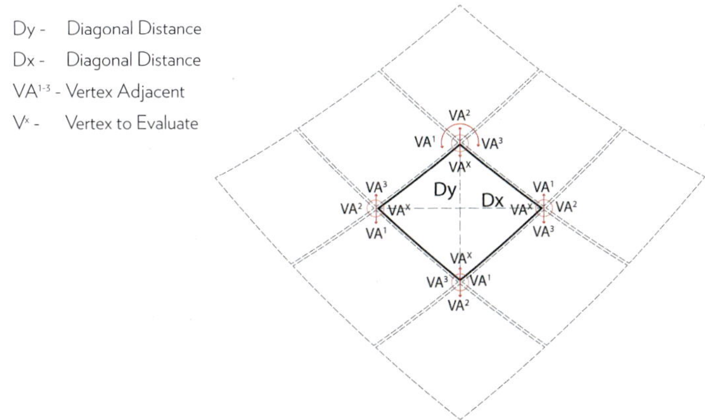

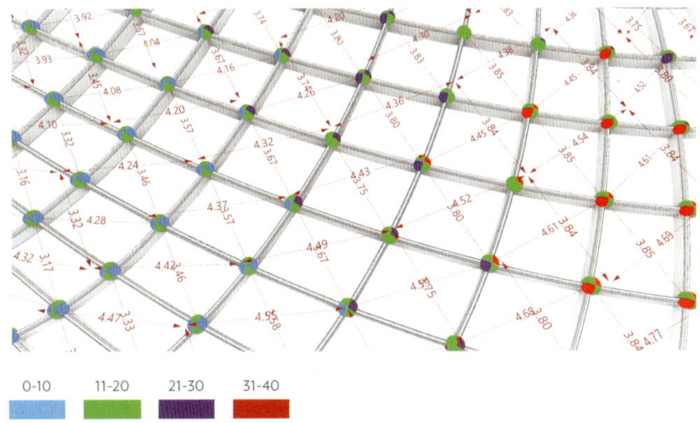

Cold Bend Vertex Distance

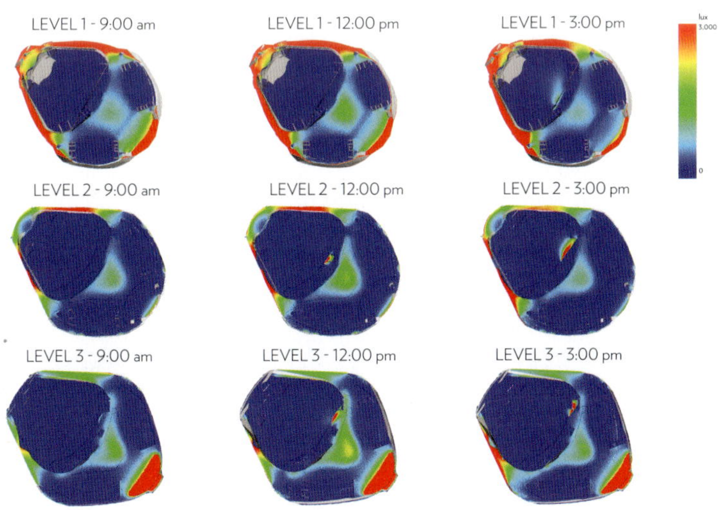

Daylight Analysis (June 21st)

Cold Bend Vertex Distance

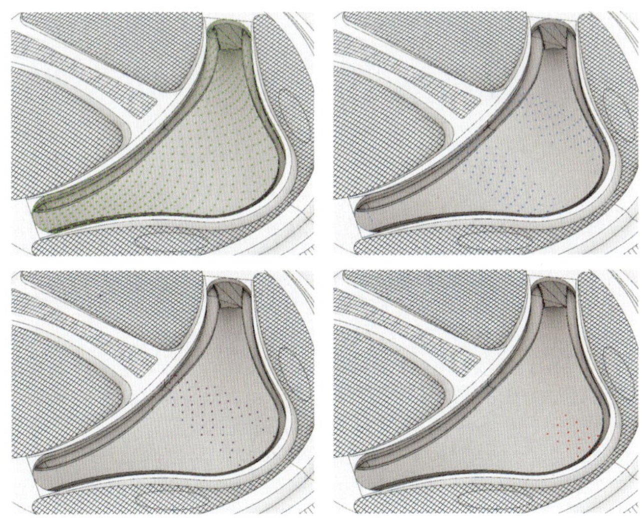

DESIGN CONCEPT | MATERIALS

The exterior facade required a parametric workflow to synthesize the assembly into simple and constructible elements. From the outset, strict guidelines were established to achieve the fluid form. Constructing the foundational surfaces as developable lofts ensured that the surfaces could be easily subdivided into planar panels. Subdivision strategies required an approach to accent the fluidity of the primary creases, while maintaining manufacturability.

Following the quadrilateral subdivision process, a cross validation process was implemented to ensure gap tolerances were uniform and that corner points were within the allowable distance of adjacent corner panel points. The overall process ensured the rapid fabrication of the cladding panels using a CNC beltline process that was fed with aluminum coil.

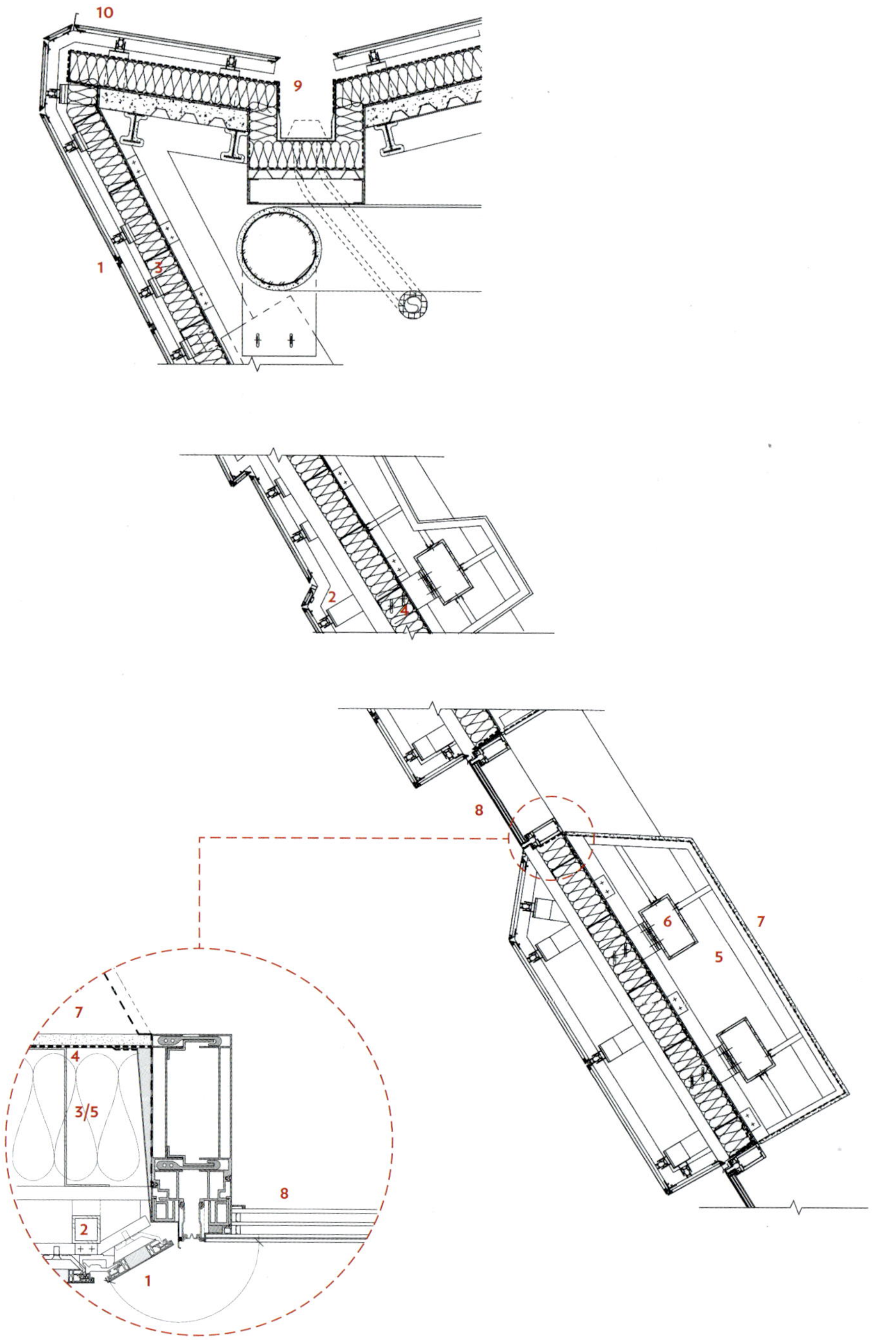

Exterior Wall Section

1 Composite Cladding
2 Cladding Tracks
3 Insulation
4 Waterproofing Membrane
5 Light Steel Framing
6 Structural Steel
7 Interior Finish
8 Triple Pane IGU
9 Gutter
10 Snow Guard

Several aspects of the design required in-depth research and analysis to realize the best solutions to address function, constructability, and intent. For example, the acoustical performance of the auditorium was crucial to the success of the space. Controlling the sound levels in such a large space presented a unique case study during the iterative design process.

Reverberation is controlled through both absorptive and diffusive tactics. Absorption is achieved through micro perforations within the ceiling and wall wood paneling, which was also lined with a sound absorptive fabric. This reduces the amount of noise and the overall reverberation in the room.

Diffusion of the sound waves was achieved with non-parallel surfaces on the ceiling and walls. This pleating reduces parallel reverberation. Analysis of various iterations studying the trajectory and number of incident collisions of sound waves with respective surfaces led to optimized and irregular perimeter surfaces compared with the original smoother concepts.

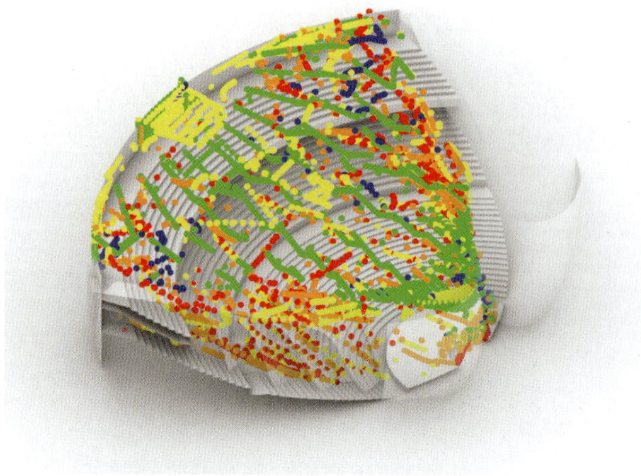

Simplified Reflectance Impact Study

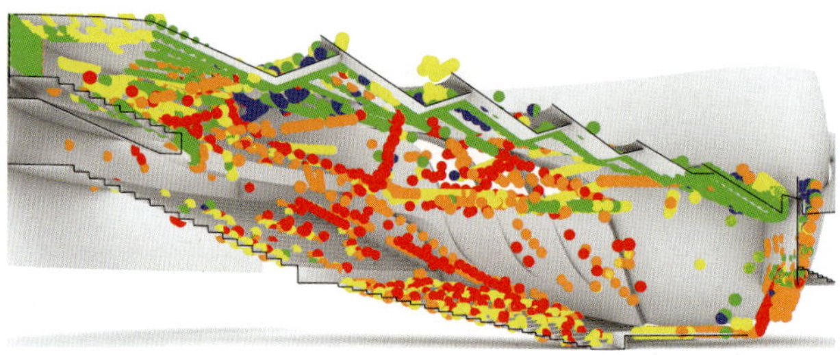

1 2 3 4 5

Reflectance Impact Count Along Ray

Acoustical Reverberation Investigation

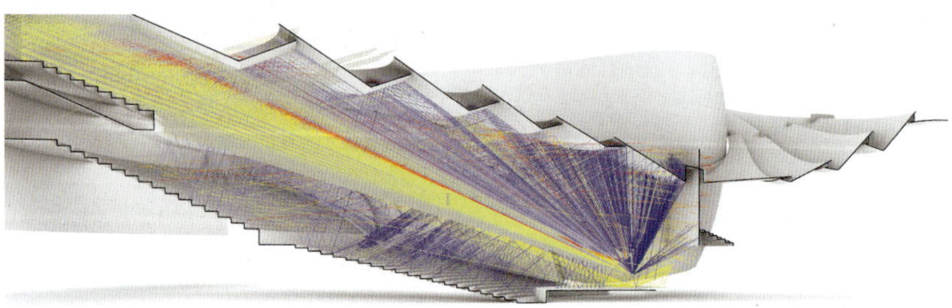

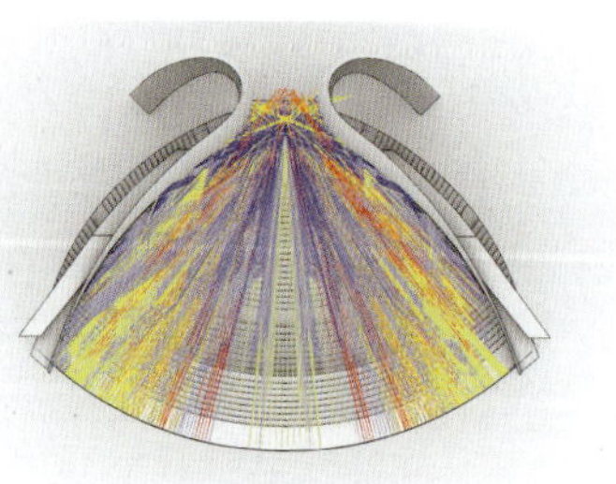

0-39 40-79 80-119

Reverberation Distance Traveled

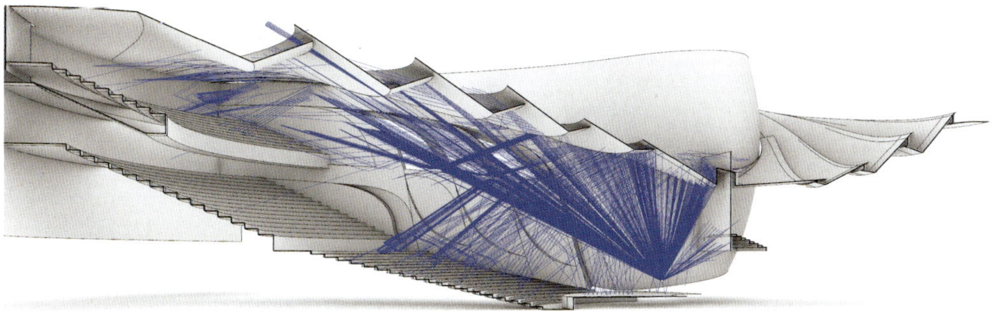

0-39

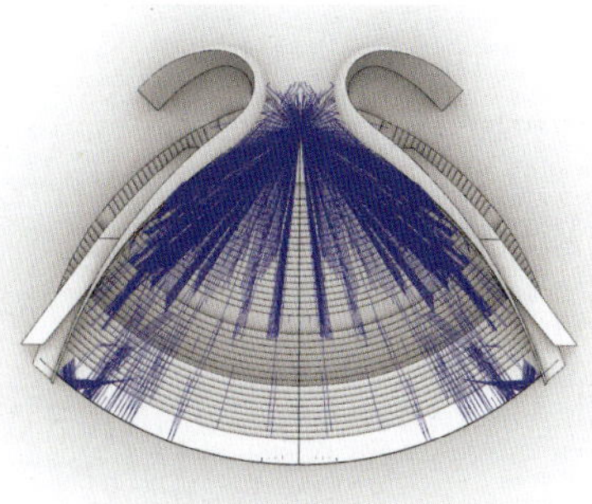

Plan

40-79

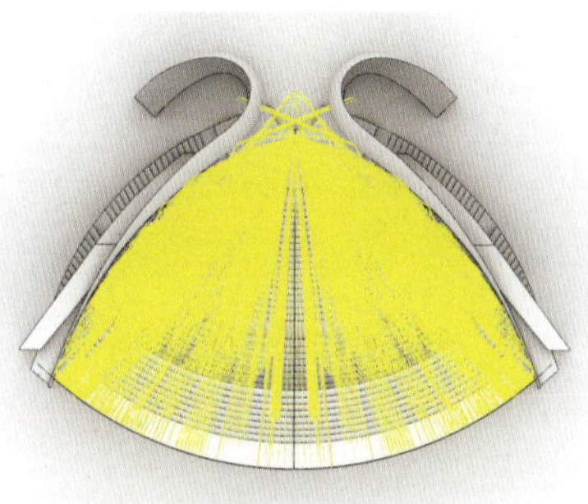

Plan

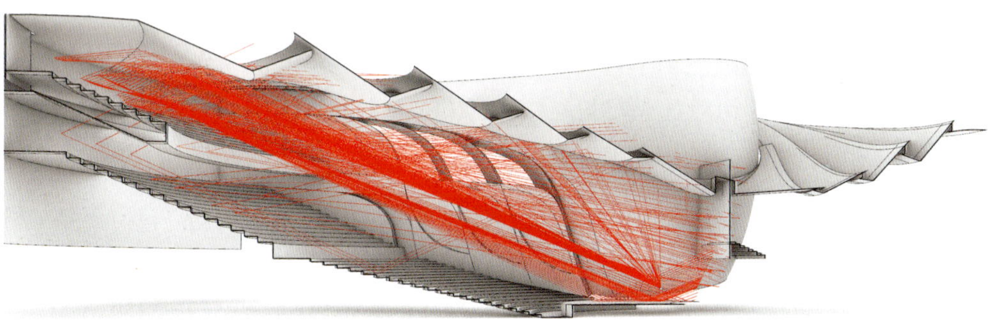

80-119

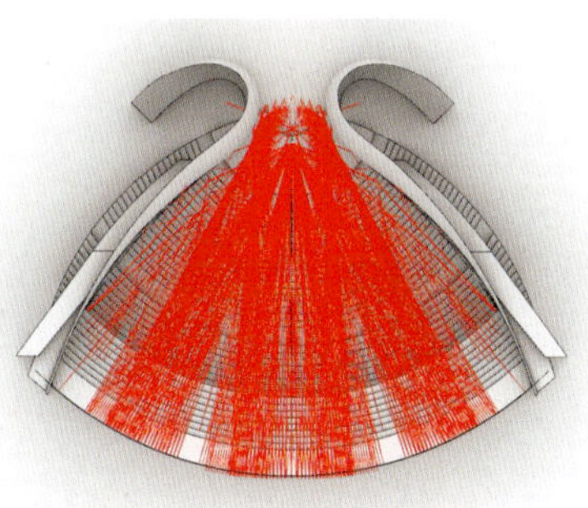

Plan

0-39 40-79 80-119

Reverberation Distance Traveled

A sightline analysis is a critical component of the design process for any performance space. Ensuring that every participant has access to unimpeded visual acuity to the primary performance stage is essential to the success of the space and informs the seating's design and rake.

The process is rooted in a viewer's average "resting eye" position, which is typically between 0-15 degrees from the horizontal. A maximum limit threshold of 25 degrees above horizontal and 35 degrees below zero represent the extremes. To produce optimal viewing angles, the project thresholds were set to 20 degrees above horizontal and 20 degrees below horizontal.

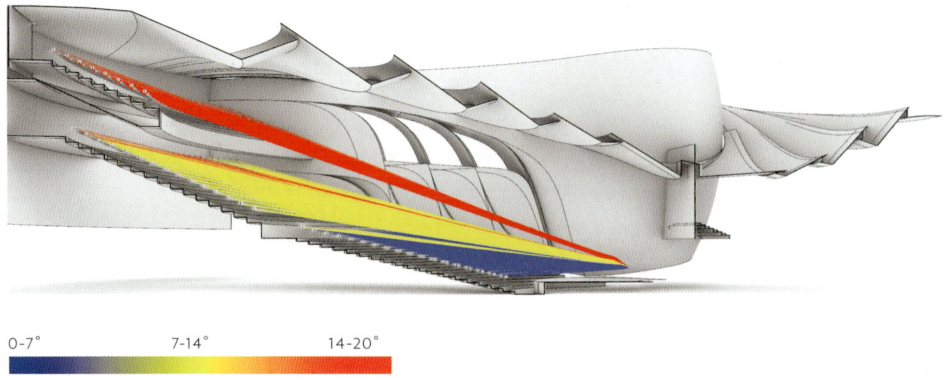

Stage Viewing Angle

Angular Range Principle

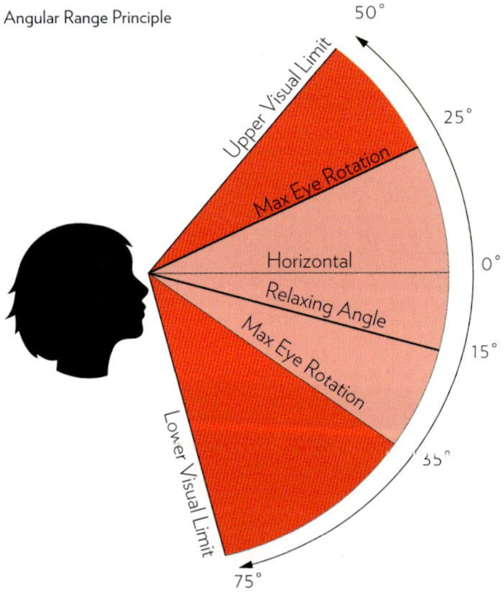

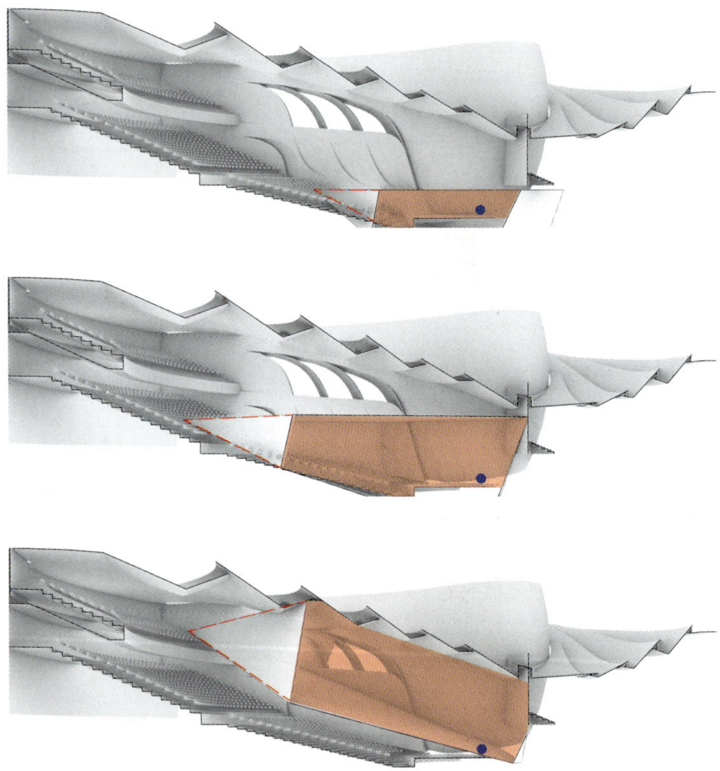
Angular Range Validation Per Seat Location

Sightline Analysis

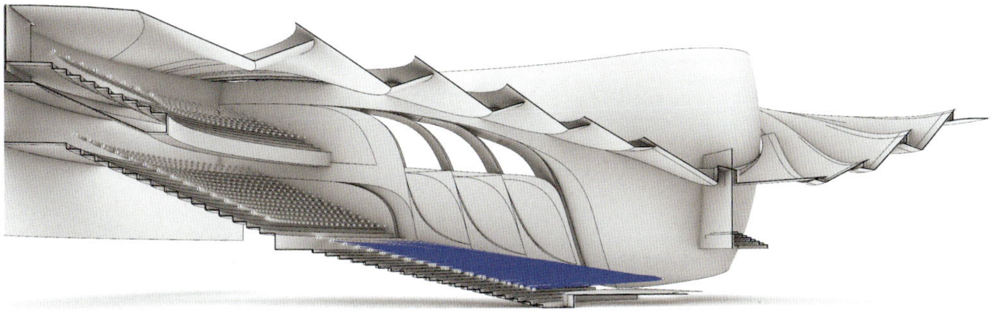

0-7°

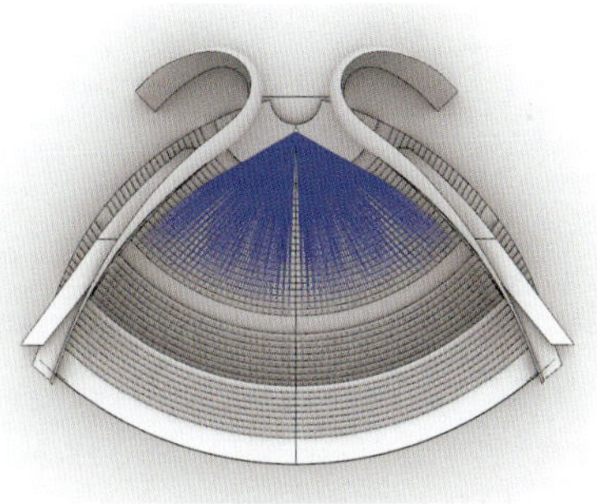

Plan

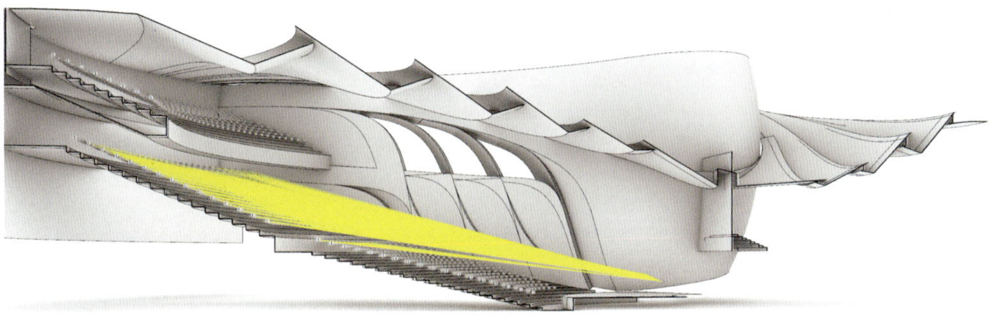

7-14°

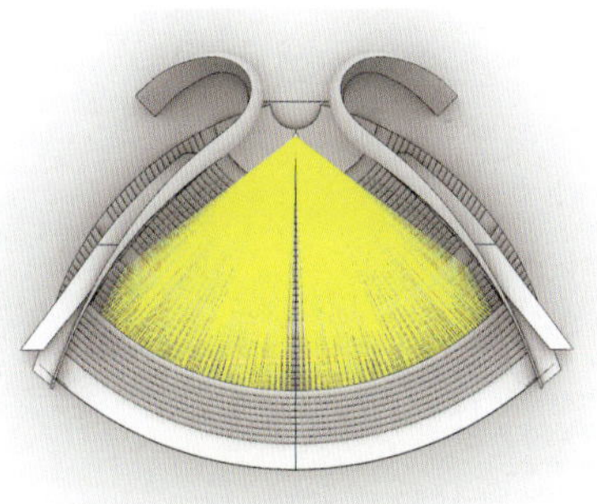

Plan

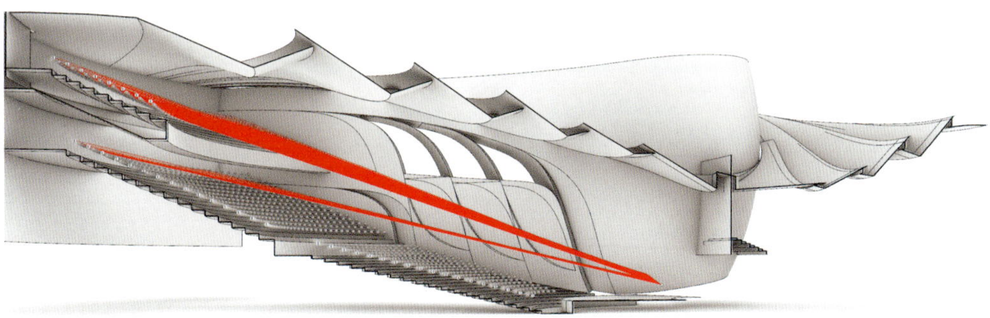

14-20°

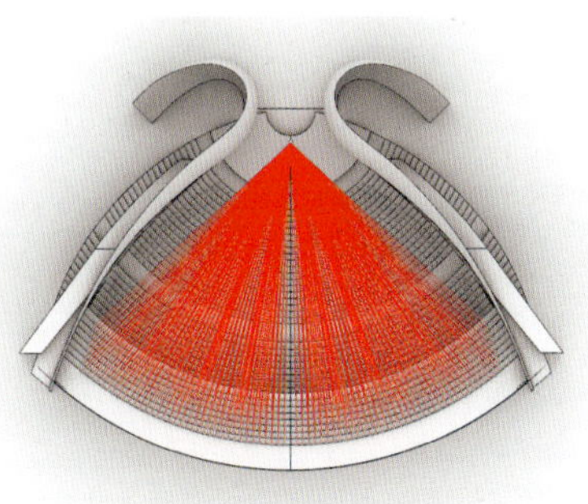

Plan

WILLOW CREEK NORTH SHORE

Glenview, Illinois, USA

Willow Creek North Shore is a non-denominational church and designed as a community center and multi-functional venue rather than a standard place of worship. The client's aim was for the 72,000-square-foot building to reach people who may be intimidated by a more traditional, staid church structure.

Willow Creek features a central auditorium flanked by two landscaped outdoor terraces, as well as administration offices, flexible ministry rooms, and several educational classrooms for a variety of community strengthening activities. A youth worship room, located at the north end of the building and opposite the auditorium, offers activities such as music performances and motivational talks. The Promiseland daycare and play area can accommodate up to 400 children.

Willow Creek North Shore is located in a quiet suburban setting along Shermer Road in Glenview, Illinois. Founded in 1975, Willow Creek is an interdenominational, intergenerational church foundation. The building is contextual to its natural setting, surrounded by green space when viewed from afar. To the north is a cemetery, to the southwest a residential community, and across the street is a public golf course. The building is carefully sited and designed to be seen, but set back from, the main road with landscape screening on the residential sides of the property.

Function: Religious + Community Center | **Status:** Built, 2016 | **Client:** Willow Creek North Shore | **Awards:** The Chicago Athenaeum, American Architecture Award, 2017

DESIGN CONCEPT | SITE

Several months of construction were dedicated to site works, which elevated the church by five to eight feet from its original grade, creating a gentle plateau with views of the surrounding community. A large retention pond was also constructed near the entrance of Shermer Road, as well as surface parking for over 700 vehicles, and access drives to and from the site.

In a study done prior to construction, the client found that patrons using the church have little to no effect on current traffic patterns, if certain criteria were met. Several recommendations were followed including adding turning lanes at key intersections, adding a traffic signal at West Lake and Shermer Road, and hiring volunteers to direct traffic on Sunday mornings.

> *Willow Creek North Shore is a project built around a community, for a community. Though it does not reach the tall heights of AS+GG's other buildings, the firm's signature form and style are undeniable.*
> *- Matthew Messner, Contributing Editor, The Architect's Newspaper*

Site Plan with Traffic Pattern

1 Youth Ministries Entrance
2 Staff Parking Lot
3 Service Entrance
4 West Parking Lot
5 Courtyards
6 Main Entrance
7 Signage Point
8 Residential Development
9 Retention Pond
10 East Parking Lot

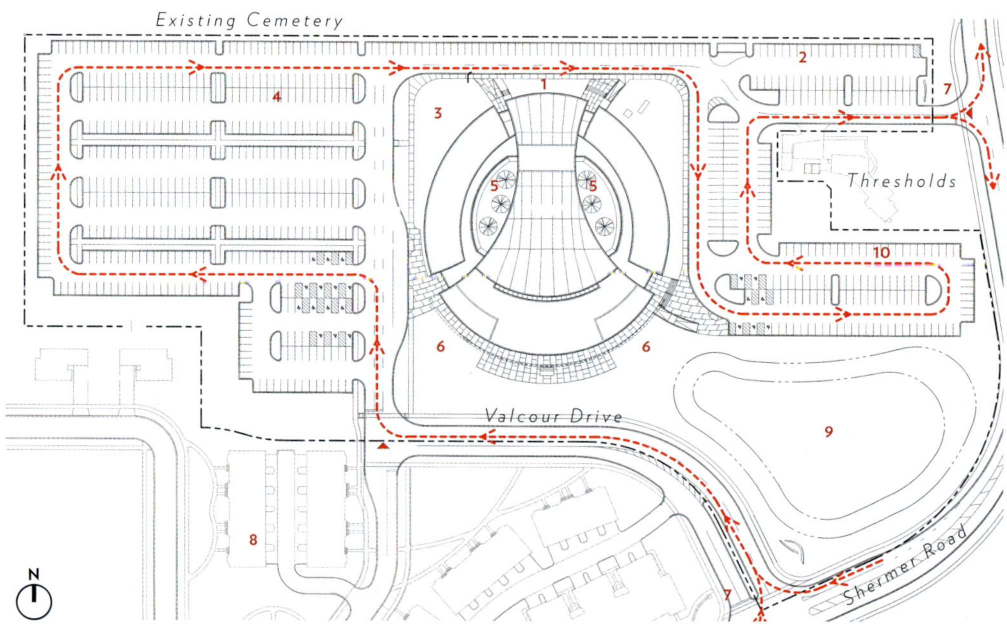

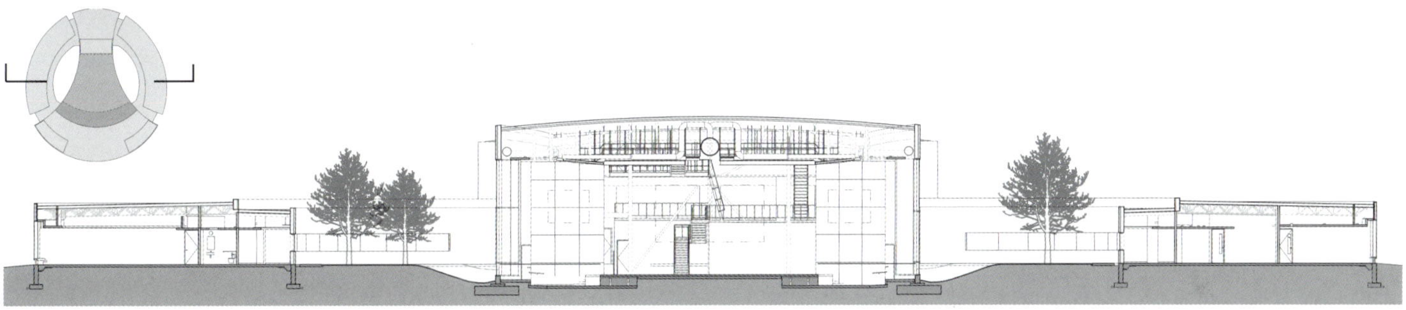

Cross Section

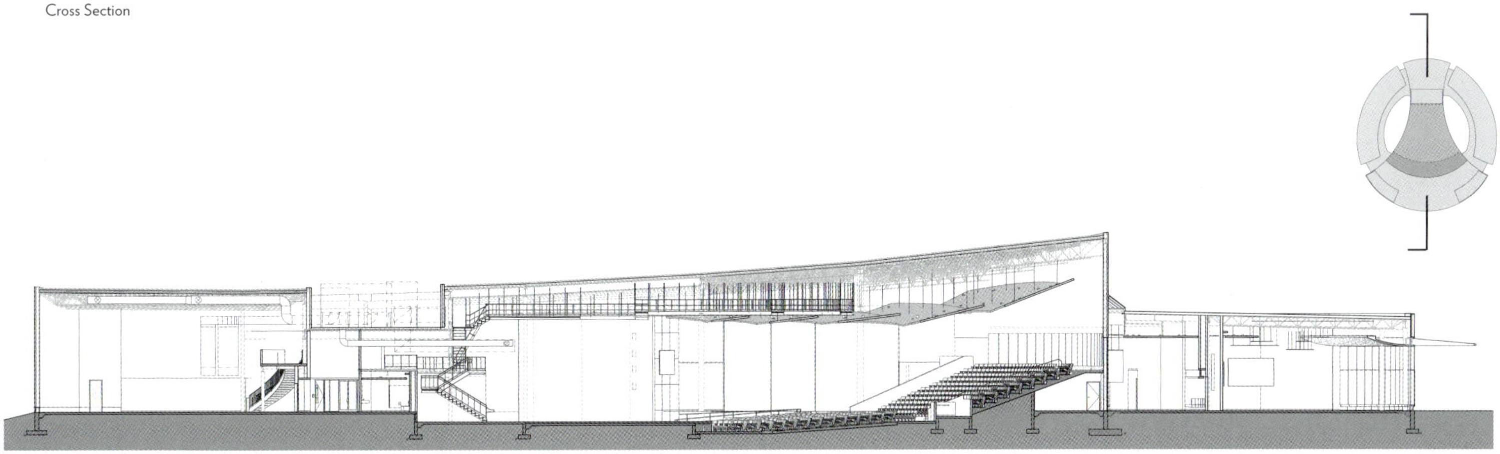

Longitudinal Section

DESIGN CONCEPT | PROGRAM

The building consists of five sections that link together to form an oval shape, with the main worship space at the center—and pinnacle—of the design. Surrounding the main worship space are the east and west wings, which house the educational and administrative spaces and the south wing, which has public gathering and pre-function spaces.

The spacious pre-function lobby establishes a welcoming feeling and a clear diagram that is understandable for both those who attend on a regular basis and the first-time visitor. The lobby's wayfinding guides visitors to the main sanctuary or other gathering points throughout the building. Gently curving circulation paths allow occupants to flow through the space while enjoying views of the outside.

Flexibility was key to the entire design building. For instance, administration offices are used by the church employees Monday through Friday but are available on the weekend for adult ministry services and can provide additional opportunities for classes, workshops, and fund-raising activities.

North Elevation | Pre-function Lobby (Right)

Floor Plan

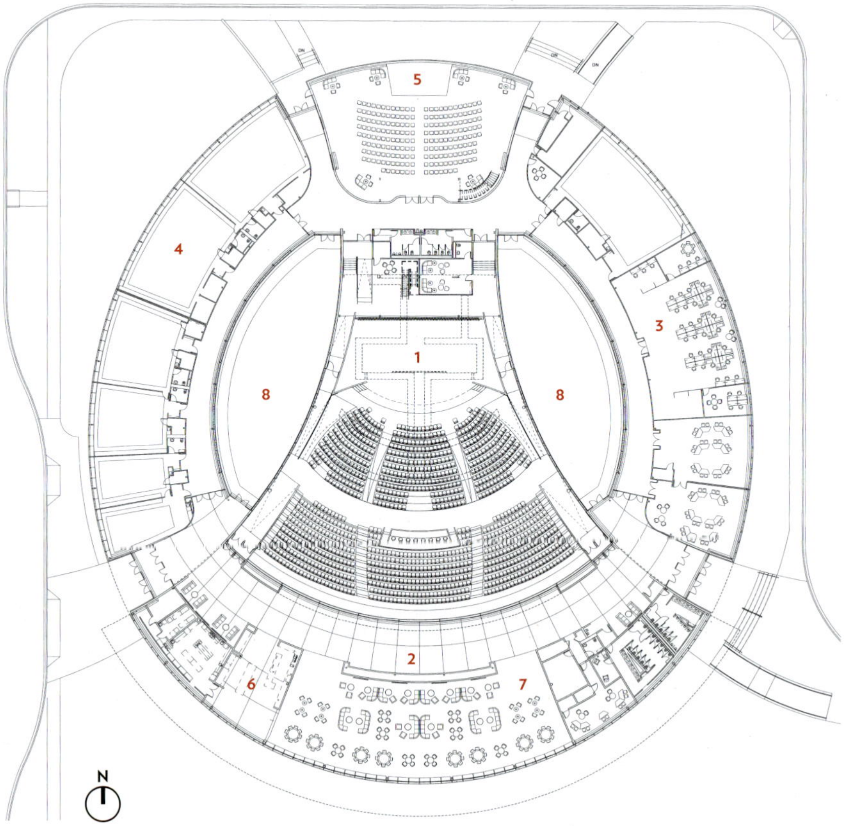

1 Main Auditorium

2 Pre-Function

3 Administration

4 Promiseland

5 Youth Group

6 Food Service

7 Meeting Space

8 Courtyard

COME
&
SEE
EASTER
AT
WILLOW CREEK
Welcome Center

DESIGN CONCEPT | FORM

The design is inspired by the form of a mustard seed, a biblical metaphor that means even if your faith is smaller than a mustard seed, you can still move mountains. This sentiment reminds attendees that no amount of faith is too small—that everyone is welcome to this community-based church.

The mustard seed also represents the building's association with nature. The geometry is based on a symmetrical, circular shape in plan. Two wings wrap around two central courtyards that can be viewed from the auditorium and the administrative offices. This green space seeks to connect building users to the outdoors, translating the mustard seed inspiration.

Design Concept

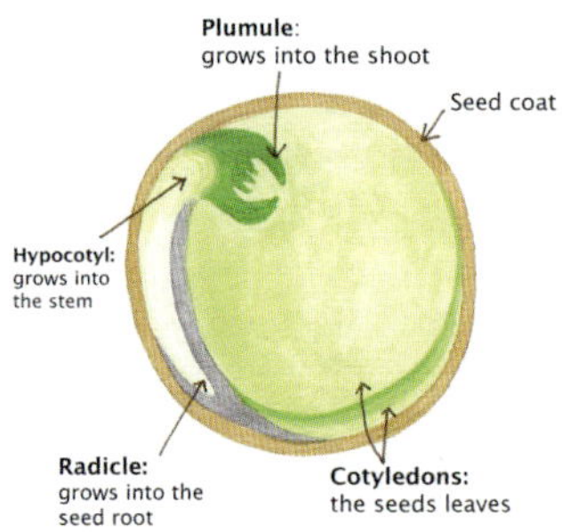

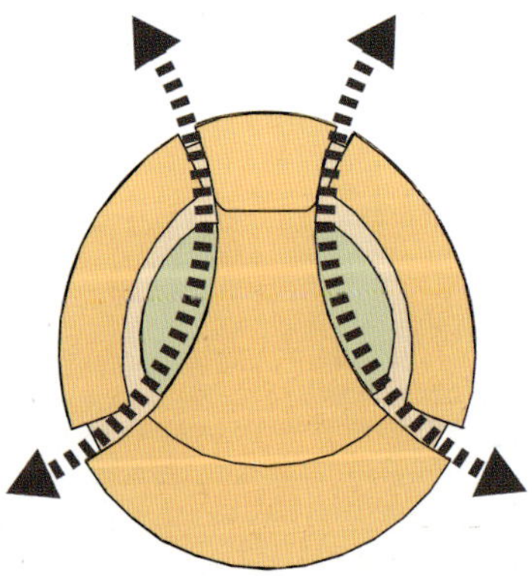

Pathways connect the program to green spaces that provide light and views.

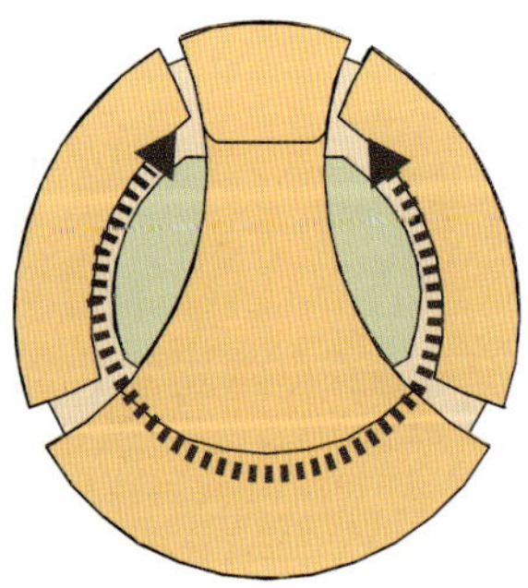

Green spaces complete the seed shape as a cohesive massing.

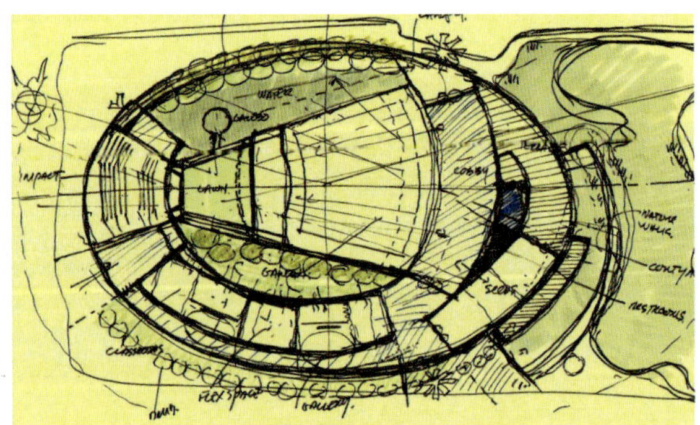

Concept Sketch

DESIGN CONCEPT | SPACE

A 1,200-seat, state-of-the art auditorium is the main worship space and is also used as a multi-functional media room that has hosted community events since the building opened. The Harvest Café, located in front of the auditorium, is used for community meetings and as a gathering space on Sundays for those who wish to watch the service on screens in a more casual setting.

Willow Creek's youth ministries groups—"Elevate" for grades six through eight and "Impact" for grades nine through 12—have a separate sanctuary on the north side of the building, facing opposite to the auditorium. This space gives students an arena to strengthen their commitment to youth ministry activities.

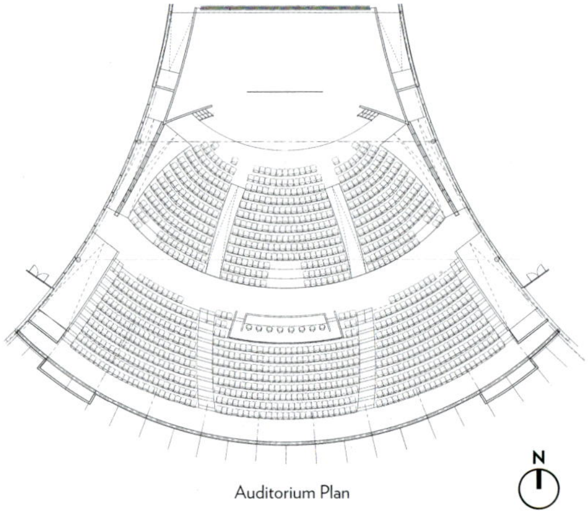

Auditorium Plan

Main Auditorium | Harvest Cafe (Right)

BECOMING US
MARRIAGE EVENT

Promiseland is an onsite children's ministry and childcare center that focuses on age-appropriate activities and teaching. The classrooms occupy the west corridor of the church and have interior design that is tailored to each age. Safe-play areas are designated for the youngest children, with small meeting and stage areas for the middle-school aged children to attend shorter worship services.

Some classrooms have movable partitions for flexibility because the amount and ages of children can vary from week to week and the space needs to accommodate for this fluidity. The design of the corridor uses a vibrant color scheme for wayfinding to each entry door and allows a generous entry area to facilitate the check-in process.

Promiseland | Corridor Color Wayfinding (Right)

Wayfinding Diagram

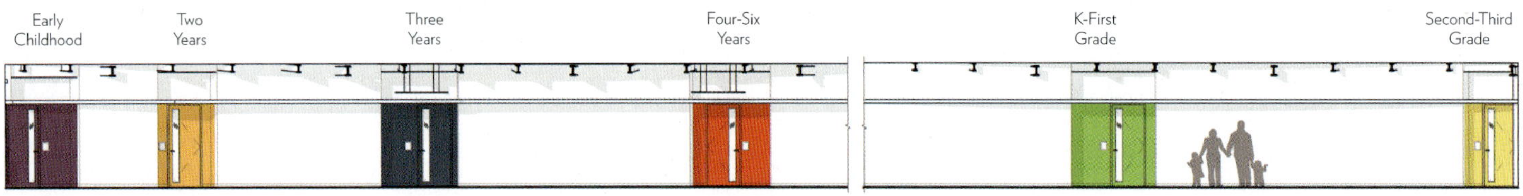

DESIGN CONCEPT | SPACE

The use of natural light is imperative to the success of this design. Floor-to-ceiling windows face outward toward the campus, providing views and natural light to the interior of the auditorium, classrooms, and office facilities. Horizontal windows face inward to the intimate courtyards providing more natural light to the interior corridors, strengthening the building's connection to nature. Skylights carved into the roof also provide daylight into the interior corridors, while adding visual interest to the ceiling and walls.

A long skylight in the center of the pre-function space was designed so that the sun shines directly into the space, washing the outside wall of the auditorium with light as people enter before the worship services. The light's positioning changes throughout the day, allowing more connections to nature for the building's occupants.

Main Auditorium | Pre-function Skylight (Right)

Landscaped Courtyard

DESIGN CONCEPT | MATERIALS

The materials used on both the exterior and interior of the building are elegant and simple. Externally, creative construction methods and materials were used to keep the budget at approximately $200 per square foot. With a limited budget and a desire for maximum transparency of the facade, simple measures were undertaken to reduce the carbon footprint of the building and achieve energy and cost savings. Strategies include using a heavily insulated exterior wall, a 30% glazing ratio, and high-performance glazing.

High-performance glass coupled with heavily insulated solid walls keep the building warm in the winter and cool in the summer, decreasing the operation costs compared to similar sized buildings. Internally, the structure is exposed throughout the public spaces, increasing the ceiling height and the feeling of openness. To achieve these results a combination of 150-foot clear span trusses, bar joists, and cantilevered steel framing was used. Polished concrete floors are used in the youth and pre-function spaces.

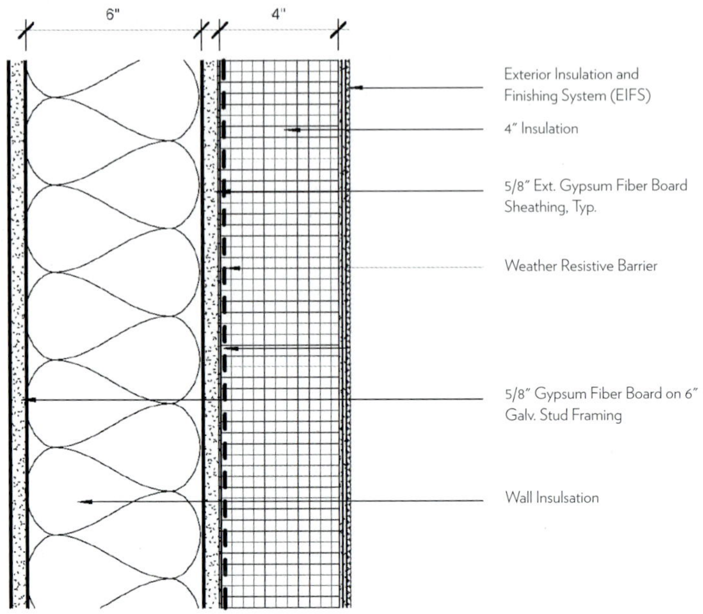

Typical Solid Wall - 10" Insulation

North Elevation

South Elevation

East Elevation

West Elevation

1 Stucco Wall

2 Glass + Aluminum Facade

3 Aluminum Base

4 Glass + Aluminum Facade with Stainless Steel Sunshade

RESEARCH + DEVELOPMENT | ANALYSIS

The sunshade canopy is one of the building's defining architectural features. Its primary purpose is to shade the exterior wall's glass to prevent excessive glare and heat gain in the assembly space. The design also emphasizes the main assembly space at the front of the building and identifies the building as a unique place. The materiality and constructability of the canopy on a limited budget was a great challenge and opportunity. Several options were studied during early design phases.

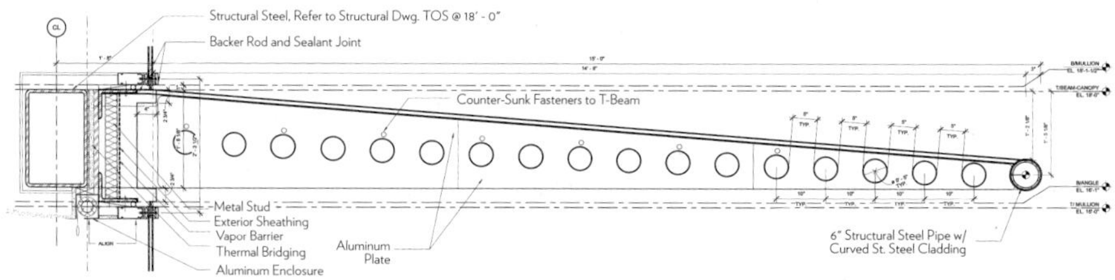

Canopy Section

One initial option that was considered was the installation of Thin-Film photovoltaic panels laminated into glass to form the canopy. Although the panels would have experienced generous exposure to the sun and would have provided the necessary shading, it was found that the framing and glass itself was beyond the budget.

Many other materials were considered, but it was decided that a light-weight aluminum tubular sunshade was the most cost effective, the most durable, and the simplest to install. The design team worked with a local fabricator to procure the aluminum and to optimize the design for easy installation.

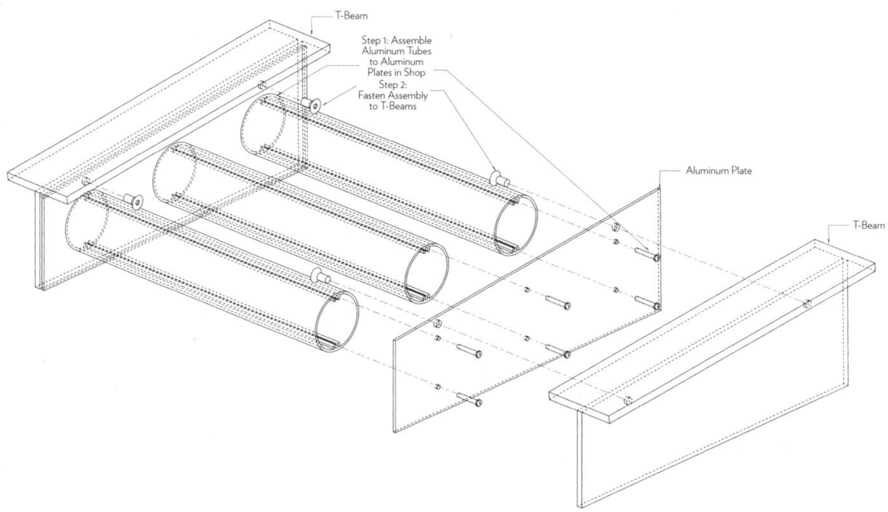

Perspective View

A cassette system was derived to allow the necessary tolerances for installation and for structural movement. Neoprene spacers were installed between the aluminum and the steel canopy supports to prevent galvanic action. The cassette system allows the tubes to be brought to the site before assembly and then are installed after the steel is erected.

Studies determined the optimal size and spacing for the tubes in terms of cost-effectiveness, efficiency, functionality, and control. As a final cost savings measure, the canopy tubes were eliminated on the sides of the building where the restrooms and kitchen were located because these spaces have solid walls and did not require shading and the steel structure was left in place to complete the gesture of the canopy element on the main facade.

Concept

Construction

Execution

The building design exceeds the required ASHRAE baseline by saving 20% of its energy costs.

- Predicted EUI in kBtu/sf/yr excluding on-site renewable energy contribution: 35.92
- Predicted EUI in kBtu/sf/yr including on-site renewable energy contribution (carbon offsets will not be counted): 35.92
- Predicted % regional energy reduction per Energy Star Target Finder: 22%

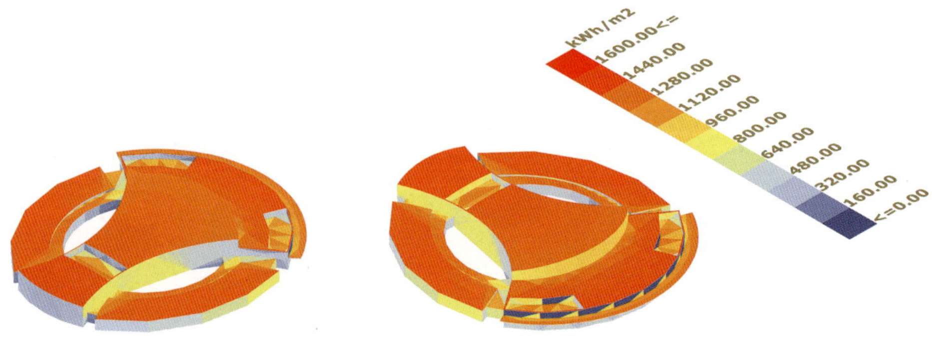

Northeast

Southwest

Radiation Analysis

North

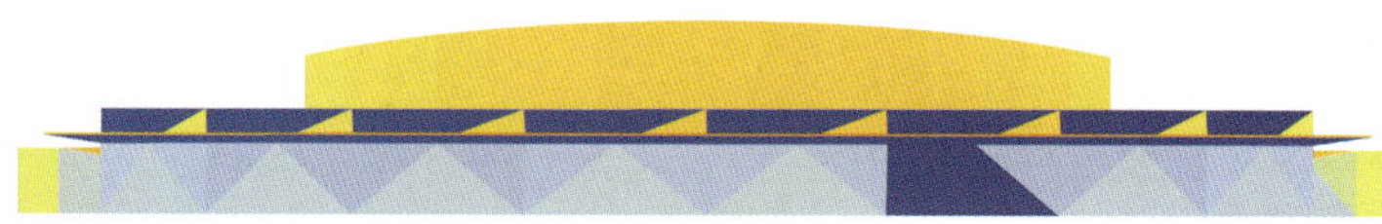

South

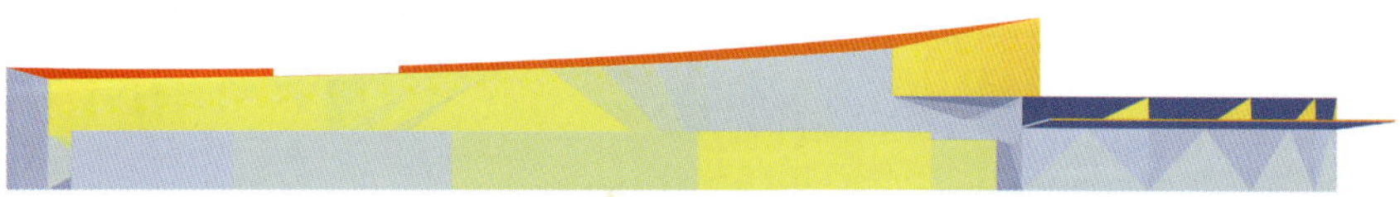

West

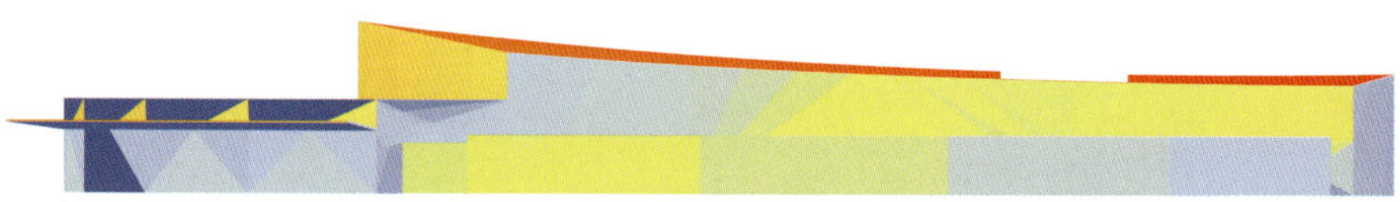

East

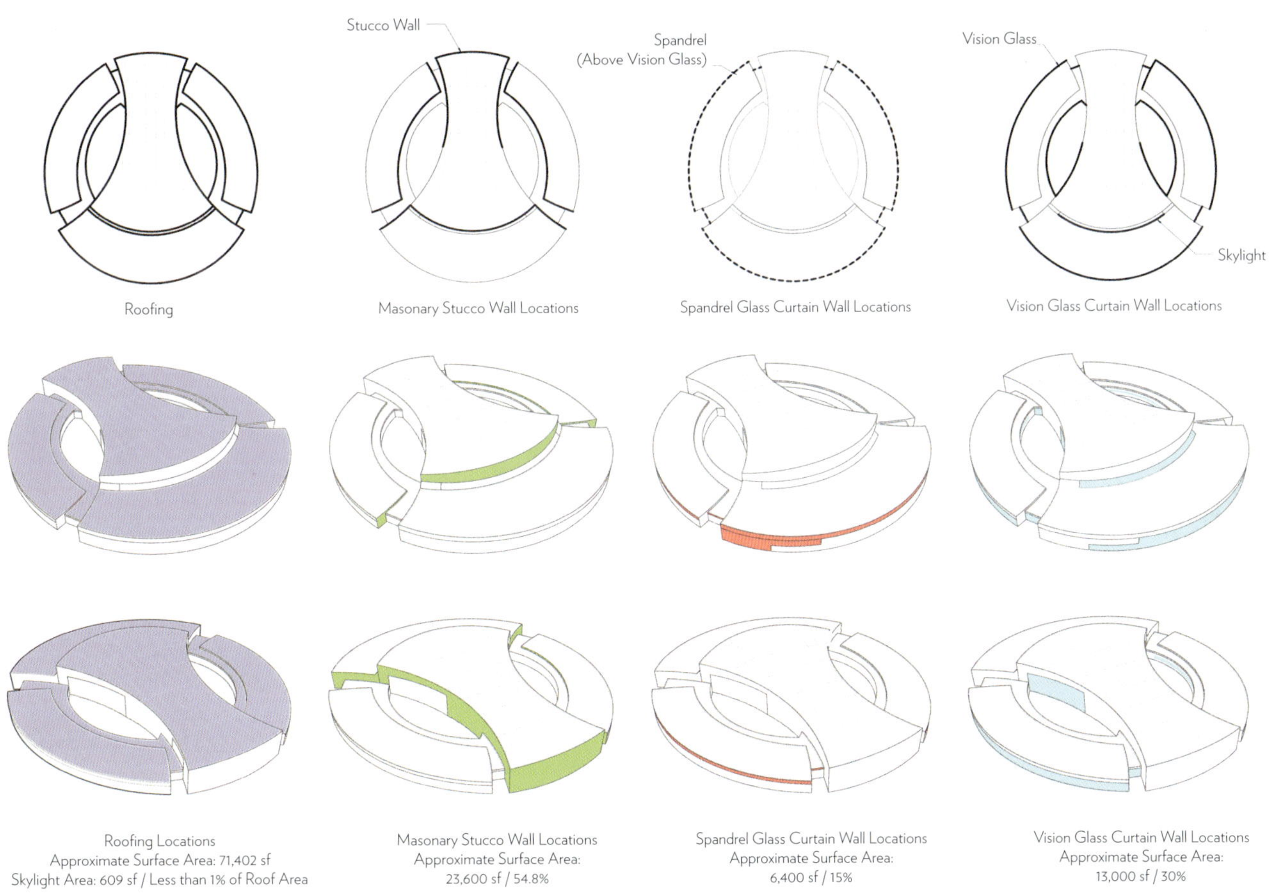

Glazing Ratios (up to 30%)

THE YARD AT CHICAGO SHAKESPEARE THEATER

Chicago, Illinois, USA

The Yard at Chicago Shakespeare Theater at Navy Pier in Chicago, Illinois, is integral to the pier's Centennial Vision and reimagining of the Midwest's most visited leisure destination. The new and renovated features are designed to expand Navy Pier's impact and audience, showcasing a vibrant cultural, educational, environmental, and recreational landscape.

The Yard is a next-generation performance venue that reflects Chicago Shakespeare's multi-faceted artistic vision as it redefines the traditional relationship between artist and audience, taking the theater production, performance, and audience to a new level. The project features flexible seating towers and a new entrance lobby that connects to the existing theater, introducing Chicago to a global trend in theater architecture, which focuses on flexible, adaptive, and sustainable design.

Navy Pier, located in Chicago, Illinois, opened to the public in 1916 as the "Municipal Pier," designed by Charles Summer Frost and based on Daniel Burnham's Master Plan Vision for Chicago. It originally served as a dock for freight, passenger traffic, art expositions, pageants, and indoor and outdoor recreation. Today, the pier still functions as an urban amenity with more than fifty acres of parks, gardens, shops, restaurants, family attractions, and exhibition facilities, drawing nearly two-million visitors annually.

Function: Performance Hall | **Status:** Built, 2017 | **Client:** Chicago Shakespeare Theater | **Awards:** AIA Innovation Awards, Stellar Architecture, Honorable Mention, 2017; The Architecture MasterPrize, Honorable Mention in Architectural Design, Cultural Architecture, 2017

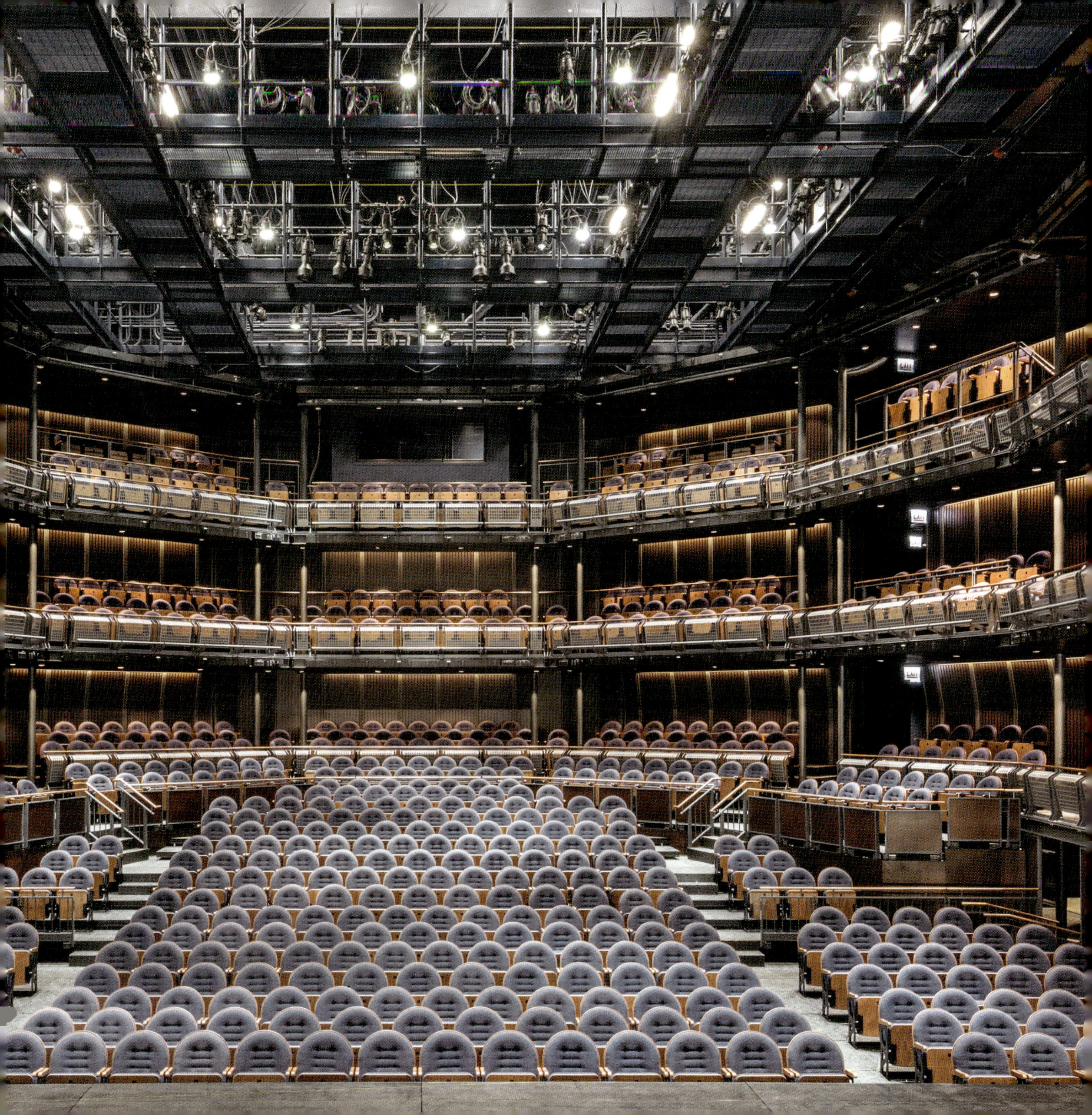

DESIGN CONCEPT | SITE

The design repurposes the theater's outdoor venue, the Skyline Stage, by constructing a fully enclosed, indoor theater chamber beneath the iconic white tent, utilizing the existing stage house and backstage support spaces. The client wanted to preserve the tent because of its landmark value and visibility from Lake Shore Drive and downtown Chicago. The white canopy further promotes the project's visibility as a canvas for artistic light projection effects.

The longitudinal section of the site illustrates the complexity of the site and the relationship of The Yard to the pre-construction site conditions. The form of the theater box shell was developed through a tight negotiation of requirements defined by the height of the program requirement for three-story seating towers and theater catwalks against the existing constraint of the complex form of the tensile structure.

Cost was another major factor in the design. Chicago Shakespeare is a non-profit organization; therefore, a modest budget was determined. The budgetary decision to keep the existing tent significantly reduced the cost of the core and shell, allowing a higher budget for the interior spaces, stage engineering, and audio-visual systems. By working with the existing architectural design, the total cost of $35 million is less than half of the projected estimates for the new construction of a similar technically advanced theater.

> *Like all good theaters, the Yard accentuates the drama on stage and the connection between audience and actors.*
> *- Blair Kamin, Architecture Critic, Chicago Tribune, 1992-2021*

Navy Pier, Chicago, Illinois, USA | Section Rendering (Right)

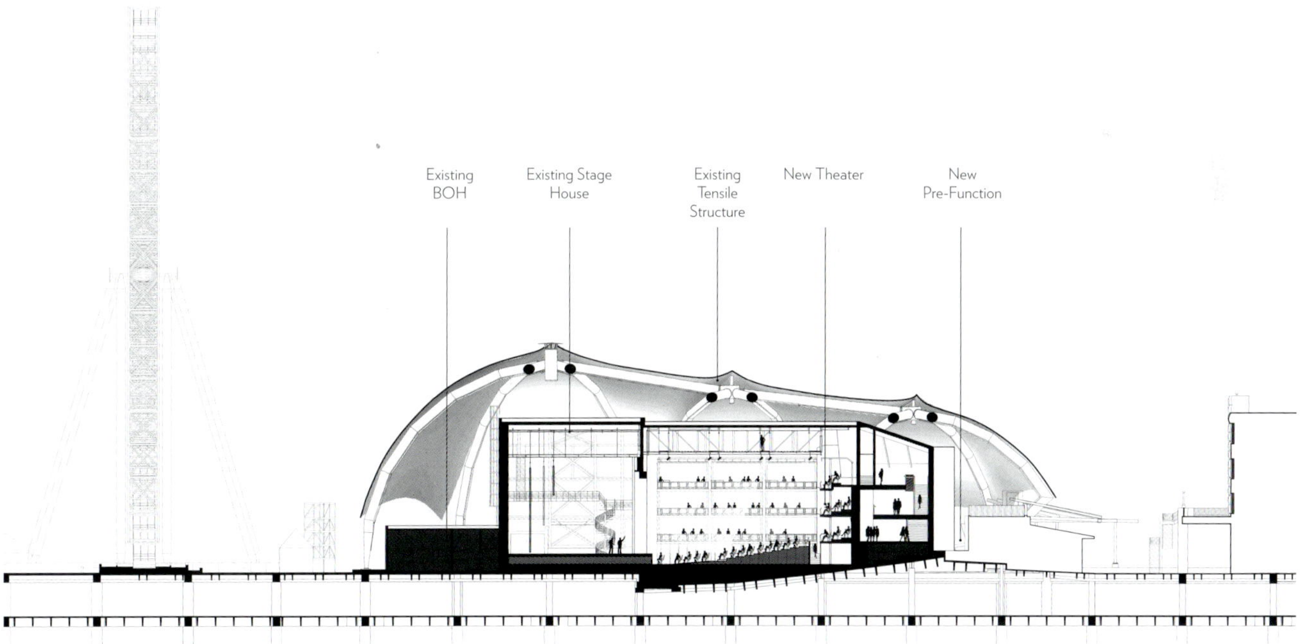

East-West Section

The 33,000-square-foot addition is connected to the existing theater with a glazed two-story lobby and reception space that was designed to negotiate the floor level differences and bring the two spaces together. Aligning the elevations of the new theater to the existing theater proved to be a significant architectural design challenge.

The pre-function space connects to the lobby by two ramping corridor "links" at Level 0 and Level 1, which are spatially minimized to reduce the demolition of existing site conditions. The lobby gently ramps along the main stairs to align with the existing theatre lobby levels.

A new floor for the auditorium was constructed over the existing raked seating, supported by three-foot-deep steel girders that span 60 feet. The resulting cavity is utilized as a plenum for the mechanical system and raceway for the several thousand feet of conduit serving the many building system, stage engineering, and audio-visual systems.

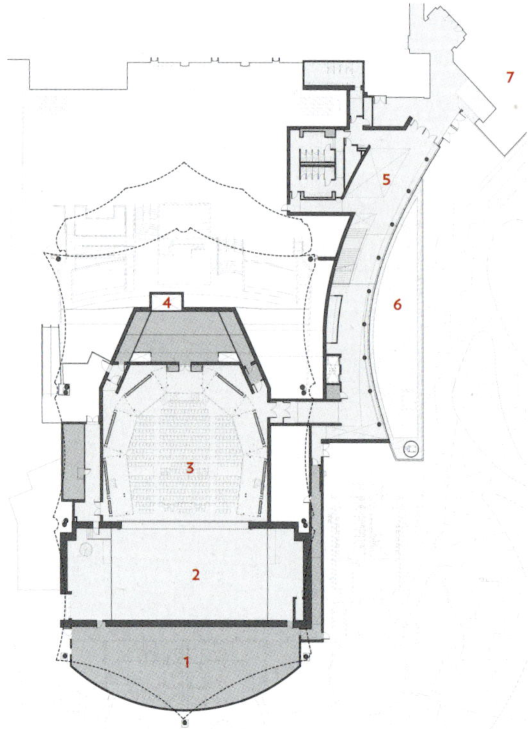

Floor Plan

1 Existing Back of House
2 Stage House
3 Theater
4 Storage Room
5 Lobby
6 South Planter
7 Existing Theater

N

Southeast Elevation

Southwest Elevation

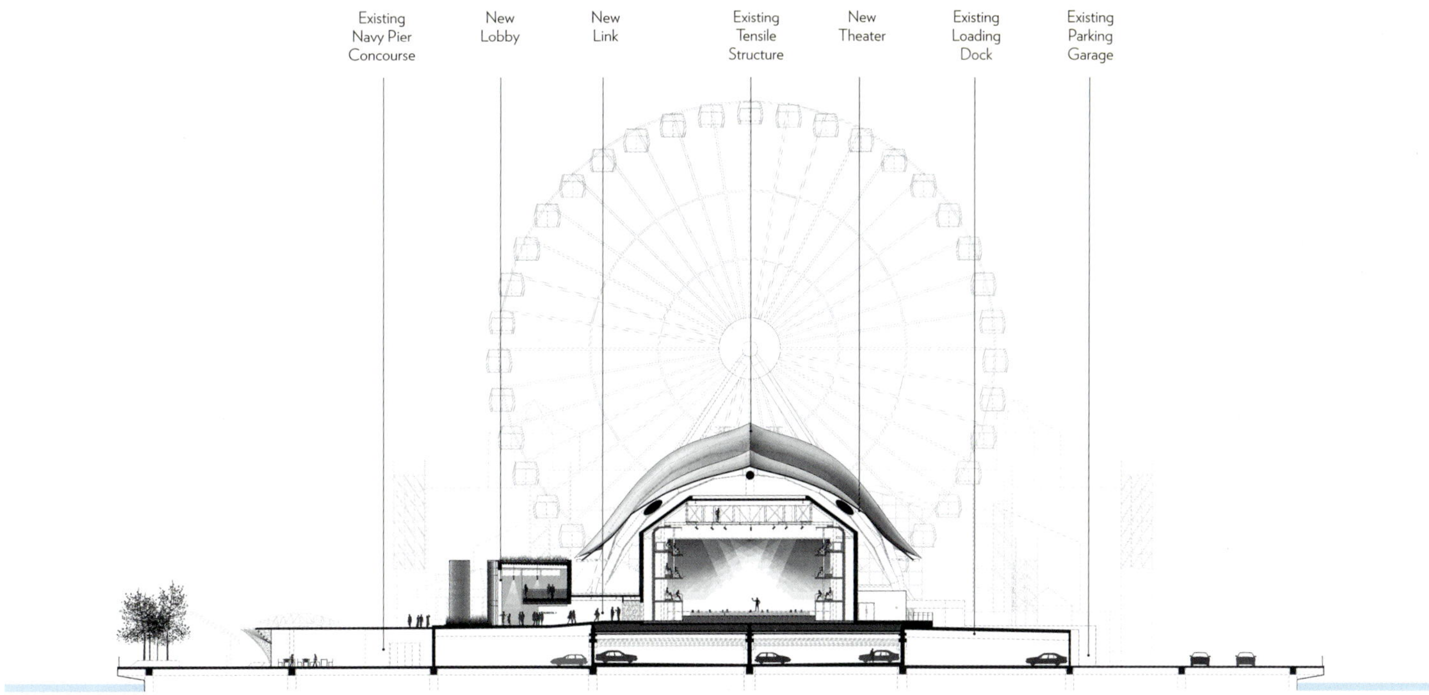

North-South Section

The theater can be customized for the purpose, size, or type of audience. The towers can be configured to accommodate 150 to 850 people, depending on which of the nine seating tower arrangements are used. Several days are needed to reconfigure the layout because of multiple components involved, and while the speed of changeover was a concern, achieving configurations that felt permanent was more important.

Seating Configurations

Large End On

Small Thurst

Thrust

Cabaret

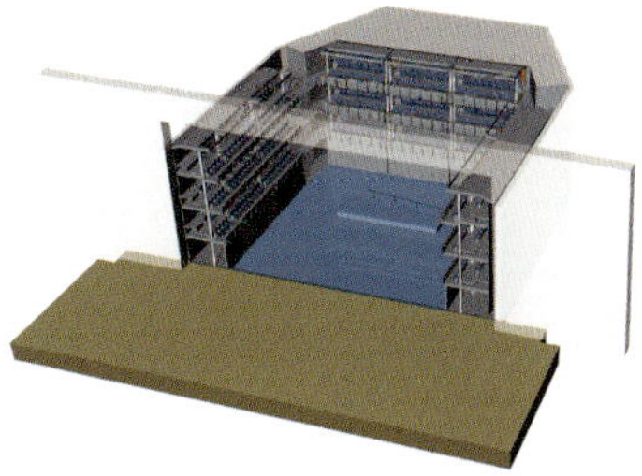

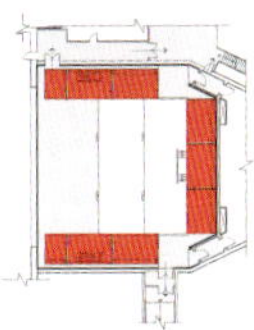

Standing Room
(890 audience)

Seating against three walls, with an open floor for maximum standing capacity. Used for large performances.

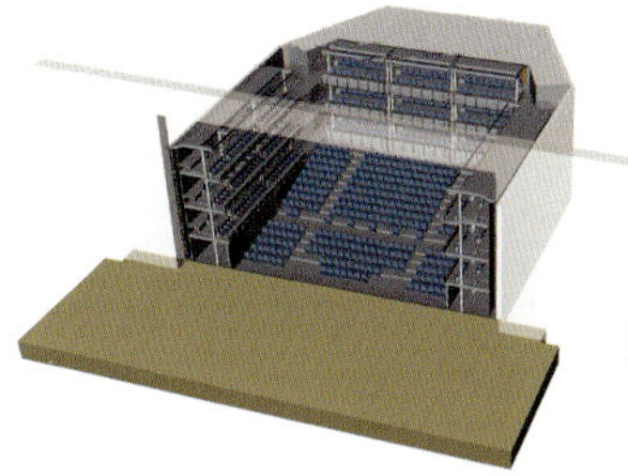

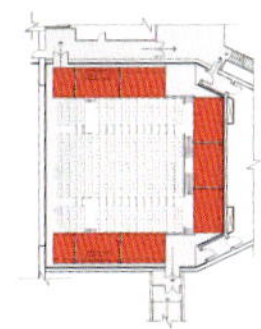

Large End-On
(870 audience)

The seating towers are placed flat against the back and side walls, main floor seating is maximized, and the stage extends slightly beyond the proscenium.

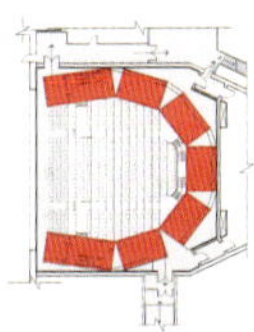

Horseshoe
(800 audience)

Similar to an opera house or European theater setting, seating is in a U-shape for ideal audience sightlines for large-scale theatrical programs. The main floor is filled with racked platforms for additional seats.

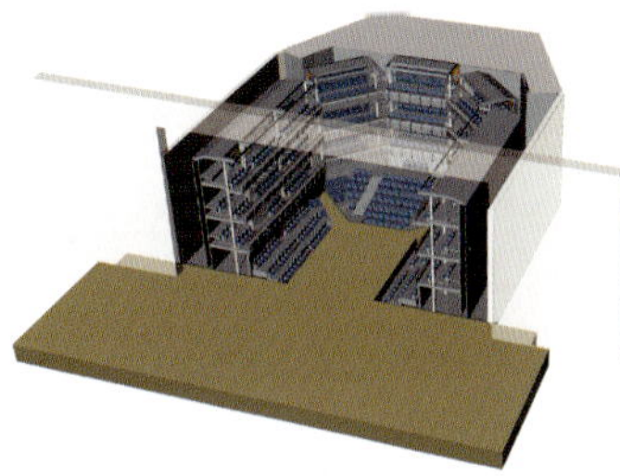

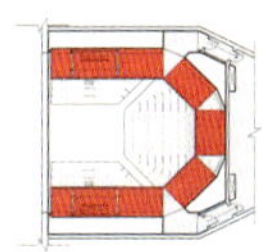

Thrust
(575 audience)

Stage juts into the house with audience seated on three sides. Allows the performance out of the proscenium into the house, with large scenic elements typically placed near the rear of the stage.

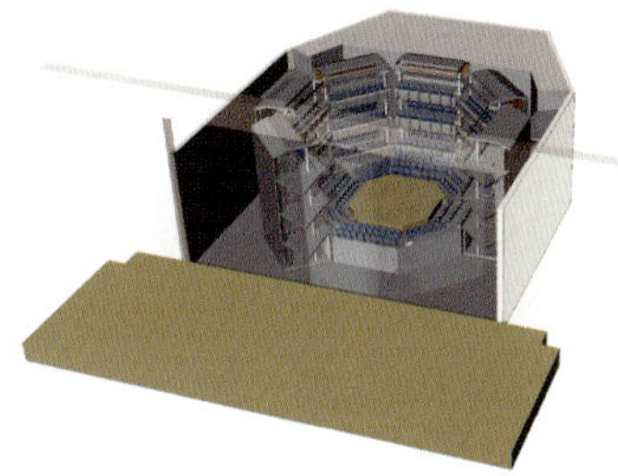

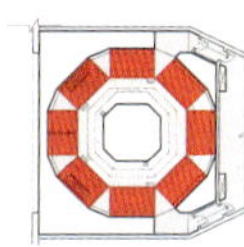

In the round
(469 audience)

This "arena" configuration includes a stage surrounded on all sides by seating towers. This most intimate configuration puts the audience in direct view of each other.

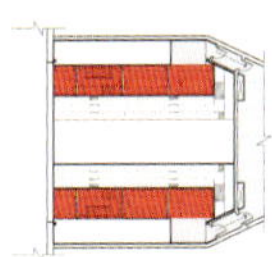

Traverse
(424 audience)

The "alley," configuration forms a catwalk down the center of the theater chamber with audience on two sides facing each other.

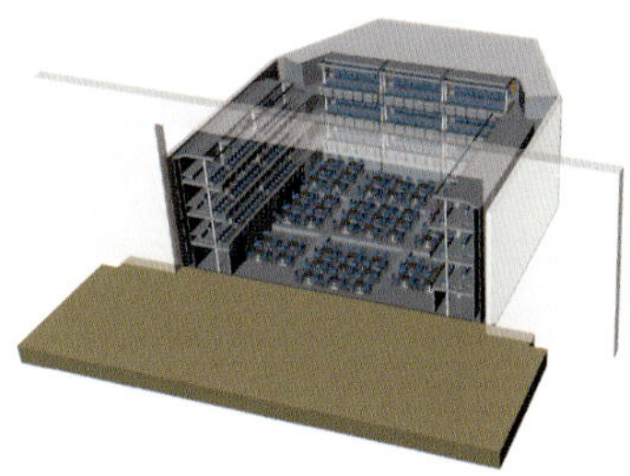

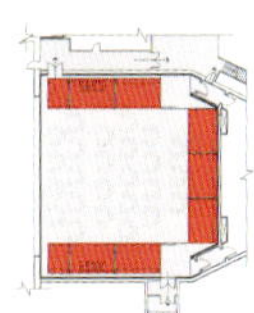

Cabaret
(400 audience)

Tables with chairs are arranged on the main floor with seating towers along three walls, simulating a nightclub or restaurant.

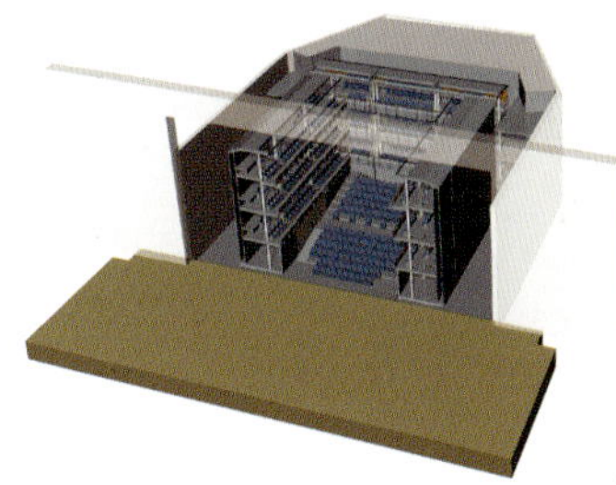

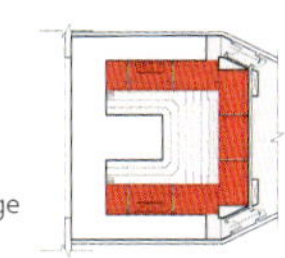

Small End-On
(350 audience)

Smaller version of large end-on configuration. Towers move away from the wall toward the center of the room, still offering plenty of stage space for performers and scenery.

DESIGN CONCEPT | SPACE

Several design goals were determined for the lobby spaces through a collaborative process between AS+GG, the theater consultant Charcoalblue, and the client. First, the space must be an imaginative, creative space for storytelling. Second, the space must provide the audience with a singular theatrical experience. Third, the space must maximize the audience density and their relationship to the stage.

The resulting space is bright and multi-functional. It serves as a place to meet before and after the show, to have a drink, or to enjoy views of Lake Michigan. The lobby's open-concept space is flexible to accommodate fundraising and social events, small-scale performances, and cast meet-and-greet opportunities. The furniture, including the concierge desk, drink rails, and seating, is fully adaptable. Nothing is fixed, which reinforces the flexible design concept.

Entrance Lobby | Rendering (Above)

Mezzanine Lobby | Rendering (Below)

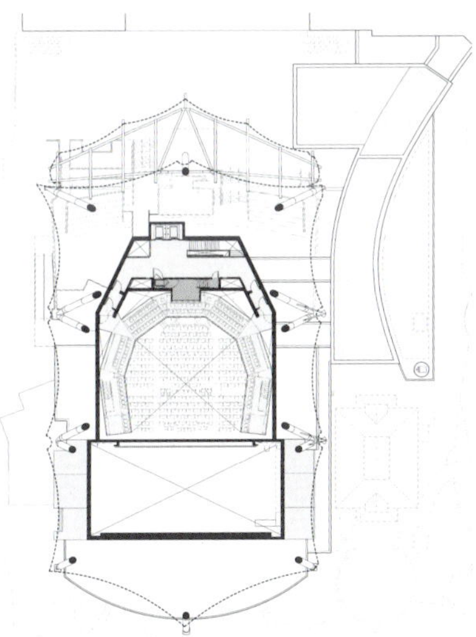

N Mezzanine Level Plan

Industrial technologies are repurposed to allow the seating towers to function accurately and smoothly. At the base of each tower, air casters carry the burden of the lifting capacity, giving greater steering control than more typical applications, such as swivel casters. Between productions compressed air-skid technology, commonly used in industrial and aeronautical settings, lifts each of the 35,000-pound towers 3/8" off the ground on a bed of air, allowing them to be moved by a three-person team.

Each mobile tower is about the size of a city bus standing on its end, with three levels of seating. These complex structures, pioneered specifically for this design, hold extensive theatrical technology, and connect into a network of HVAC components and sprinkler systems that help accommodate audience comfort and safety. Additional modular main-floor seating risers and custom-built stage decking complete each configuration.

This new use of a previous technology was successfully shown to meet the requirements of national codes, the City of Chicago, and provided the flexibility necessary to Chicago Shakespeare Theater to minimize operational downtime.

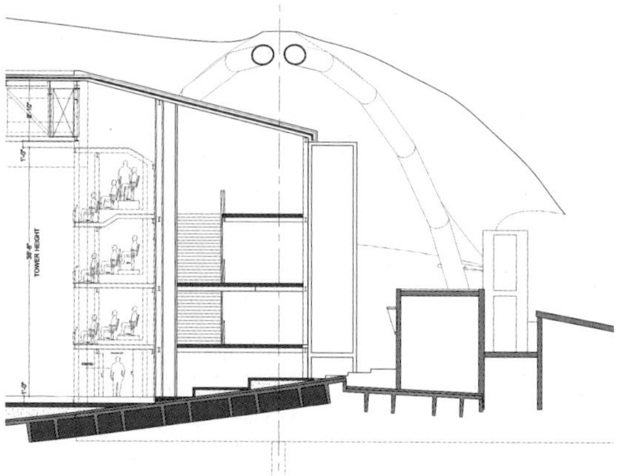

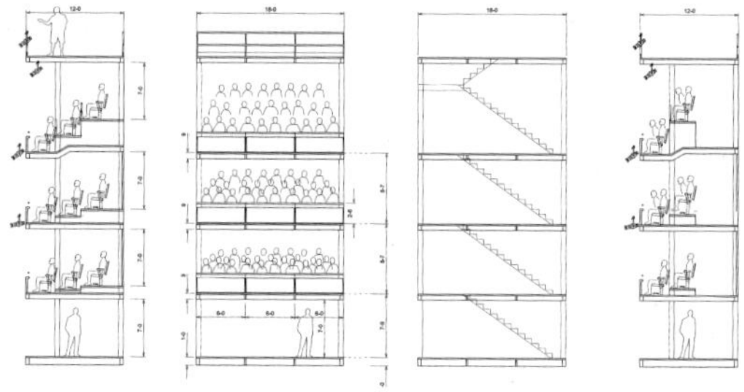

Tower Sections

Seating Tower Sketch

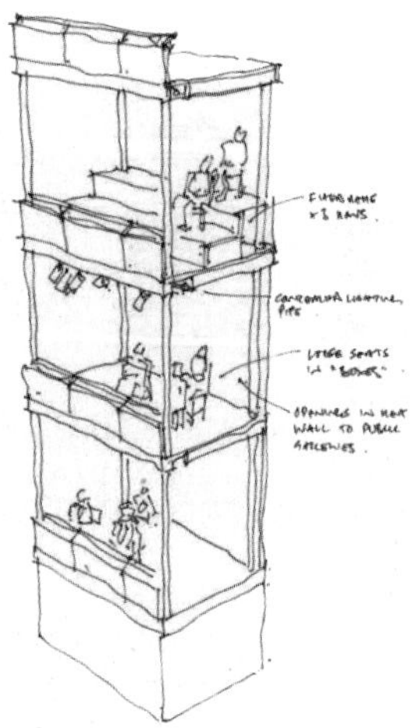

Mechanical System

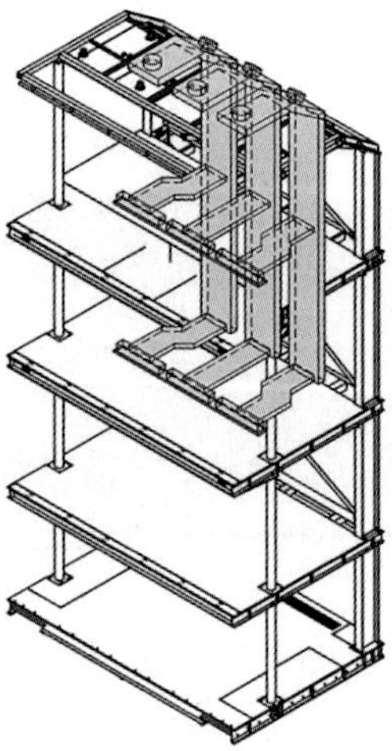

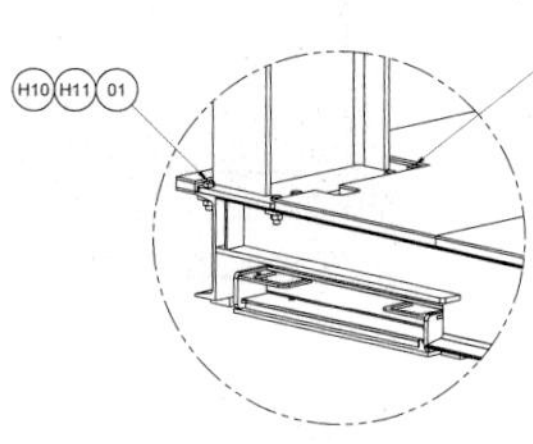

Air Caster

Flexible Connection

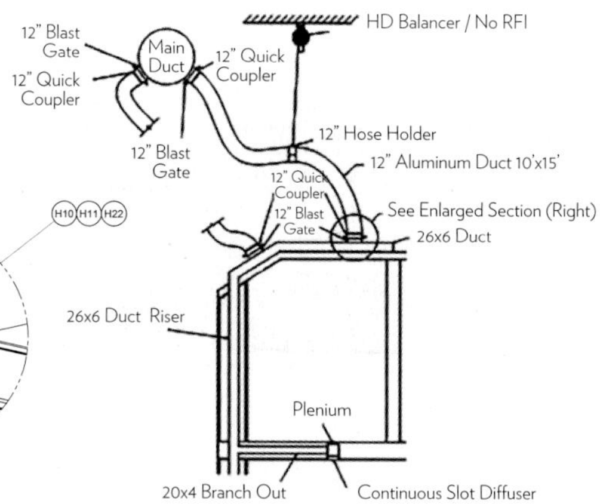

The Yard, 2019 | Interior Rendering (Below)

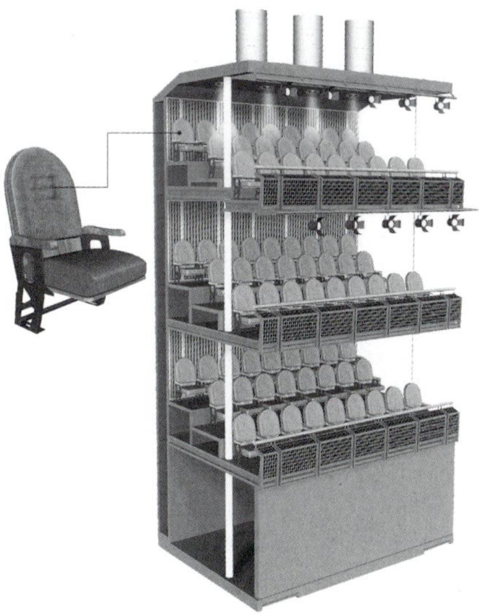

Seating Tower Diagram

The elegant, curved south curtain-wall facade was developed through an interactive design process. The gentle geometry frames the southern views of Lake Michigan and the Chicago cityscape, extending the exterior into the interior lobby. The glass selected for the lobby facade creates an architectural relationship between the existing building and the new building and frames views in both directions, interior and exterior.

Because the lobby facade faces south, SageGlass® electrochromic glass was installed to control the heat gain. Sensors on the roof signal the glass to tint according to the positioning and intensity of the solar radiation throughout the day and over yearly seasonal variations. Using this system, the theater has an 11% total energy reduction, a 44% cooling demand reduction, and 21% operating cost reduction. Traditional low-E glass requires a larger HVAC system initial cost, as well as increased energy usage, lighting and cooling costs, and peak-demand charges. Electrochromic glass further reduces energy usage because it maximizes daylight in the lobby, so the installation and maintenance costs of interior shades and blinds are eliminated.

The ability to control the tint also helps to dramatize the space. The artistic possibilities through various pattern combinations are endless. The interior's neutral palate compliments the color from the varying tint intensities of the electrochromic glass. The space is animated by the tinting glass and shadows from the perforated panels that are constantly changing as the sun rises and falls across the electrochromic facade. When the facade is fully opaque, from the exterior visitors naturally become engaged with the site. The glass reflects the viewer within the crescent shaped city view and lake view behind them, providing self-documentation opportunities.

SageGlass® 60% VLT

SageGlass® 10% VLT

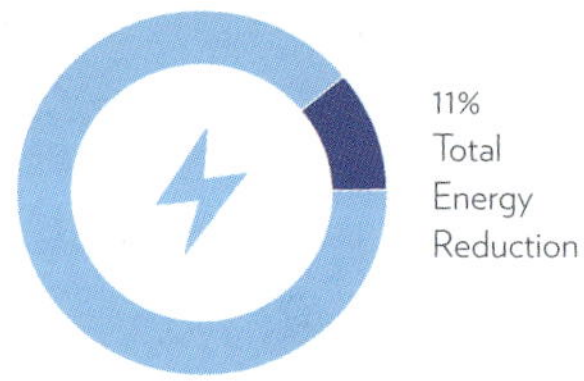

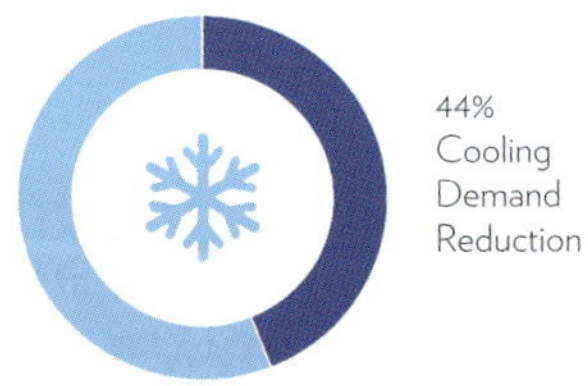

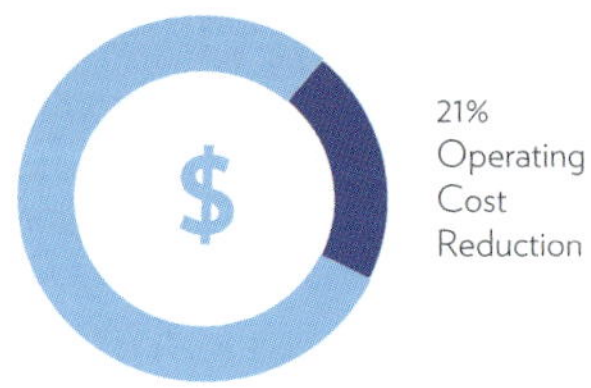

Electrochromic Glass Comparison

VLT - SHGC

- 1% vlt - 9% solar gain
- 6% vlt - 10% solar gain
- 18% vlt - 15% solar gain

Summer Morning

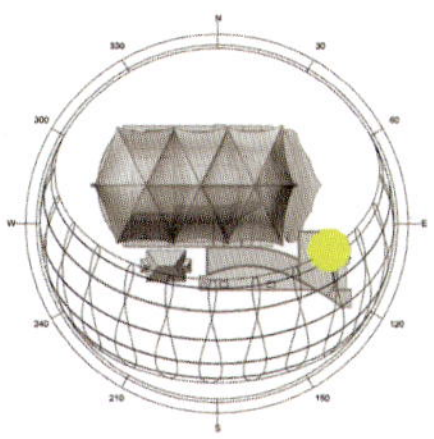

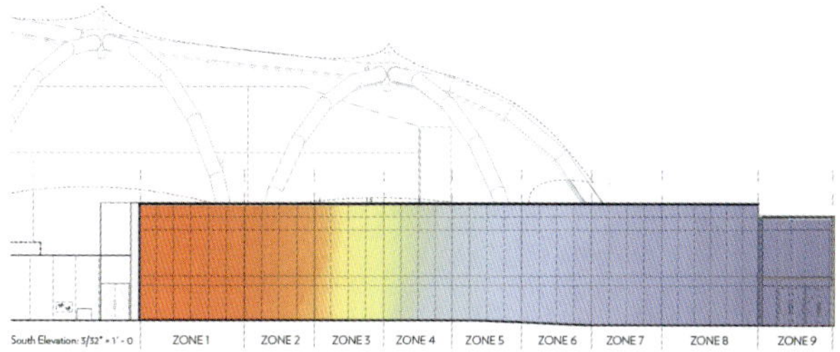

Conventional Glass
Summer morning solar gain: 16 kW

16 kW

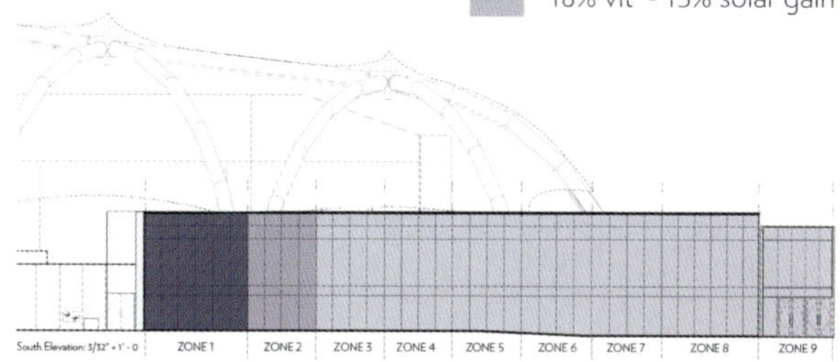

SageGlass
Summer morning solar gain: 3 kW
(81% reduction)

3 kW

Summer Noon

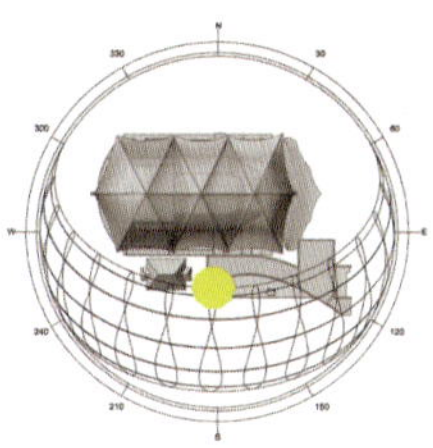

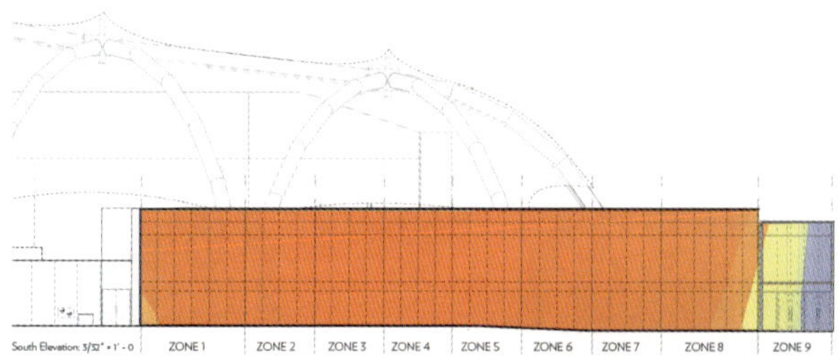

Conventional Glass
Summer noon solar gain: 29 kW

29 kW

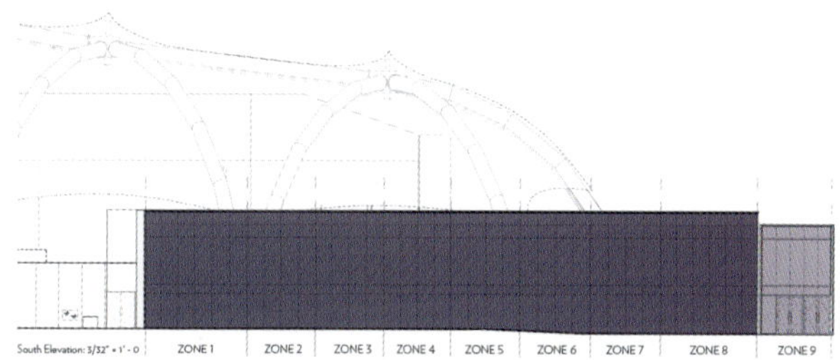

SageGlass
Summer noon solar gain: 5 kW
(83% reduction)

5 kW

Summer Afternoon

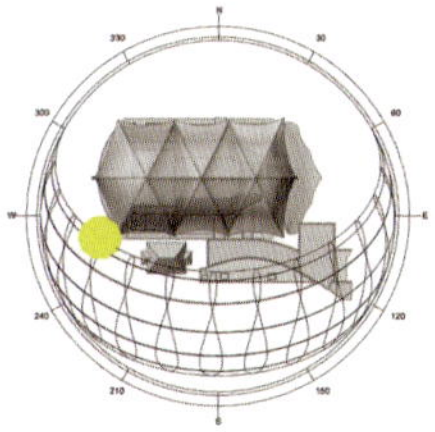

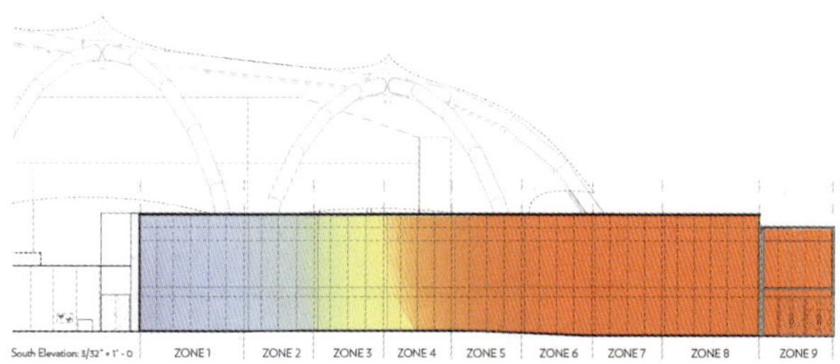

Conventional Glass
Summer afternoon solar gain: 33 kW

33 kW

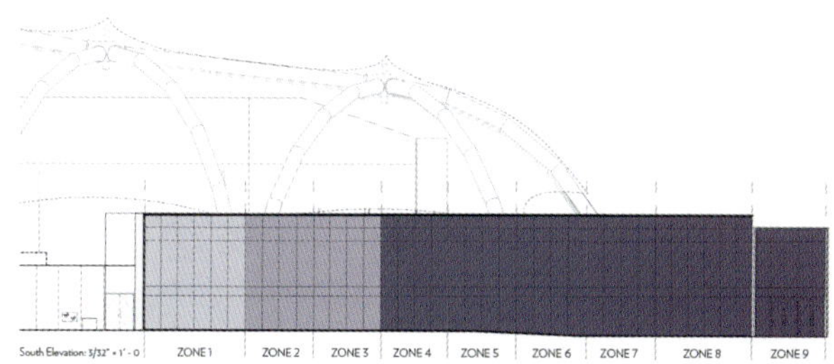

SageGlass
Summer afternoon solar gain: 6 kW
(81% reduction)

6 kW

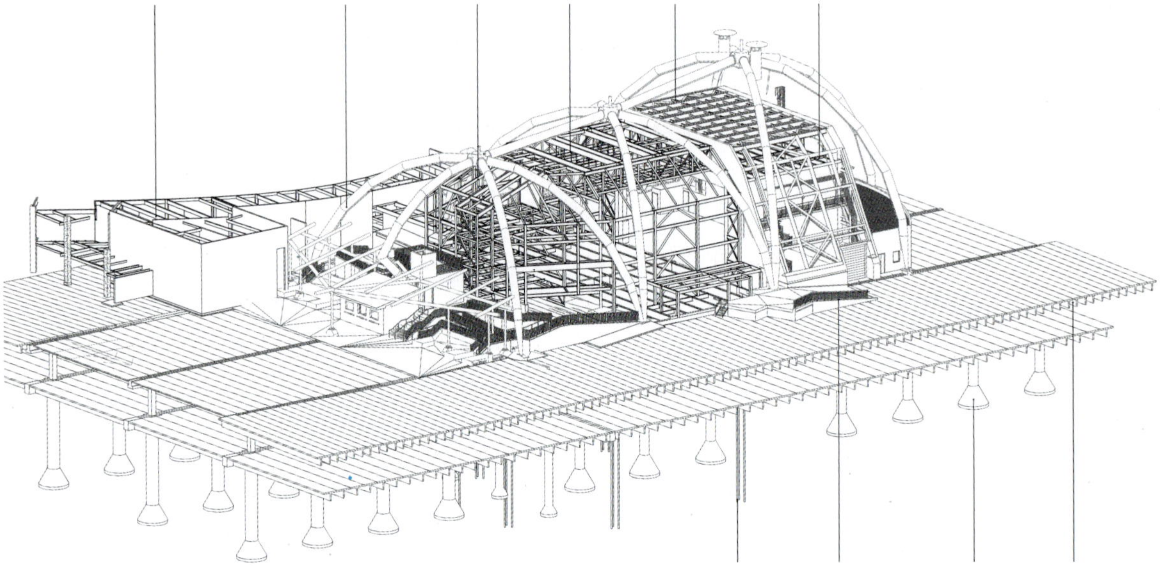

Revit Model, 2016

Construction conditions on Navy Pier are complex. The Yard's auditorium floor is built over the Skyline Stage's raked seating and is supported by three-foot-deep steel girders that span 60 feet. The resulting cavity is used as a plenum for the mechanical system and as a raceway for the several thousand feet of conduit serving the many building systems, stage engineering, and audio-visual components.

The form of the theater box shell was developed through a tight negotiation of requirements defined by the height of the program restrictions for the three-story seating towers and theater catwalks, and against the existing constraints of the tensile structure's form. Supplemental micro-pile foundations below the pier and shear walls at the parking garage levels support the structure. Construction was coordinated so that operations of other tenants at Navy Pier were not interrupted.

An extensive collaborative analysis determined the theatrical loads needed for the various seating tower configurations and the multiple possible overhead grid configurations. Dimensions between structural members were coordinated down to the fraction of an inch to ensure the proper spacing needed for load hoisting with the constrained space for construction and the need to maximize indoor space for the towers. Smaller members were favored over larger ones to avoid potential issues for the construction crane when setting steel below the tent.

Masonry load bearing structure and structural steel framing composes the organization of the lobby. The masonry block along the north and east walls was chosen as a structural strategy to reduce costs where the program did not require large openings for fenestration. The Level 1 mezzanine floor is supported by structural hangers, hung from the roof deck, to minimize beam depth and maximize ceiling heights.

THE YARD

STEPPENWOLF THEATRE CAMPUS EXPANSION

Chicago, Illinois, USA

In the summer of 2021, the expanded Steppenwolf Theatre, now known as The Liz and Eric Lefkofsky Arts and Education Center, opened its new building at 1646 N Halsted in Chicago, Illinois. The state-of-the-art, multi-purpose hub of creativity is conceptualized based on the collision of physical and programmatic spaces.

The expansion introduces a new theater experience for patrons, the surrounding community, and Chicago. The project features an intimate 400-seat theater-in-the round, which at only six rows deep will center the actors with the audience surrounding the stage. No audience member will be more than 20 feet from the stage, blurring the lines between the actor-audience relationship.

The design process and methodology levers experimentation by pushing boundaries of the meaning of theater and exploring how a performance building can best present itself to a city.

Founded in Highland Park in 1974 by Rick Argosh, Leslie Wilson, and Gary Sinise the Steppenwolf Theatre Company is locally, nationally, and internationally acclaimed for their high-quality productions and actors. In 1991, they built their main theater at 1650 North Halsted Street in Chicago. The new theater is on a tight site directly connected to the existing theater to the north and a parking garage to the south. Now in its fifth decade as a professional theater company, Steppenwolf has received unprecedented national and international recognition, including a series of Tony Awards and the National Medal of Arts.

Function: Theater + Arts Education Center | **Status:** Built, 2021 | **Client:** Steppenwolf Theatre Company | **Awards:** AIA Chicago, People's Choice Award, Cultural Cateogry, 2023; Architizer A+ Awards, Hall/Theater, Finalist, 2023; AIA Illinois, Honor Award, Excellence in Interior Design, 2022; Architect's Newspaper, Best of Design, Editor's Choice, 2022; Chicago Building Congress Merit Awards, Commercial Construction Under $50m, Winner, 2022

Steppenwolf has long had a strong understanding of the social constructs and neighborhoods across Chicago. Architecturally, the new theater is carefully stitched into its neighborhood context, recognizing the significance of its presence along Halsted Street, while respecting its neighbors.

The former Ethan Allen furniture store directly north of the existing theater was acquired by Steppenwolf in 2016 as a Phase 1 in the project. It now houses a cabaret theater and a new coffeehouse and bar. Phase 2 includes the new theater-in-the-round, which is directly connected to the existing theater on a tight site between an existing parking garage to the south and the existing building to the north. Its prominent facade faces east along Halsted Street, with the north and south facades abutted by buildings and the west facade facing toward a public alley.

The theater is in an urban setting, with mostly three to four story buildings and residential areas in its immediate context in Chicago's Lincoln Park neighborhood. Therefore, at the neighborhood level it was important that the theater be transparent in its function and invite participation from the people who live, work, and visit Lincoln Park and Halsted Street. At the city level, it was important to be inclusive to the diverse, multicultural Chicago communities that Steppenwolf serves. At the individual level, the audience, patrons, staff, artists, and the storied ensemble's needs must be met, as they have driven the theater's success for 30 years.

> *It is clear Gill has understood and given form to his client's goals, and there's no shortage of architectural drama in his ambitious, animated, and nicely resolved production.*
> *- James Gauer, Architectural Record*

Floor Plans

1	Pre-function	5	Stage Set Assembly	9	Meeting Room
2	Bar Cafe	6	Dressing Rooms	10	Offices
3	Stage	7	Pantry	11	Classroom
4	Seating	8	Costume Workshop	12	Balcony

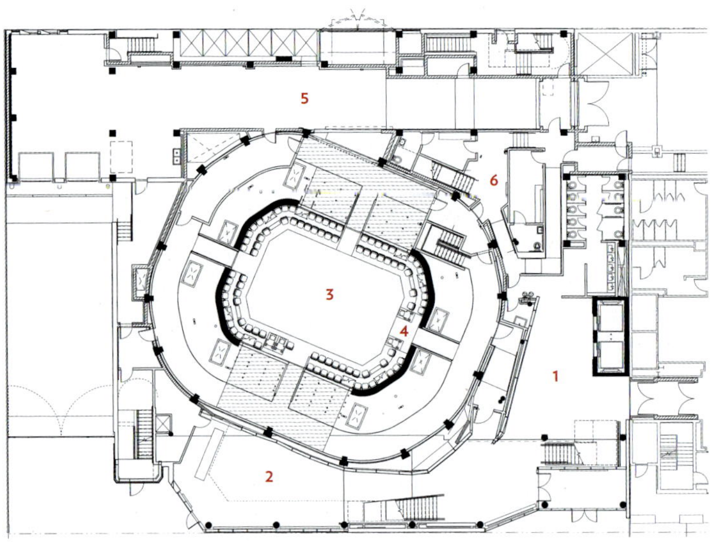

N Ground Level

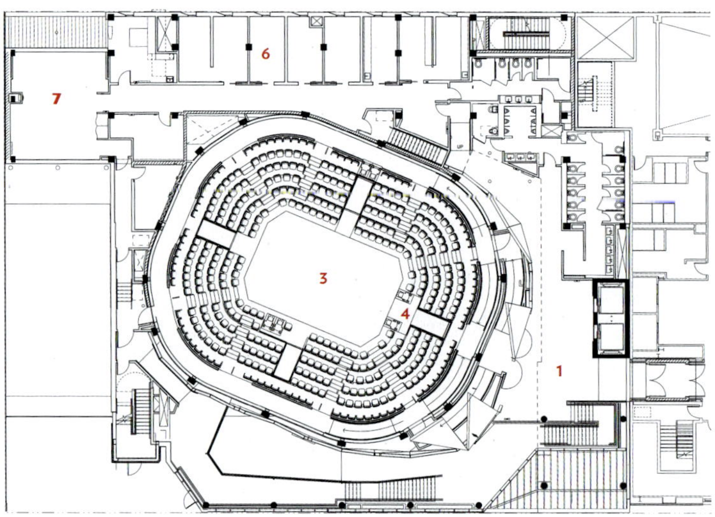

N Level 2

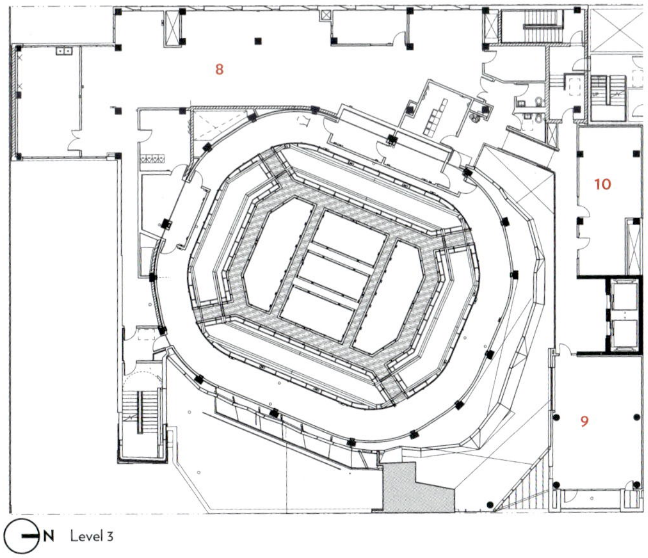

N Level 3

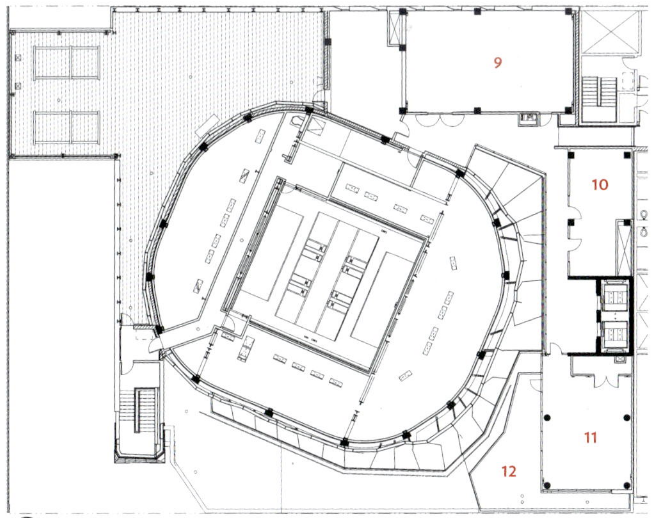

N Level 4

DESIGN CONCEPT | SITE

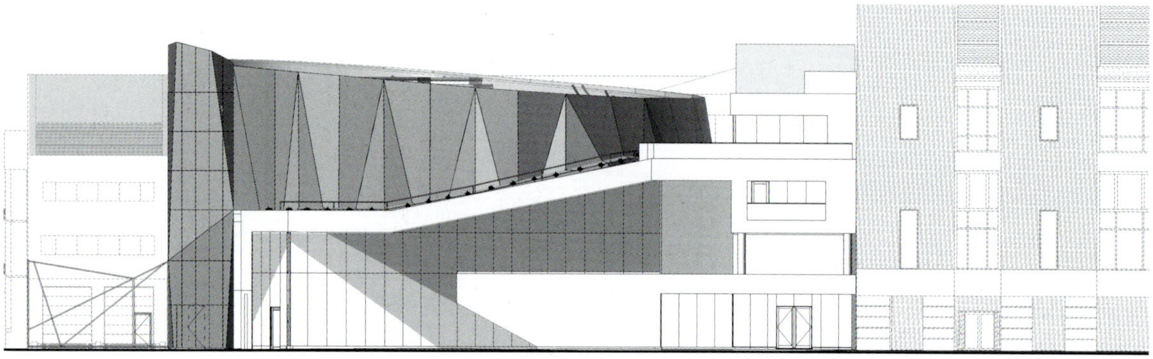

East Elevation

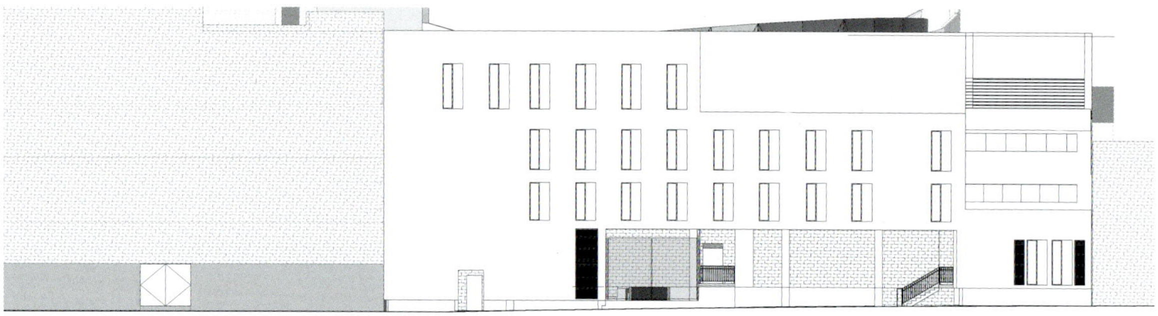

West Elevation

Cross Section

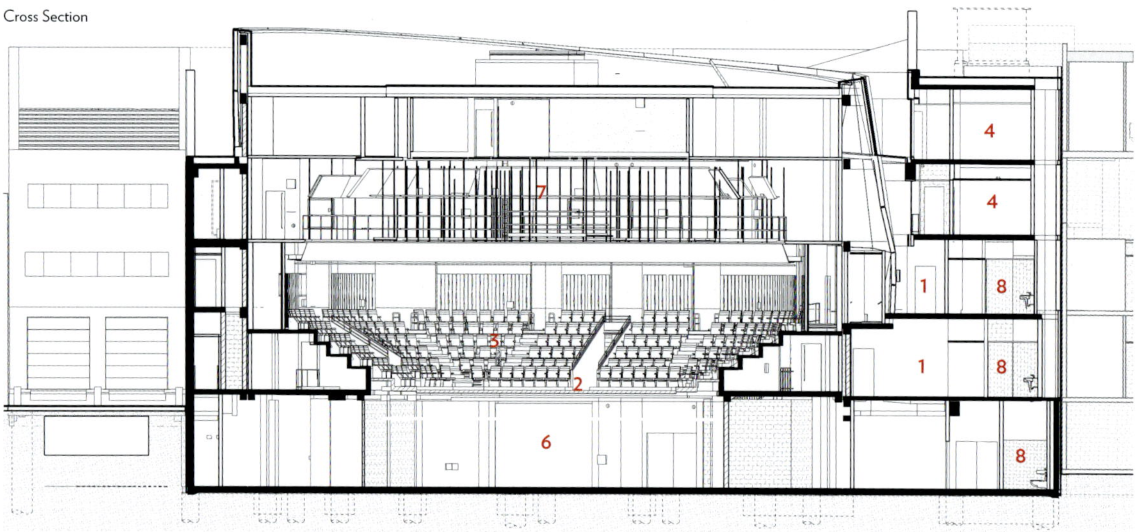

1 Pre-Function
2 Stage
3 Seating
4 Offices
5 Classroom
6 Trap and Costume Storage
7 Lighting Grid
8 Toilet Room

STEPPENWOLF

DESIGN CONCEPT | PROGRAM

During the concept design phase, the client and design team explored stage forms, developing both regular and asymmetrical settings. Unlike more traditional modern theater forms, it is the stage area and the seating capacity that dictates the shape of the room. The final design is an intimate space with 400 seats that grows from the stage, with the audience rising on all sides.

Other additions include a dedicated education floor, a two-story atrium lobby, as well as space for Steppenwolf's costume shop and other updated production amenities. A new wine bar and sidewalk lounge increases the social gathering spaces where artists and audiences can converge.

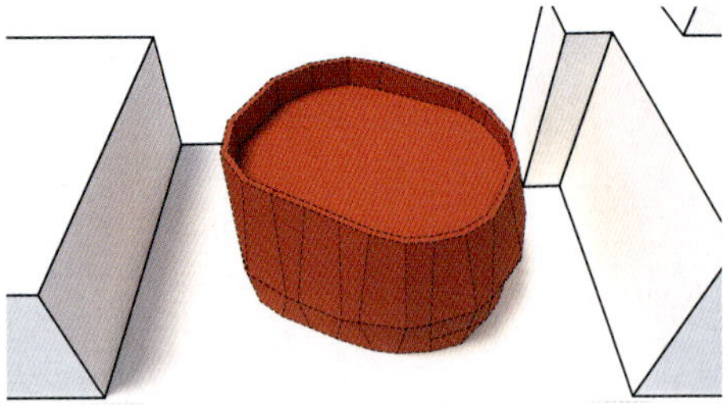

Theater Form

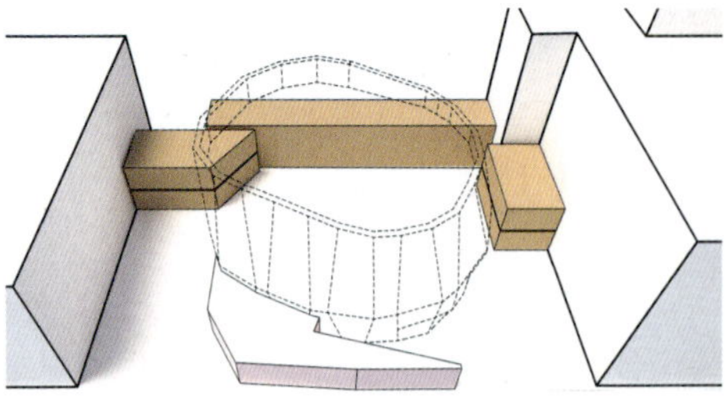

Levels 1-2

Aerial View Rendering

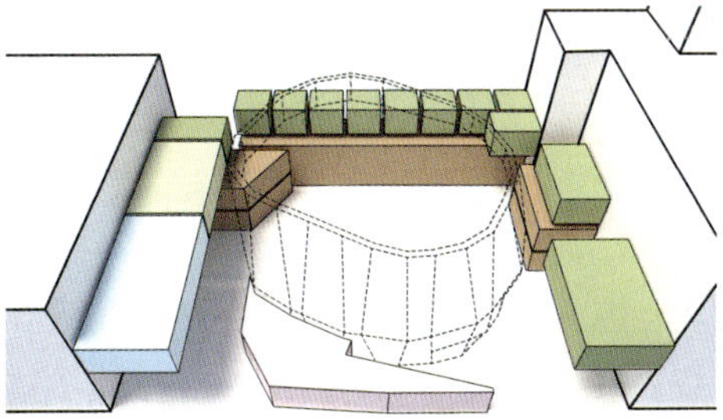

Level 3

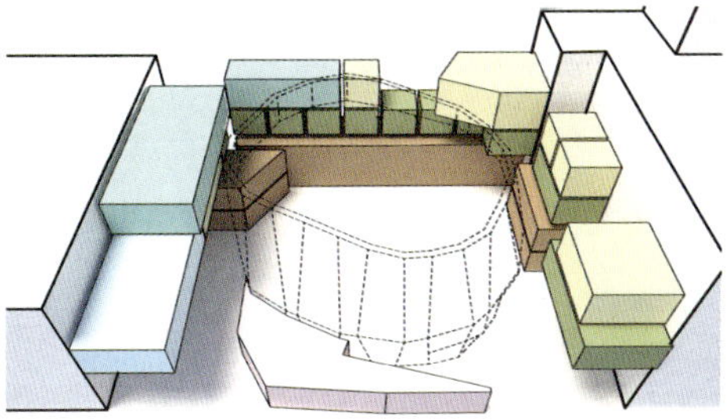

Level 4

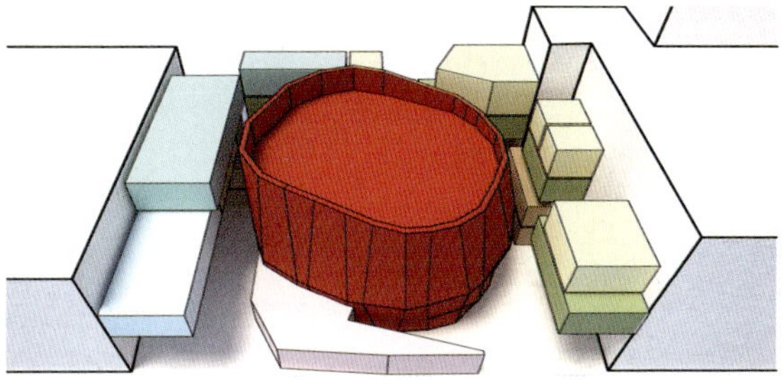

Program Massing

Program Diagrams

- Theater
- Restaurant
- BOH / Assembly
- Offices
- Wardrobe
- Costume Workshop
- Dressing Rooms / Green Room
- Rehearsal / Classrooms

East Facade Facing Halstead Street

DESIGN CONCEPT | FORM

The theater's form is based on the idea of collision: that the interactions between the actor and the audience serve to establish dynamic and intimate spatial relationships throughout the space. The in-the-round theater design was determined to be the most beneficial arrangement for this design goal.

In-the-round theaters are challenging for production teams and actors because the configuration limits certain elements, such as scenery that needs to be finished on all sides, the stage may be limited in height to maintain sightlines, and costumes must be more detailed because of the close proximity of the actors to the audience.

However, in-the-round seating embodies the ethos of Steppenwolf. The format creates a space that requires performers to occupy the stage, as they are no longer performing to a fourth wall but inhabiting a location that is observed from all sides.

The tradition dates to ancient Greek and Roman theaters but lost popularity through the history of theatrical performances as the stage moved to the end of the auditorium. Its popularity was reignited in the United States in the early 20th Century among many universities. In the 1920's, the form shifted into the world of professional theater when Gilmore Brown founded Pasadena's flexible Fair Oaks Play-box.

The configuration was further advanced in the hands of Glenn Hughes when rebelling against the immediacy of cinema he experimented with theater shape and with John Conway when he established the first dedicated in-the-round venue, the Penthouse Theater, which was built in Seattle in the 1940s. With the completion of the building, the style gained influence around the world, also taking root in the United Kingdom. In the US in 1950s, Stephen Joseph became another leader in this form.

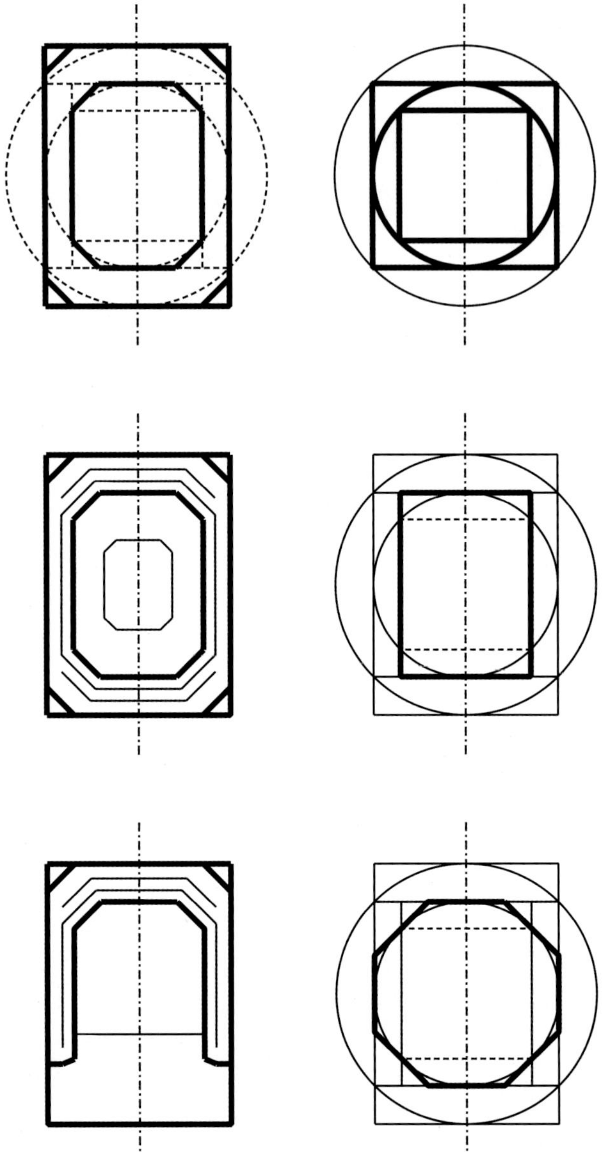

Room Geometry

Early Design Studies

DESIGN CONCEPT | SPACE

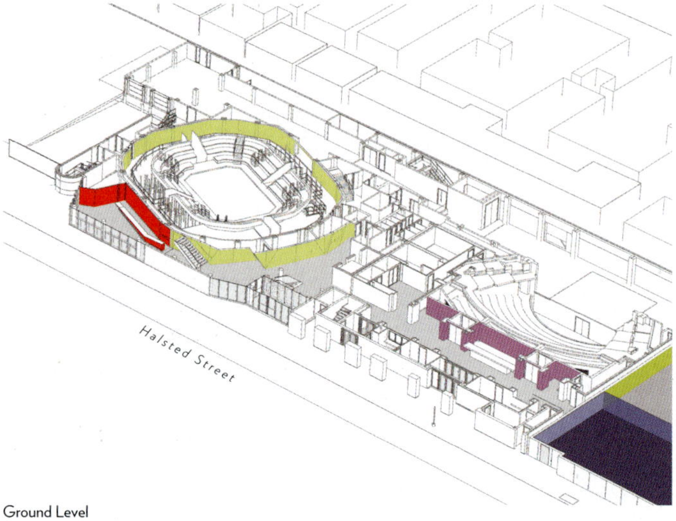

Ground Level

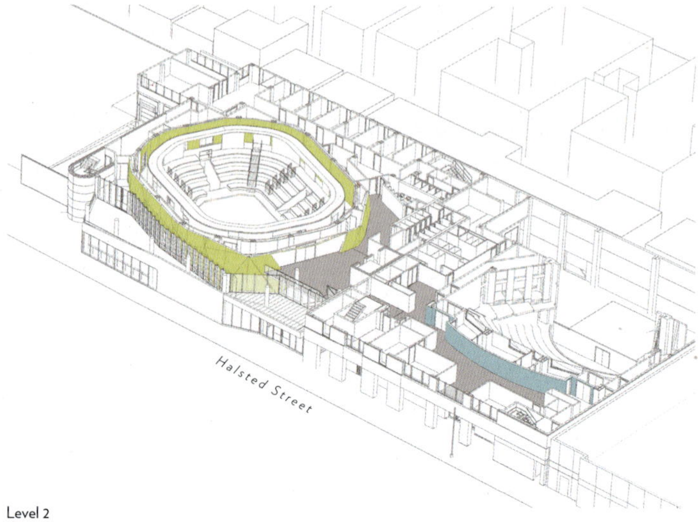

Level 2

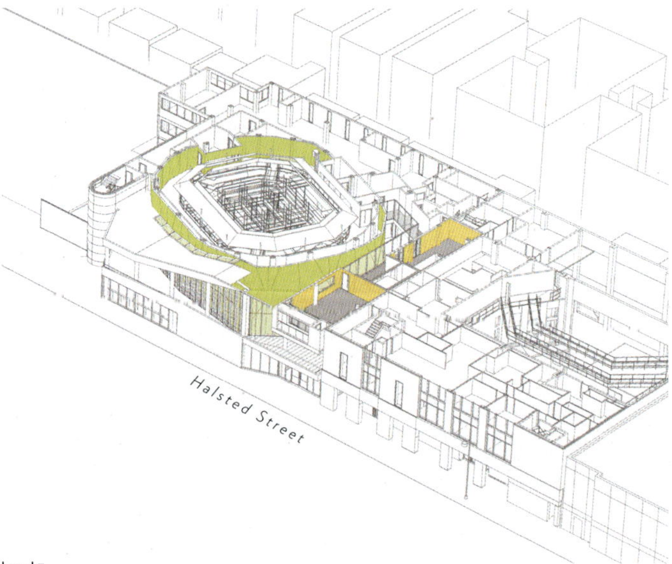

Level 3

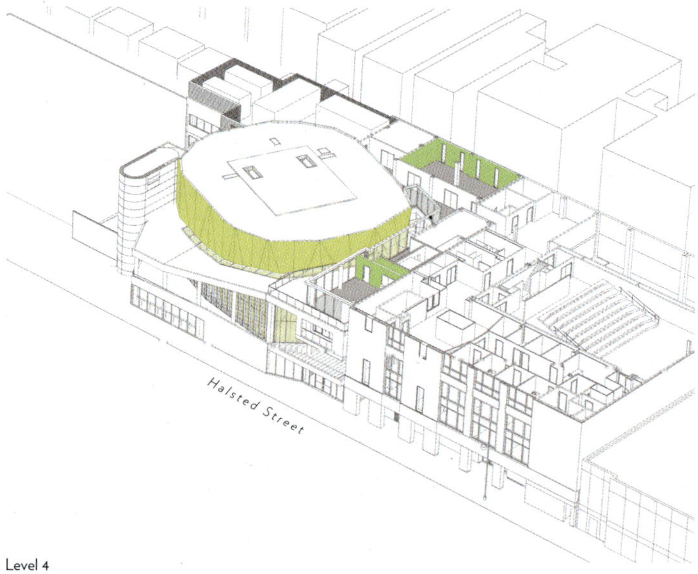

Level 4

STEPPENWOLF

DESIGN CONCEPT | SPACE

The main audience entrance is on the second-floor through two sound and light locks. This pre-function space features polished concrete floors and wood ceiling baffles with acoustical insulation felt that introduces the pallet of the theater interior.

Elements such as perforated wood screens above the stairs and the orange elevator facade create easy wayfinding throughout the building. Patrons arrive at their seats through stepped aisles that are spaced around the perimeter. Underneath the seating tiers, but within the theater volume, is a corridor for actors and technical staff to access the stage via two fixed vomitories.

The stage level sits on the first floor of the building. This configuration is an effective utilization of space by not having a large off-stage area. The lobby and audience circulation surround the theater at the front side with technical support and assembly areas to the rear. This further blends front of house and back of house spaces revealing to the audience member the craft of what is happening on stage.

Second Floor Theater Lobby Space Renderings | Second Floor Theater Entrance (Right)

DESIGN CONCEPT | MATERIALS

The interior design is an honest expression of materials that relates to the building's architecture. The ceiling and walls are treated as overlapping planes with acoustical plaster, wood panels, acoustic slats, perforated metal, EIFS, or concrete. These planes are veils that allow views to the spaces while still providing a sense of discovery.

All finishes were chosen to create an inviting sense of warmth in the spaces. Color is introduced to highlight wayfinding and circulation paths throughout the building. A sky-lit atrium promotes a dynamic expression by introducing natural light that establishes a three-dimensional visual connectivity between the various levels of the building.

Design Studies, 2012-2017

Entrance Lobby Looking South

Entrance Lobby Looking North

The short ends of the theater's seating banks are fixed in configuration with a single, central seat entrance. The longer sides are flexible, allowing entrances in multiple locations and are configurable per production. A single audience entrance at this level allows wheelchair users access to the lower section of seating.

The design offers eight wheelchair positions as a base, with two in the first row near the fixed vomitories and six positioned around the space at the back row. It is possible to add additional spaces around the auditorium if required for alternate formats. The rear circulation is fully accessible with seats offered through the space when coupled with front row access.

Although the new theater is a fixed format, the design needed the ability to be modified to allow for maximum creative flexibility. Through the design team's research, a system was developed for the theater to be adjusted through a series of demountable platforms that enable alternative configurations, with differing sized stages, entrance locations, and seat numbers.

The main flexible elements are contained in the first two rows, or six feet from the stage edge. A 24-foot section of removable stepped platforming on the long sides can also be reconfigured. This flexible area can be lowered and raised to create a playing space on or below the stage or a platform for a "Juliet balcony" above. The design anticipates that the seating will be frequently reconfigured to provide changing stage shapes and audience sizes within the base format.

The pitch of the seating rake steepens as it ascends, maximizing downward sightlines and maintaining the backstage circulation route beneath. This "cupping" increases the intimate feel of the theater and the feeling of audience density through the space, as it allows a direct connection from actor to audience, even from the back rows.

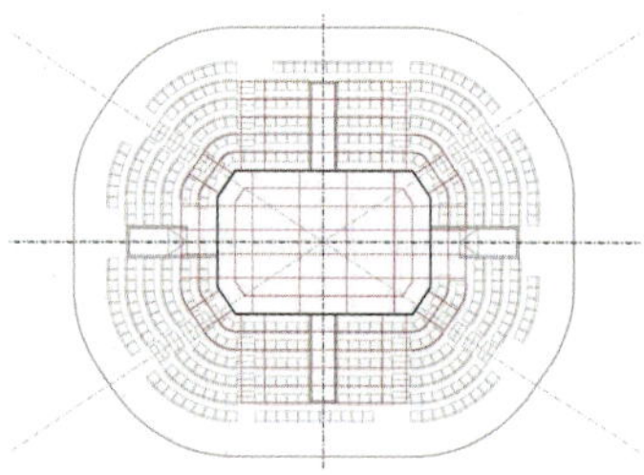

Orchestra Plan Illustration Rostra Layout

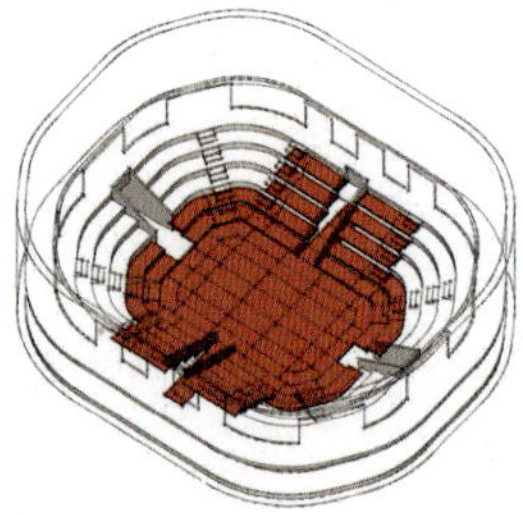

Rostra Diagram

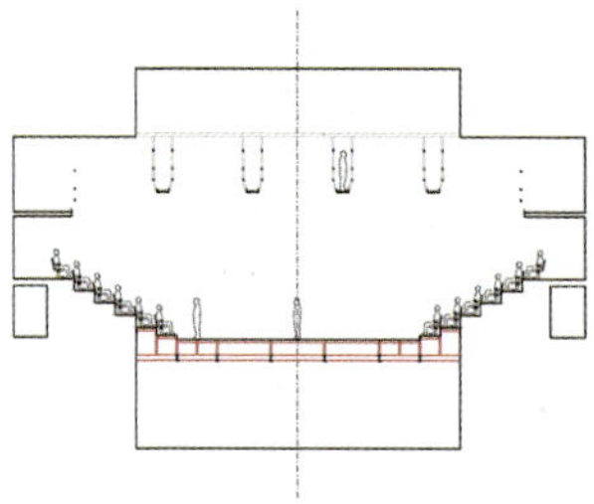

Long Section Illustrating Rostra Layout

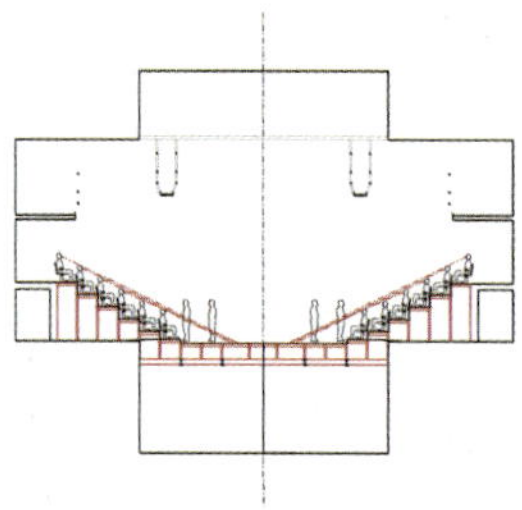

Short Section Illustrating Rostra Layout

Anton Chekhov's *Seagull*, May 2022

View Across Stage

View Across Stage

View From Actor Entrance

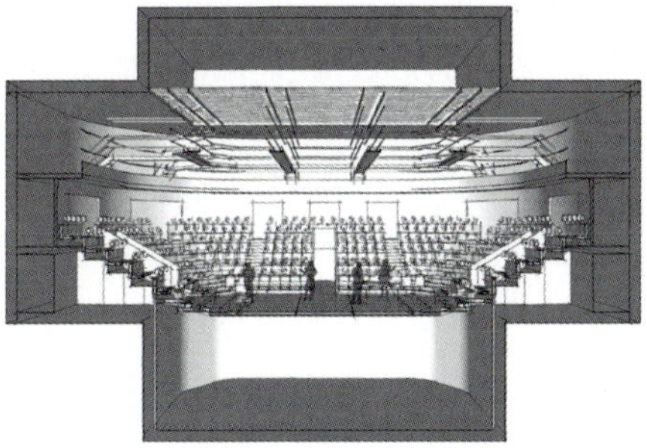

Sectional View

The maximum stage size is 36-feet by 24-feet, with a base seating capacity of 402, set over six rows. This capacity is determined by three-foot deep rows and 22-inch seat widths. The audience rows rise from the stage with the first row set seven inches above stage level and then a rise of 14-inches for the second row and 21-inches for each subsequent row.

At the third level is a technical walkway around the perimeter providing access to a network of catwalks for suspended technical equipment. Also at this level, is a suite of control rooms that provide enclosed spaces for the operation of technical equipment. These two elements provide excellent technical capabilities but also create the feeling of a ceiling, helping to focus the room towards the acting area.

Encompassing the entire fourth floor is The Loft, Steppenwolf's first-ever dedicated arts education center. The spaces are accessed through a corridor with a palate that is carried through from the theater floors, featuring polished concrete floors, linear ceiling lightings, and a double-glazed exterior wall system.

The Loft designates some of the most prized space in the center for young people to explore and create in a bright, safe space that is designed specifically for them. The education center includes three learning rooms for theater and visual arts with a private outdoor balcony overlooking the neighborhood.

The space signifies the theater's commitment to hands-on education and mentoring the next generation of Chicago artists with The Loft's "Teen Arts Project." The after school drop in program features, gallery walls for artwork created by Chicagoland youth, spaces for quiet study, maker workshops, and conversations series with local artists and educators.

Fourth Floor Corridor

Instructional Room | The Loft with Rooftop Terrace (Right)

CHAPTER 2

LEARN + INTERACT

Exhibit + Assembly

Exhibit and assembly cultural spaces cater to those who visit for a specific purpose: to view a theatrical production, to join a religious service, or to attend a professional conference. There are also assembly spaces that are intended to give visitors a more exploratory experience, both within the building and with one another. These venues can be educational in nature and include museums, expositions, and public gathering spaces.

The architecture of a public space can enhance the experience of the visitor, with the site design and the incorporation of building elements helping to draw people inside the main spaces. The design of the public space around the building and the building's entry can be just as important as the contents inside.

New exhibit and assembly spaces encourage fully interactive experiences with special enclosure pre-function areas for social interactions that are facilitated by the architecture. These spaces build excitement, directing visitors into the main event and facilitating informal, yet important, interactions between guests and hosting additional events or popup exhibits. Exhibit and assembly spaces are increasingly focused on the overall experience, allowing occupants to be educated through light, sound, and other emerging technologies.

FKI Tower Conference Podium - Nur Alem Museum of Future Energy - Astana Arts Center - Chicago Architecture Center - Mobility Pavilion

FKI TOWER CONFERENCE PODIUM

Seoul, The Republic of Korea

First occupied in January 2014, the head office building for the Federation of Korean Industries (FKI) is a major new addition to the skyline of Seoul, Korea. The project includes an iconic tower, a podium containing the auditorium/events spaces, and landscaped public areas.

The podium is available for the tower's tenants but is also a stand-alone venue that is rented to the public for events. Its unique, sculptural form creates a dramatic pre-function space with special outdoor terraces and a sunken garden plaza. The space is now one of the premier locations in Seoul and regularly holds memorable events such as weddings and banquets.

The Federation of Korean Industries (FKI) represents over 500 companies, including major Korean firms such as Samsung, LG, and Hyundai Motors and oversees up to 80% of the total exports from Korea. FKI is a driving force for South Korea's economy and is a major part of many Korean's life and livelihoods. FKI built the new tower as a symbol of Korea's free market economy and as a center to establish trustworthy business enterprises that are competitive in the global marketplace.

Function: Conference Center | **Status:** Built, 2014 | **Client:** Federation of Korean Industries | **Awards:** The Architecture MasterPrize, Architectural Design, Tall Buildings, Winner, 2017; Re-Thinking the Future, Sustainability Award, First Award, Commercial, 2016; The Chicago Athenaeum, Green Good Design Award, Green Architecture, 2015; Civic Trust Awards, Civic Trust Award, 2015; Korean Architecture Award, Excellence Award, 2014; AIA Chicago, Distinguished Building Award, Citation of Merit, 2014

DESIGN CONCEPT | SITE

FKI Tower is built on the same land as FKI's previous headquarters and is conveniently located in Seoul's Central Business District about 20 minutes from Incheon International Airport. The site is within close proximity to excellent local transportation links, including MRT stations and bus routes. The site has an intended and significant inclusive design component; it was important that the public be able to use and enjoy the site and its amenities.

To better serve the public, the site organization was rearranged from the original competition brief by sliding the tower to the west. This unlocked more site frontage and allowed the podium to be closer to the street, giving the podium a presence and identity unavailable if it was located behind the tower.

The new arrangement also allows more space for outdoor landscaped courtyards for public use. The building's site takes advantage of the neighboring parks, positioned so that arrival sequences for pedestrians, subway commuters and parkers are landscaped to extend the park setting into the building ground plane.

Flexibility of the public spaces was key to the design. The spacious and elegant banquet hall in the podium is an efficient multi-purpose space. Operable partitions make it easy to separate into up to three banquet rooms. Other breakout spaces in the podium and in the tower are available as community gathering points.

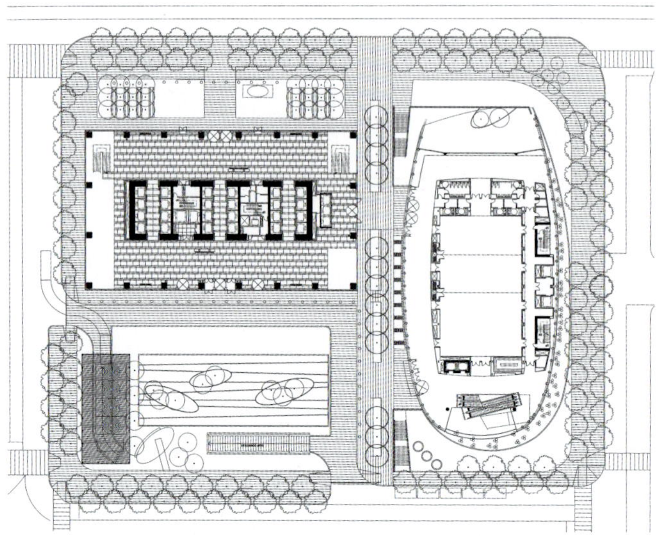

Site Plan

> *FKI Tower is what a modern building should be: intelligent, high performing, and forward-looking, while still exhibiting timeless and enduring qualities.*
> *- Civic Trust Awards, Juror Comment, Winner, International Project, 2015*

DESIGN CONCEPT | PROGRAM

The podium's program includes a main ballroom on the first floor, several smaller second-floor meeting and conference rooms, and a third-floor main auditorium. The podium can accommodate business events for the tower's tenants as well as a range of world-class events including association conferences, weddings, banquets, lectures, and small conventions. For flexibility and convenience, each floor has multiple breakout spaces.

The design has proved to be resilient over the past 10 years. In today's competitive commercial office space market, it is important to have first-class meeting spaces that are available to tenants. A multiple purpose, flexible podium onsite makes the value of the tower more competitive, so tenants do not seek outside venues for their assembly needs. It also increases the company's presence and goodwill in the community.

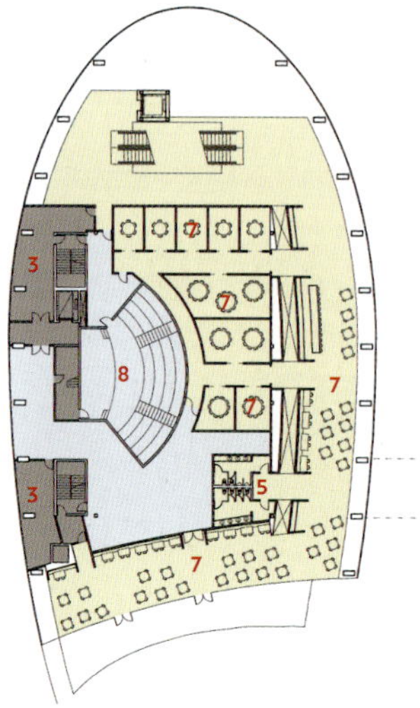

Level 2

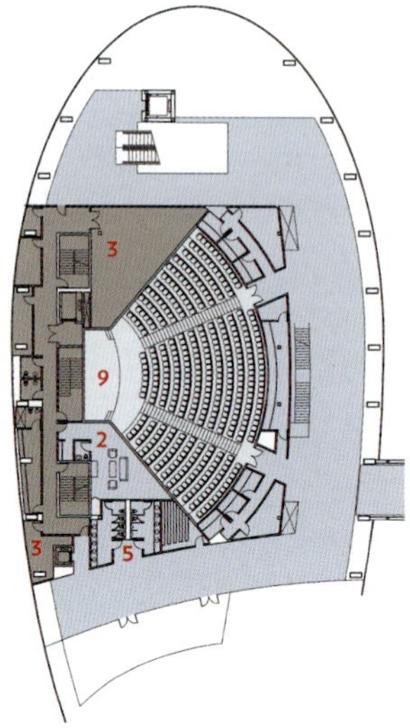

Level 3

Level 1

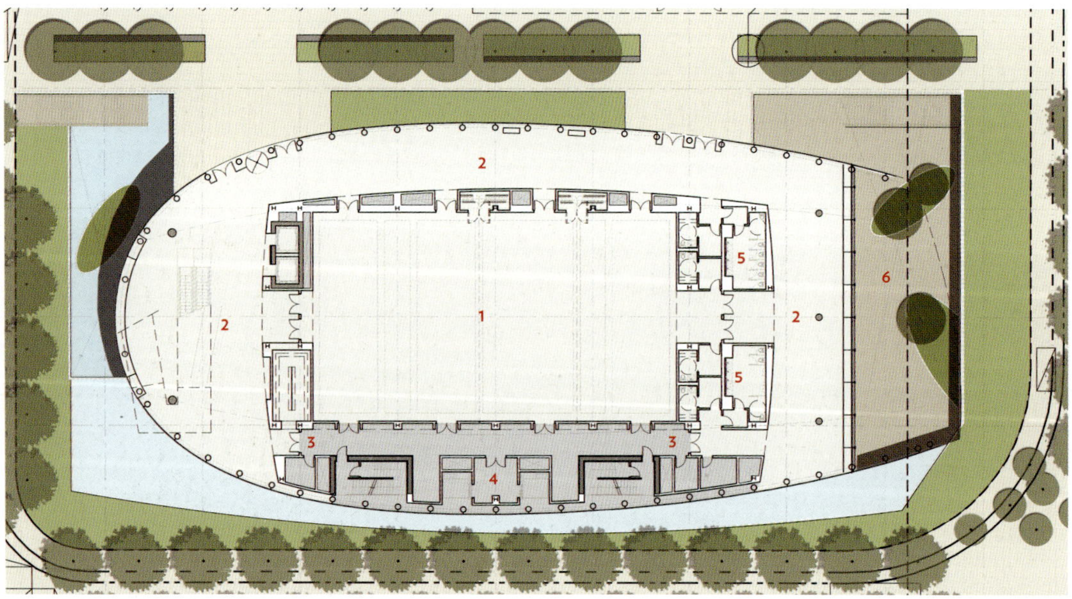

1 Ballroom/Banquet Hall
2 Flexible Pre-Function
3 Back of House Functions
4 Freight Elevator Lobby
5 Restrooms
6 Sunken Garden
7 Conference Rooms
8 Lecture Hall
9 Conference Hall
10 Restaurant
11 Parking

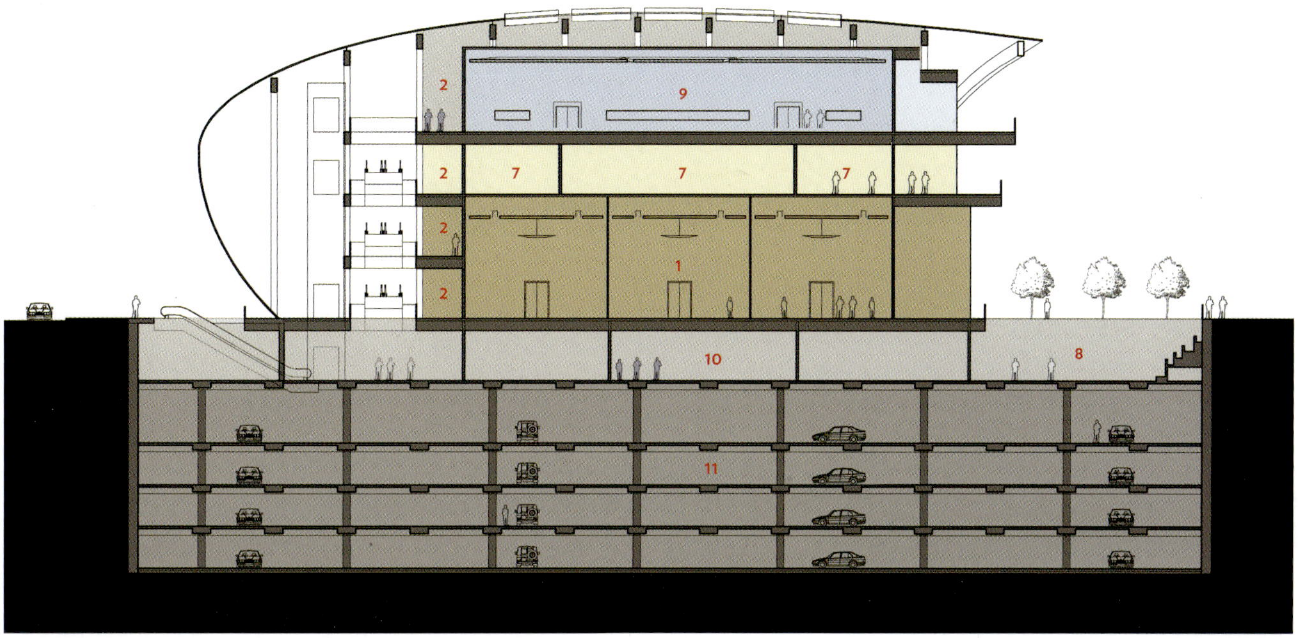

Program Section

Lecture Hall

Conference Room

Restaurant

DESIGN CONCEPT | FORM

The sculptural form of the podium was envisioned as a counterpoint to the pure Miesian geometry of the tower, enveloping the public program elements within a pure shell. In addition to contrasting the overall form, the smooth, double-curved glass surface differentiates itself from the sawtooth regularity of the tower. These differences reflect the two programs: the tower contains regular and repetitive office floors, and the podium contains public banquet and various conference spaces.

The form of the podium is further refined to respond to the surrounding urban and environmental context. The shape enables unobstructed views into the program and pre-function space, as well as to the core elements of the building. It also allows pedestrians to have unique views of the service spaces in the building.

Podium Section | FKI Tower + Podium (Right)

Marriott

DESIGN CONCEPT | SPACE

FKI's podium is flexible and adaptable to the needs of the user. The first-floor ballroom has divisible walls to adapt to a variety of sizes. Flex spaces on each floor can accommodate presentations, meetings, or small performances. The facilities take advantage of the dimensions, using every inch possible for functional space. The third-floor auditorium, for example, has sloped seating that dips below and into part of the second-floor volume to increase the usable square footage.

One end of the podium is sliced to create a vertical surface that reveals views of the adjacent park and neighborhood. The opposite end completes the overall elliptical geometry into a space that anchors the drop-off area and houses the entry and vertical circulation. This end also holds the service core that has back-of-house, mechanical, and exiting functions.

Because it was important to provide an appealing and continuous facade, the core is clad in metal panel and the stairs are expressed through the glass wall. The core is integrated into the architecture, allowing the building to meet all the exiting requirements for the assembly occupant loads. The podium is connected to FKI Tower through a bridge at Level 3. Several incarnations were designed before the final structure was approved.

Bridge Studies, 2012

Level 3 Bridge to Podium | Podium with Tower Connection (Right)

CAUTION
CAUTION

FKI
전국경제인연합회

DESIGN CONCEPT | MATERIALS

The podium features high-quality, low-maintenance finishes and fixtures throughout the building and podium. Materials were chosen specifically for each of the two main functions within the building: the public program elements and the service core, which have two very different material needs.

The materials selected for the public program elements have natural tones. Naturally finished slatted wood and unfilled matte silver limestone seek to create a warm tactility experience for the building's public users. All of the lighting is low-energy LED and is precisely integrated with signage into the ceilings, soffits, and walls.

The service elements of the building are revealed behind the podium's glass enclosure, with each component carefully considered, from the exposed freight elevators to the open fire stairs. These elements are exposed to the outside through the exterior wall so minimalist materials such as linen-finished stainless steel and white back painted glass are used.

The podium's exterior has an integral glazing and structural system that helps maintain a minimal expression and achieve a visually flush outer skin without exposed outer pressure caps or drainage interruptions. This method allows the facade to avoid dirt lines near the joints that can appear after rain.

The system consists of glazing units that are linearly supported on each of the four sides with structural silicone sealant shop applied onto anodized aluminum carrier frames, which are then bolted to a steel substructure on site and wet-sealed with weather silicone over backing rods. This system is simple, with a high-performance, low maintenance, minimal expression.

Podium Flex Space Corridors (Above + Right)

When designing the podium, a series of studies were completed to achieve the complex form and to optimize the environmental performance. Early solar studies indicated that the highest level of protection was needed on the roof. Although the building was envisioned as a pure continuous form, it was important to have a material change at the roof to increase insulation that protects it from the sun and allows daylighting into the interior functions. Therefore, the exterior glass transitions to an insulated metal panel system that matches the same overall geometry but provides a much higher level of performance.

Another challenge was to control the heat gain on the glass. The form is self-shading and therefore offers benefits in performance by virtue of its sectional shape. This was accounted for when determining the density of frit protection in the various areas of the building which is tuned to best reflect out the harshest solar radiation. A gradient frit pattern—white dots toward the outside and black toward the inside so as to block the least views—was selected to meet the energy goals of the project.

The greatest challenge in adhering to the desired form was the complex curves required; in some cases, double-curved glazing was necessary. Facade panelization analysis was done to understand various exterior panel configurations from a smooth/irrational double-curved surface to flat panels. Initially the panelization strategies were developed by the design team and then evaluated by the facade fabricators for production time and project cost which was fed back to the design team.

This iterative process was critical to understand the possibilities of fabrication and to negotiate a blended strategy which balanced the design teams desire to have double curved panels with the repeatability needed to meet the project budget and technical requirements. The glass fabricator achieved the design using bent glazing on the curved portions of the facade.

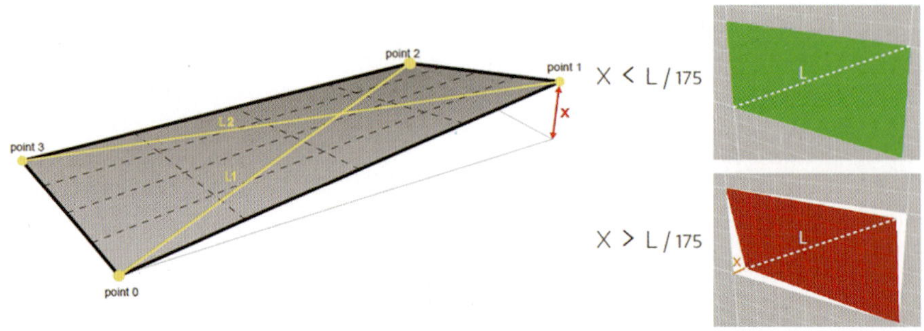

Planar Analysis Diagram

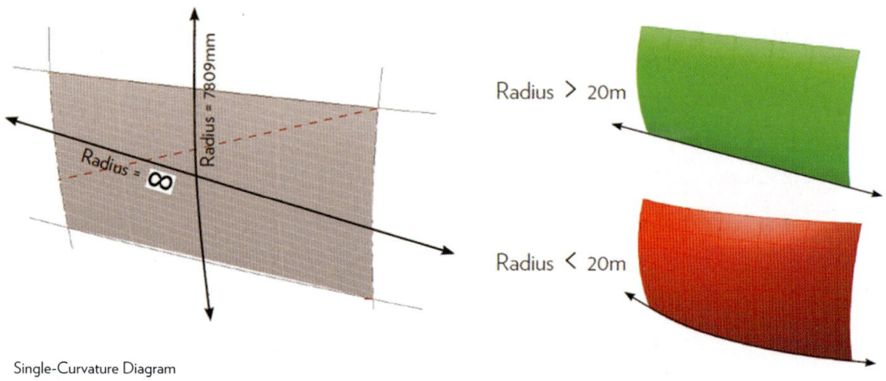

Single-Curvature Diagram

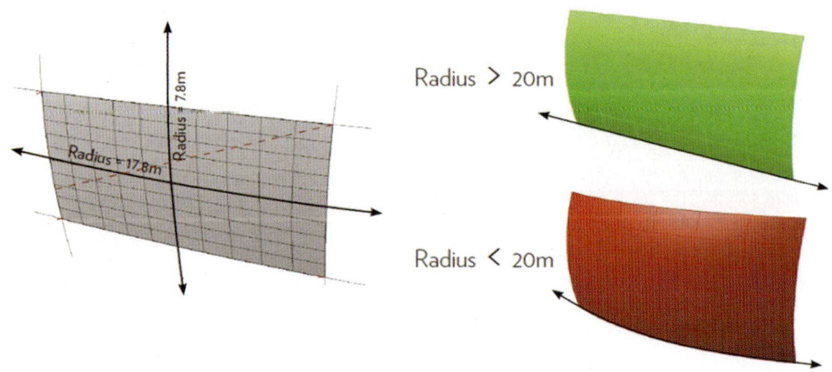

Podium Panelization Explorations

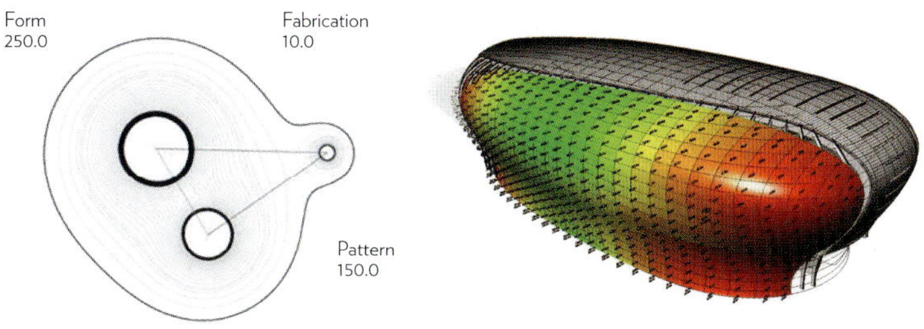

Method 1 - No Compromises

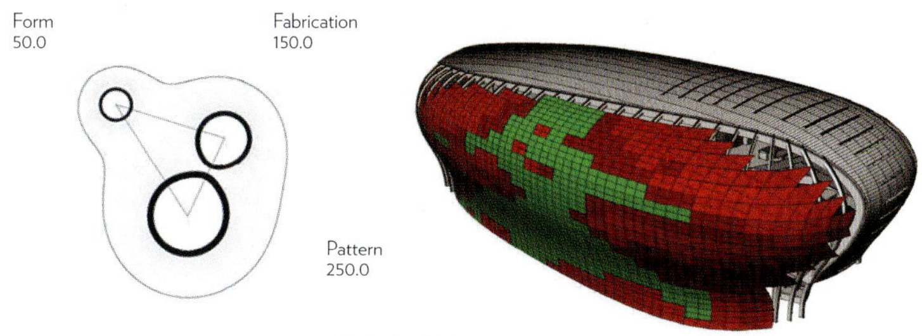

Method 2 - Scales

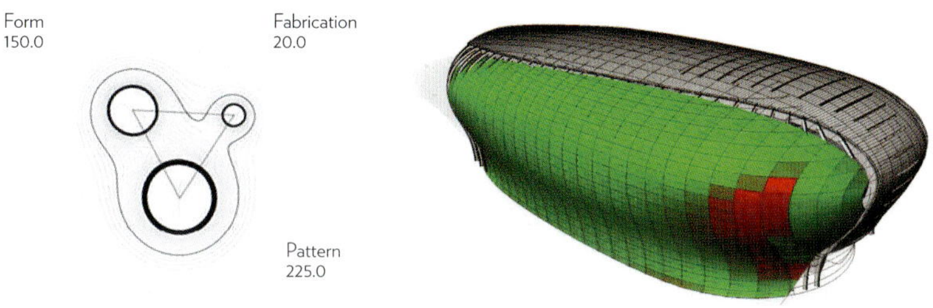

Method 3 - Hybrid

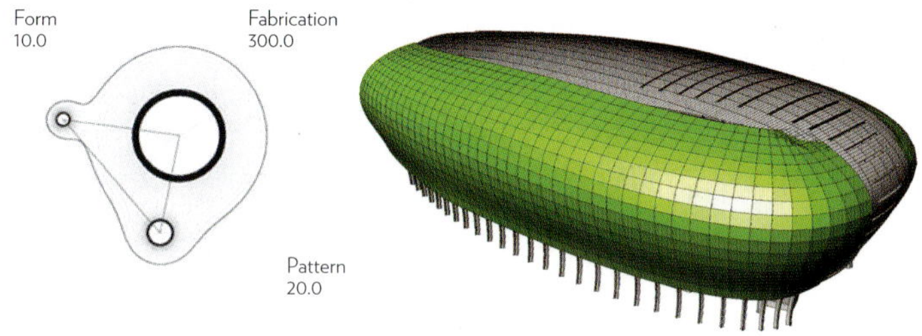

Method 4 - Blunt Rationalization

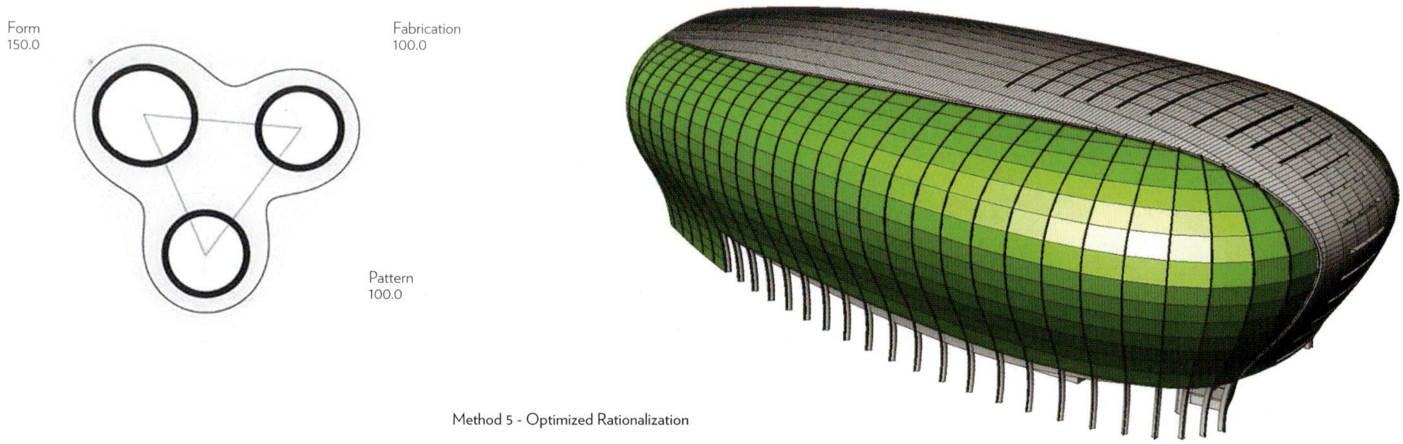

Method 5 - Optimized Rationalization

NUR ALEM MUSEUM OF FUTURE ENERGY

Astana, Kazakhstan

Nur Alem Museum of Future Energy, formerly known as the Kazakhstan Pavilion, was the iconic, high-performing centerpiece for Expo 2017 in Astana. Post-exposition, the building has transformed into Astana's premiere science museum. The building accomplishes the client's goals of a spherical-shaped building, while also meeting the programmatic and sustainability goals.

The theme of the expo, "Future Energy," reflects a broader community interest in the problem of energy consumption, which is having an increasingly negative impact on our planet. A major objective of the exposition was to engage people in a call for responsibility, one that fosters a discussion and works to develop a knowledge that will enable people to plan and control energy consumption on our planet and to minimize damage to the environment.

AS+GG won an international competition to design the master plan and associated buildings for Expo 2017. The International Exposition took place from June 10 to September 10, 2017, in Astana, Kazakhstan. The theme "Future Energy," was aimed at creating a global debate between countries, non-governmental organizations, companies, and the public on how to ensure safe and sustainable access to energy for all while still reducing CO_2 emissions.

Function: Science Museum | Status: Built, 2017 | **Client:** Expo 2017 | **Awards:** The Chicago Athenaeum, American Architecture Award, 2019; Rethinking the Future, Global Architecture & Design, Second Award, 2018; AIA National Tap/CCA Innovation Awards, Stellar Design, Astana Expo City, 2016

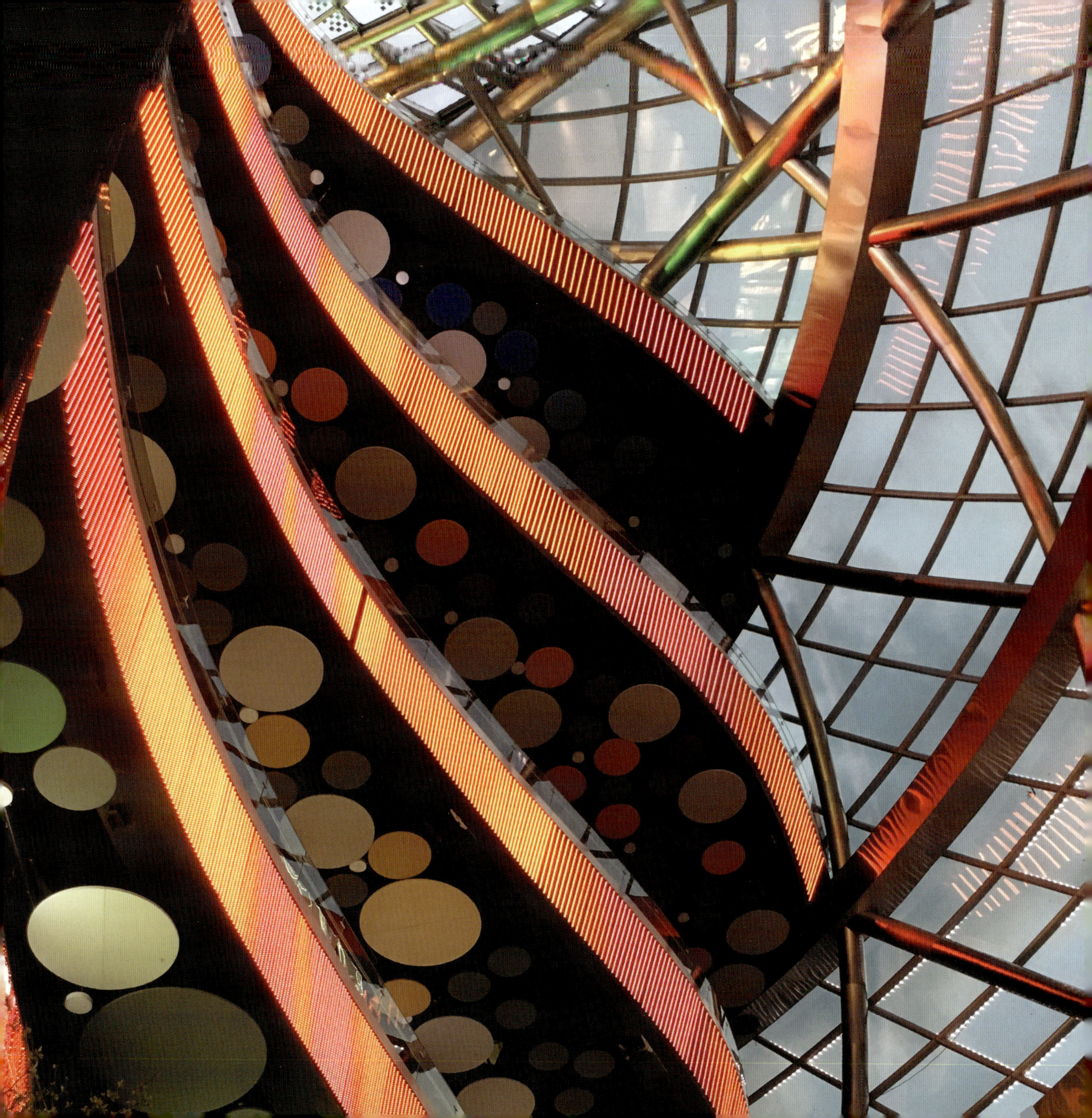

DESIGN CONCEPT | SITE

Located south of Bayterek Tower and east of Nazarbayev University, Nur Alem is now a significant landmark for Astana and is one of the first examples of how to extend the use of an exposition site. The site is close to urban amenities and is easily accessible to the rest of the city with multiple public transportation options.

In studying the fate of previous international expositions, the design team learned that most sites fall into disrepair and are unused and discarded. To avoid this, the design team collaborated closely with the client and the governments in Astana and Kazakhstan to develop a building that challenged the established standards for exposition structures. The team successfully procured and implemented a sustainable building that was designed to catalyze the expo site in a new way.

AS+GG knew early in the design process that their roles as architects and planners would go beyond the delivery of standard design. The goal was to design a building that would be a symbol of pride for Astana; a building that holds a higher standard for urban development and architectural design; a building that serves the needs of a diverse 21st-Century community.

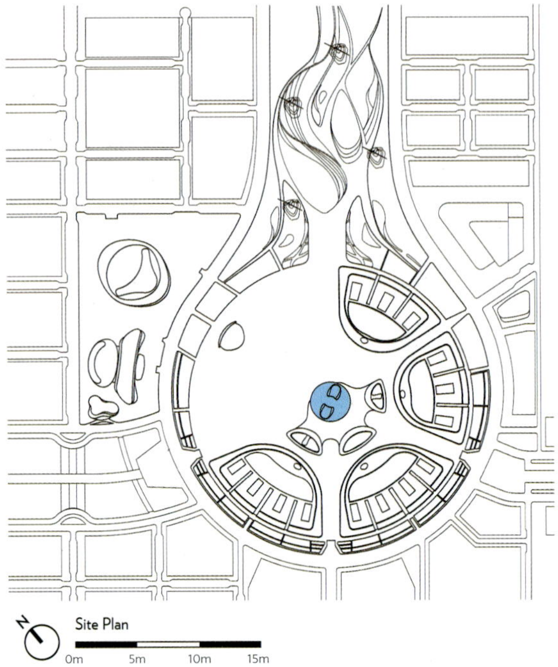

Site Plan

Nur Alem Museum of Future Energy Aerial View | Exterior View (Right)

The podium's 20,000 square meter exhibition space was the only program area noted in the client's design brief. The ground level plaza, central atrium, side atria, and terrace spaces and associated functions were not originally required. One of the important outcomes of the design process was to discover new opportunities to add to the vision of the project. The final design creates value for the building, the users, and community.

The building is supported by a central double core that organizes the stairways and other support functions such as service elevators and restrooms. The central atrium is surrounded by eight passenger elevators where visitors can travel in glass volumes from the ground level plaza to the top observation and event space. The central atrium also allows light to permeate the internal area of the building.

Nur Alem has seven levels of uninterrupted, column-free exhibit space with a floor-to-floor height of nine meters. The resulting seven-meter clearing leaves substantial space for exhibits. At the base, a covered access plaza organizes the entry sequence to the museum floors and provides additional exhibition space. Visitors can walk under the sphere and look into the interior spaces for alternative vantage points. Levels 2 through Level 7 are designated exhibition floors, while Level 8, the highest floor, is an event space that features a viewing platform with optimal views of the city. The space has playful interactive exhibits that display the building's high-performance functions.

Side terraces are accessible from each exhibit space so visitors can rest and reflect in the sun-drenched atria. The atria also link the floors, directing the visitor's traffic flow to ascend on the elevators and descend using the stairways. This flow helps control peak crowds and enhances the visitor experience. The building is accessible to people with disabilities, with access for wheelchair users at all levels and spaces of the building. Exhibits are multi-sensory, meaning they can be enjoyed by people who are hearing or visually impaired. The building was designed for all ages and abilities in mind, with interactive displays at different heights, for different educational levels, and different interests.

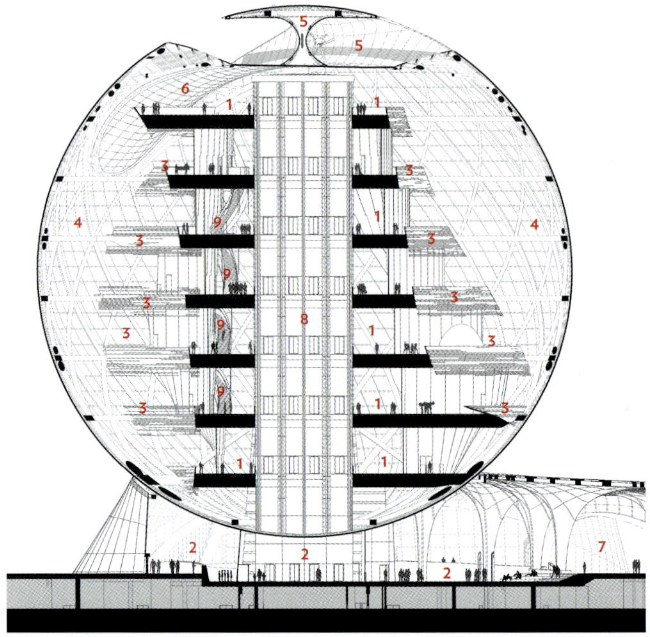

1 Exhibit Space
2 Special Exhibit
3 Balcony
4 Atrium
5 Wind Scoop Turbine
6 PV Solar Array
7 Covered Street
8 Elevators
9 Grand Stair

0m 5m 10m 15m

Section

Level 1 Entrance Exhibition | Elevator Experience (Right)

R ENERGY

DESIGN CONCEPT | FORM

Building Information Modeling (BIM) software helped the design team explore multiple design iterations of the spherical form in a virtual space, prior to documentation. The options were analyzed for design expression, energy impact, and structural integrity, in a coordinated international team effort. The sphere structure was modeled as an idealized design expression, then the structural team analyzed and engineered the structural forces of the complex grid shell and proposed further optimizations. The refined designs were evaluated in an architectural model, which were then further coordinated and refined. The process was repeated in a feedback loop to push the design to be a fully integrated solution that expresses the design shape and allowed the desired building integrated systems.

> *"The project is innovative in energy and resource conservation. Design indicators show the complexity of the project from interoperability, optimization of form, and performance.*
> *- AIA National, Juror Comment, Winner, The Technology in Architectural Practice (TAP) Innovation Award, 2016"*

Physical Model

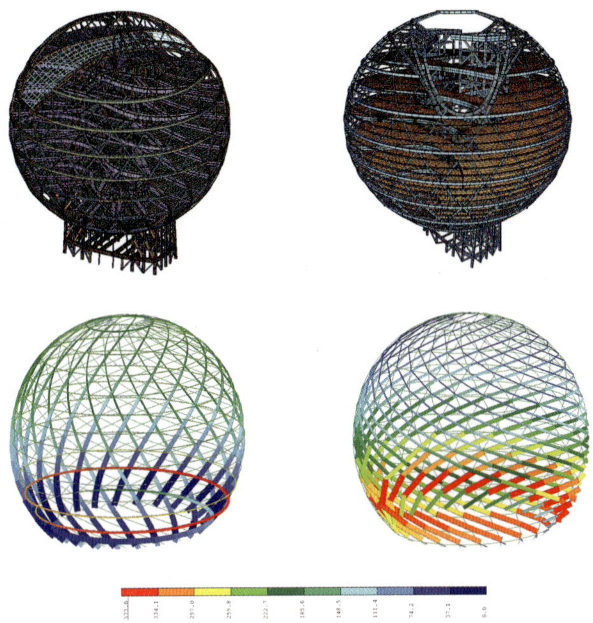

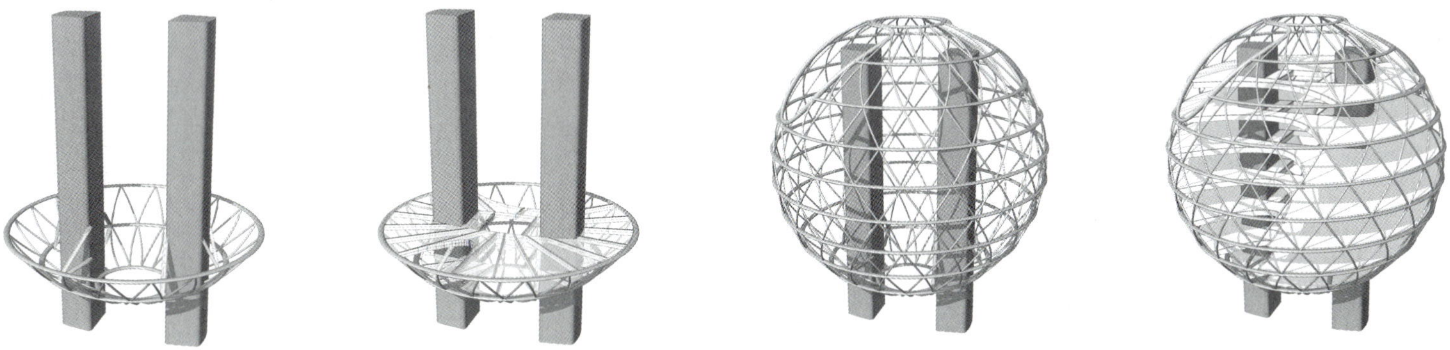

Structural Models

Two atrium spaces rise upward through the building, landing outside of each exhibition floor to give visitors a place of respite with interior and exterior views. The first faces primarily north toward the central district of Astana and the Baritek Tower. The second looks south to the linear green park. The atrium edges are programmable with LED displays that can be changed throughout the exhibition cycle, enhancing the exhibit experience. These "light ribbons" are seen from the exterior, particularly at night, allowing the building to visually draw in visitors. The atria also keep the floor lease spans at the appropriate size rather than creating deep floors that can lead to dark environments that are unable to access daylight.

The atria's spiral shape visually connects the different exhibition levels and features smooth, curved lines that soften the rigidity of the materials used to form organically shaped terraces. Each terrace is fully landscaped, incorporating seasonal and permanent plantings, especially on the south-facing space. The terraces are flexible in their use, providing event planners and building operators with an open platform.

During the design phase, atria options and overall carving of the floors were studied. Factors considered include solar performance, structural efficiency and constructability, flow of visitors, amount and configuration of the space, and experience of the space from the visitor perspective.

Level 1 Exhibit Spaces

Atrium

Level 1 Plan

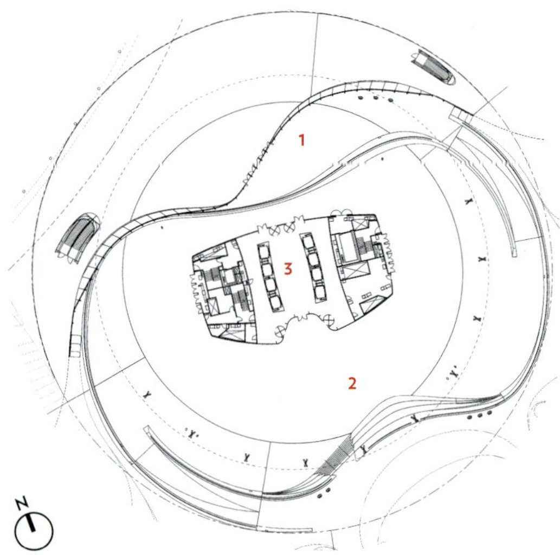

1 Entry

2 Exhibit Space

3 Elevator Lobby

Mid Level Plan

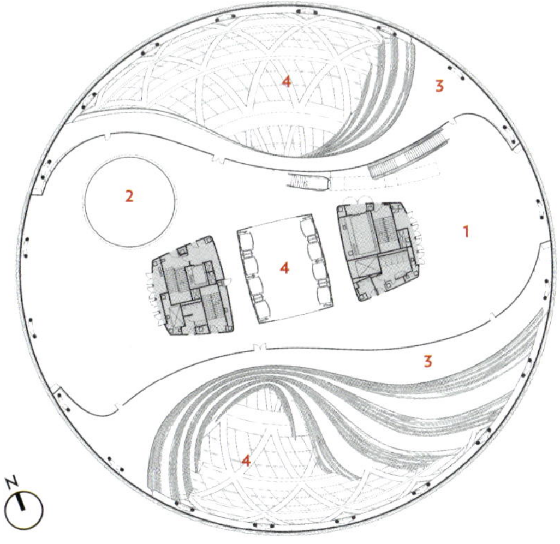

1 Exhibit Space

2 Special Exhibit

3 Balcony

4 Atrium

Mid-Level Exhibit Spaces

DESIGN CONCEPT | SPACE

The most engaging exhibition space is the observation and event space on Level 8, which features displays that are flexibly designed for a variety of educational, scientific, and art displays.

The wind turbine, a key feature of the overall form of the building, is exposed and can be experienced in motion. From the same area, visitors can view the Building Integrated Photovoltaics (BIPV) that are embedded into the glass exterior for shading and energy generation.

Floors are connected by the elevator system and a series of sculptural stairs connect the exhibit floors, dynamically curving to align with the shape of the terraces and exhibition floors and are clad in curved metal panels and integrated LED lighting.

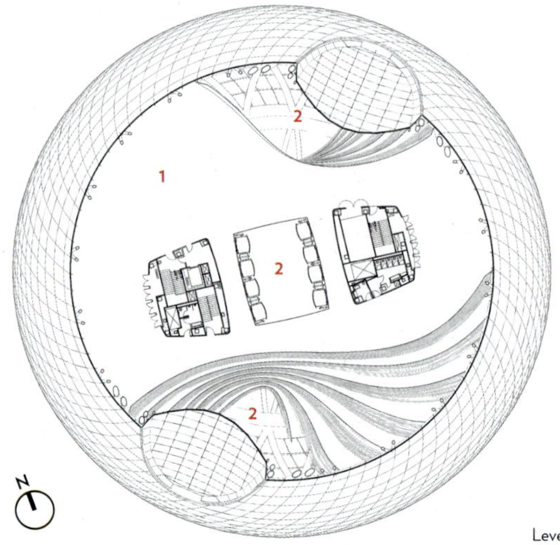

1 Observation + Event Space

2 Atrium

Level 8 Plan

Level 8 Exhibit Space with Photovoltaics + View (Right)

Sculptural Stair

50%

The facade, seen prominently from the interior, is part of the overall visitor experience. The sphere is smooth, not faceted like a typical geosphere structure. Its innovative, double-curved-glass exterior wall gently curves in three dimensions. To achieve these results, the fabricator heated the glass in special ovens until the material was soft enough to take the form of a mold, and then slowly cooled. The glass has high-performance, insulated laminated panels that are panelized in a spiral pattern for maximum repetition.

The cladding is attached directly to the structure, following a diagrid panelization. The clean diagrid was the most efficient cladding, adding to the elegant expression when coupled with the fully integrated structural design. A frit pattern is used to shade the south glass. The exterior wall consists of:

- Glazed unitized curtain wall with thermally broken double-curved insulated glass units (IGU) with aluminum mullions supported by the building's primary structural tube system and secondary members.
- The horizontal mullions support a perforated enclosure with a radiant heating tube system.
- The steel tube structural system is thermally isolated from the unitized glass wall.
- The inboard and outboard lite of the double-glazed, insulated-glass unit has laminated glass units. The outboard laminated lite includes a pattern of ceramic frit.
- The glazing is ultra-clear, low-iron glass with low-E coating and ceramic frit in a varied pattern.
- LED illumination and graphic system is integrated into the exterior curtain wall mullion system.
- A Building Management System (BMS) controlled shading system is integrated into the exterior wall mullion system.

Exterior Wall Diagram

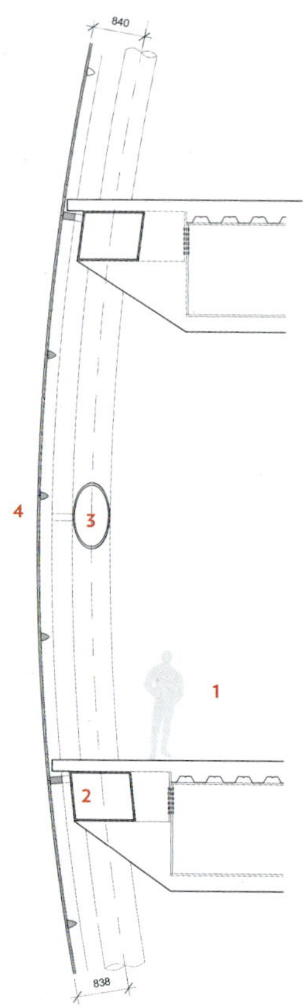

1 Stainless Steel Grating

2 Primary Structural Ring Beam

3 Primary Diagonal Structural Member

4 Double Curved IGU With Laminated Low-Iron Glass

Exterior Wall Curved Glass Panels

Typical Exterior Wall Vignette

Astana Expo 2017 Opening Night

One of the building's design goals was to maximize its means of communicating with the local and international community. As a central piece of the expo event and the legacy district, its ability to engage with local and global audiences is a part of its success. When geometry is considered, the design relates to its context as a 360-degree platform. The glass facade becomes a programmable canvas, where digital content can be integrated to form a rich dynamic expression. Options ranging from LED meshes and other interior and exterior systems were considered.

In the final and built solution, LED strips were installed into the exterior wall panels, aligning with the organic and dynamic expression of the sphere cladding. The physical, static architectural elements that define the Nur Alem during the day come to life at night, saturating the building with various light displays, messages, and colors.

Details were developed to incorporate LED strips, which are integrated with the aluminum supports at each side of the joint and protected from the exterior environment. Maintenance and installation work are done from the interior of the structure. Even though the separation between the LED strips is significant, and the overall density of the LED points is low, therefore the vast size of the sphere and the movement of light at the panels help make the system successful.

LED Integrated Lighting

A detailed design analysis was conducted using Rhino/Grasshopper to refine the spherical form and maximize the sun exposure for the Building Integrated Photo Voltaic cells (BIPV). Many investigations were completed and evaluated to integrate the solar panels, while balancing the requirements of other critical building components such as MEP surface area requirements, collision with other architectural elements, maximizing wind swept area for the turbines, and the rationalization the double-curved minimal surface geometry.

Monocrystalline semi-transparent BIPV were installed and integrated into the glazing of the scoop at the top of the sphere. During the testing phase, the energy model predicted 81,056 kWh/year of electricity or 2.21% of total energy demand. The PV percentage integration into glazing panels ranged from 40% to 80% density. Monocrystalline wafer was specified for the BIPV, spaced to allow a percentage of natural daylight to pass through. The light transmittance varied depending on the location.

Daylighting Analysis

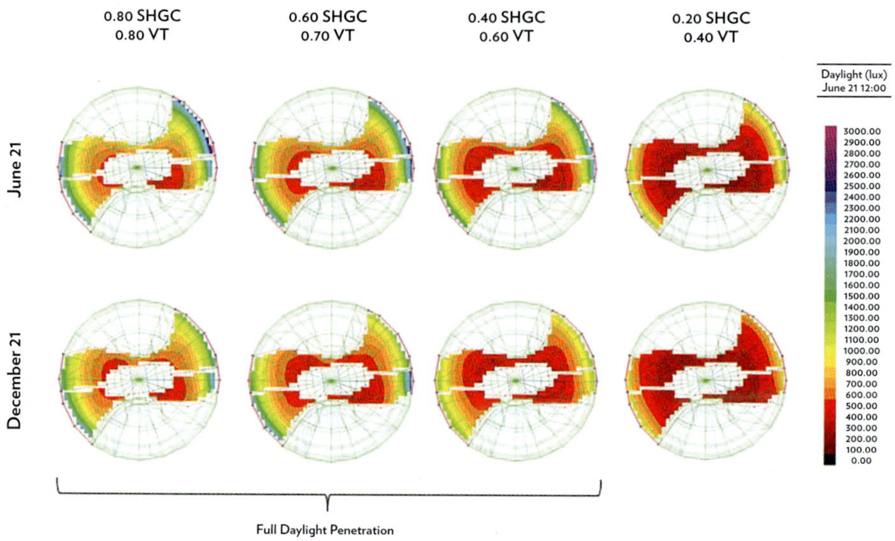

Solar Radiation Analysis

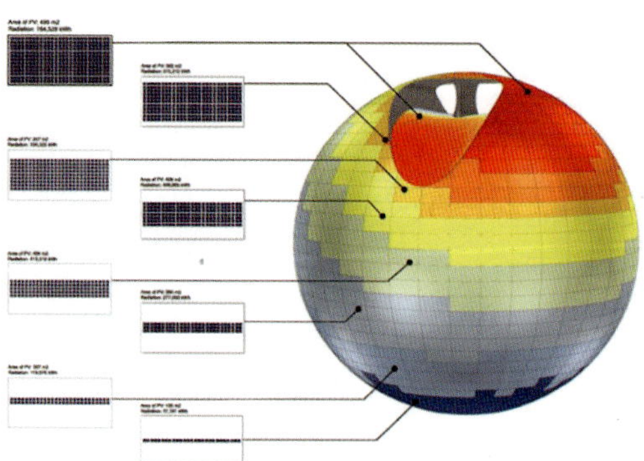

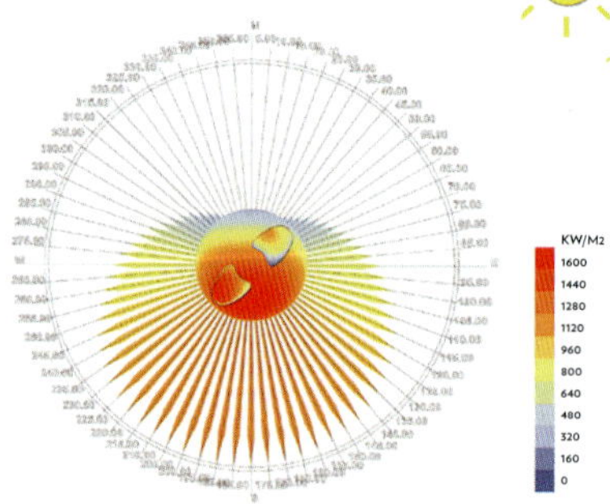

Total Radiation (kWh/m2)
UACC Astana
1 Jan - 31 Dec

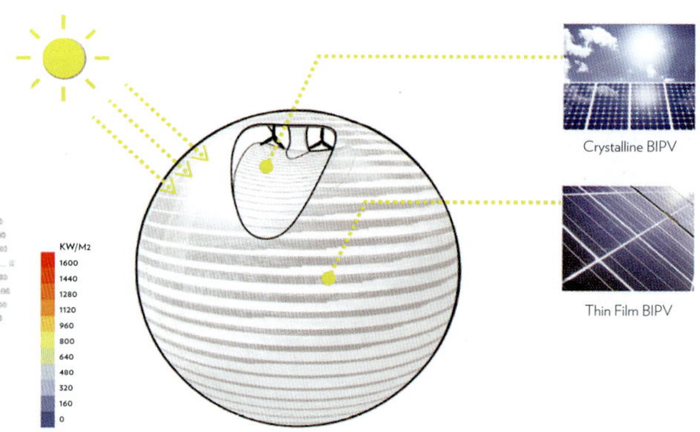

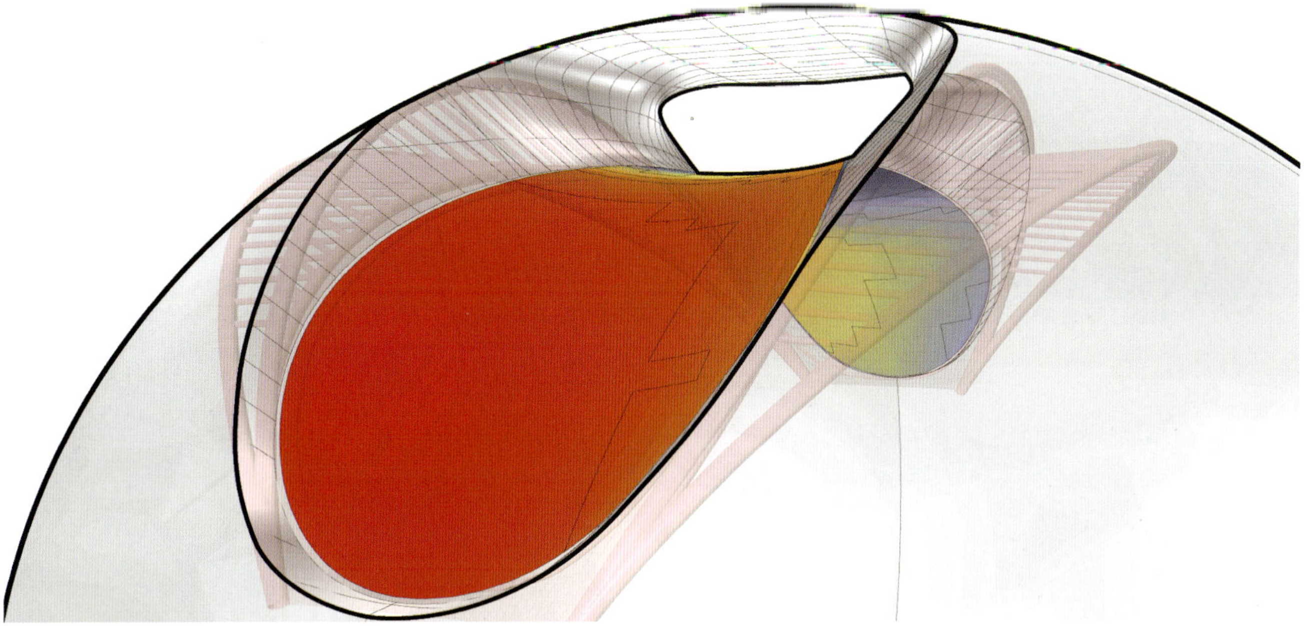

Panelization Rhino Model

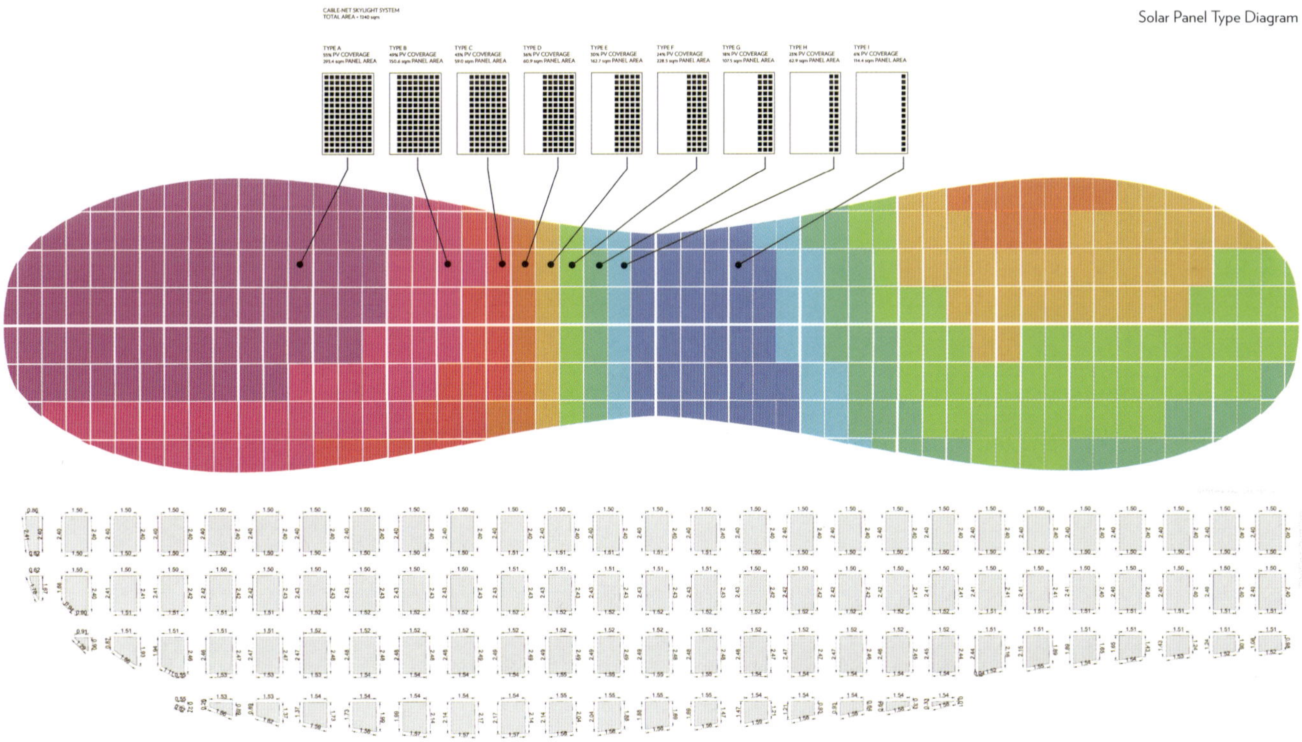

Solar Panel Type Diagram

To improve energy generation, several designs were modeled and assessed to find an appropriate form that responded to the programmatic requirements and optimized the amount of energy generation possible. A final analysis determined that building integrated wind turbines can produce energy through an inlet carved from the top of structure.

The design team worked closely with the wind engineers to design and test multiple overall building forms and eventually the shape of the inlet on the surface of the building. Predominant southwest winds are channeled to activate the turbines that were designed specifically for the harsh winter conditions of Astana. When evaluated, the turbines produce a total of 52,700 kwh/year of electricity or the equivalent of 1.6% of the building's total electricity demand or 0.9% of total energy demand.

2017 Wind Turbine Installation | Building Integrated Wind Turbines + BIPV (Right)

Wind Flow Diagram

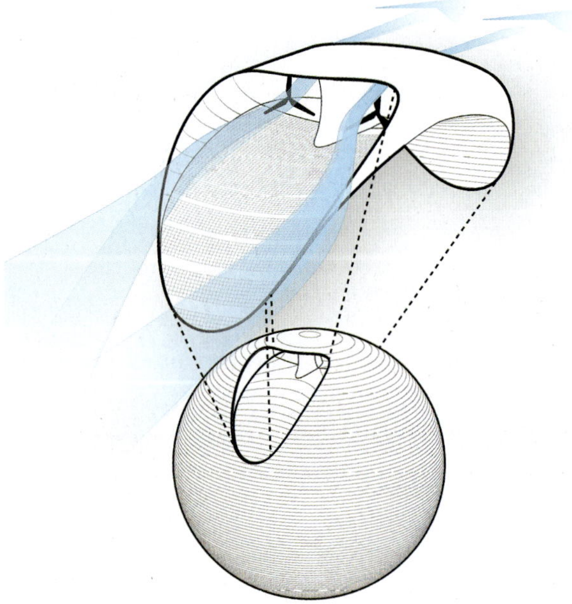

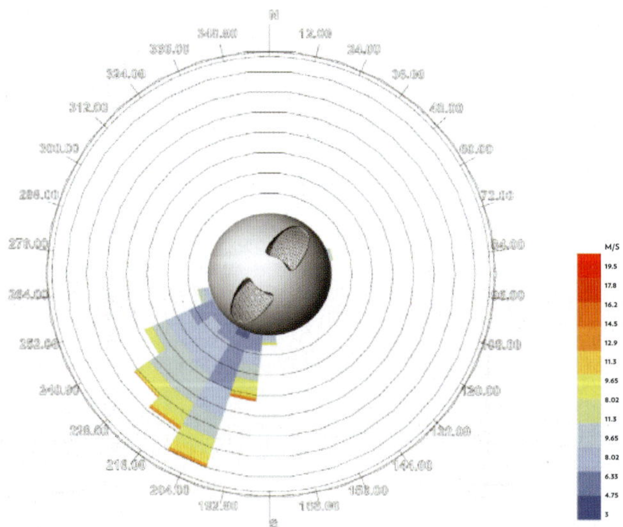

Wind Rose
1 Jan - 31 Dec
Wind Speed > 3m/s - 74% of Total Hours

ASTANA ARTS CENTER

Astana, Kazakhstan

The conceptual design for Astana Arts Center was approached as a high-performing building designed to be operational during Expo 2017, the three-month international exposition in Astana, Kazakhstan. After the completion of the exposition, the building was designed to transition into a permanent art museum for local international art events.

The design fully integrates into the exposition's site with a gently sloping landscaped roof that becomes a platform to expand the reach of the outdoor amphitheater designed for adjacent site. The roof also thermally and acoustically insulates the museum as it creates multiple viewpoints and gathering points for visitors.

The award-winning design for the 5,000 sm Astana Arts Center was conceived for Expo 2017, Kazakhstan's International Exposition, which ran from June-September 2017. Although unbuilt, the building is an excellent example of how an exposition building can be repurposed for future use once the exposition ends its initial run.

Function: Art Gallery + Museum | **Status:** Conceptual, 2015 | **Client:** Expo 2017 | **Awards:** The Chicago Athenaeum, International Architecture Award, 2019; Rethinking the Future, Global Architecture & Design Awards, First Award, Cultural, 2019; AIA Chicago, Unbuilt FORWARD Award, 2018

DESIGN CONCEPT | SITE

Facing the cultural axis, near the center of the Expo 2017 site, the arts center was designed to allow the exposition park to gracefully ascend to form the roof of the art museum. A series of wide stairs and ramps direct visitors toward the rooftop sculpture garden or to the main entrance at the east side of the building.

The main entrance is oriented toward the exposition site, taking advantage of the views of Nur Alem, the science museum discussed in the previous section. A sculpture garden is featured at the peak of the rooftop promenade. Access and exit for services and utilities is available at the north entrance, where mechanical equipment is also discreetly located.

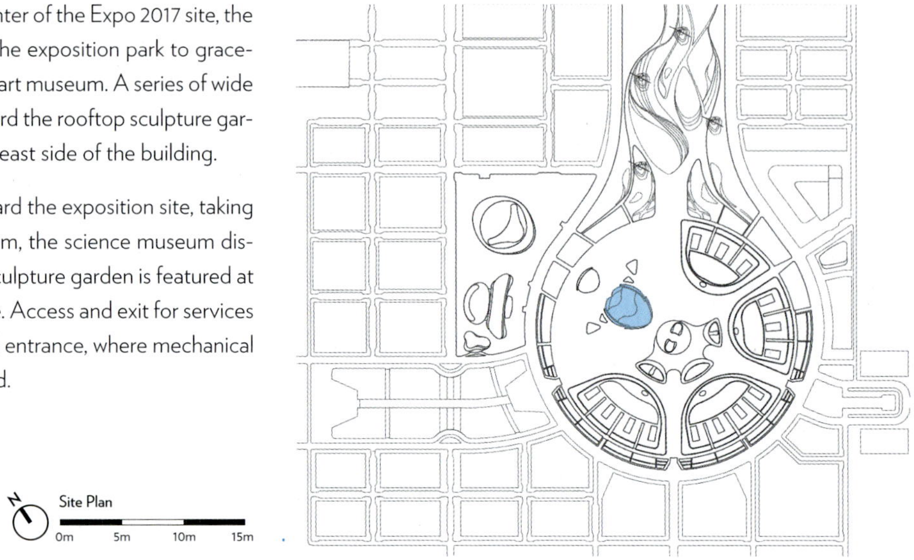

Site Plan

Cultural Axis View

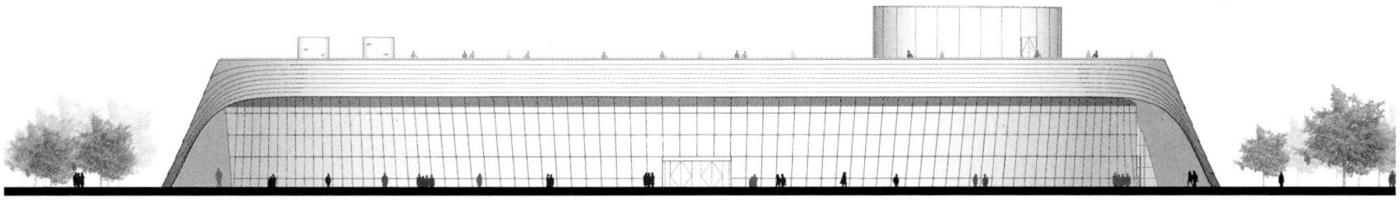

Southeast Elevation

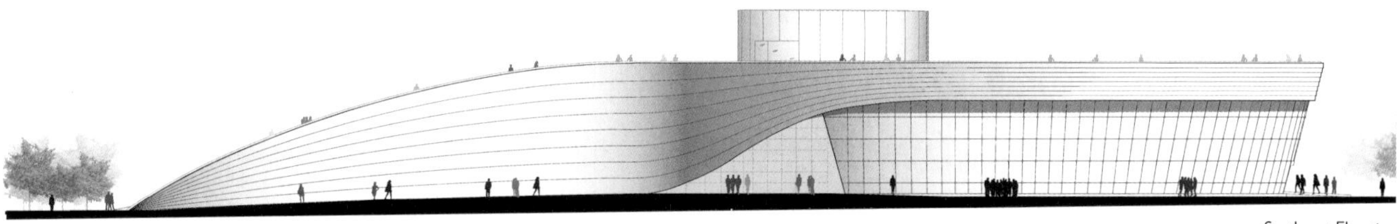

Southwest Elevation

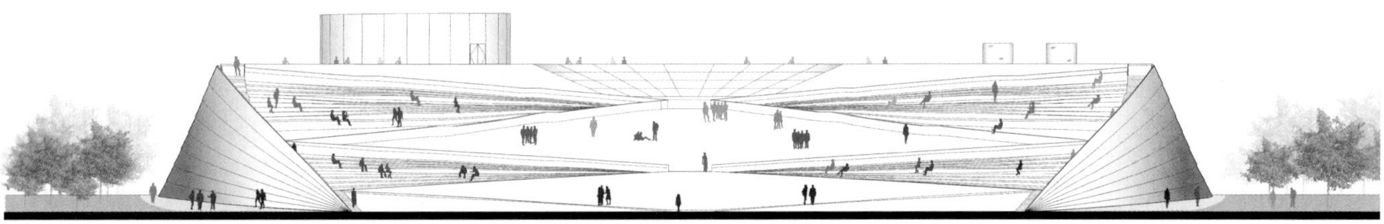

Northwest Elevation

At the opposite end of the first-floor galleries is a set of dynamic spiral stairs that lead to the mezzanine level and other gallery exhibition spaces. This partial mezzanine contains several smaller galleries and a viewing platform toward the larger gallery double height space below.

> *The Art Center's design is strong; it is elegant and also solves program issues.*
> *— AIA Chicago, Juror Comment, Winner, Unbuilt Forward Award, 2018*

Level 1 Floor Plan

1 Public Gallery
2 Private Gallery
3 Exhibition Space
4 Offices
5 Entry
6 Storage + Services
7 Gallery OTB
8 Stair to Mezzanine

0m 10m 20m 30m

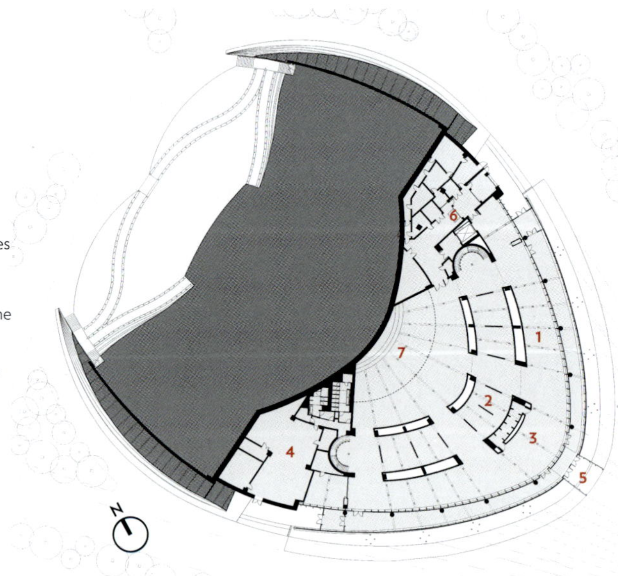

Level 1M Floor Plan

1 Stair to Mezzanine
2 Mezzanine Gallery
3 Offices

0m 10m 20m 30m

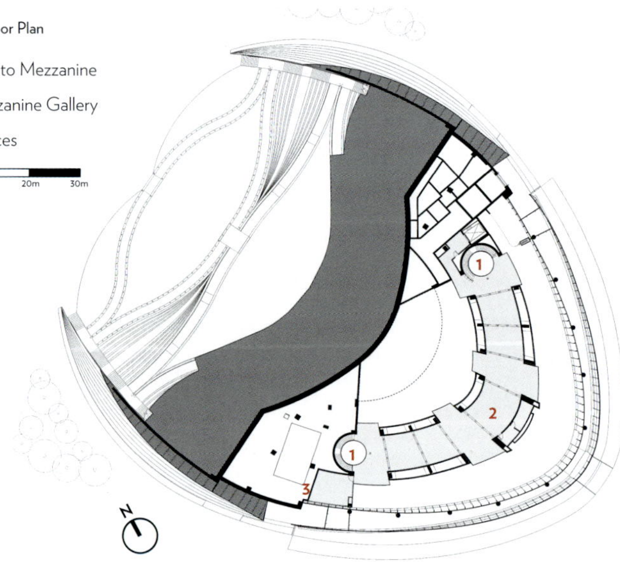

Roof Plan

1 Observation
2 Lawn
3 Sitting Stairs
4 Skylight
5 Sculpture Garden

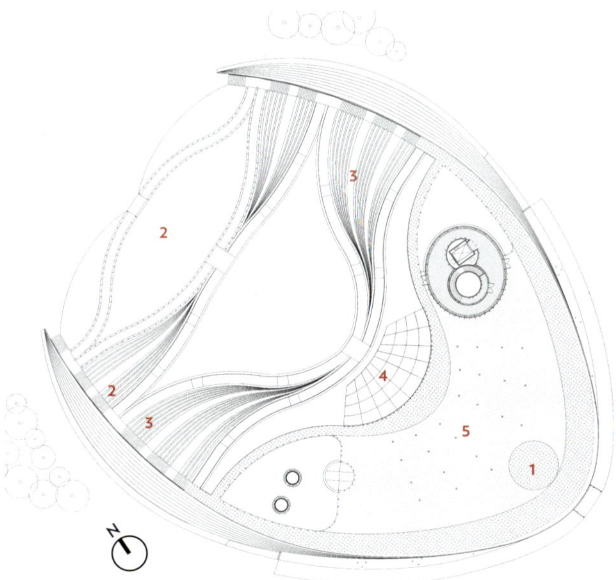

The landscaped roof is a key feature in the design. The public is invited to enjoy the promenade, which provides areas to sit and enjoy the views or to watch large events. An outdoor sculpture garden on top of the roof garden further integrates art into the context, encouraging visitors to access the space at any time of the day or night, with direct views into the center of the expo park.

DESIGN CONCEPT | FORM

Inspired by the gently rolling hills of Kazakhstan, the goal was to design a high-performing form that complements diverse sizes and scales of art. The design incorporates a double-wall facade system that will insulate during the region's humid summers and harsh winters, making it one of the most efficiently designed buildings in the region.

The landscaped roof, and its positioning, was critical to determining the building's form. Various iterations were studies to determine the architectural articulation and language of the terraced space and which design enhance the building performance rather than deter from it.

The berm sides were originally designed as green landscaped sloped surfaces. However, with further development of the design, it was determined that a fully landscaped implementation, considering Astana's harsh climate, meant that it would be difficult to maintain a "green" planted sloped surface with such a geometrical configuration. A sculptural copper wall system was developed, which maintained the desired natural and colorful tone.

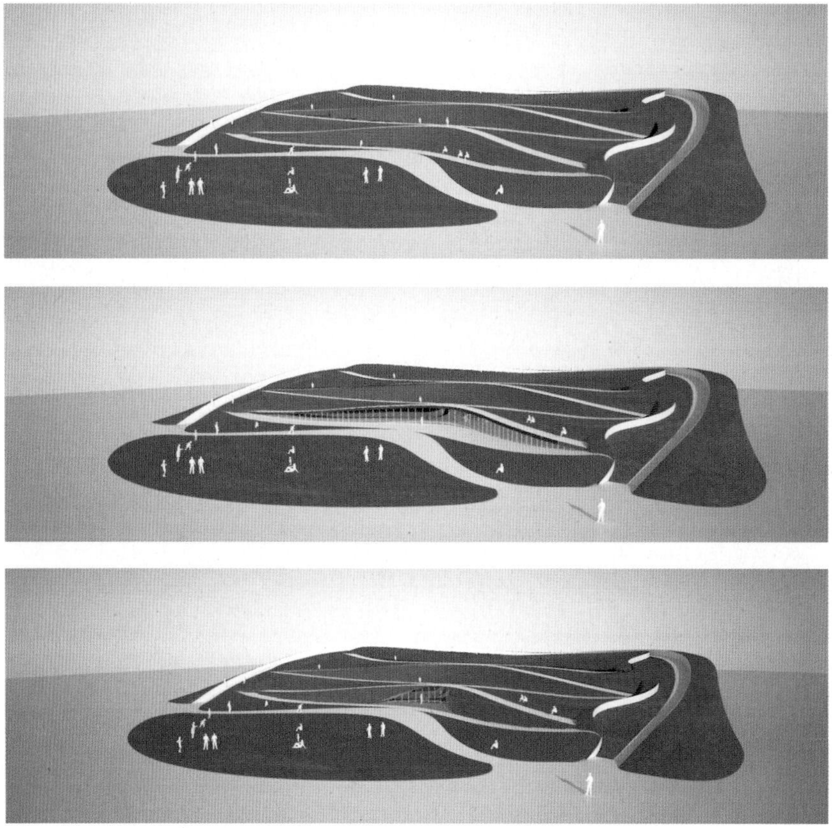

Landscaped Roof Options

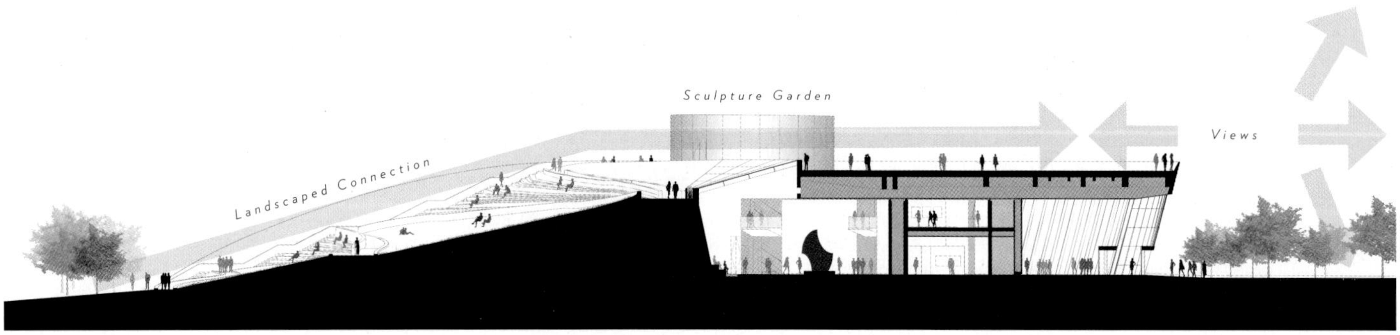

Design Concept

The exterior form filters indirect light that is preferred for art exhibits and display spaces. The perimeter entrance gallery features an angled cable wall that provides ample natural light and acts as a buffer zone during cooler and warmer days. This "room" relates to the impact of Astana's climate and studies were completed during the design process to determine the correct size, materials, and spacing for the optimal comfort levels of the building users.

The mezzanine level is equally bright, naturally lit through a wide PV integrated skylight that spans several galleries. A daylighting analysis helped determine the shape and size of the atrium skylight, as well as the density of the solar cells integrated into the glass.

Mezzanine Level Gallery with Skylight (Above + Right)

Entrance Gallery

The exterior wall has a sloped, triple-insulated, glazed cable net facade that features one-way cables supported with panels of clear double-insulated low-iron glass. Stainless steel cables and stainless-steel fittings and attachments are anchored to the steel truss structures above and the concrete structure below.

This solid portion of the exterior wall consists of a sloping zinc metal clad honeycomb backed rainscreen panel system with concealed fasteners. Waterproofing and rigid insulation are installed behind cladding and supported directly by the secondary steel framing attached to primary structure.

Glazed Cable Net Facade

Option 1
Double Glazing Outer Wall
Double Glazing Inner Wall

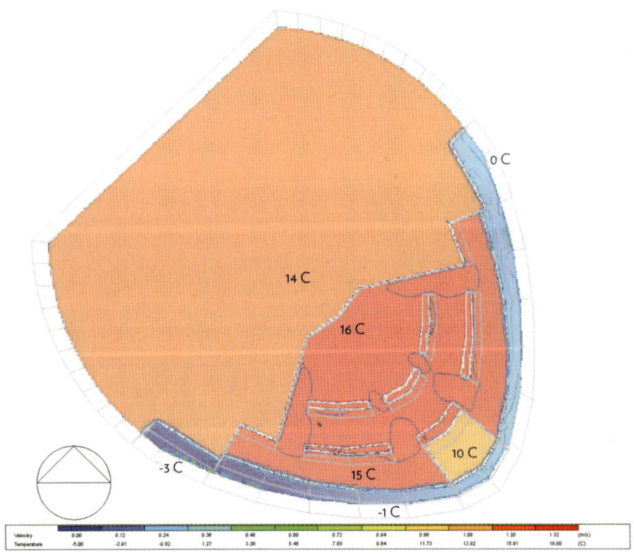

December 1st 12:00 pm
Outside Temperature -25.8 C

Option 2
Triple Glazing Outer Wall
Single Glazing Inner Wall

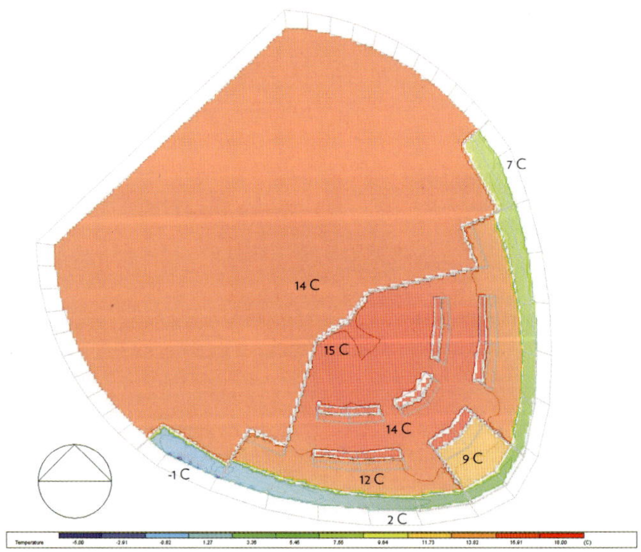

December 1st 12:00 pm
Outside Temperature -25.8 C

Cooper Facade Sections

The facade's berm sides were originally designed as green landscaped sloped surfaces. However, with further development of the design, it was determined that a fully landscaped implementation, considering Astana's harsh climate, meant that it would be difficult to maintain a "green" planted sloped surface with such a geometrical configuration. A sculptural copper wall system was developed to maintain the natural and dynamic tone of the building.

The art center's design has an optimized form and orientation to reduce energy and carbon loads, while also incorporating passive design philosophies to further reduce energy usage. A daylighting analysis established the shape and the size of the atrium skylight, and the density of the solar cells integrated on the skylight's glass. A solar radiation analysis determined that the ideal position for the rooftop photovoltaic panels was for them to be tilted downward to minimize solar radiation on the walls.

The facade features two types of double-glazed exterior glass walls. The first type is a sloped double-glazed cable tension facade with a one-way cable support system. The IGU consists of low iron, vision glass panels with double silver low-e coating. The second system is a double-glazed butt glazed system with vertical glass fins and white horizontal mullions. Horizontal rolling shades help minimize heat gain on the interior side of the curtain wall.

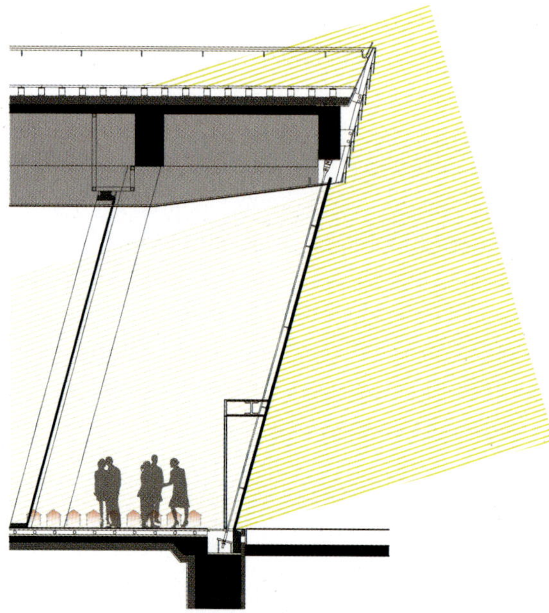

Exterior Double Wall Facade

Exterior Double Wall
Passive Design

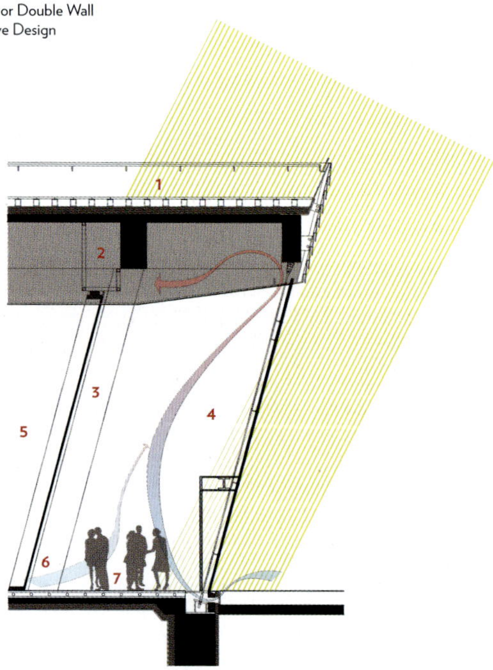

1 Solid roof with integrated photovoltaic pavers.

2 Ceiling cavity utilized for the reuse of natural air exhaust for makeup air.

3 (Galleria) used for passive natural ventilation during warm days and the containment of light from direct solar glare and heat gain.

4 Double thermal control coated glass cable wall system maximizing comfort and contained daylighting.

5 Second entrance wall with clear low iron laminated glass fins used to keep away aggressive high summer sun while allowing sunlight in during cold winter months maximizing comfort and contained daylighting for art display space.

6 Radiant floor heating for cold months.

7 Operable grill for passive natural ventilation during comfortable months.

All aspects of power generation were investigated, and several were incorporated into the building-design guidelines, including high-performance glazing that maximizes solar heat gain in winter, while providing shading in summer; energy piles that will reduce energy demand and provide temperature modulation during winter; and energy storage capacity that can meet two days of emergency demand. The predicted EUI in kBtu/sf/year excluding on-site renewable energy contribution is 184. The predicted EUI in kBtu/sf/year including on-site renewable energy contribution, not including carbon offsets is 178.

The site-wide infrastructure concept is an integration of occupants, buildings, and utilities. These include a smart-energy grid, smart recycled water grid, integrated waste management system, water reduction and waste to landfill reduction targets. Strategies incorporated into the building's designs include high-performance energy piles that will reduce energy demand and exposed thermal mass that will provide temperature modulation within the buildings during both summer and winter; 100% of rainfall from a 100-year storm event will be managed on site; and 90% of waste generated on-site will be diverted from a landfill. Reducing waste content was particularly important for the structures designed for Expo 2017. Because of the strict budget and tight timeline, it was critical that hauling waste was not part of the primary expenses so 90% of waste generated on site was diverted from a landfill.

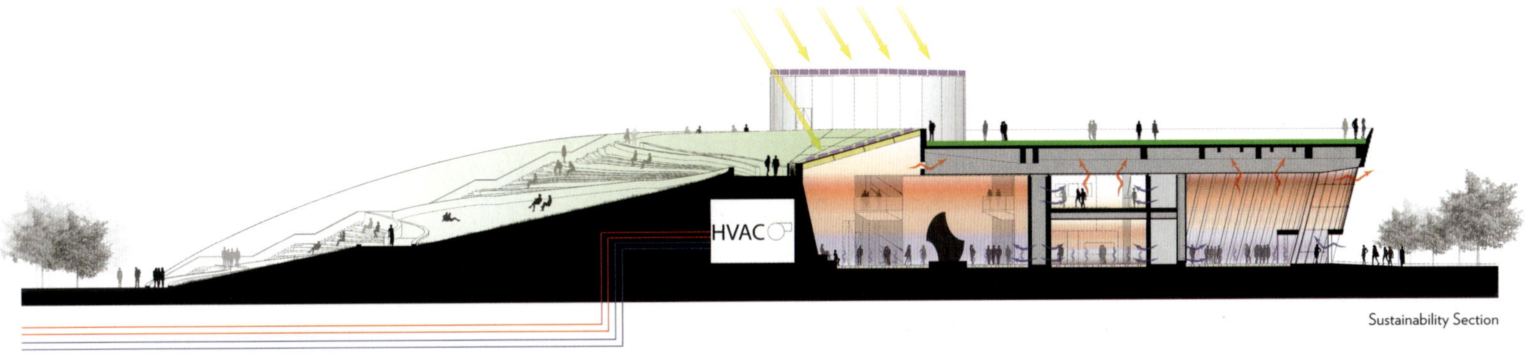

Sustainability Section

Annual Average Solar Radiation Analysis

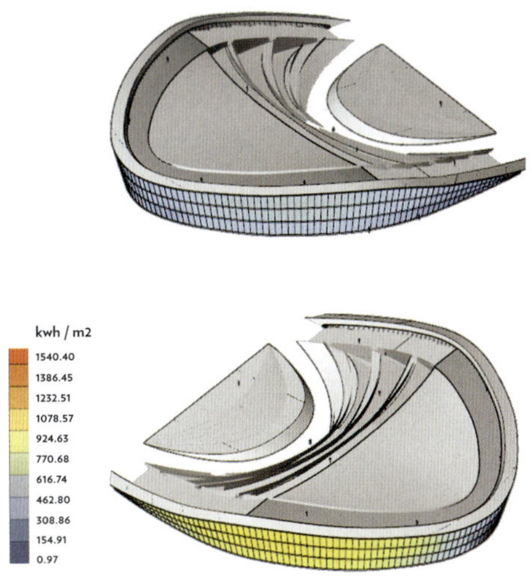

CHICAGO ARCHITECTURE CENTER

Chicago, Illinois, USA

The Chicago Architecture Center (CAC) was designed from an under-utilized retail space and recently enclosed exterior terrace at the Illinois Center in downtown Chicago, Illinois. The CAC was able to consolidate their influence into one general location by relocating the center to a site adjacent to the Chicago River and above the dock for the center's architectural riverboat cruises.

The CAC has become one of the largest cultural organizations in Chicago serving 700,000 people annually. Their mission is to inspire people to discover why design matters. Participation has grown since the opening, fueling the rediscovery of Chicago architecture's role in society.

Opened in August 2018, the Chicago Architecture Center, or CAC, is the new visitor experience and exhibition space for the nonprofit cultural arts organization formerly known as the Chicago Architecture Foundation, which was founded in 1966.

Function: Exhibit, Retail, Education | **Status:** Built, 2018 | Client: Chicago Architecture Center | **Awards:** AIA National, Interior Architecture Award, 2022; AIA Chicago, Interior Architecture Award, Citation of Merit, 2021; GCFD Special Achievement Real Estate Award, 2019; Chicago Building Congress, Merit Award, Finalist, 2019

CHICAGO
ARCHITECTURE
CENTER

DESIGN CONCEPT | SITE

The CAC outgrew the location of their previous facility on Michigan Avenue. Although options were explored to expand their footprint within the existing building, it was an inconvenient location in terms of the CAC's walking and boat tours as well as their expanding exhibit and educational programs.

The new location is adjacent to the Chicago River and above the dock used for the center's CACF Architectural River Cruise, which is one of the most popular tourist attractions in the city. The new site links CAC's cultural attractions in one walkable district.

The design leverages its location to create a cultural corridor that reaches people visiting other cultural attractions like Millennium Park, Navy Pier, and the museums on the Cultural Mile, as well as patrons of the retail establishments on the Magnificent Mile on Michigan Ave.

The site is also conveniently connected to Chicago's downtown central area with access to local and regional transportation options within walking distance. The space is also easily accessed by bike lanes and if driving is necessary, parking is available on site.

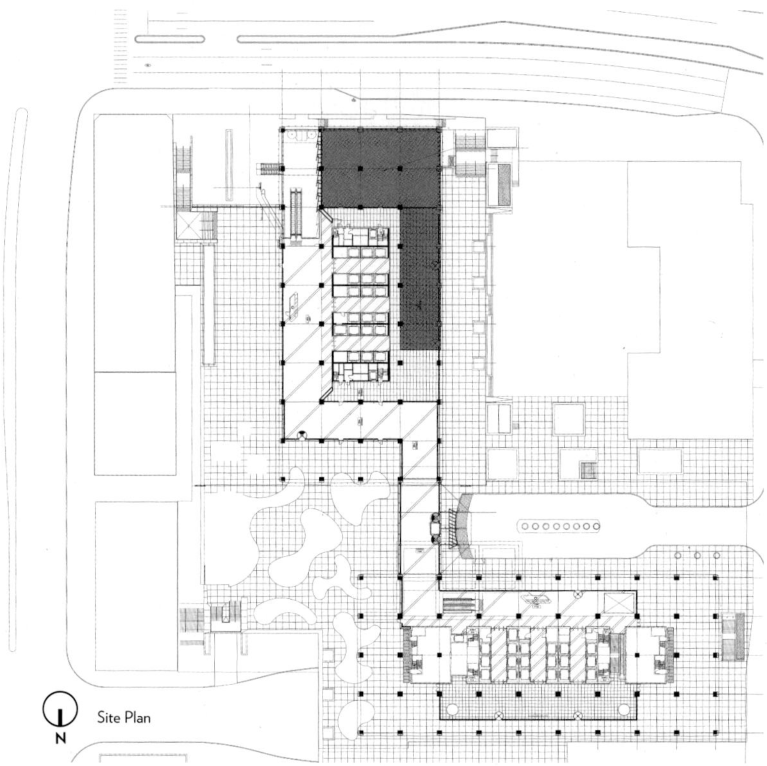

Site Plan

East-West Section

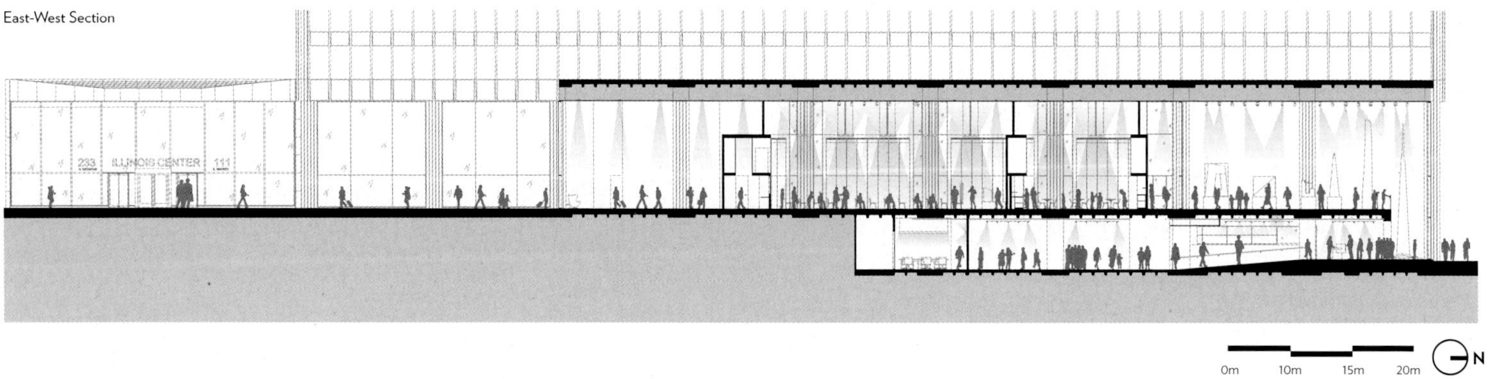

Chicago Architecture Center with River Cruise Boat Dock

DESIGN CONCEPT | PROGRAM

The project's program is part exhibition, part retail, part educational center, and part lecture hall. The 20,000 square foot space is adaptable for its various functions, operating as a full-service community cultural center for Chicago's residents and visitors.

The program features two permanent exhibits and rotating exhibit galleries, meeting spaces for the CAC's river and walking tours, a lecture hall for workshops and lectures, which is also available to rent, and a Design Studio for youth outreach programs in architecture.

The CAC's museum shop has a variety of design books, home decor, and CAC-branded merchandise. Proceeds from CAC's tours, gift store, and donations support their educational mission with free workshops, grants, and sponsorships.

The CAC is committed to remaining fully inclusive and accessible to everyone and is fully ADA compliant ramps and elevators available to make the space easy to navigate for any level of mobility. Sign language interpretation is available, and the lecture hall is equipped with an FM Assistive Listening System. A large family/gender neutral restroom is also available.

CAC Museum Shop | Entrance Lobby (Right)

Plaza Level N

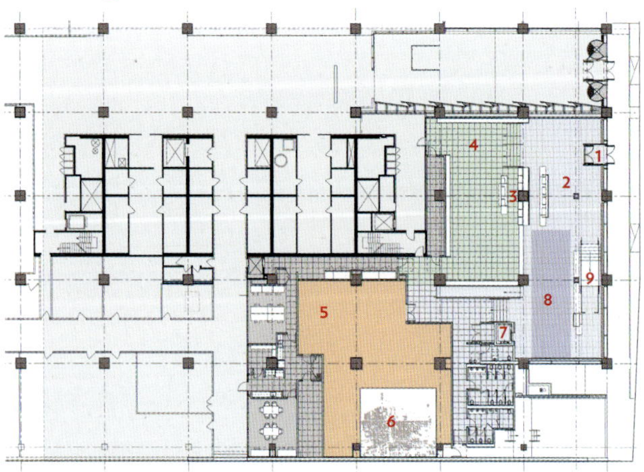

Concourse Level N

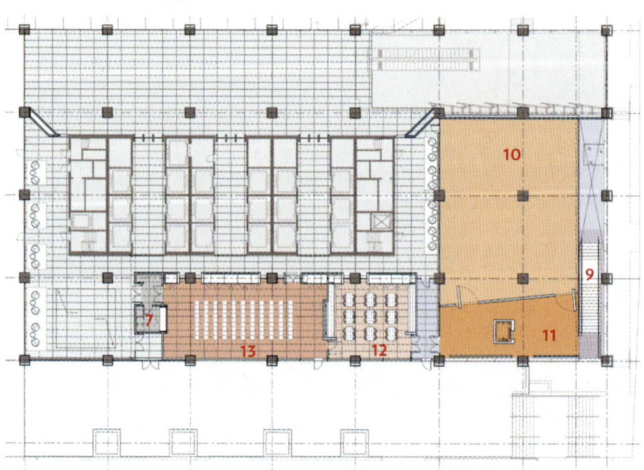

1 Front Entrance
2 Lobby
3 Ticketing
4 Museum Store
5 Chicago Gallery
6 Chicago Model
7 Restrooms
8 Tour Meeting Point
9 Grand Stair
10 Skyscraper Gallery
11 Rotating Gallery
12 Design Studio
13 Lecture Hall

DESIGN CONCEPT | FORM

The form of the center's interior was designed to be flexible and work seamlessly for both the public and paid exhibition programs. A two-story atrium connects the programs and highlights views of the Chicago River and Lake Michigan. A unique experience is formed for both the internal and external visitor by having the front portion of the program open to the street front. The galleries are enhanced by the light entering the atrium, activating the circulation of the program.

The main arrival point is the grand stair, which orients the visitor to city views that function as a panoramic backdrop for the entrance lobby and plaza level gallery. Unlike other galleries that conceal stairways toward the back or side of exhibition spaces, the steps at the CAC are central to the design; they are the vehicle that flows through the interior, enticing visitors to take the journey through the space. The configuration takes advantage of city and river views, encouraging users to slowly experience this unique perch.

The stairs are light and floating, crafted of wood, metal, and glass which allows added light to penetrate into the adjacent spaces. Solid wood treads have perforated stair risers with lighting embedded into their underside to glow during late evening and after hours.

> *The new Chicago Architecture Center is the latest jewel in Chicago's architectural crown.*
> *- Blair Kamin, Architecture Critic, Chicago Tribune, 1992-2021*

The Grand Stair with Pre-Function Gallery | Exterior View with Lit Stair

20
50
CHICAGO
ARCHITECTURE
CENTER

DESIGN CONCEPT | SPACE

The CAC's interior architecture contrasts the austere classic Mies van der Rohe elements with moments of raw architecture. It was important that the project's aesthetic be classic and timeless, yet provocative and forward thinking. The energy of the space is to engage visitors with its ability to appeal to the serious architecture scholar and not be intimidating for inquisitive tourists or locals. The design applies red, the CAC's brand color, for wayfinding or spatial organizational elements to create hierarchy and orientation within the center. At the Concourse Level where visitors enter, the ticketing directs them to the various programming elements. Trained Exhibit Hosts and Docents lead dozens of tour options and meet their groups on the Chicago Loop floor graphic, which serves as an entry point to discussions on Chicago Architecture.

Entrance Lobby at Plaza Level | Orientation Graphic (Right)

CAF was founded in 1966 to save Glessner House, one of Chicago's oldest residences.
The largest Tiffany stained glass dome is in Chicago.

The Chicago City Model Gallery is on the Concourse Level behind the Museum Store. The entry corridor is a rotating gallery for architecture exhibits and other Chicago-focused displays. The gallery leads visitors to a physical scale model of 3,000 buildings in downtown Chicago. This exhibit, which has been expanded and modernized from the Chicago Model at the center's previous location, tells the story of how Chicago became the epicenter of modern architecture and design through a mixed-media presentation of video and light. A film and coordinated light display follow Chicago's early growth, from the rebirth after the Great Chicago Fire to the first-ever skyscrapers to today's modernist masterpieces of steel and glass. The viewer can dictate the experience by choosing which building or section of the Loop with digital tablets stationed around the model, creating an interactive experience.

Entry Gallery

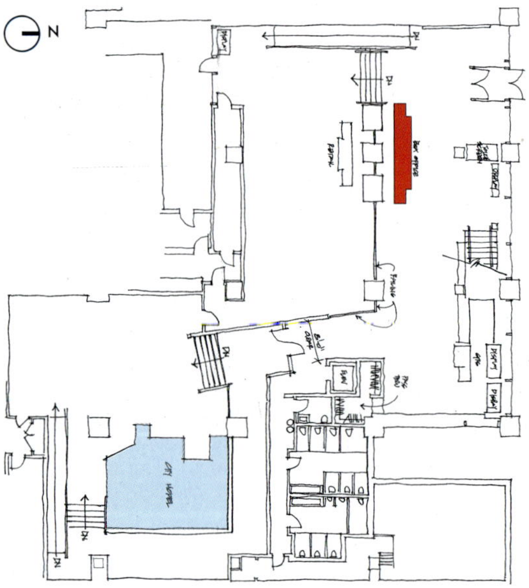

Plaza Level Plan Sketch, 2017

Chicago City Model Gallery (Above + Right)

CHICAGO:
CITY OF ARCHITECTURE

To access the Plaza Level gallery and educational spaces, visitors ascend the grand stair along the north elevation of the space. Much of the center has direct views to the outdoors through floor-to-ceiling windows that provide an abundance of natural light to the lobby, exhibition spaces, and corridors. Forty-foot windows let the city spill into the interior space, filling it with light and views of the unique waterfront site. The space also offers iconic, rare street level views of the Chicago River, the Equitable Building, the DuSable Bridge, and the Wrigley Building, fully ensconcing visitors in a special Chicago view. The spaces that lack views and daylighting are intentionally positioned to allow for intensive audio/visual presentations. A rotating gallery serves as a pre-function space for the Skyscraper Gallery, the Design Studio, and the Lecture Hall. Exhibits in this space rotate every three months and focus on various topics related to architecture and design. The space is highly flexible. With rotating walls and pedestals on wheels, countless configurations can be achieved.

Rotating Gallery | Grand Stair (Above + Right)

STATE
AWARD WINNERS
LIVE

THE INHERITORS

DESIGN CONCEPT | SPACE

The Plaza Level Skyscraper Gallery features scale models of some of the world's tallest and most iconic buildings in the exhibit, "Building Tall." The exhibit reveals how design and engineering innovations have spurred a "race to the top," to build higher into the sky.

The models—either on loan from local, national, and international architecture firms or made by a local Chicago model maker—examine the ways that architects have broken boundaries to build structures like the Home Insurance Building (one of the world's first skyscrapers) and the Willis Tower (previously Sears Tower), which held the title of world's tallest building for nearly 25 years.

Front and center, spanning the full height of the atrium space is AS+GG's 40-foot-tall model of Jeddah Tower, which will be the world's tallest building when completed.

Plaza Level Plan

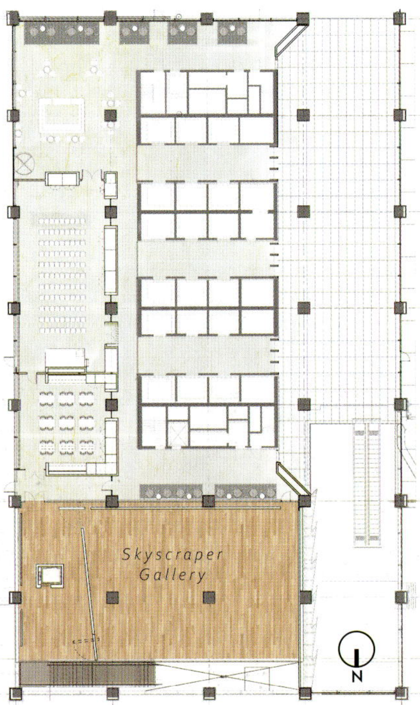

Building Tall Exhibit, Plaza Level | Jeddah Tower Model (Right)

3250ft
1000m
2750ft
800m
2250ft
OF THE ART
MEGATALL
600m
1750ft
WILLIS
TOWER
1,451ft
(442m)
400m
1250ft
SUPERTALL
300m
WORLDWIDE
AMERICAS
EUROPE
MIDDLE EAST
& AFRICA
10 YEAR
AWARD
URBAN
HABITAT
AWARD
AMERICAN
COPPER
BUILDINGS,
NEW YORK
THE SILO,
COPENHAGEN
ZEITZ MOCAA,
CAPE TOWN

DESIGN CONCEPT | MATERIALS

To improve daylighting conditions, the interior architecture has floor-to-ceiling windows that offer an abundance of natural light to the lobby, exhibition spaces, the design studio, corridors, and the lecture hall. The natural light is further transferred into the core of the building by narrow slots of glass at each existing column, which also sets the new architecture off the existing aluminum clad columns.

The design studio and the lecture hall are single and double spatial cubes, respectively, taking advantage of the same unique proportions. The studio has interactive walls of writable surfaces to be used in classroom settings and the lecture hall has a state-of-the-art audio-visual system, allowing this space to be used for many different types of events.

An abundance of storage allows for secure spaces for educational materials, student laptops and class projects. Both spaces feature acoustically designed ceilings that are installed with suspended, modern lighting. All lighting is low-energy LED and Greenguard Certified furniture is used for workshop and conference spaces. Sustainable touches are throughout. For example, dry eraser wall surfaces in the design studio minimize the need for printing educational projects and promotes collaboration.

An abundance of storage allows for secure spaces for educational materials, student laptops and class projects. To improve daylighting conditions, the interior architecture takes advantage of the floor-to-ceiling windows of the exterior wall, offering an abundance of natural light that is further transferred into the building by narrow slots of glass at each existing column, which also sets the new architecture off the existing aluminum clad columns.

Lecture Hall

Lecture Hall + Design Studio Renderings

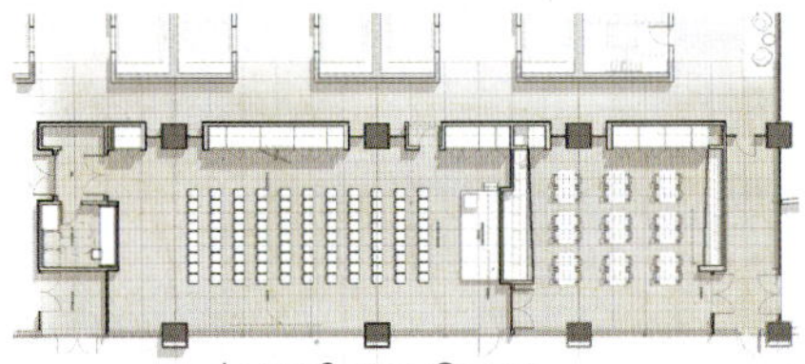

Lecture Seating - Option 1

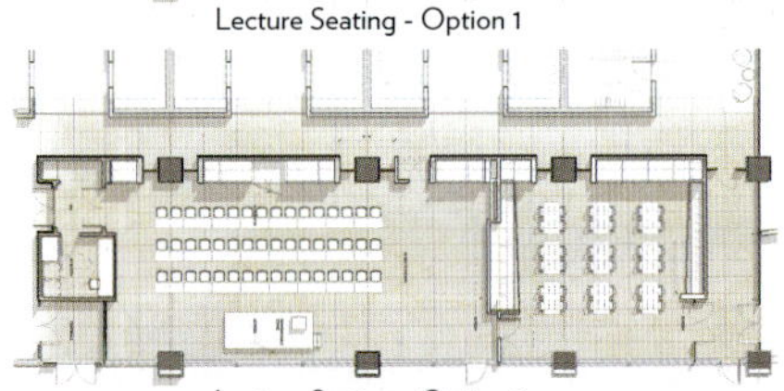

Lecture Seating - Option 2

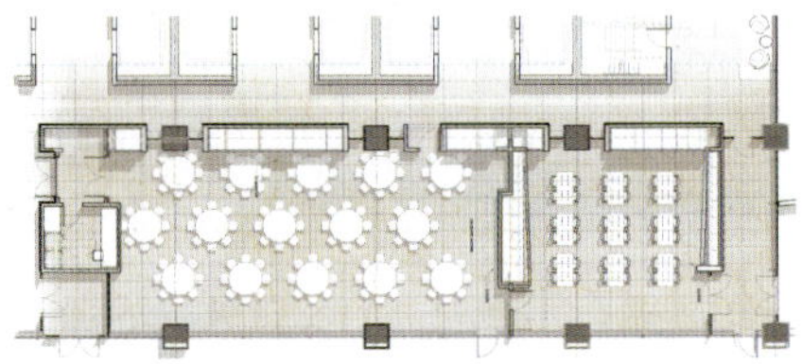

Dining Seating

Exterior View (Right)

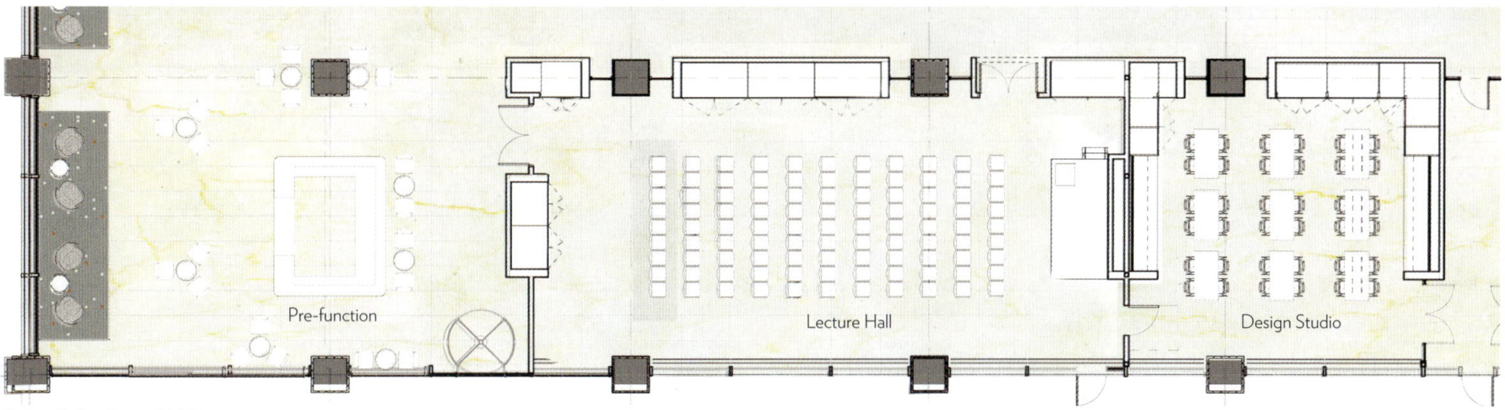

Design Studio + Lecture Hall Plan

ZAHA HADID
ARCHITECT
1950 - 2016
Zaha Hadid was an Iraqi-British architect. It's recorded that she had difficulty commissioning people to build her structures because the designs didn't look like they could stand up. Her buildings were based off nature, such as a shell or a rock. She was the first and to-date, only woman to be awarded the Royal Gold Metal. Her design, Leeza Soho is featured in the Skyscraper Gallery of the CAC.
Hadid's, Leeza Soho, Beijing 2018
BY: SARAH LOUGH, GRADE 7
JEANNE GANG
ARCHITECT

MARION L. M. GRIFFIN
MARGARET BURROUGHS
EDUCATOR, ARTIST, POET
FLORENCE KNOLL-BASSETT
DESIGNER, ENTREPRENEUR
FRIDA ESCOBEDO
ARCHITECT

GLOBAL MOBILITY PAVILION

Dubai, United Arab Emirates

The concept for the Global Mobility Center was designed to be a node within the larger network of Dubai Expo 2020 and in the post-expo legacy district. The form is a simple shell that is easy to erect and clad in tile, a material that is indigenous to the region. The colors and attributes of the design are easily recognizable as contemporary, compact, and adaptable.

The structure is adaptable and can be infilled as floor area needs and uses change. As designed, the open space concept is programed for exhibition and museum uses that are themed on sharing information. The interior surfaces and exterior walls function as screens that project living data. Open spaces connect from floor-to-floor allowing information to be seen and shared between groups throughout the building.

AS+GG's Global Mobility Pavilion was designed for an invited international competition for one of the three themed signature pavilions at Expo 2020 Dubai: Sustainability, Opportunity, and Mobility. In responding to the competition brief, AS+GG envisioned a project that supports the public exhibition activities during the Expo stage and its legacy stage conversion into the Global Logistics and Supply Chain Management Institute, supporting Dubai's role as a global transport hub. The eight-week competition was held in 2015 and included submissions from AS+GG, Foster and Partners, Santiago Calatrava, Shigeru Ban, and Asif Kahn.

Function: Exhibition Center | **Status:** Conceptual, 2017 | **Client:** Expo 2020 Dubai LLC

EXPO
2020

DESIGN CONCEPT | SITE

The Global Mobility Pavilion was designed to play a key role in the site plan organization and crowd flow circulation patterns at Expo 2020. Situated within a large plaza in the space framed by a series of exposition buildings, the pavilion is strategically positioned to maximize its visual impact as seen from the south entrance gate and the main pedestrian circulation routes. A relationship between the entrance of the surrounding buildings is coordinated to provide clear sight lines and travel paths to the pavilion.

In addition to creating memorable ground level views, aerial views of the expo are choreographed as seen from a network of gondolas envisioned for the event. The striking form of the structure, together with the sculpted ground plane and contrail directional lines, establishes a unique visual identity as seen from above.

The pavilion can be approached from each sides and when visitors move along the edges of the building, they will be shaded by the sloped shell overhang. The central courtyard serves as an open gathering space to organize visitor arrival and entry sequences. When entering, visitors are received in a space between the thematic exhibits. A vibrant and clear means of circulation is understandable and large enough to gather people through and direct them to the individual exhibit spaces.

When arriving, the design envisions each guest is given a number and color logo. This information is activated on the pavilion ceiling as a permanent point of light that identifies the guest as a living document of their visit. In the future, these points of light become a galaxy of stars, connecting everyone who has visited the pavilion. If the visitor returns to the pavilion at a later date, their star is identified by the previously assigned number and color.

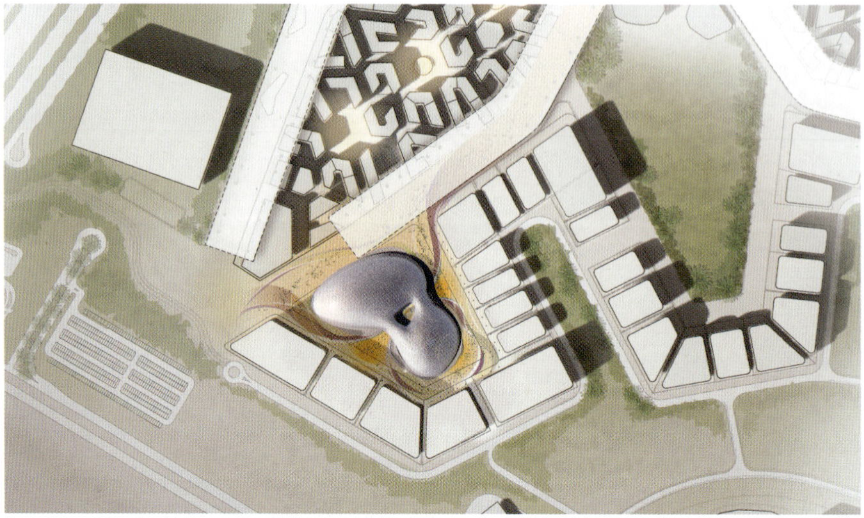

Site Plan

Visitor Flow Diagram

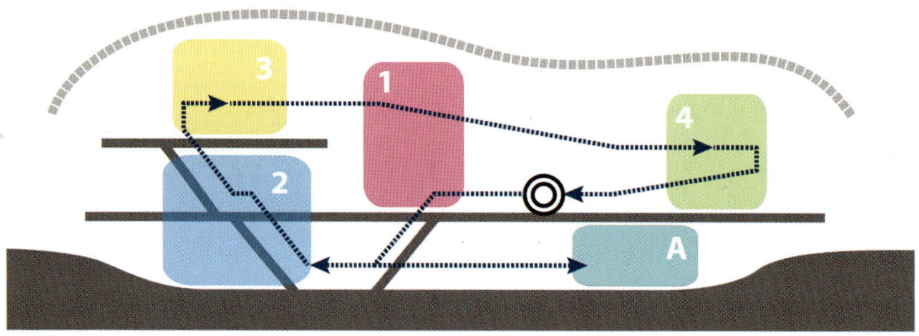

REGULAR VISIT - APPROXIMATELY 30 MINUTES

TIME	4 MIN	5 MIN	5 MIN	5 MIN	5 MIN	4 MIN
	ENTRY INTRODUCTION	**THEME 1** PERSONAL MOBILITY EMPOWERING PEOPLE THROUGH MOBILITY	**THEME 2** RESOURCE MOBILITY DISTRIBUTING GOODS AND RESOURCES	**THEME 3** INFORMATION MOBILITY CONNECTING DATA AND INFORMATION	**THEME 4** UNIVERSAL MOBILITY FUTURAMA 2020	**EXIT** FINALE
PEOPLE	200	250	250	250	250	200

DESIGN CONCEPT | PROGRAM

In their design, AS+GG fully realizes the program. The first themed exhibit is an interactive, mobile experience that reflects how mobility has evolved with humans. A 360-degree panoramic projection shows the evolution of mobility from nomadic movement with camels and horse drawn carriages to the first automobiles, zeppelins, the early days of aviation, science fiction images from the 1950s, contemporary congested highways, and future intergalactic space travels.

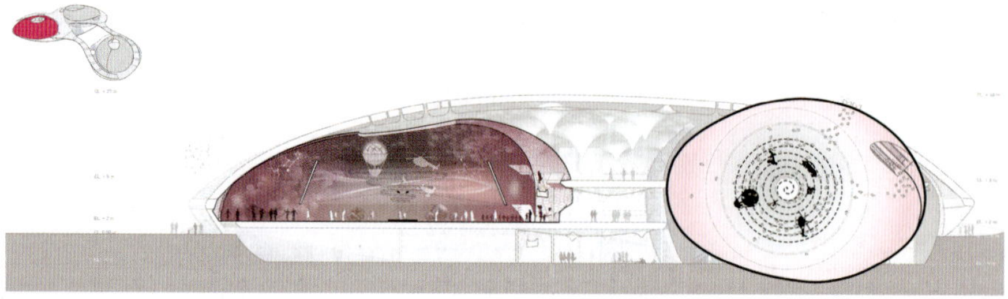

Empowering People Through Mobility

The images are mixed with animated infographics that demonstrate the mobility of vehicles through range, radius of action, and speed. A low platform in the center of the gallery features additional projections of prehistoric art, industrial inventions, and future visions that highlight the importance of human ingenuity. At the heart of this platform, special spotlights are integrated into the floor to help highlight physical objects in the installation.

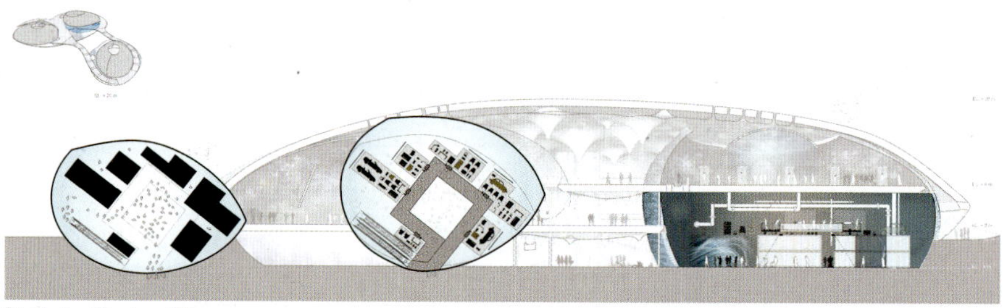

Distributing Goods and Resources

The second themed exhibit is divided over two levels. Visitors entering the space on Level 4 step into an industrial world of containers and pipelines, to learn about the planning and transportation of resources and goods. The center of the space is left clear to form a plaza where visitors view the story of global distribution showing giant container ships, freight trains, and air-cargo planes, emphasizing the constant flow of goods and resources. The images shift and push forward, as if they are the containers being lifted and stacked.

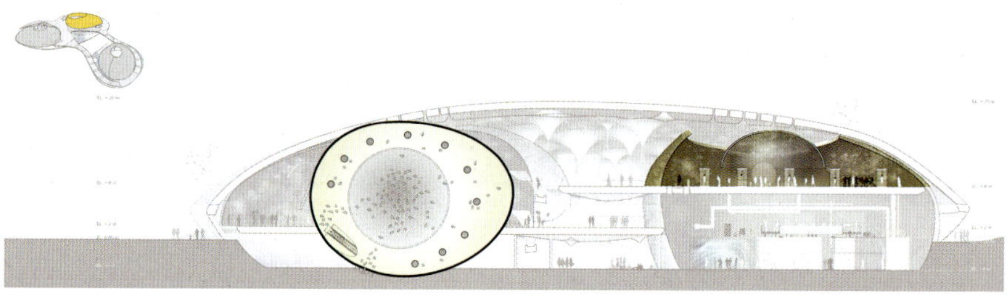

Connecting Through Data and Information

To reach the second level of the exhibit, visitors flow up a three-meter-wide elevated pathway and are invited to interact with six families from six different continents using touch screens and scanners connected to the guardrails. Visitors are prompted to scan products from the tablet display to learn about the product's origins: where the goods are produced and how far they travel to their destination. The exhibit features families that were chosen to demonstrate the contrasts in wealth between various parts of the world and their corresponding contrasts in mobility.

Futurama 2020

When entering the third themed exhibit, visitors are surrounded by an immersive digital space. The central element is a large projection dome with LED tiled floors. Projections on the inside of the dome and floor create a dynamic environment featuring topics including global connections through satellites, the growth of telephone traffic, the role of data centers, big data collection, and opportunities for driverless cars enabled by a global satellite network.

The fourth and final exhibit focuses on the relationship between mobility and cities recalling "Futurama," the General Motors Pavilion from the 1939 World Expo in New York, designed by Norman Bel Geddes. In this pavilion the visitor was transported to a future car-friendly city in 1960, presenting an ideal world of tomorrow. Visitors to the new Futurama exhibit enter after descending one of two ramps from an overlook that reveals the content below. The centerpiece is a large city model of Dubai surrounded by a digital projection screen.

The model is projected with images, while light and sound are arranged in a synchronized show presenting different future scenarios. Visitors exit the space underneath the model or continue to learn more detailed information concerning the presented future scenarios in Dubai. For this purpose, touch screens pads are found on the tribune.

DESIGN CONCEPT | FORM

The design concept was developed using the form of a cell, a simple form that is capable of multiplying and splitting, a compact form that is inherent to every human being and at the heart of the universe. From the universe to the subatomic level, all things are in a dynamic equilibrium, constantly in motion, and infinitely connected. At the center of these systems lies the human being; people who connect, communicate, and create systems and technology that affect us all. This combination of movement and connectedness is essential to the development and the mobility of a truly global society. Like a cell, the Global Mobility Center was designed as a living node within the larger network.

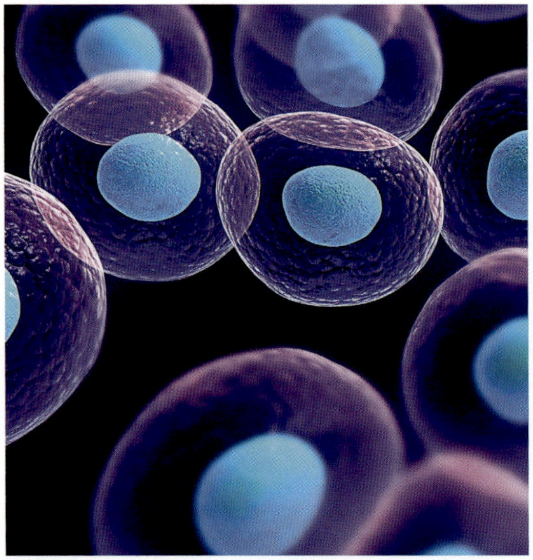

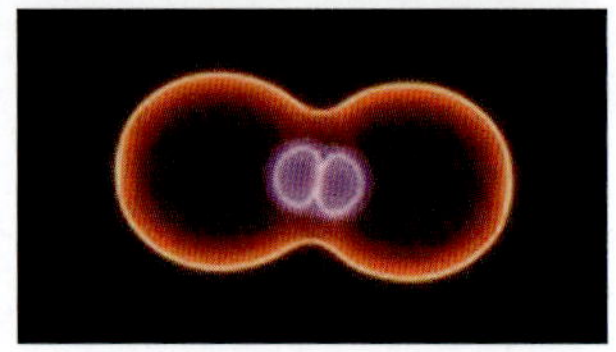

Mobility Pavilion Rendering | Design Inspiration (Above)

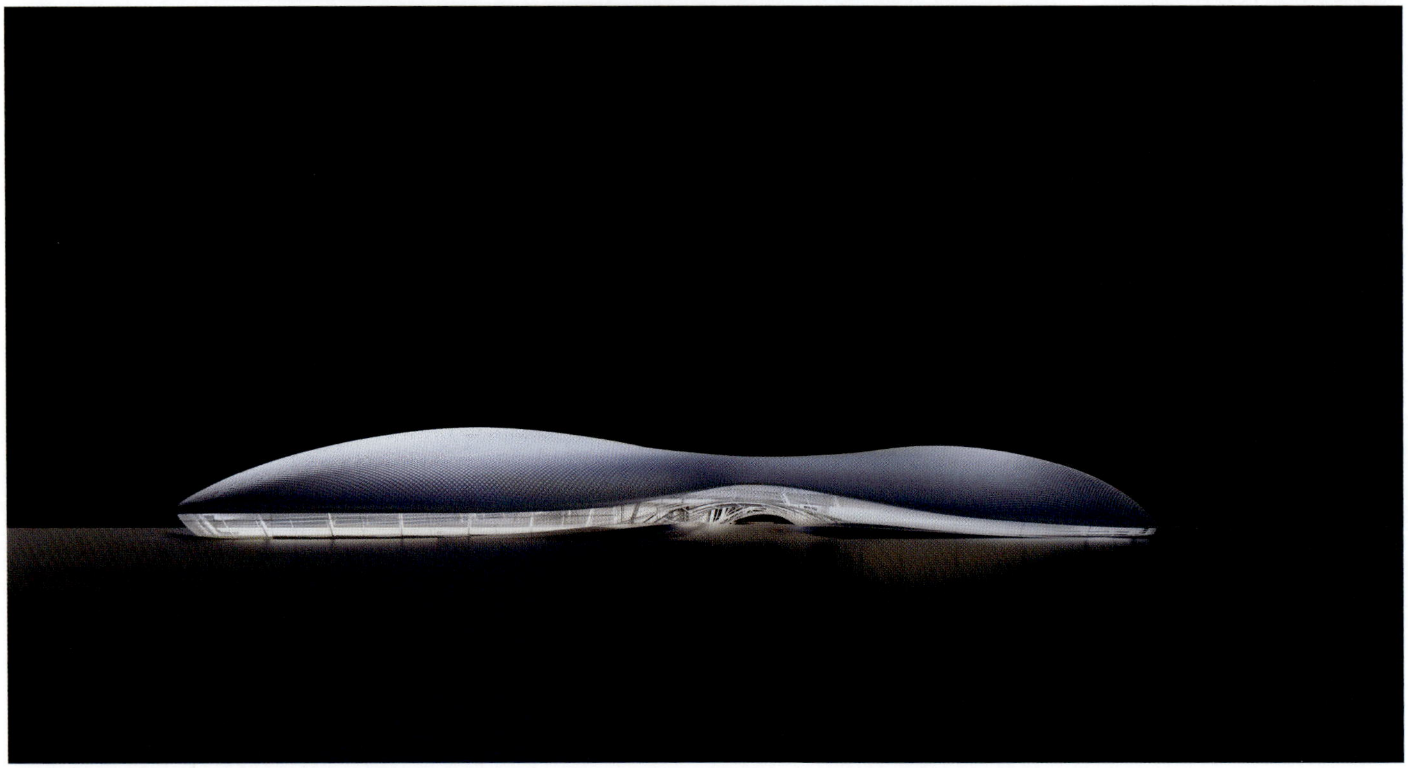

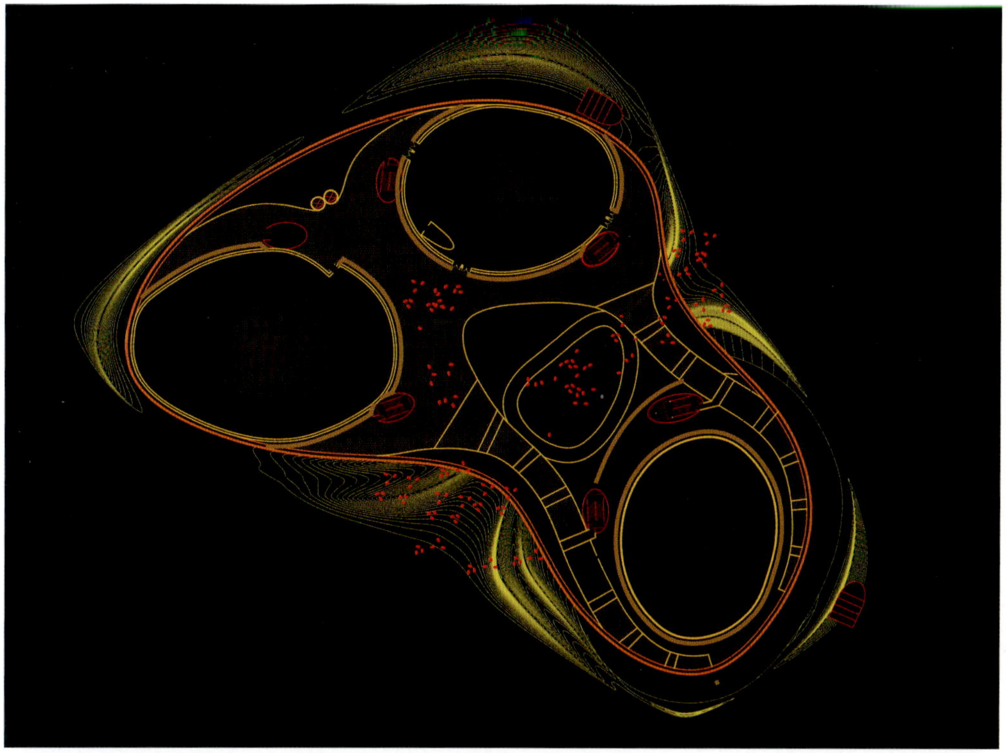

Plan Analogy | Physical Model (Below)

The pavilion features active energy-generation techniques as well as low-tech, passive solutions. The inward sloping exterior facade is self-shading, which significantly reduces direct solar radiation through the glazing. Diffused light and light reflected from the adjacent buildings and surfaces enters the space, helping maintain comfortable levels of natural daylight. Glare is managed using internal daylight-controlled roller shades. Shade glazing units meet the required performance from the master plan's sustainability guidelines, targeting a solar heat gain coefficient of 20-25% and a U-value of less than 1.2 W/m2K.

Diffused light penetrates through the outer shell through mirrored tubes and fiber-optic strands. This light is further circulated and controlled by actuated fabric cones resulting in dynamic and textural illumination. The light tubes can be artificially lit if necessary and can be completely closed off through using an internal diaphragm.

Electricity produced from the PVs provides a minimum of 25% of the overall energy needs with 350mm PV discs clipped directly into prefabricated unitized roof panels. Air cools the PV by circulating behind and through the prefabricated panels through a void behind the disc within the panel. This void allows condensation drainage of that forms during the night at certain times of the year.

Intermittently spaced operable vents release heat and smoke exhaust using two kinds of operable vents: ventilation of the plenum behind the PV cells and ventilation of the occupied spaces below the roof assembly. Each PV cell is individually monitored for performance and temperature. As the air temperature within the PV cavity increases, the vents around the PV open, expelling the hot air. To maintain a constant air flow through the warm air buoyancy effect, each vent remains open only for the period necessary for heat exhausting. All vents open at night to ensure cooling of the roof cells.

Sustainability Section

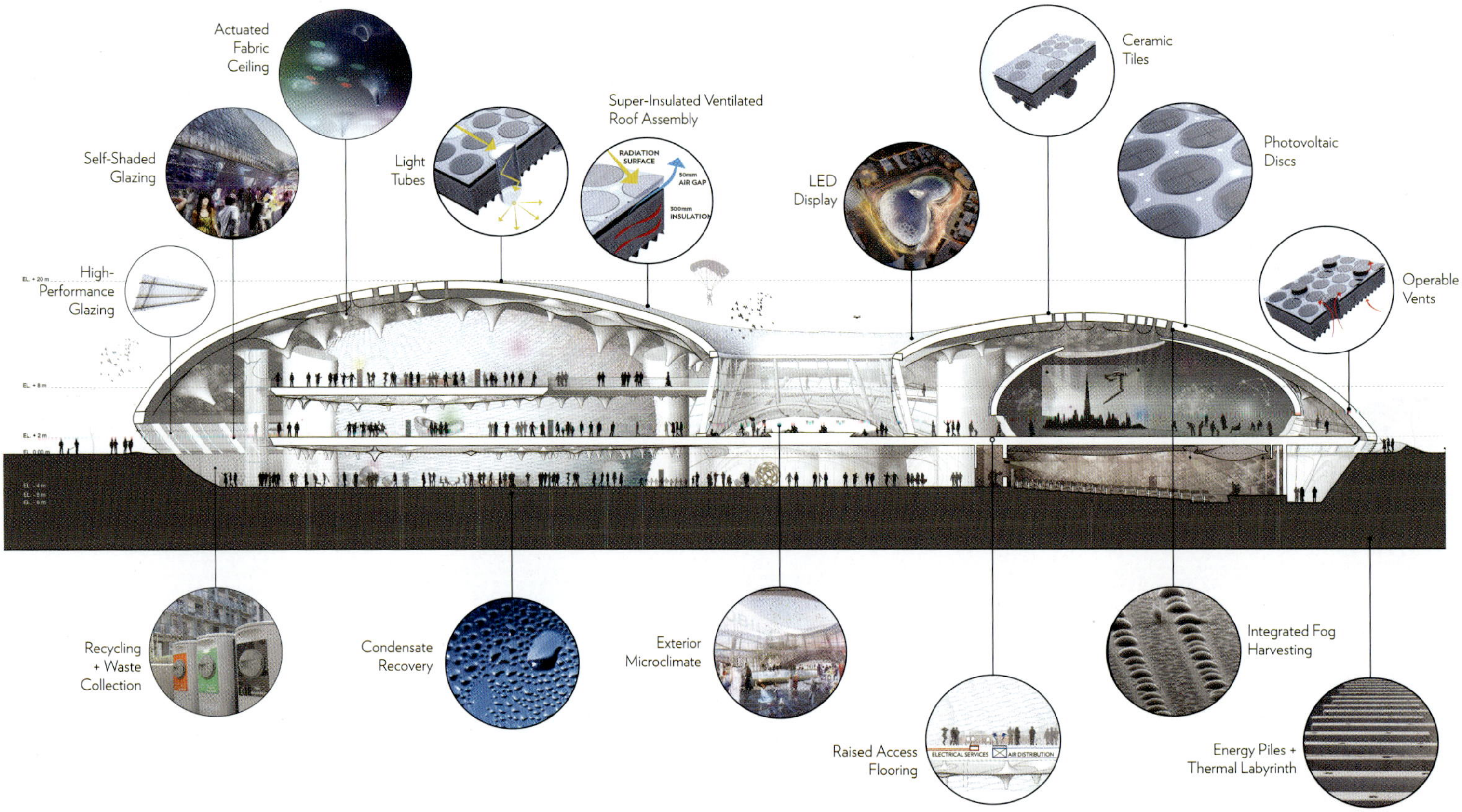

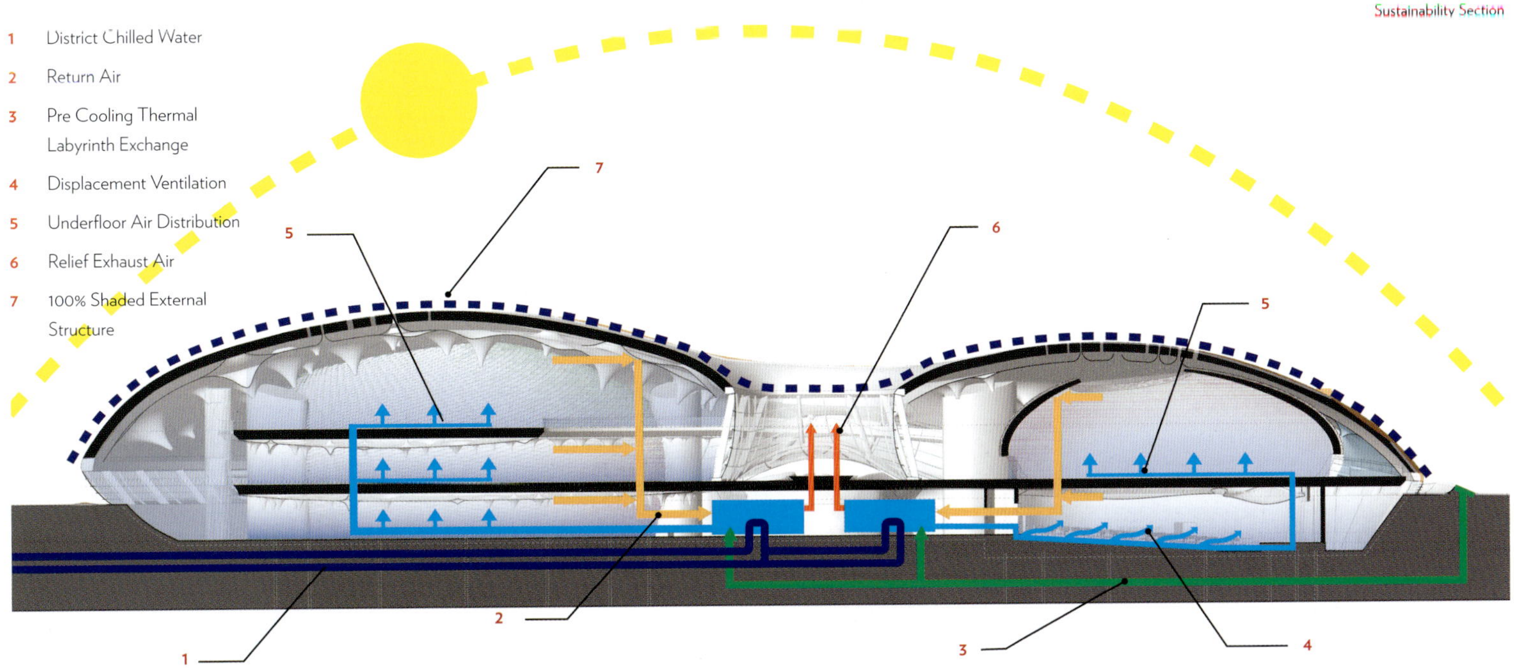

The master plan recommends a minimum of three stream waste segregation including dry mixed recyclables, food waste, and non-recyclable waste. In a public building, it is likely that food waste is co-mingled with residual waste so further discussions with the site-wide waste management planning team are necessary. The master plan also recommends vacuum waste for food collection and conventional waste collection for the remaining waste, both recyclable and non-recyclable. For vacuum waste collection, a single port located adjacent to the waste storage room within the building can be used by the cleaning staff for centralized waste disposal.

Condensate is collected from all sources including air handling units, local fan coil units, and refrigerators. Cold water also has energy stored as coolth, which can be used to pre-cool outdoor air that passes through the thermal labyrinth into the air handlers. Collected condensate is combined with greywater in a short-term storage tank and then treated to the appropriate DEWA standard, stored, and distributed as recycled water for toilet flushing and irrigation. PV cells are used as surfaces to condense and collect moisture. Desert insects in the UAE harvest dew in this way, and the same principles can be applied to the outer skin of the building. As the system uses no additional components beyond those already planned in the roof, there is no cost premium, and it is just a matter of developing and refining the system so that it serves this multi-purpose role.

A raised access flooring system is recommended for its two distinct advantages. First, Under Floor Air Distribution (UFAD) provides the most flexible and energy efficient means of providing displacement ventilation. The system is easily controlled and moved by occupants to accommodate different display configurations. Eliminating the need for ductwork in a plenum space is the most cost-effective solution.

The module-ready raised floors can be removed and replaced by prefabricated office, bathroom, or kitchen/pantry pods. Plumbing fittings within the floor space can be connected seamlessly and the space can be transitioned from exhibit to office and back with minimal waste and at minimal cost.

Ground source heat pumps reduce cooling demands through using the constant temperature of the ground to pre-cool air. The master plan recommends that the only cost-effective way to incorporate this technology is through using geothermal energy piles. The design explores using a thermal labyrinth with grade changes (to minimize construction costs) that are used to pre-cool intake air for the air handling units. The thermal labyrinth can be ground connected through energy piles, which use a closed loop system to reject heat from the labyrinth into the ground water.

Dubai has a tropical desert climate with hot, humid summers and warm, short winters. The cooling season is more predominant than the heating season, therefore cooling is needed year-round. Most days are sunny throughout the year, with a high intensity and distribution of solar radiation. Rainfall is infrequent and only lasts for short periods, mostly from December through March. The wind direction is from the west and northwest throughout the year.

Through environmental analysis, it was determined the building should be self-shaded to protect against solar radiation and the surface area to volume ratio should be minimized to reduce solar heat gain. Minimizing the exposed thermal mass also reduces solar heat gain, while super insulating the building prevents cool air from escaping and heat from penetrating the skin. Reflective materials with high albedo finishes are also recommended. Potential for condensate recovery and rainwater harvesting were studied and considered essential to keep operation costs down.

A solar radiation analysis was conducted to estimate the incident direct radiation on the surface of the roof and to calculate the potential electric power generated by photovoltaics. The solar radiation study also helped determine the ideal placement of the photovoltaic discs to optimize the roof design and maximize energy generation. The highly efficient building design and systems reduced the operational energy; the estimated onsite energy generation with photovoltaic discs on the roof exceeded the 25% target.

Life Cycle Analysis (LCA) is a method used for estimating the impact of a product on the environment over a defined period. LCA was undertaken to evaluate the options available for reducing the carbon dioxide emissions of the building materials. The materials manufacturing stage, which typically accounts for a high percentage of CO_2 emissions during the building life cycle, was studied for a steel diagrid structure roof in comparison to a structural concrete roof.

This stage accounts for the cradle-to-gate manufacturing of the construction materials of the building, including extraction of raw materials, transportation to the manufacturing location, processing, and assembly. A steel diagrid shell was selected over a concrete roof to reduce structural materials and save 310 tons of CO_2 eq, 16% less of the carbon emissions of concrete.

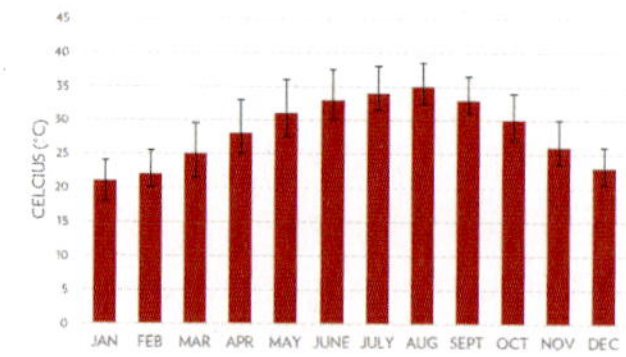

Average Temperature

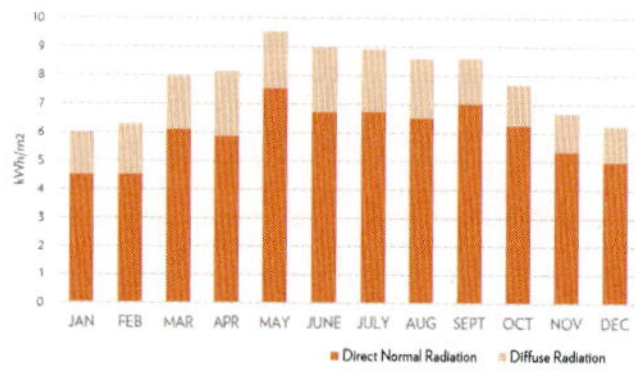

Average Daily Radiation

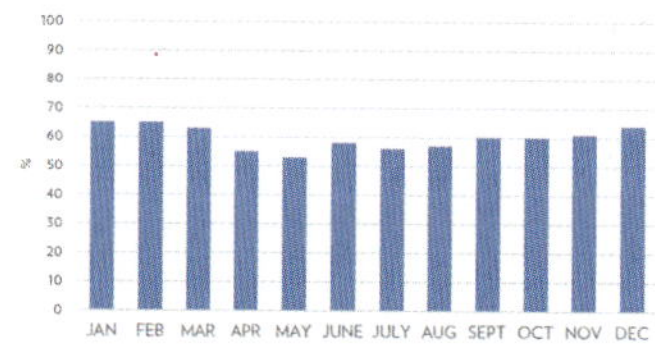

Relative Humidity

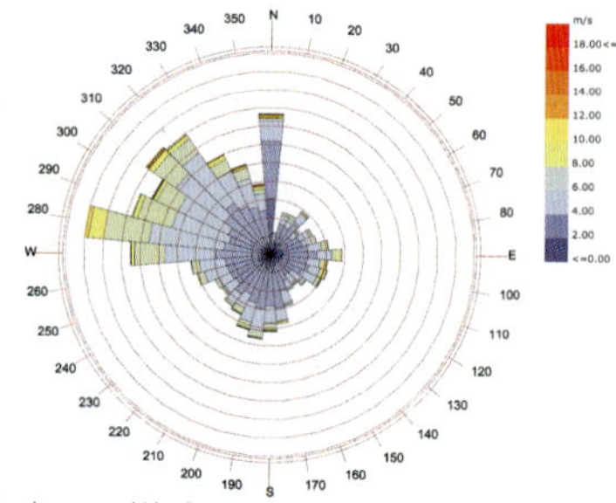

Predominant Winds
All Year

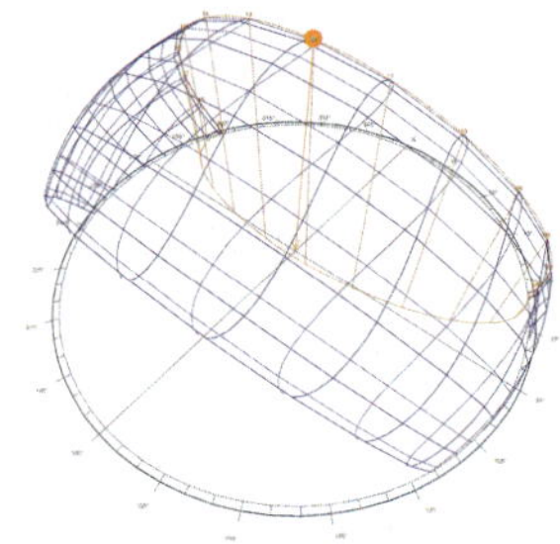
Sun Position - Summer Solstice at Noon
Azimuth: 130.3° / Altitude 85.0°

Exterior Wall Sustainable Strategies

Environmental Stategy

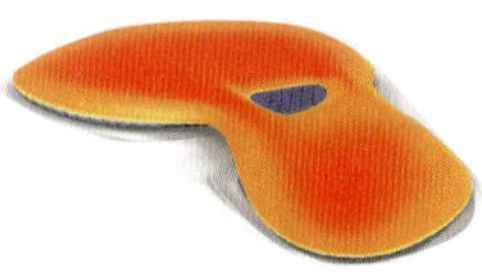

Energy Performance

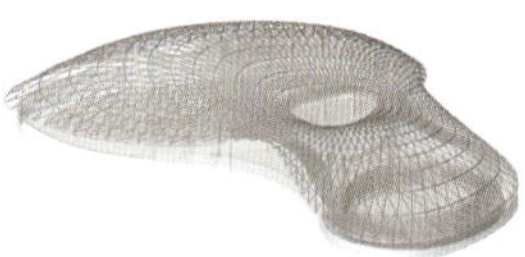

Low Embodied Carbon Materials

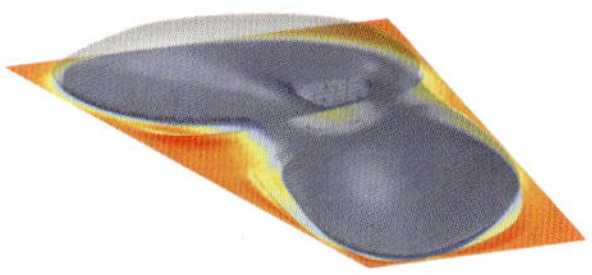

Themal Comfort

The structural system utilizes an efficient steel diagrid shell roof that encloses a conventional reinforced frame. The shell is used to efficiently support the long pavilion roof with no additional internal columns and a minimized structural depth allowance. The shell can achieve this by introducing additional curvature to portions of the roof to minimize bending in elements and maximize the membrane action of pure tension and compression. As a result, the geometry is a derived form, taken from the constraints of the roof loads, roof spans, support locations, and shell height limits. The structural system includes a diagrid steel shell, a perimeter steel tension tie, and steel tube columns to support the tie and diagrid.

The use of shell structures to provide dramatic long-span interior or sheltered spaces is well tested. Historically, shell shapes were either derived from simple mathematical forms or through experimental testing. This history resulted in shells that were either basic in form that required basic boundary conditions, or forms that were susceptible to inaccuracies in measurements. Modern analytical "form-finding" routines have made it possible to more accurately develop and test more complicated forms.

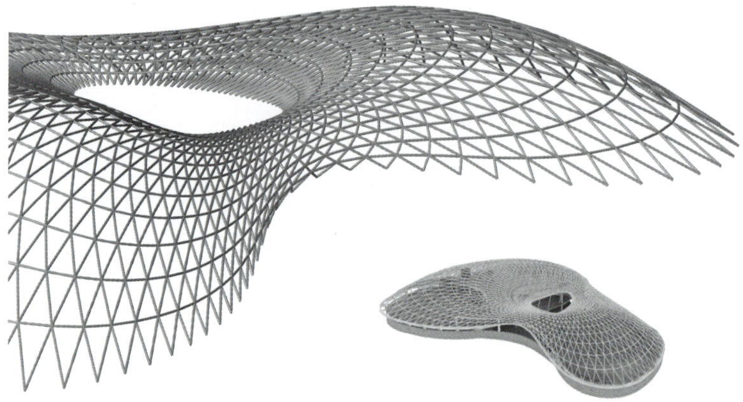

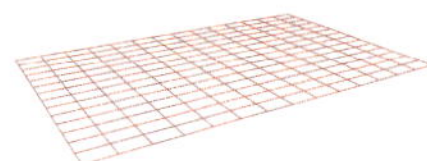

Base Model

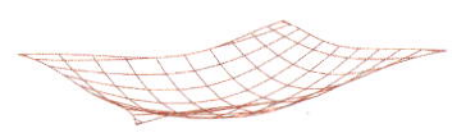

Tension Membrane

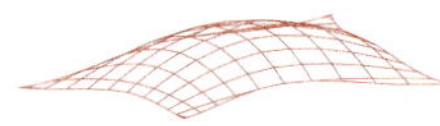

Shell Inverted Membrane

Structural Diagrams

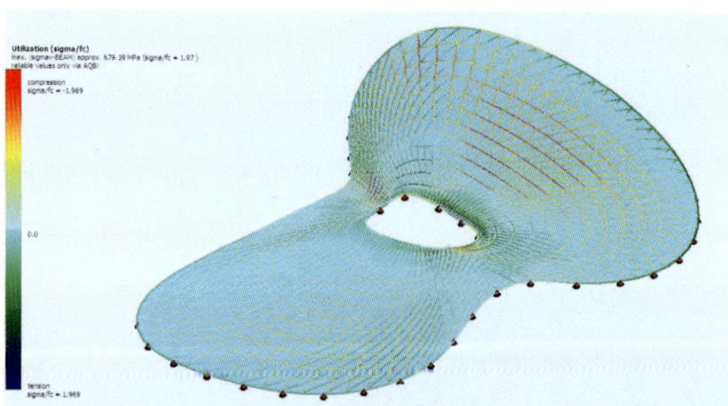

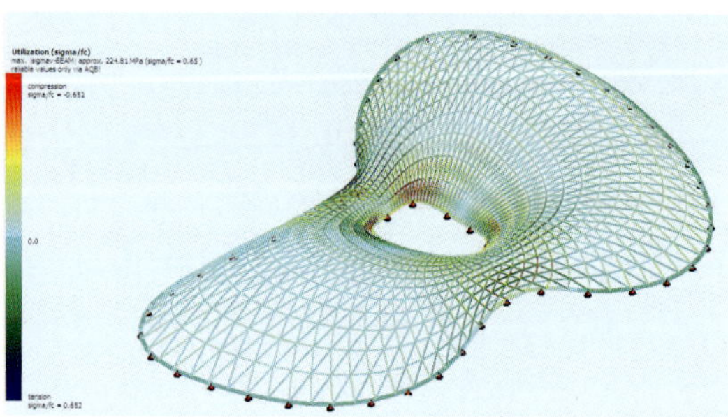

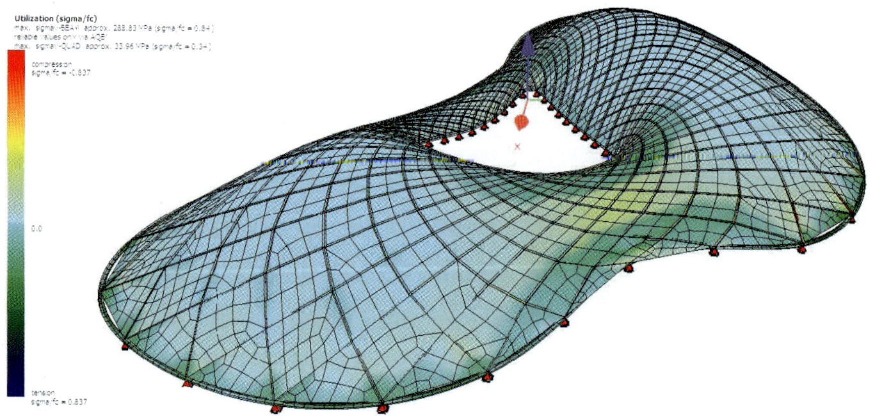

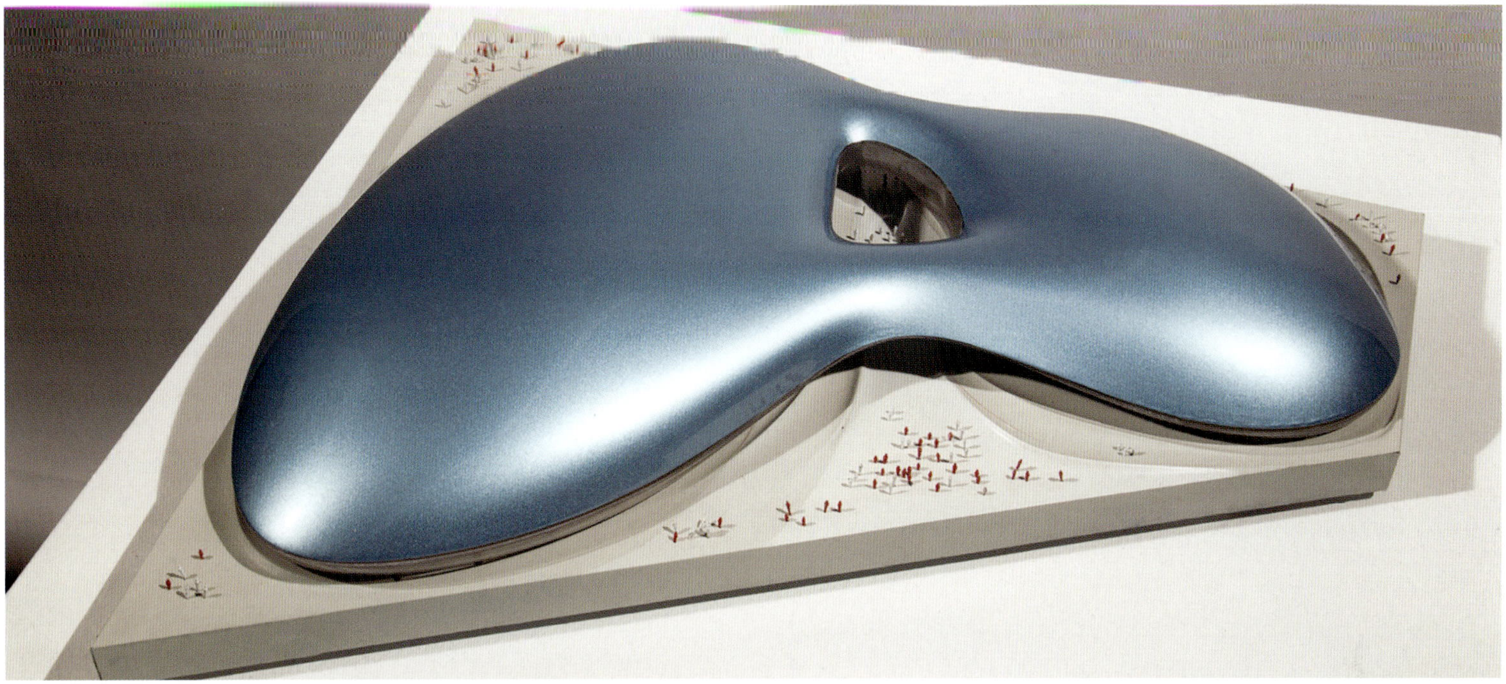

Physical Model

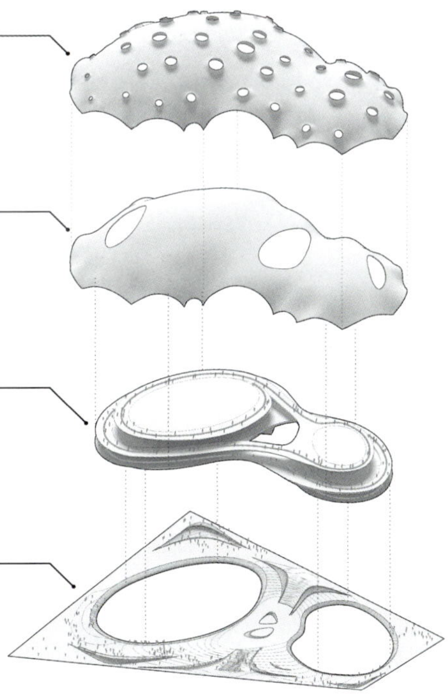

Using form-finding routines and nature's constraints to develop the roof geometry creates a true form, not forced. There is nothing arbitrary about the shell's shape. The payoff for being disciplined in the development of the shape is that the structural system's cost and structural depth are minimized, and dramatic long-span interior space is maximized.

Externally, the structural grid shell shades and protects the vision glass and program spaces within and performs additional functions such as renewable energy generation, daylight mediation, natural ventilation, physical movement, and digital information display. These are easily accommodated within the roof tile system to allow the integration of sun tubes that allow diffused daylight into the center of the internal spaces or by using photovoltaic cells instead of tile to achieve the 25% renewable energy requirement.

An LED system is integrated into the roof and offers the expo a fifth elevation: the building's roof. Easily visible from the grounds and aircraft, the pavilion is designed to broadcast information and imagery on its roof using the theme of mobility.

The exterior walls have an integrated water misting spray to cool the area for potential outdoor programming and overflow queuing, while the sculpted soffit surfaces increase the natural wind flow. LED light fixtures, speakers, flag poles with large banners and flags add a festive and inviting atmosphere during the day and night activities.

CHAPTER 3

PARTICIPATE

Experiential Spaces

As Architects, we believe that as technologies advance and become more readily available, performance and assembly spaces will become increasingly important to the communities that surround them. While the last 20-30 years saw the exponential increase in the processing power of computers and advancements in digital graphics and projection, the next century is predicted to be strongly affected by advances in artificial intelligence and machine learning.

A new generation of assembly spaces can expand the perspective with the types of experiences they provide. We envision spaces that use three-dimensional and interactive digital displays that are responsive to the user.

In the field of supertall buildings and large-scale exhibitions, owners are looking for innovative ideas to distinguish their buildings. Supertall towers are typically built with the goal of creating a destination and an icon for a city. But height is not the only way to achieve this. Dramatic lighting, video displays, and unique assembly or observation spaces can also create unique experiences. When placed within the tallest floors of a tower, they have the opportunity to become the experiential spaces of the future.

Similarly, large outdoor venues in cities are striving to develop special cultural spaces where digital media is used to exemplify the next generation of public, world-class assembly attractions.

1 Dubai Space Show - Kingston Leadership Plaza - The Portal at Runmao Tower - Shimao Tower Observatory - Al Wasl Plaza - Astana Discovery Center

1 DUBAI SPACE SHOW

Dubai, United Arab Emirates

1 Dubai is a trio of supertall towers with heights of at least 600 meters. The towers are joined near the base to form a "city within a city" at the center of AS+GG's 2008 conceptual master plan, Jumeirah Gardens. On its tripodal base, 1 Dubai rises over a canal to form a lofty oasis. Grand arched entrances allow boats to travel underneath the building and into the central atrium space.

On special occasions, the oasis transforms into one of the world's most unique event and performance spaces with a floating stage surrounded by barges that double as seating banks. State-of-the-art sound and light shows featuring giant holograms are projected in the air and onto the building's mosaic-like glass and aluminum skin.

Although the project went through Construction Documentation, 1 Dubai was placed on hold in 2010 because of the world-wide economic downturn. The tower remains unbuilt.

Dubai is one of the most important business centers in the Middle East and for the past 20 years boundary pushing architecture has been developed at a rapid pace. Meraas, the developers of 1 Dubai, sought to build a landmark structure for tourism-focused Dubai that would complement and frame the nearby Burj Khalifa. Through an international design competition in 2008, AS+GG won the contract to build the innovative three tower scheme as one of the tallest and largest mega-structures in the world.

Function: Assembly + Observation | **Status:** Conceptual, 2008 | **Client:** Meraas Development

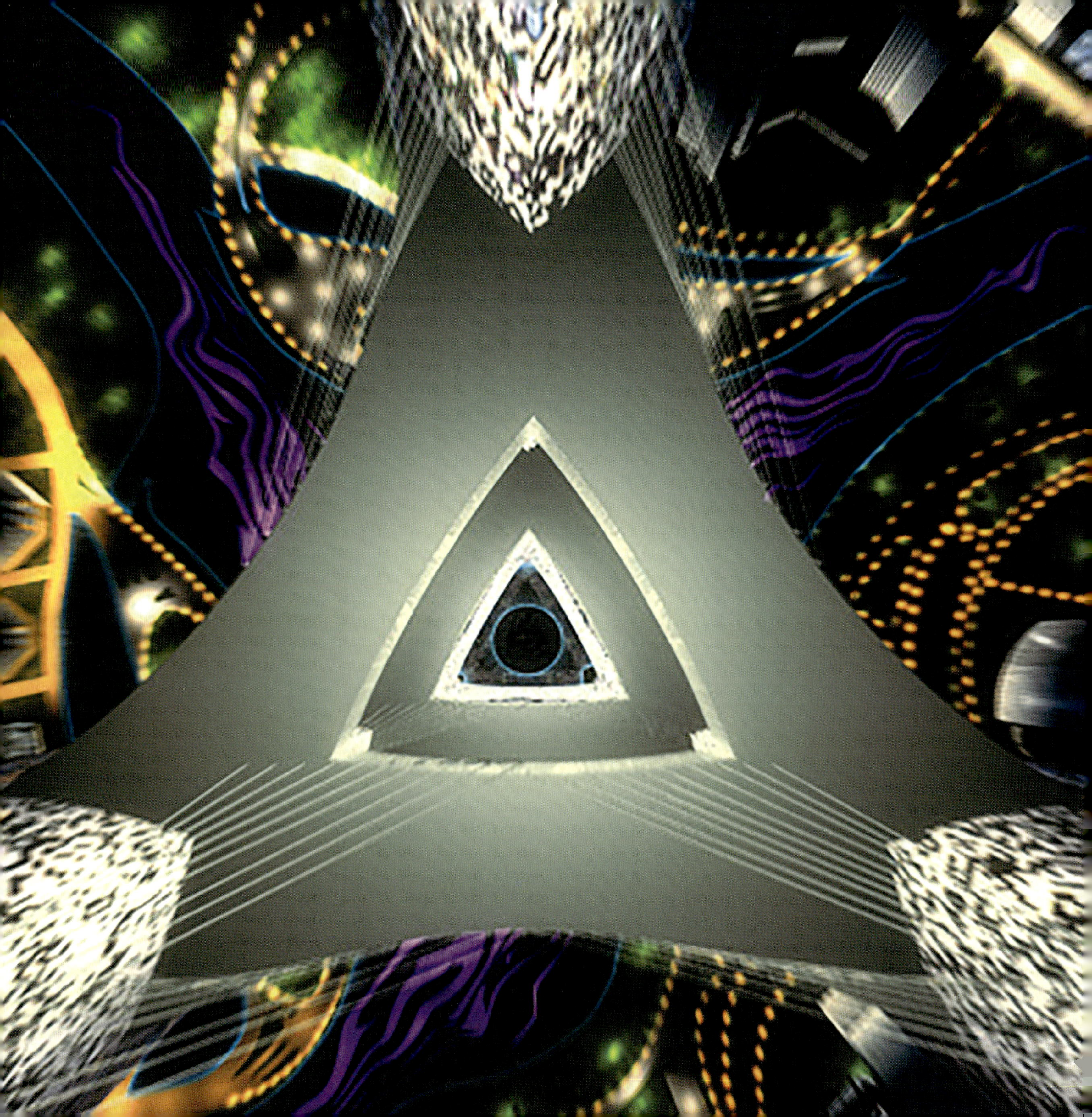

DESIGN CONCEPT | SITE

1 Dubai's site is directly across from a main Dubai throughway, Sheik Zayed Road, at the heart of the Jumeriah Gardens master plan, framing the adjacent Burj Khalifa. The design includes the creation of a central canal that complements the walkable district. The canal is an active, continuous system that runs through multiple parks, plazas, and pathways.

Most of the development is within a five-minute walk from multiple local transportation options supported by cultural and retail functions. The promenade incorporates water taxi stops and connections to the floating theater and islands beneath the tower. The atrium beneath the tower and along the canal is used for various entertainment functions.

The Space Show is a light and sound of the attraction that is visible from nearby developments, acting as an attractor for this center of activity and community.

Jumeirah Gardens Master Plan | Site Plan + Atrium Space (Right)

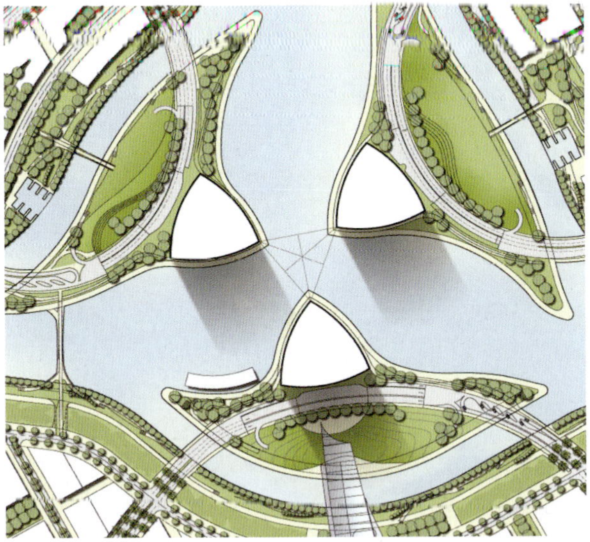

0
100
200
300
400

PERSHING

DESIGN CONCEPT | PROGRAM

1 Dubai is composed of three towers connected by a set of four programmed bridges. The mixed-use tower includes two world-class five- and six-star hotels, office floors, residential floors, and retail spaces. The tallest of the three towers features one of the world's highest clubs and observation halls.

Other facilities and amenities include two trading floors with 8.4-meter floor-to-ceiling heights, ballrooms, conference facilities, a spa, gym facilities with full-size basketball courts, volleyball courts, and an Olympic-sized swimming pool.

The program places a high importance on social gathering spaces for visitors, occupants, and community residents. Sky bridges offer stunning views of Dubai and the Persian Gulf, while the base of tower features landscaped, outdoor assembly spaces. The main public space is the floating arena beneath the tower's arching limbs.

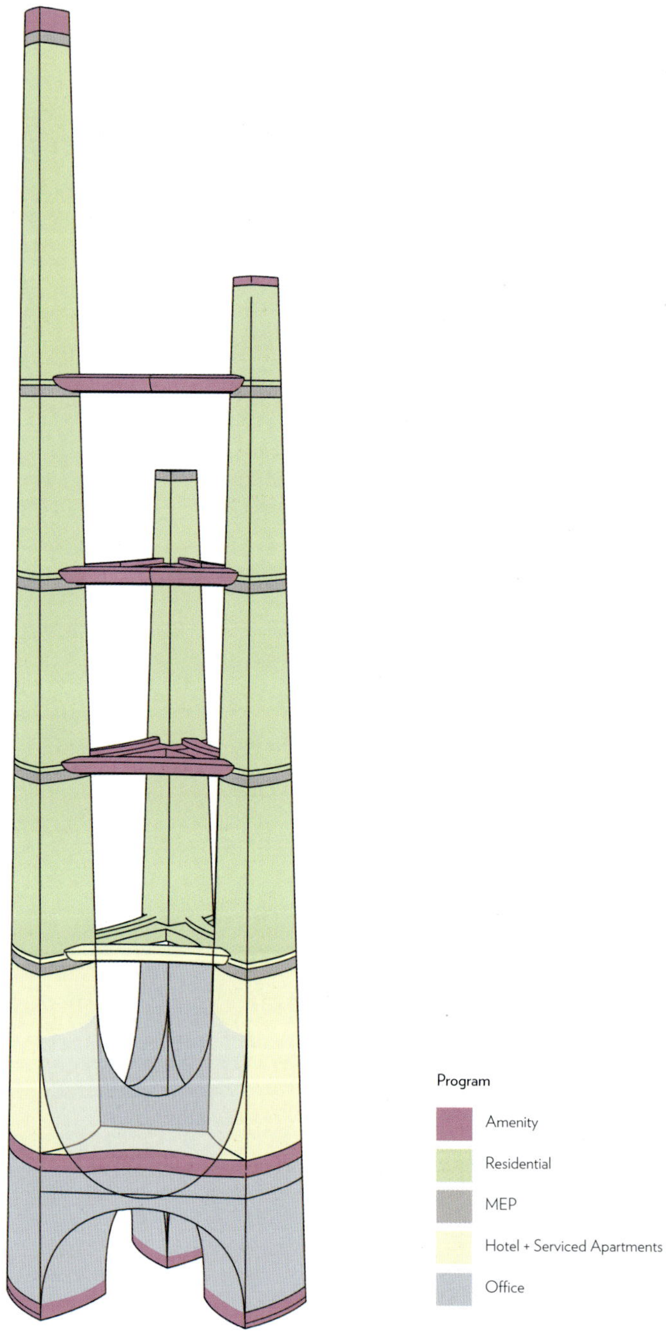

DESIGN CONCEPT | FORM

The building references specific designs found in Arabic culture. Geometric shapes that are found in Islamic mosaics, tapestries, rugs, and screens are used as formal inspiration for the design and are reflected in the patterning of the building's aluminum-and-glass diagrid skin, as well as the building's geometry.

The form is also highly functional. Soaring clusters of cables and occupiable sky bridges connect the three towers, adding structural support and providing an outdoor casing for the floating theater in the grotto-like area beneath the saddle. The digital projection and light shows use the tower's base geometry and bridges as features of the show.

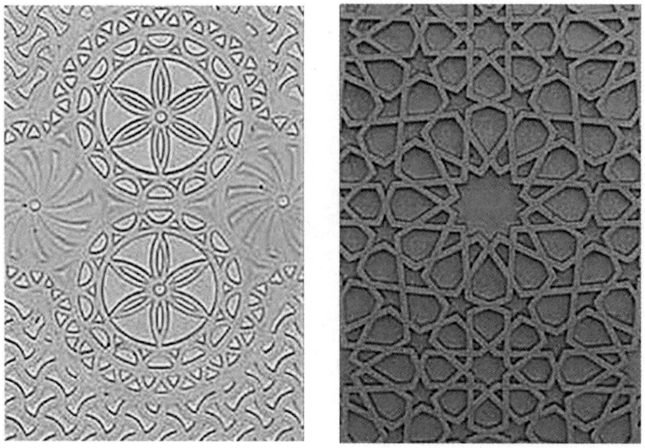

Islamic Patterns

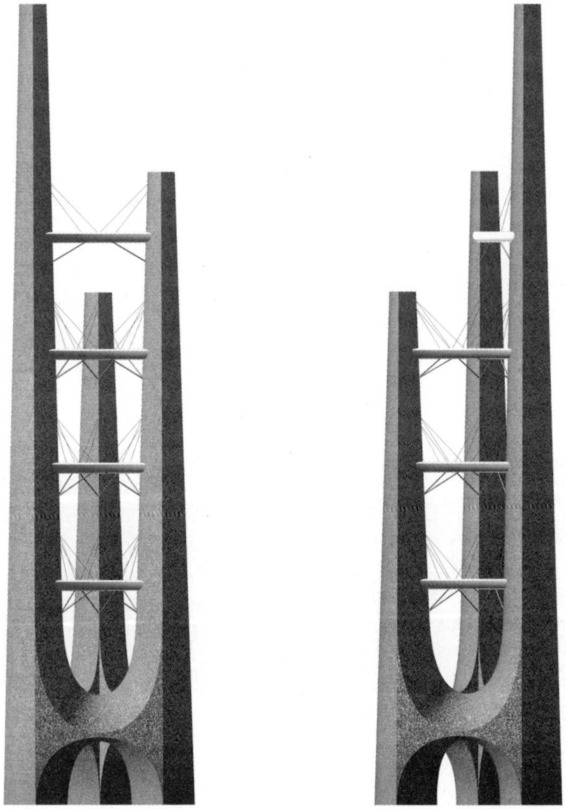

Elevations

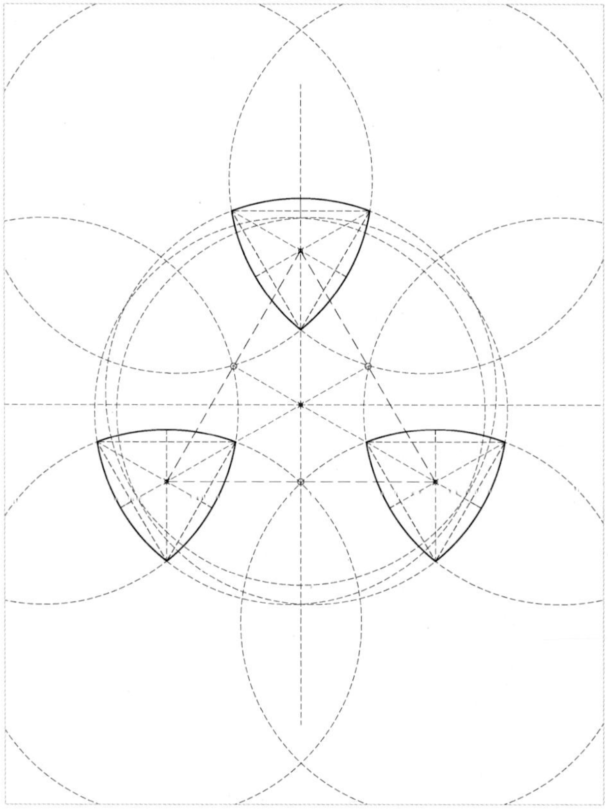

Building Geometry

The Space Show can be viewed from boats in the canal, from one of the floating seat platforms, or from above in one of the buildings' sky bridges. The design concept blurs the lines between architecture, digital media, and performance. Passengers in aircraft above have an equally remarkable view down through the center of the building.

A "virtual atrium" is formed by the V-shaped openings in the saddle structures and sky bridges, creating a virtual space and physical canvas. The use of the building as a background for projection on this large of a scale pushes the envelope of what is possible. It also opens possibilities for the client to use the building as a landmark, as well as a display surface, a public amenity space, and a city-wide attraction.

AS+GG worked with digital design experts at Scéno Plus to create the vision for the sound and lighting. The Montreal-based firm is known internationally for its arts and entertainment venue designs. The team explored storytelling techniques that helped to define the show's content and researched different ways that the media and projection can be applied.

3D digital projections create a futuristic show that will delight and astound audiences with music, lights, and holographic projections that hover above the seating and stage, with supplemental imagery projected onto the surfaces of the building skin.

Scéno Plus Conceptual Renderings (Above + Right)

Atrium Light Show

The facade above the platforms was designed using a triangulated pattern that accommodates the overall taper and curving shape of the tower geometry, particularly as it comes together at the base. Initial studies explored the use of triangular pieces made from unconventional materials, or differing amounts of solid panel versus glazing/void to create textured patterns.

The patterns are enhanced by the architectural lighting effects and further enhanced during the light show. Light rigging is integrated into the panels to create additional layers of pattern and reflection. The overall geometry of the skybridges also has the potential to create special lighting effects, particularly when utilizing the slots between the bridges in interesting ways.

The atrium's glazing system at the base of the three towers is envisioned as an electrochromic smart skin able to selectively block UV radiation and heat up to approximately 80% during the daytime while providing unobstructed dramatic views of the towers and sky at night.

Significant advancements in nanotechnology and organic chemistry have led to the development of efficient, low cost, mass produced photovoltaic films, which are ideal for architectural integration. It is estimated that the southern facing facades can generate at least 6MW of peak capacity, enough to power 120,000 square-meters of conventional office space during daylight hours.

1000 watts of energy fall on a square meter of the earth's surface during the daytime. With a targeted efficiency three times greater than that of conventional silicon-based PV, half of this energy can be harnessed into electricity. At approximately 500 mm in length, the roof of the central spine and pedestrian souks that flank the tower can provide an excess of 35MW of power.

Atrium Panelization Rendering

Section

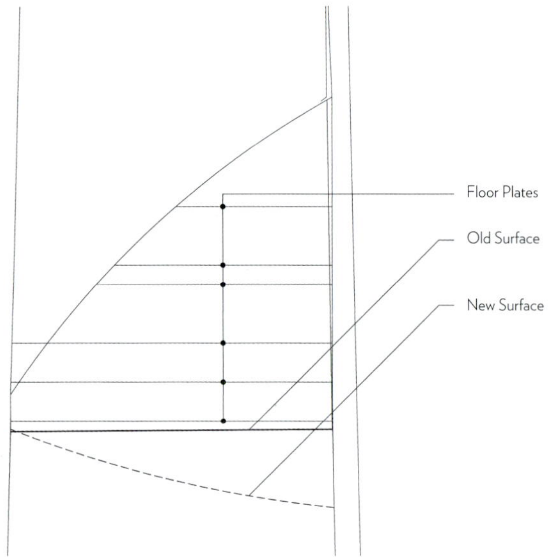

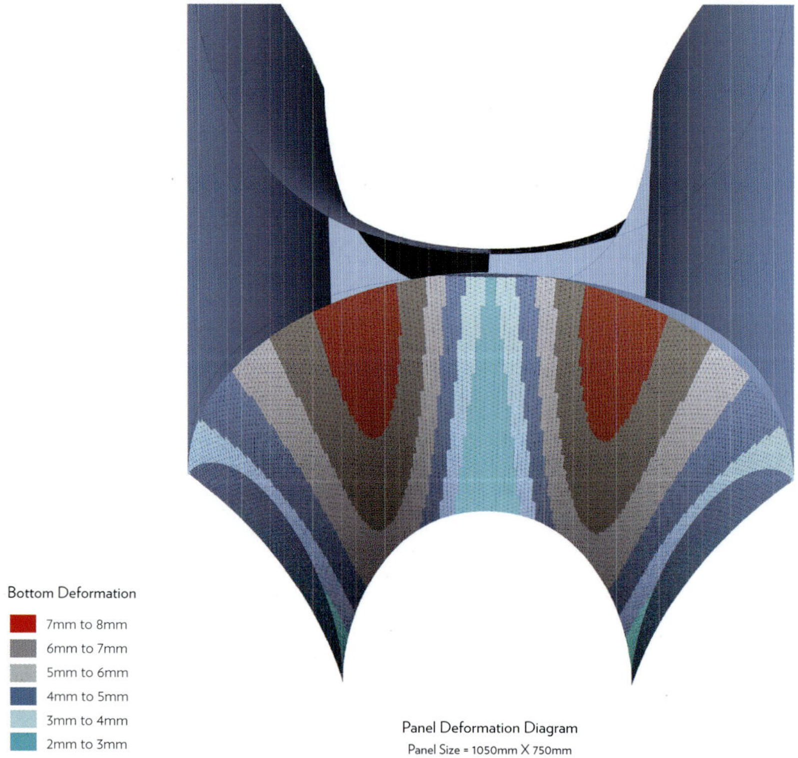

Panel Deformation Diagram
Panel Size = 1050mm X 750mm

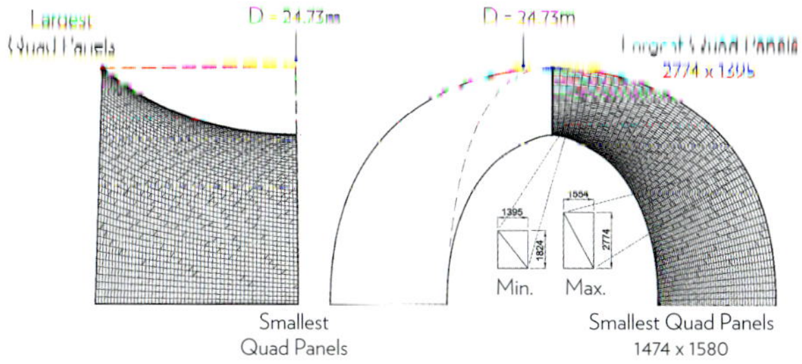

Panel Deformation Diagram
Panel Size = 1050mm X 750mm

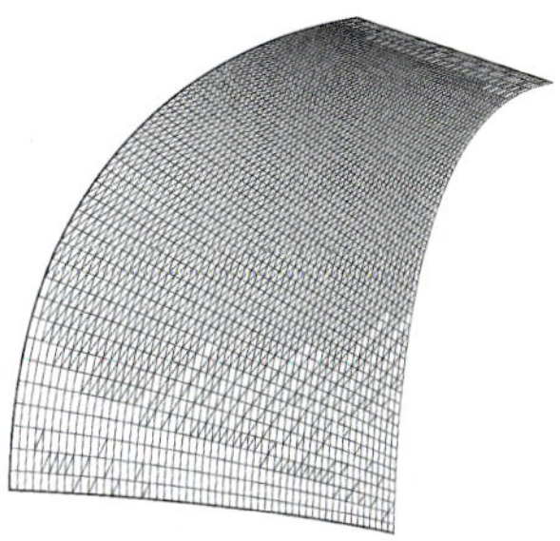

Original Unoptimized Bottom Saddle
2195 of 2610 panels triangulated

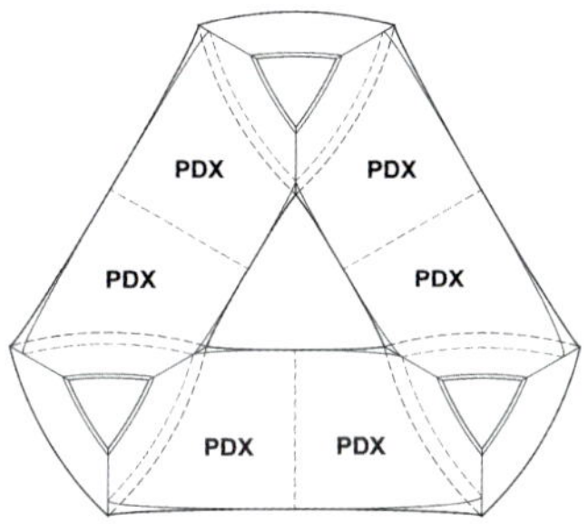

Reflected Plan
All Bottom Saddles Sim.

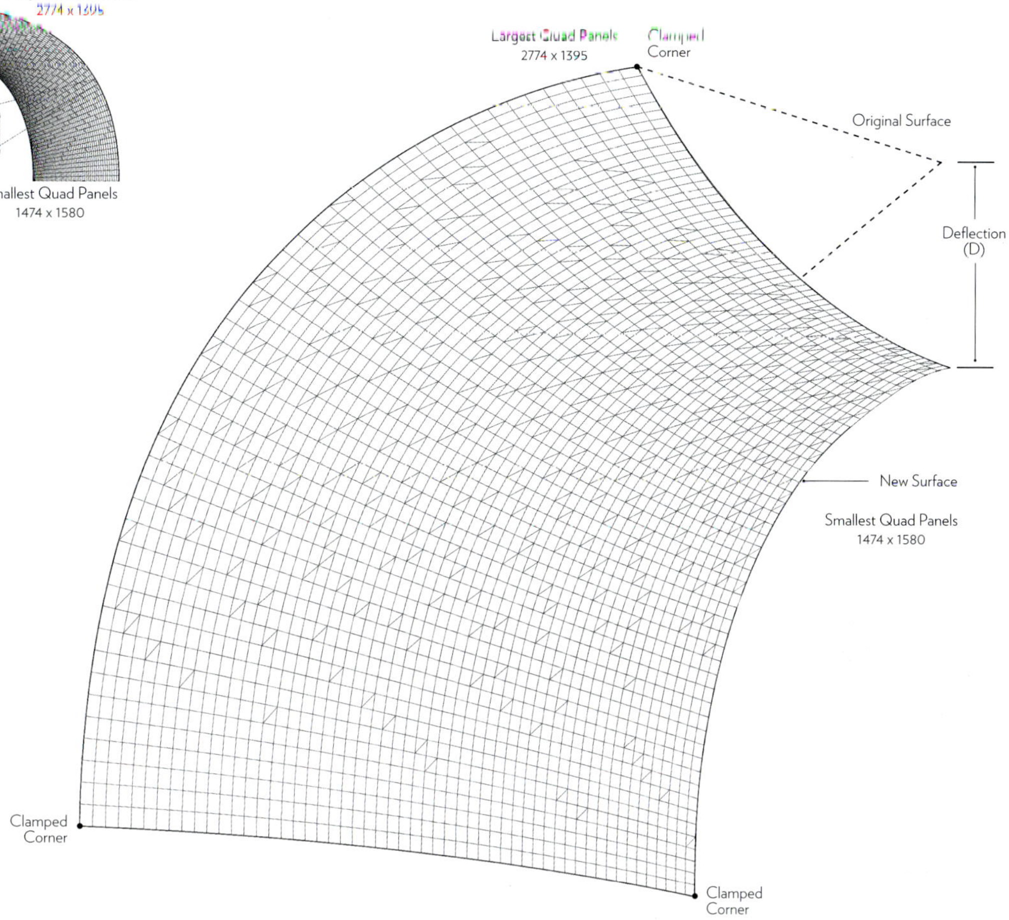

Proposed Optimized Rationalized Saddle
398 of 2610 panels triangulated

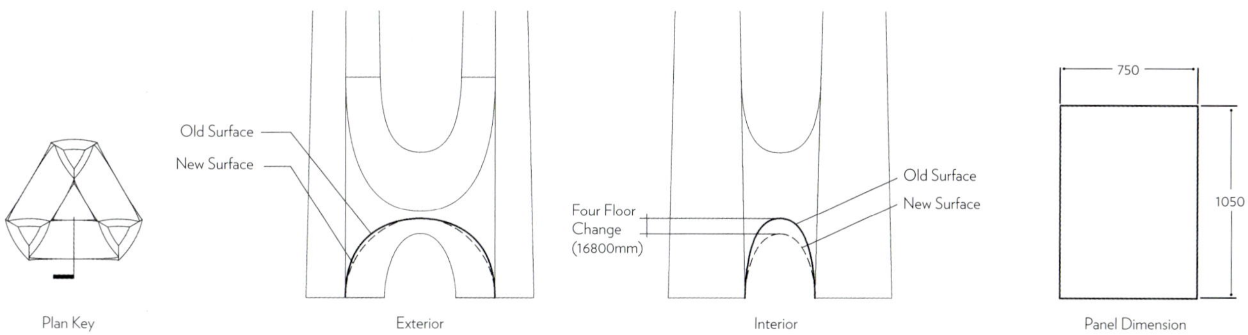

Surface Variation Diagram

KINGSTON LEADERSHIP PLAZA

Kingston, Jamaica

The new 200,000 square-foot mixed-use Kingston Leadership Plaza was designed as a beacon of outreach and service to the people of Kingston, serving as a symbol of confidence, hope, community integration, safety, and security. Envisioned as a warm, inviting space, the development houses approximately 2,000 police officers and administrative personnel in a plaza configuration with a centerpiece "beacon" and additional associated buildings.

The project was designed as a catalyst of community transformation for inhabitants of the adjacent neighborhoods to find safe and welcoming spaces for interaction, support, extracurricular activities, social integration, and growth. The innovative program seeks to be a model for urban redevelopment and can be used as a prototype for other localities in Jamaica. Education and social outreach are integral aspects of the process of design and serve to be inclusive of all stakeholders from the surrounding developments.

Located near Kingston's city center, the project is situated at the intersection of three neighborhoods southwest of where the center of government is located in National Heroes Circle. The area is the former site of Friendship Park, but now has social concerns including poverty, lack of infrastructure, and neighborhood tension. The new project aims to give back to the neighborhoods and form beneficial relationships within the community by creating an environment that provides a neutral, safe place with access to athletics, education, and music.

Function: Community Center + Park | **Status:** Conceptual, 2019 | **Client:** City of Kingston

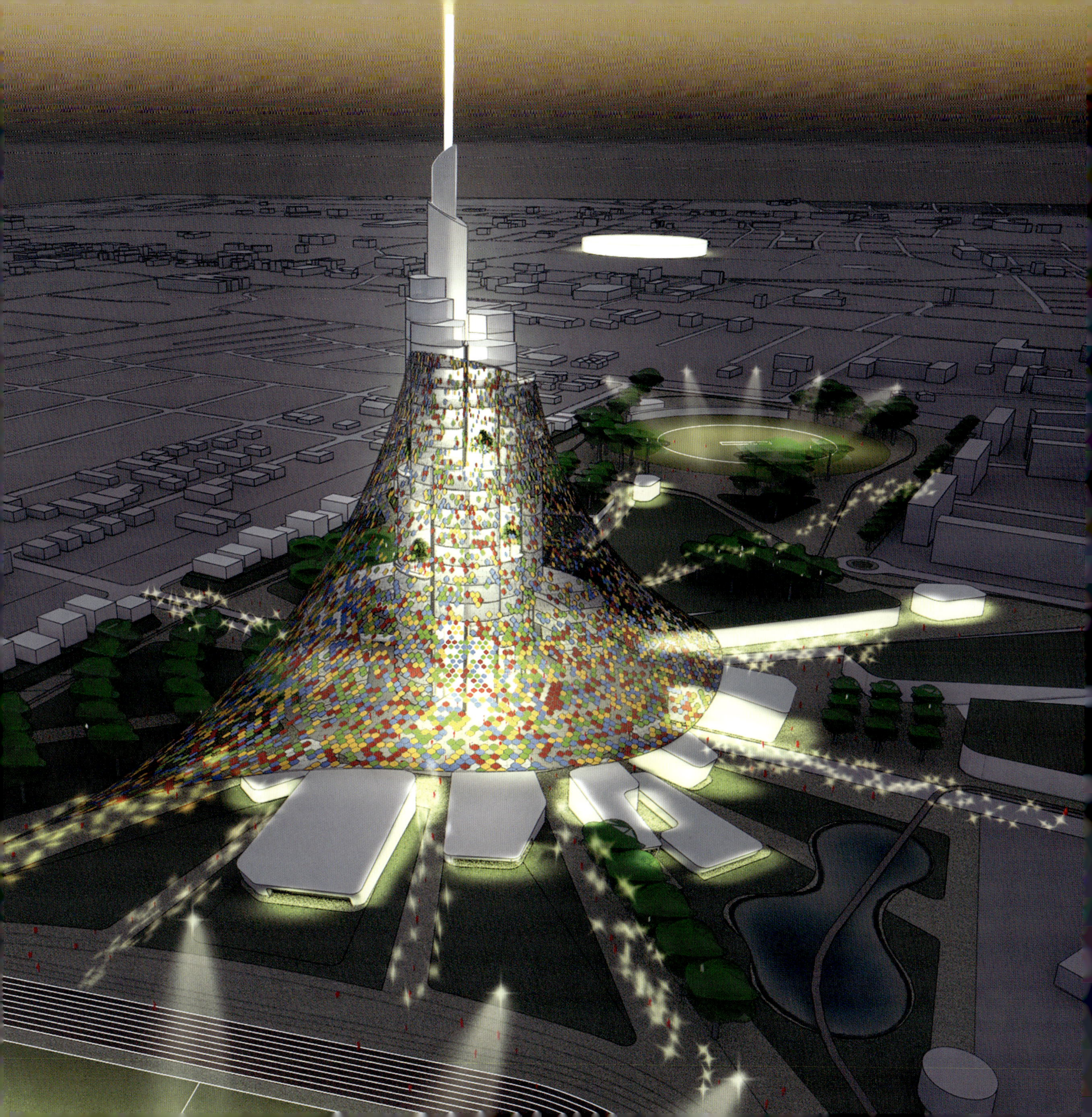

DESIGN CONCEPT | SITE

The site is comprised of three plots located between Little King Street to the west, Park Road to the east, Woodrow Street to the north, and Blount Street to the south. AS+GG first developed a master plan to ensure cohesiveness of the various components of the site and that its influence would extend beyond its physical boundaries.

The plan serves as a link to the urban fabric of the neighborhood, bringing the various components of the project together including the community, the buildings, and the landscape by setting a clear set of principles and sustainable strategies to ensure the success of the project.

A track field and other playing fields, recreation spots, leisure spaces, and spaces for energy harvesting technologies and strategies that reduce stormwater runoff and flooding problems downstream are integrated into the landscape. Drought-tolerant native landscaping seeks to minimize the need for irrigation and to better prepare the facility for drought.

The site's landscape expands beyond aesthetics and contributes to the performance of the project by providing visual continuity and promoting a sense of integration with the context and the community. The landscape's performative elements will help the goal of a net-zero or net-positive building for the site.

As a public facility that is essential for local and national safety, the onsite building is designed to achieve the highest level of performance and resiliency during and after any given emergency. The police headquarters needs to remain fully operational in the event of any natural disasters, such as earthquakes, tsunamis, and hurricanes, or man-made emergencies such as intelligence/cyber security breaches, terrorist attacks, or crime.

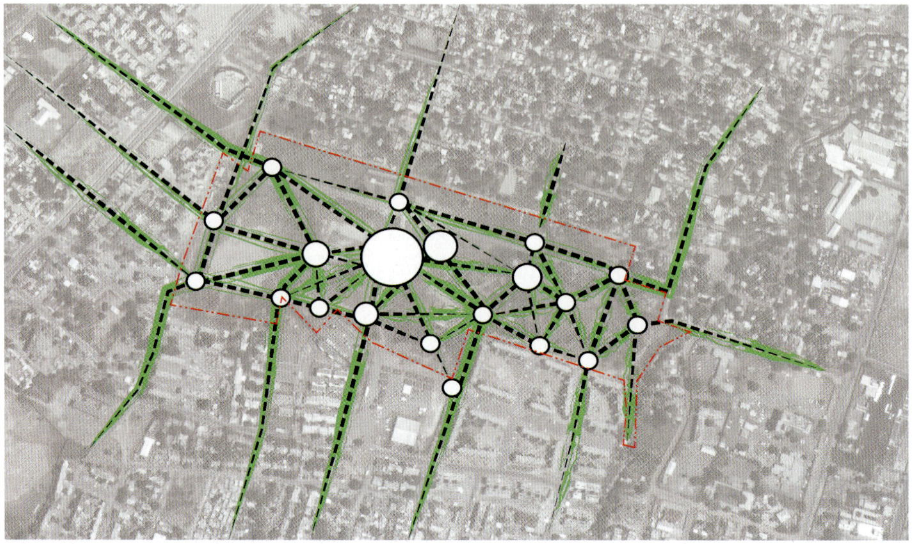

Connectivity

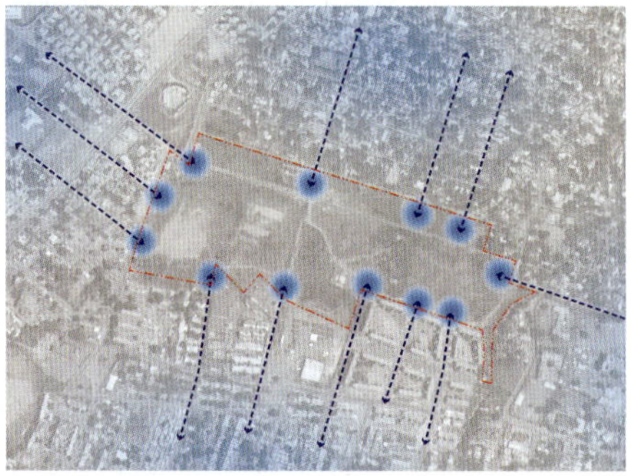

Community Integration

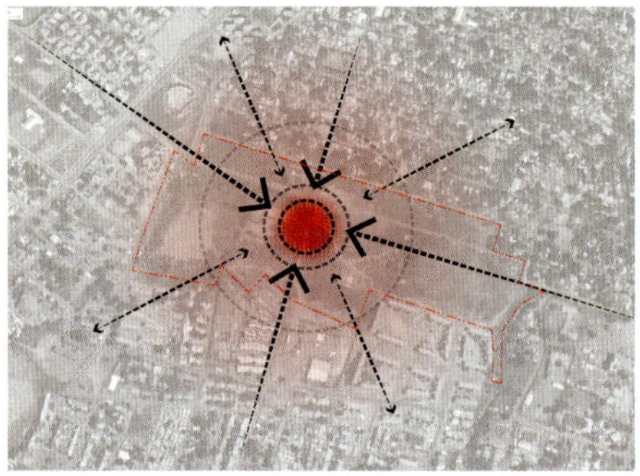

Landmark

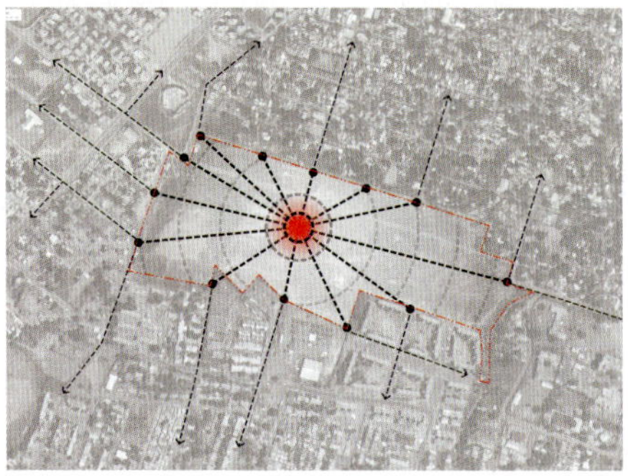

Access

Place Making

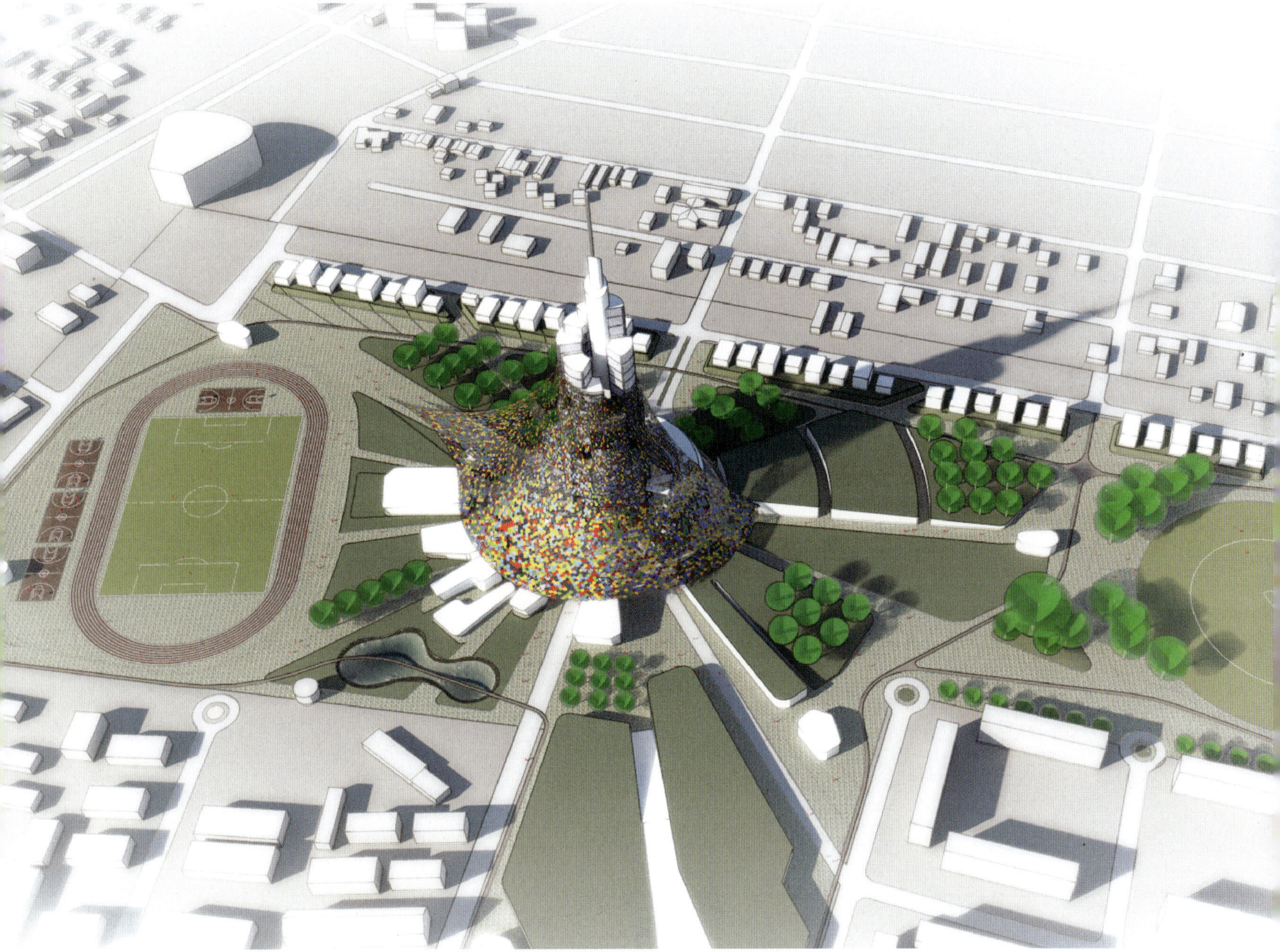

DESIGN CONCEPT | PROGRAM

The operating program accommodates spatial planning for 2,000 officers and support staff as related to secured areas, operating areas, administrative areas, and intelligence needs for the headquarters. These areas co-exist with the social and active programs for the community and provide operational support for communal activities.

The additional program for community outreach includes sports facilities, a community center, and outdoor areas for recreation. The various spaces can be used for festivals and other community gatherings such as lectures, athletics, and educational programs, increasing the community's comfortability with the police campus.

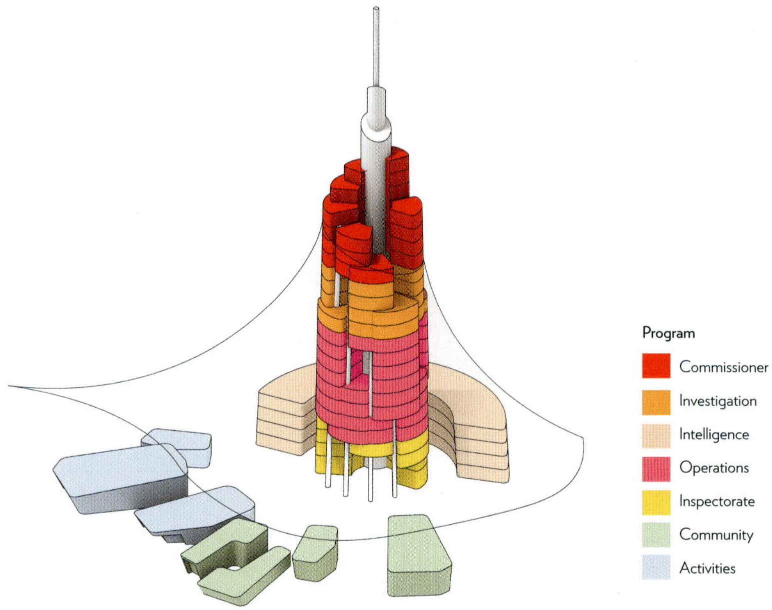

Site Plan

1 HQ Main Building Beacon
2 Intelligence
3 HQ Court
4 Fire HQ
5 Fire Trucks
6 Living Dorms / Training
7 Central Plaza
8 Large Auditorium
9 Denham Iown Community Center
10 Happy House
11 Swimming Pool
12 Gym
13 PV Veil
14 Learning Center
15 Small Auditorium

0 10 20 50 100m

N

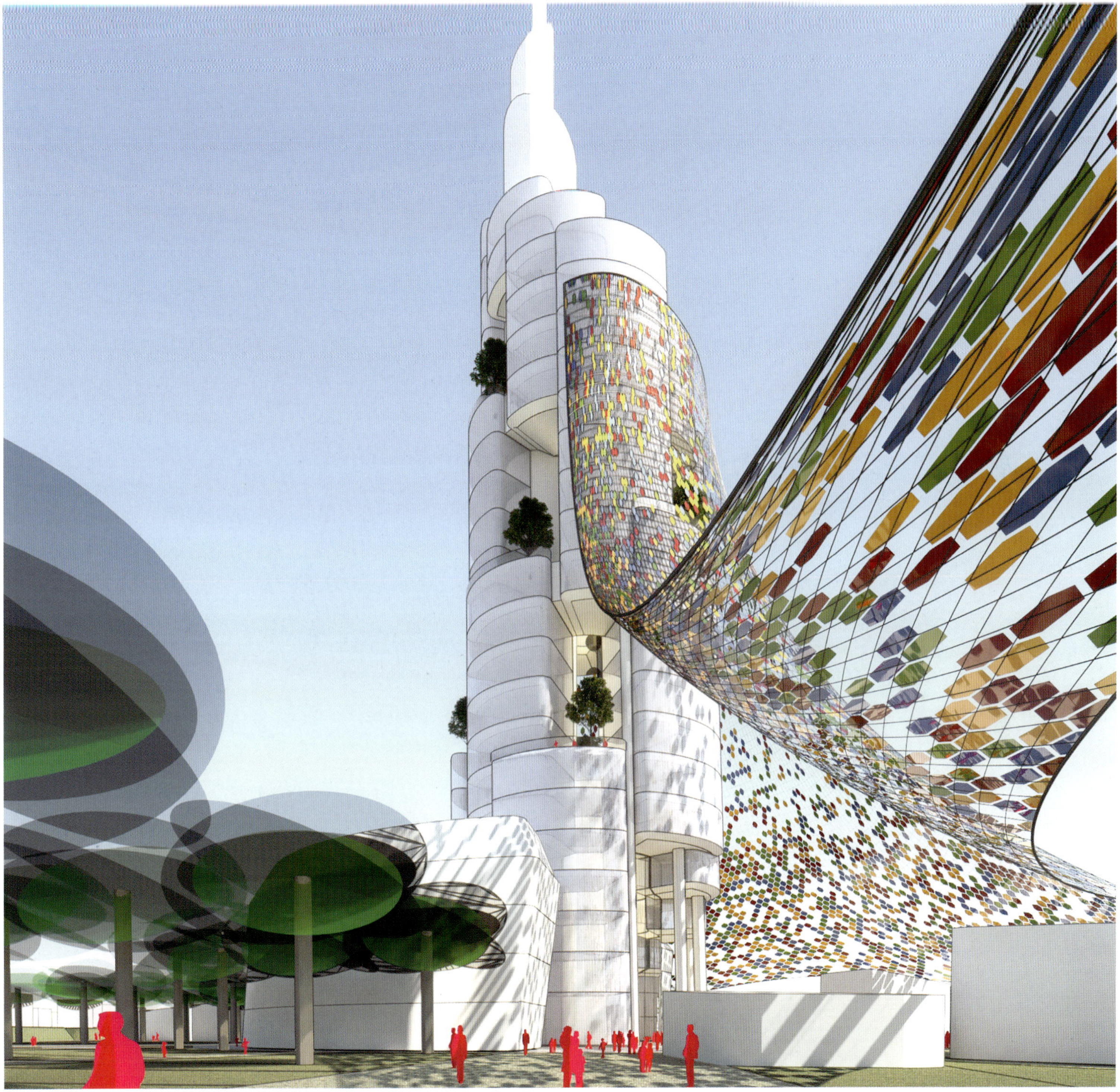

DESIGN CONCEPT | FORM

The complex is designed to be secured in a series of concentric layers, with the greatest level of security adjacent to the tower. An array of buildings containing support community programs defines the campus, while outdoor landscaped spaces emanate radially to create pathways, gardens, and fields. Uninterrupted sightlines and safety are key design factors along with ease of access and egress for police vehicles.

A single administrative tower features a cable net shield to shade and shape the public plaza. This main building is positioned to become a new icon for Kingston. The form allows for outdoor spaces that create a welcoming and safe environment for people to engage in a variety of social, educational, and physical activities.

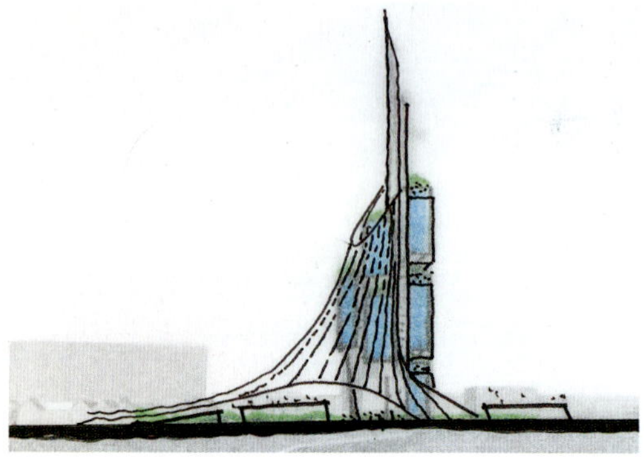

Concept Sketch, 2019

Formal Analysis

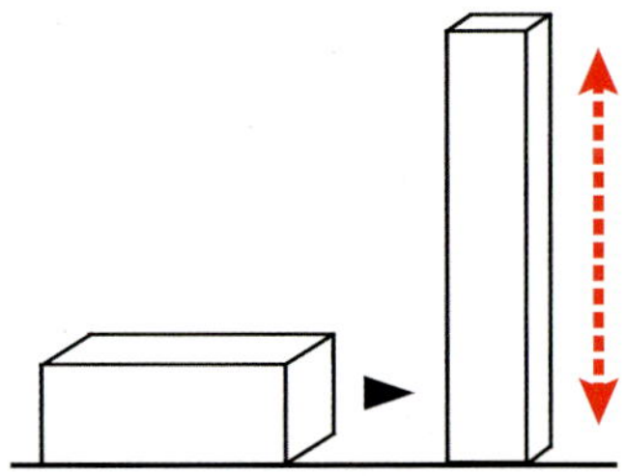

Enhance Verticality

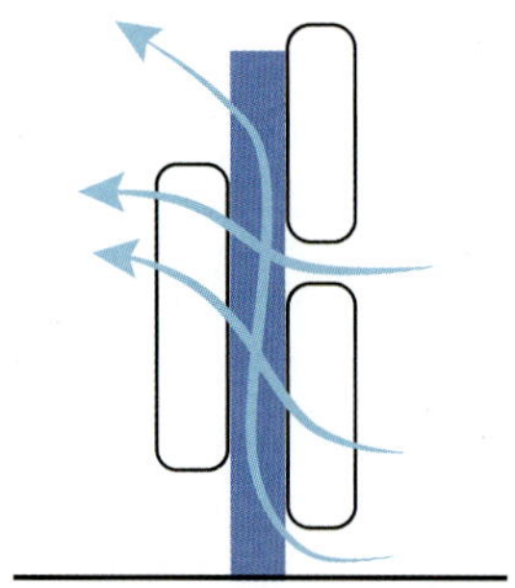

Create An Atrium

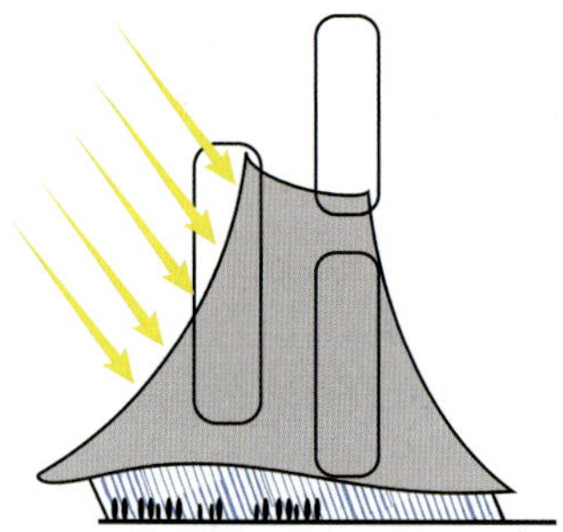

Provide Shade

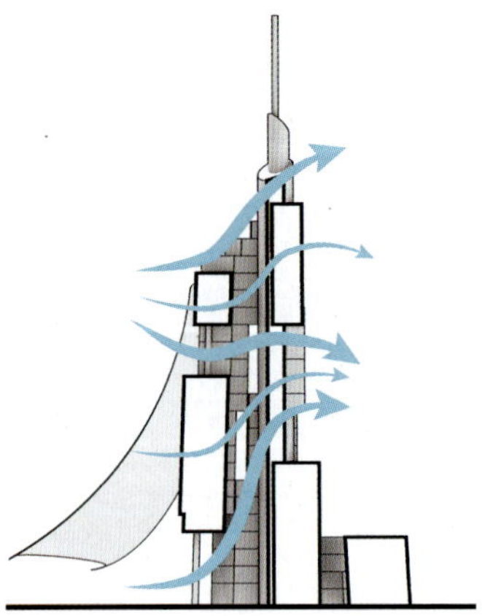

Cross Ventilation

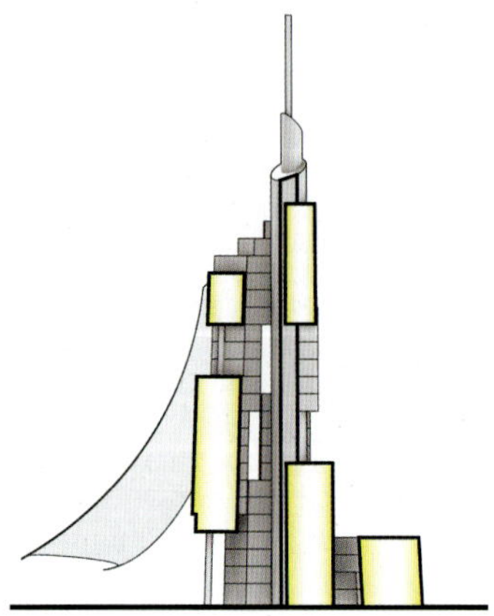

Natural Light

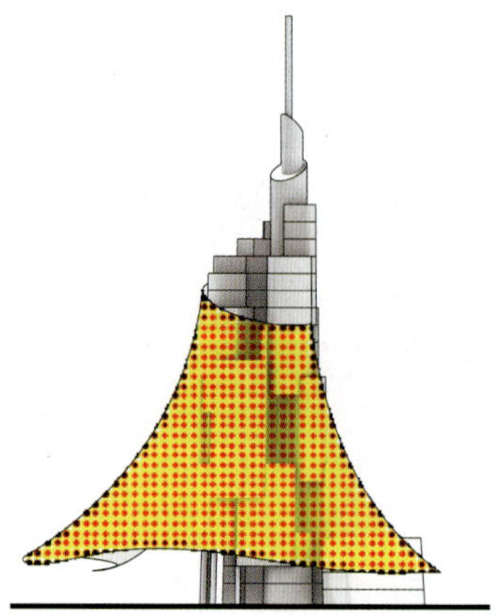

Energy Generation

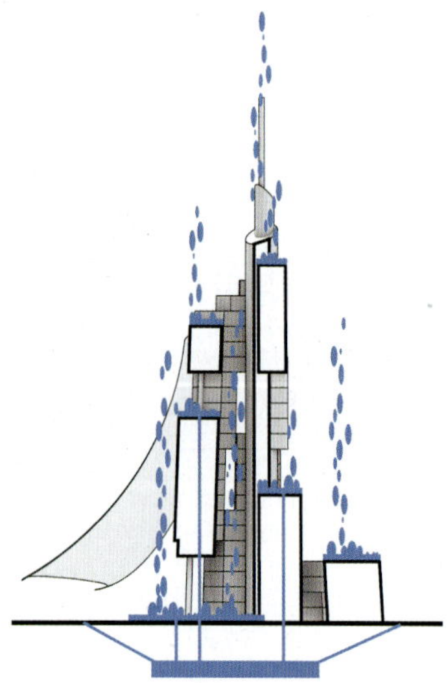

Water Conservation

The design vision includes six indicators for a clear and measurable road map to attain the advanced goals for the project:

- Lifestyle: Promote a lifestyle for its users that centers on conservation and that promotes environmental awareness.
- Health + Wellness: Promote health and wellness by providing spaces that allow and encourage physical activity and a connection with the outdoors.
- Energy + Carbon: Preserve energy and reduce carbon by being self-sufficient and by producing low carbon emissions.
- Water: Conserve water by implementing rainwater harvesting strategies such as green roofs and gray water treatment and reuse.
- Materials: Build with locally sources materials
- Outdoor Environment: Incorporate a site design that protects and enhances the local ecological value and biodiversity.

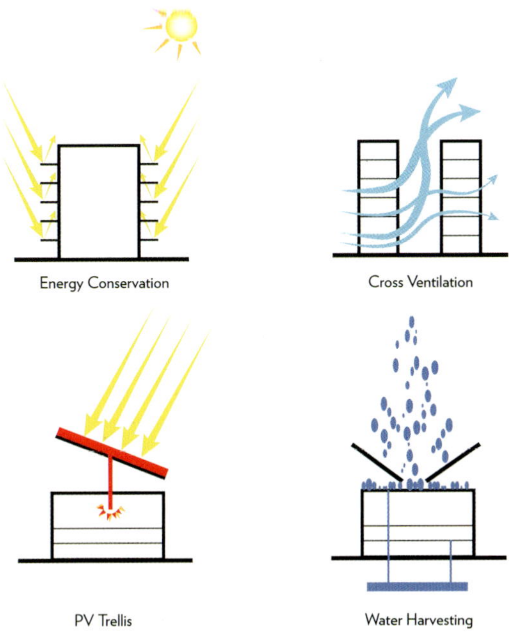

Study Models

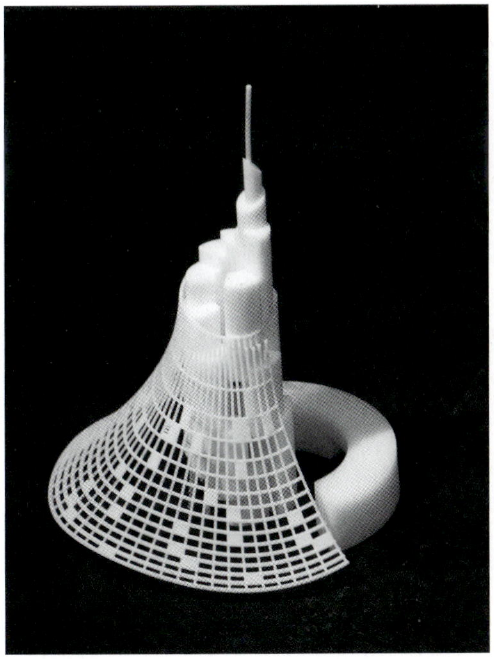

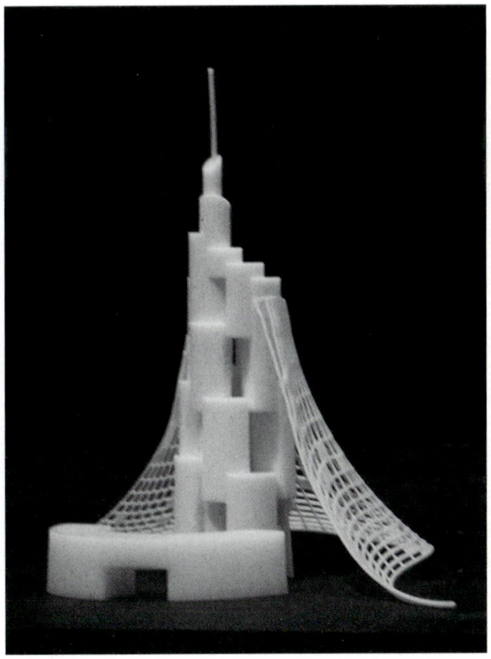

DESIGN CONCEPT | SPACE

Enabling residents to become an active part of the community was paramount, therefore treatment of the site boundary must achieve a balance between openness and safety. By providing a permeable yet secure boundary, the headquarters can create a safe sense of place where the community can be united.

Place-making is an important goal of the project's master plan as it aims to attract, support, and maintain a healthy community and social network. To create this, the project boundaries are carefully treated with landscape, program, and social activities that engage community participation and needs such as housing and retail.

With this people-centric approach to the design process, the design proposes to eliminate the distinction between roles and establish a platform for interaction and understanding for all parties involved.

The new development seeks to:

- Improve the relationship between the police and citizens, creating a more inclusive environment and making citizens feel safer.
- Enable police officers to provide swift response when required for the prevention of fatalities or disruption of public order.
- Create a strong urban presence that will also become a national landmark.
- Become a model to follow by other cities on the island or around the world.
- Set a new higher standard of building and construction guidelines that emphasize sustainability and building resilience.

Aerial View | Administration Building Canopy (Right)

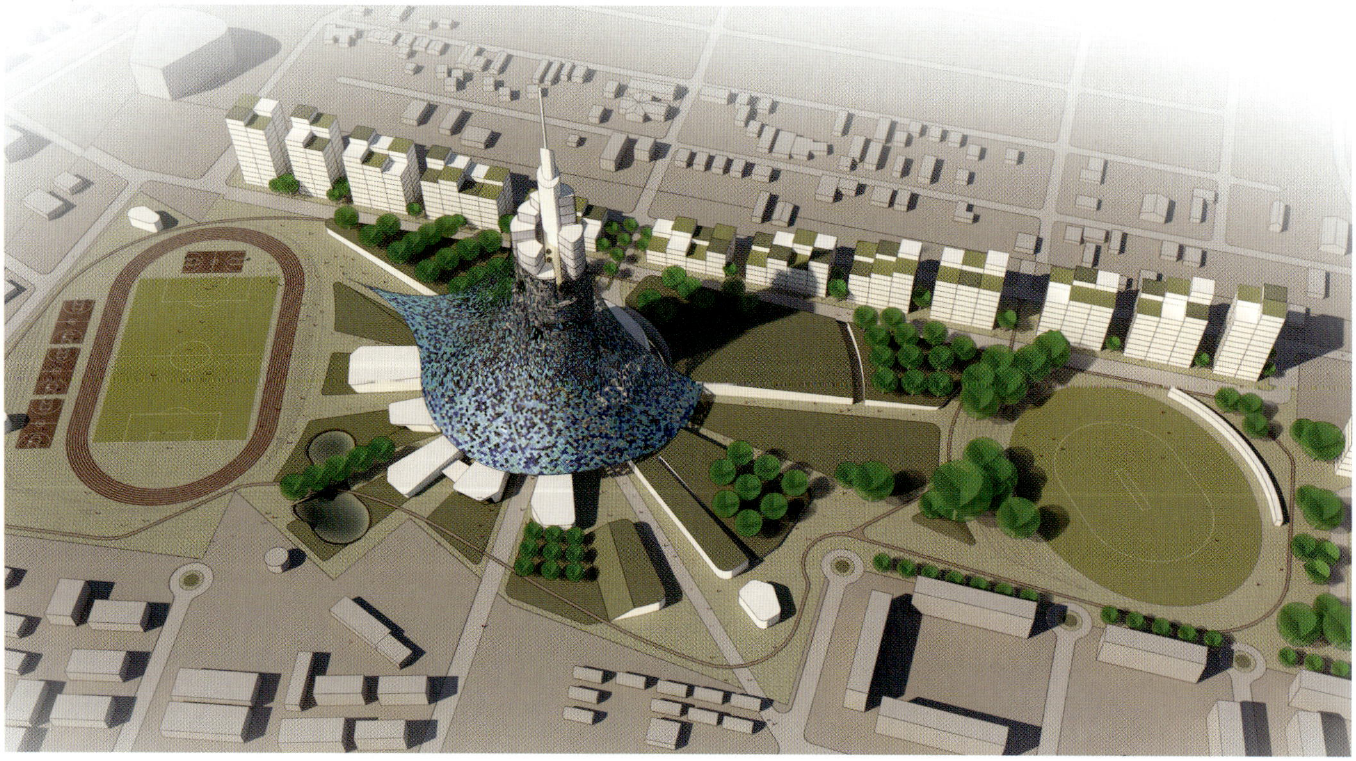

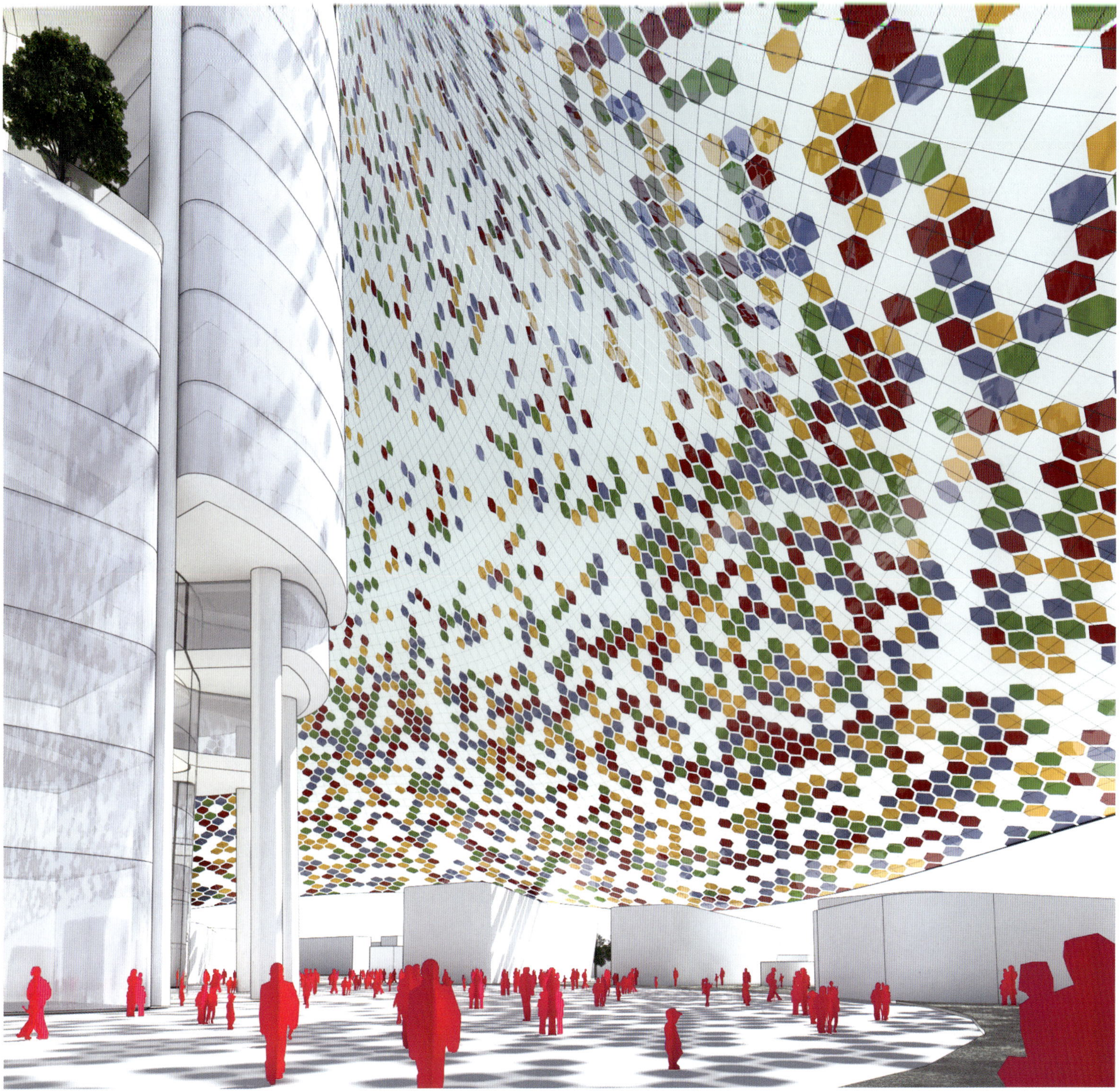

RESEARCH + DEVELOPMENT | ANALYSIS

As a facility for local and national safety, the building must achieve the highest level of performance and resiliency during and after any given emergency. This building must remain fully operational in the event of any natural disasters such as earthquakes, tsunamis, hurricanes, or other man-made emergencies such as intelligence/ cyber security breaches or terrorist attacks.

Several design and operational strategies were considered including net-zero or net-positive energy, island operations, and seismic design. To correspond with the national identity of the project, and to serve as an example for the Nation's Public buildings, the project will pursue a LEED Platinum status with a net-zero or net-positive energy target.

The project's sustainability initiatives set high targets that can be achieved both practically and cost effectively and can serve as an example for other governmental projects such as LEED platinum certification; designing to WELL platinum standards; 100% energy from onsite renewable sources; no potable water used for non-potable applications; and net-zero lifecycle emissions after 10 years.

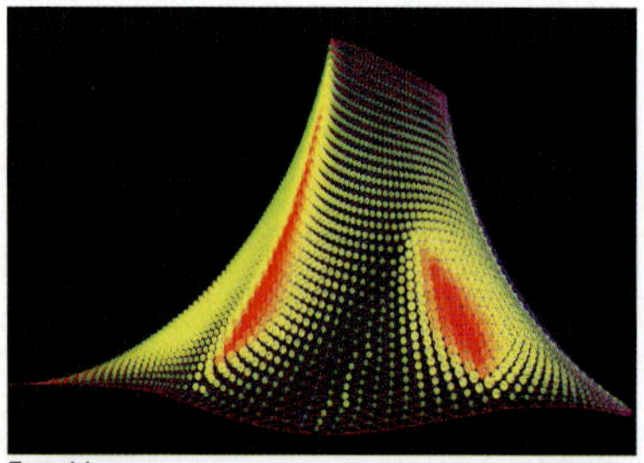
Front View

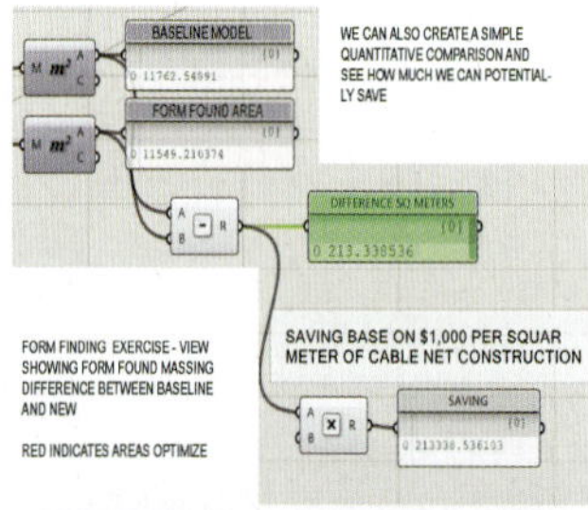

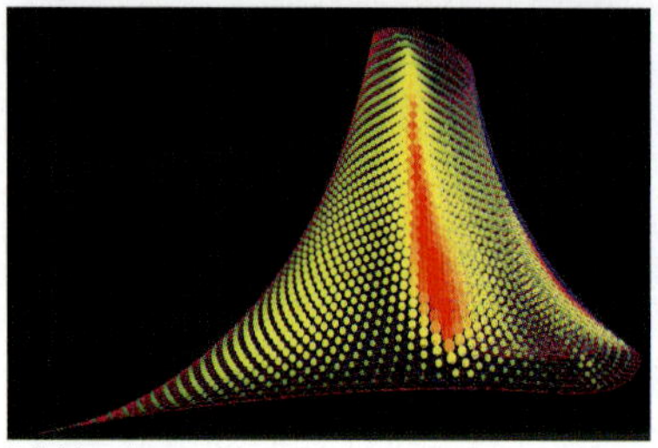
Side View A

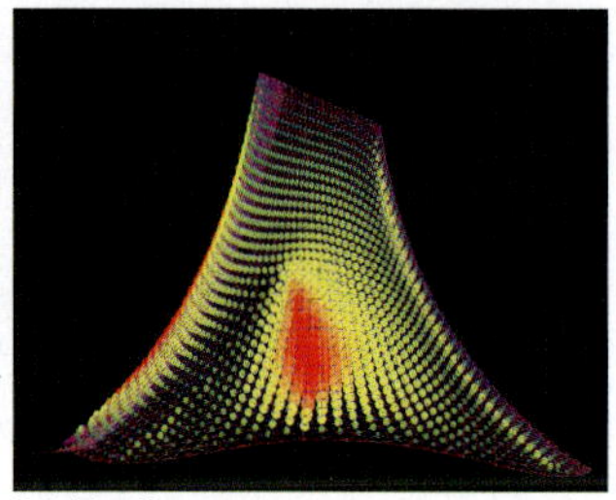
Side View B

PV Veil Structural Study

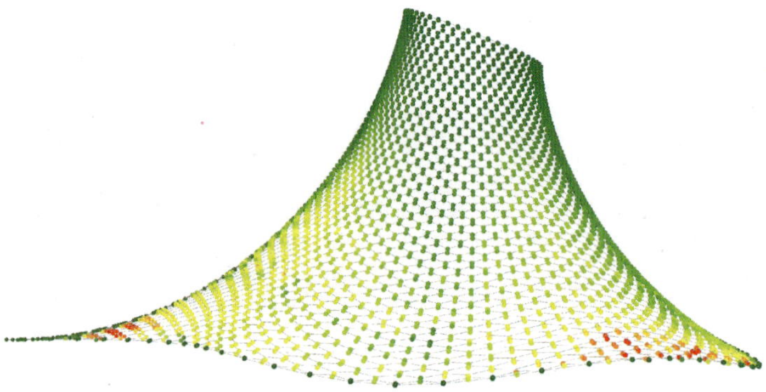
Cable Stress Analysis (Self Weight)

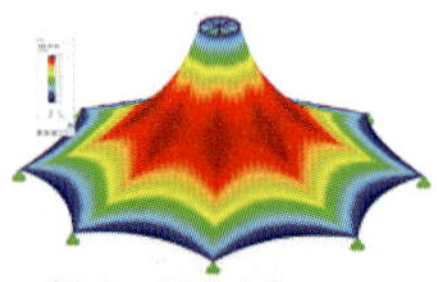
Calculation Method - Projection
Pre-Stress - Isotopic Only (for Given Axis Orientation) - Force

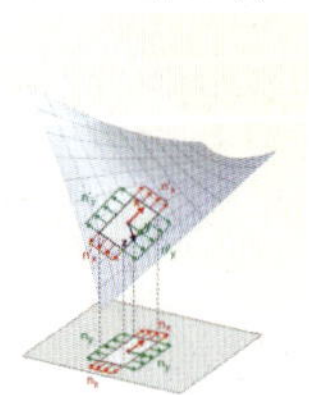
Isotropic Analysis

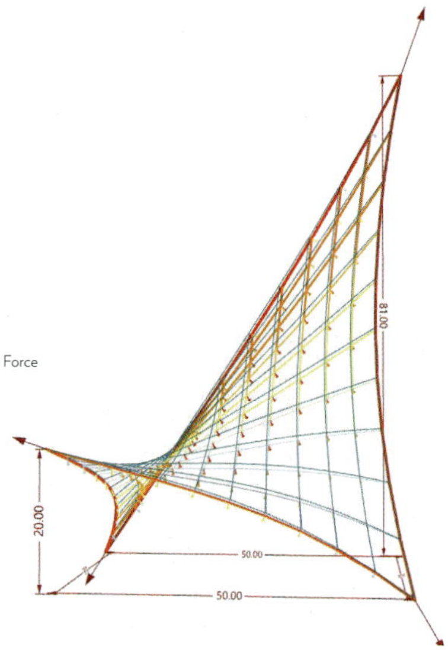

Facade Module Analysis

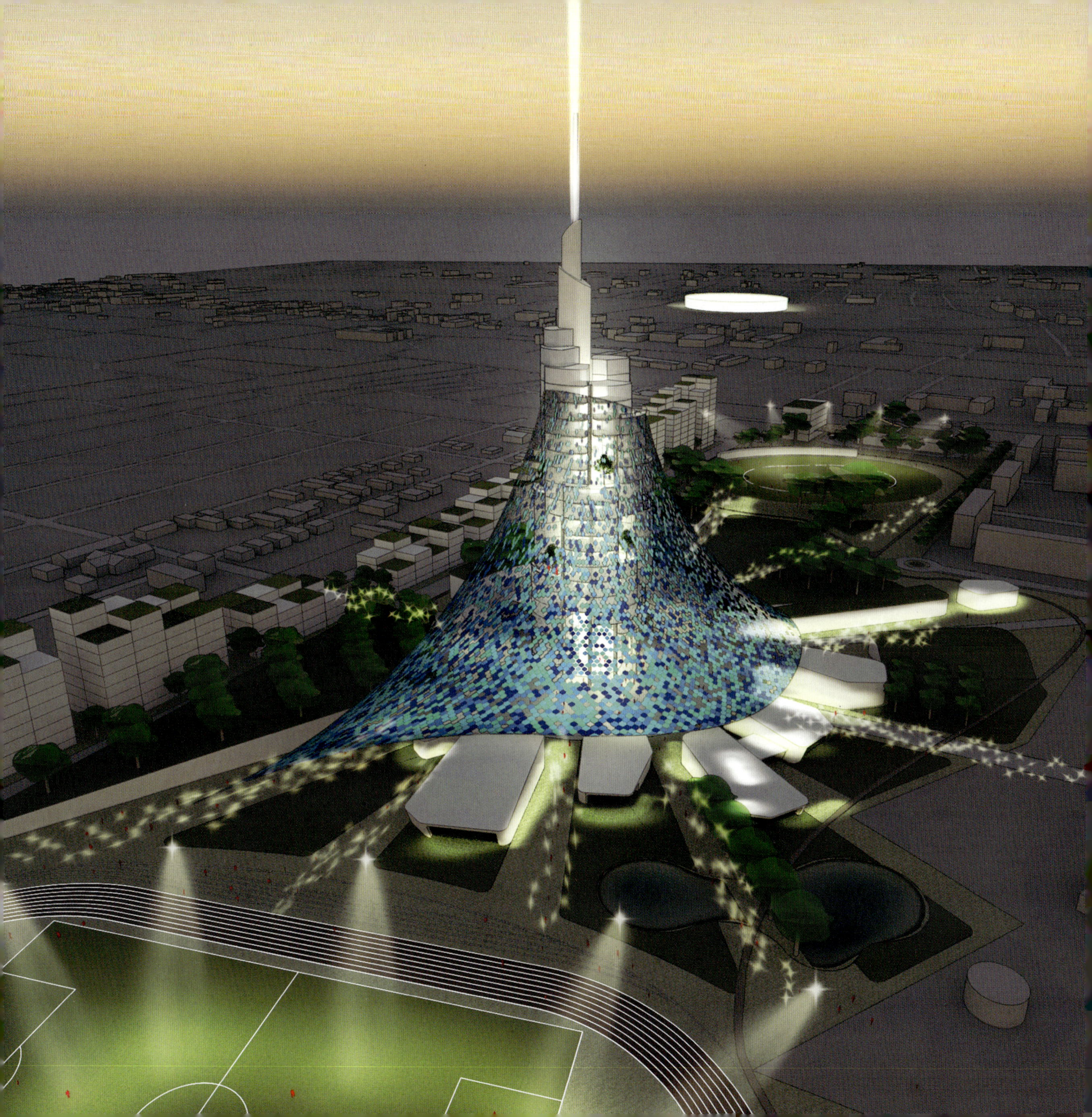

THE PORTAL AT RUNMAO TOWER

Nanjing, People's Republic of China

As experts in the supertall typology, AS+GG explores ways to create new, innovative public spaces at the top of tall buildings. These spaces seek to expand the role of supertall buildings within a community by generating wonder and contributing to the human experience with boundary pushing technological developments.

The Portal is a 360-degree open-air observatory space design for the top floors of Runmao Tower, a new supertall tower designed by AS+GG. The tower is part of an 860,000 square-meter development that anchors the surrounding district and enhances Nanjing's already iconic skyline. The tower will be one of the tallest in Nanjing at 500-meters and will be one of the tallest buildings to achieve LEED-Gold certification when completed.

AS+GG won an international design competition in 2018 to design the new South HeXi Yuzui Financial District and Tower, also known as Runmao Tower. The building, still under design, will be located at the west end of the new Hexi New Business District, facing the broad Yangtze River to the west and Jinling, the ancient capital of six dynasties, to the east.

Function: Assembly + Observation | **Status:** Conceptual, 2018 | **Client:** Jinmao Group

DESIGN CONCEPT | SITE

Supertall towers attract business, tourism, and retail in both the national and international tourist markets. This mixed-use district can increase the value of the location with networks to access the riverfront, multiple public transportation options, and new cultural, natural, and technological opportunities. Encouraging increased interaction, users are invited to experience the site as either a live-work environment or as a visitor to one of the many public parks and art centers.

Runmao Tower connects to the metro station and Yuzui Park at the west of site by two large sunken plazas. The tower's key feature is a distinctive observatory with a viewing platform that overlooks Nanjing, connecting the city to the site.

Site Plan

Runmao Tower in the South HeXi Yuzui Financial District | The Portal (Right)

The Portal is a multi-dimensional venue where visitors experience state-of-the-art virtual reality, immersive holographic concerts, and interactive 7D rides. The space also offers fine dining, a world-class sky garden, and live musical performances and other events. Glass elevators bring visitors to each level, revealing the space as they ascend to the building's pinnacle. The program includes a first-floor lobby, a central gathering space with an interactive projection screen, a hologram chamber viewed from modular pods, landscaped gardens that incorporate video screen experiences, and an open-air observation platform, aptly named the Cloud Walk.

Cloud Walk Renderings (Below + Right)

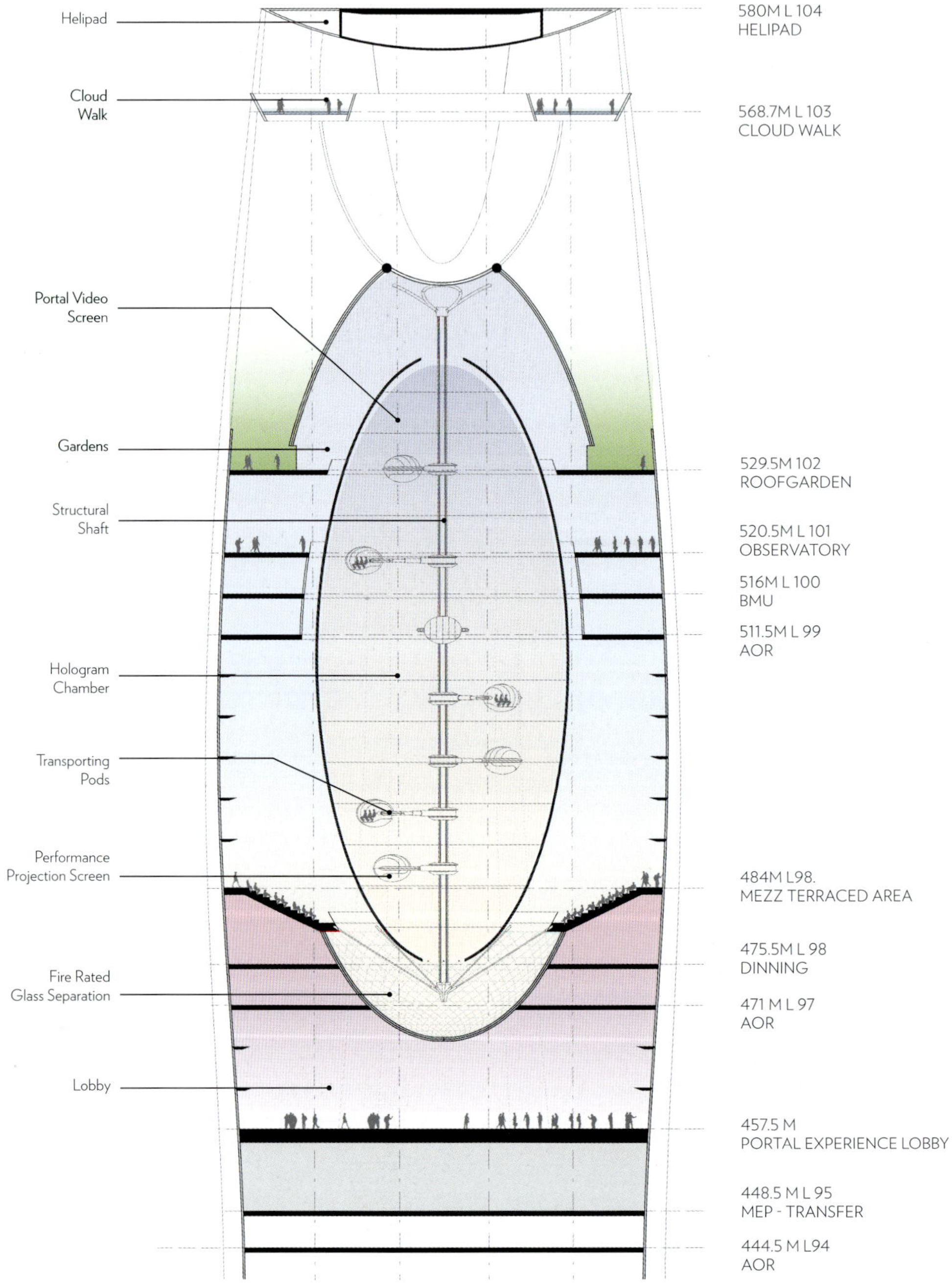

The Portal Section

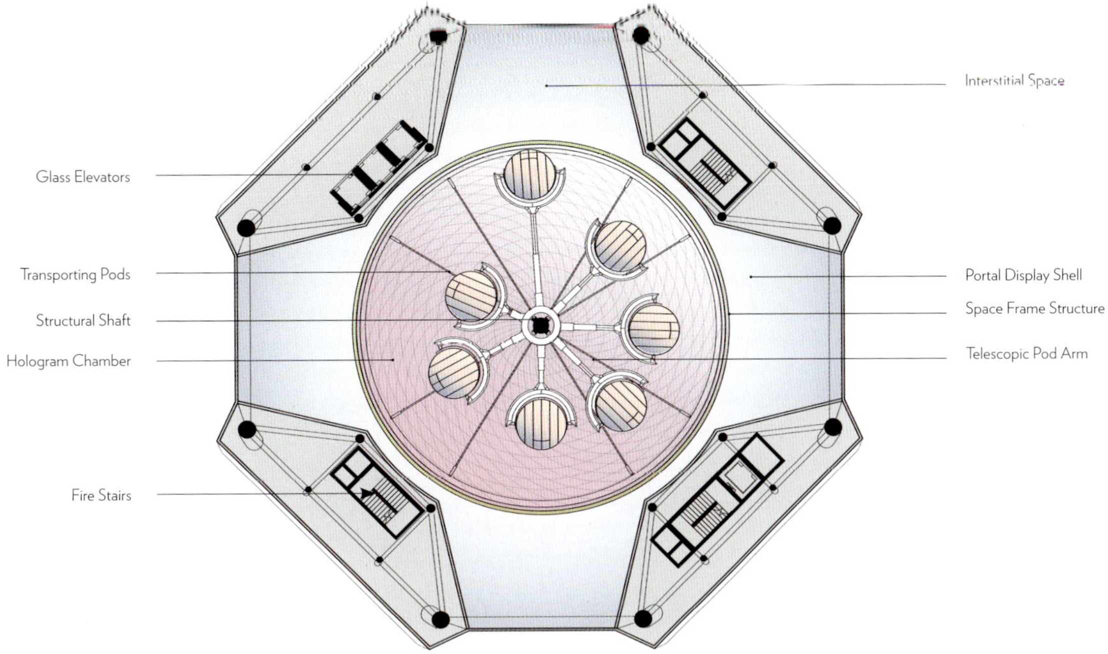

The Portal Floor Plan

DESIGN CONCEPT | FORM

The Portal's cloud-like observation function is visible through the exterior wall at the top of tower, adding interest and intrigue to encourage visitors to explore this one-of-a-kind building. An egg-like shape provides a convex surface on the exterior of the tower, maximizing its area and its visual impact. On the interior, the concave surface allows for contained and intense multisensorial experiences. The shape provides surfaces to cast visual, auditive, and sensorial information, as well as creates a media environment that can be seen and enjoyed from inside the immersive experience and from the outside the tower to Nanjing.

Conceptual Sketch, 2019

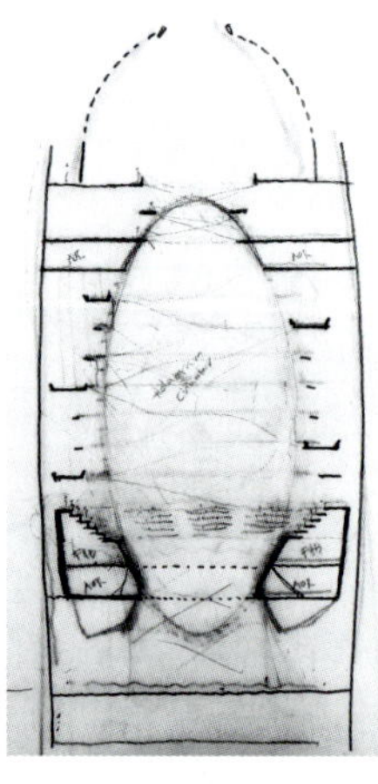

Physical Model

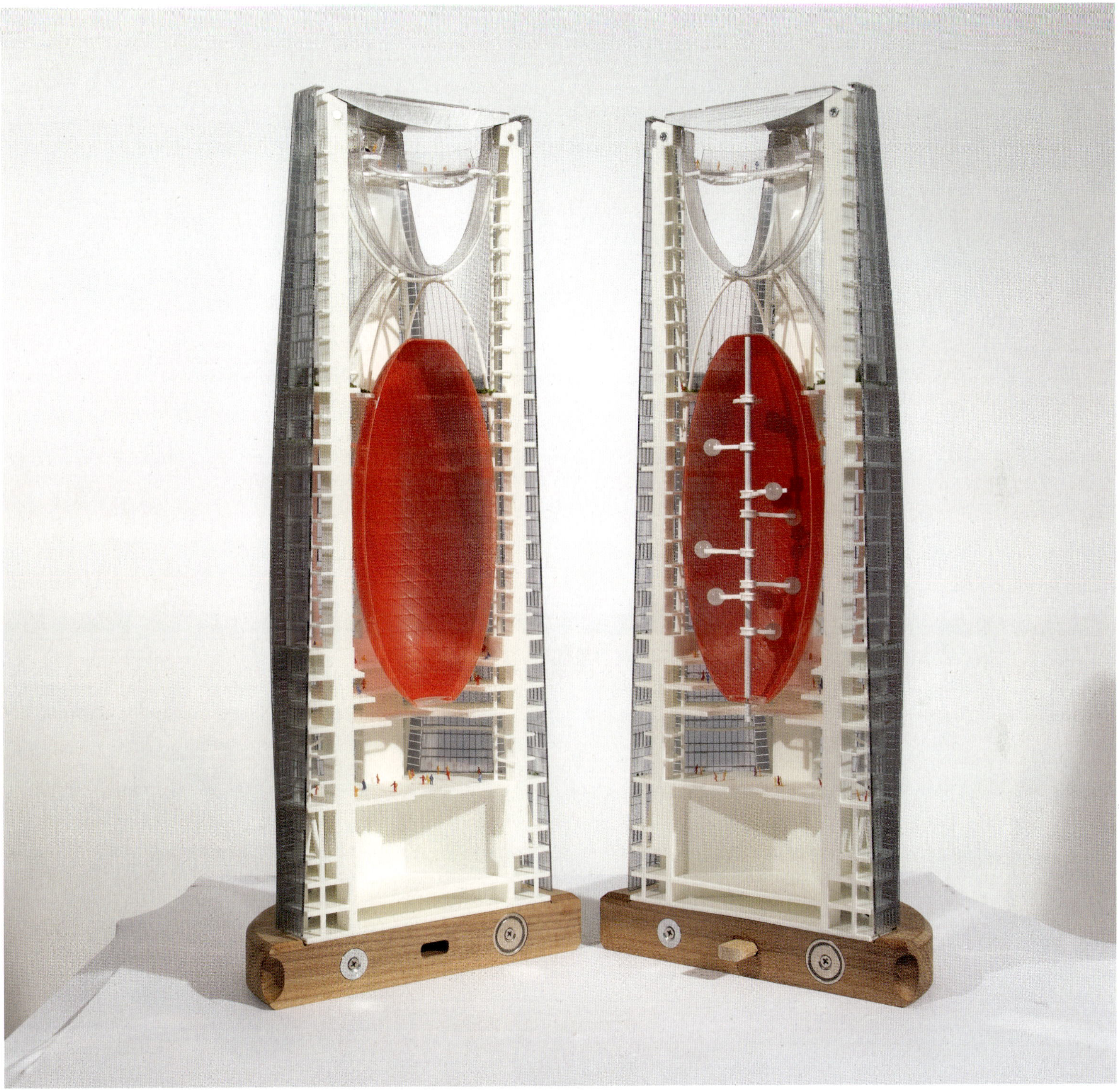

DESIGN CONCEPT | FORM

The tower's distinctive top is the integrated result of the building's programmatic requirements, the design aesthetic, fire life safety protocols, and structural requirements. To reach the iconic height of the client's original design brief, the tower was envisioned with an expansive open space at the pinnacle that provides space for new programming options.

The atrium space has entertainment functions with an outdoor glass-floor viewing deck, event spaces, and an immersive digital experience. The highlight is a glass petal-shaped pod system that hovers above a ring-shaped opening, containing The Portal immersive digital experience.

The tower's four undulating corners cantilever, creating an impressive viewing experience that overlooks the Yangzi River, the waterfront park, the canal, and the surrounding CBD. At the center, above the bridge, the underside of a polished stainless-steel convex helipad reflects the urban landscape and the landscaping of the adjacent atrium space.

In towers of this height, a helipad is required for fire and life safety and was a design challenge to visually integrate into the tower's top. The solution was to create a concave edge that maintains the required rescue landing area, while maximizing the view to the spaces below.

While the tapered building top, undulated building profile, and chamfered corners help the air dynamics of the building with wind load reduction, structurally, the helipad creates a challenge as it has a negative impact because of its weight that will increase wind loads.

The crown is hollowed at the center, leaving four corners to support the helipad and enough void space for wind to pass through, reducing the wind load and thereby improving the building's structural performance. A Hummingbird damper (a version of tuned liquid column gas damper (TLCGD) technology originated at NASA) was investigated to find if the helipad's weight can become a positive effect with the right system in place.

Physical Structural Models

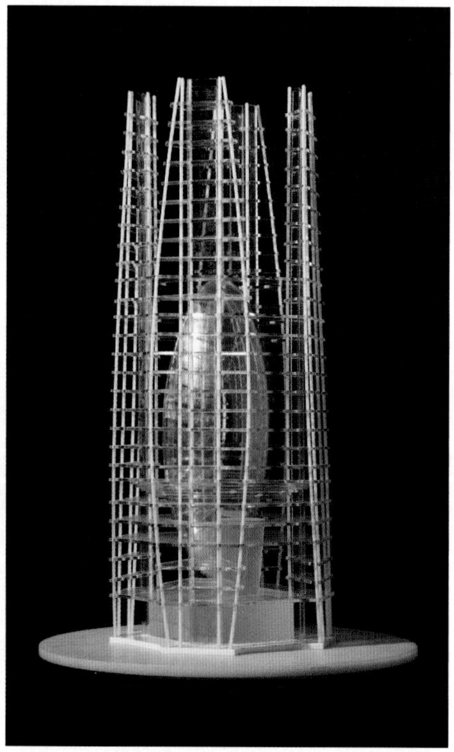

DESIGN CONCEPT | SPACE

The Portal is the next evolution in large-scale shared immersive journeys; an experience that is on the cusp of a new media revolution where real and digital worlds can be seamlessly integrated. The space harnesses today's rapidly emerging immersive tools with live equipment and utilizes them to take passengers on a transcendental communal experience.

The inside of The Portal is conceived as a self-contained world that can be accessed at various locations through a set of seven pods. The pods are small glass chambers that can accommodate up to ten people sitting in a circular configuration. The pods offer a 4D access to a digital universe that allows the visitor to become immersed in a virtual reality that surrounds them from all sides.

> *"Architecture is now being seen as a vehicle for entertainment, as much as it is a vehicle for use.*
> *- Adrian Smith, FAIA, Partner, Adrian Smith + Gordon Gill Architecture"*

The Portal Experiences Renderings

DESIGN CONCEPT | SPACE

The pods move people freely within the interior of the experience inside a "hologram chamber." In these chambers, visitors view alternative universes projected onto the interior of the pod. The experience is enhanced with light, video, sounds, smells, mist, smoke, and other mixed media.

The glass pods move effortlessly, mounted on free-wheel connections on two ends, allowing for a 360-degree rotation. The wheels are connected to a convex arm that also rotates 360-degrees on the opposite axis and is mounted to a telescopic arm that expands up to 15 meters and reduces to three meters.

The seven pod assemblies are mounted to a 60-meter vertical shaft at the center of The Portal that expands the totality of its height. The pod assemblies can rotate around the shaft and move up and down with a range of 20 meters. This wide range of motion allows for a realistic experience as movement and gravitational forces are coordinated with the other censorial stimuli.

Pod Studies

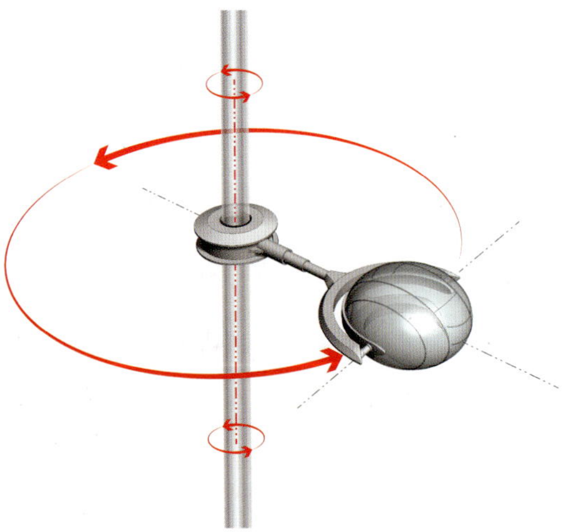

Rotation Axis 1

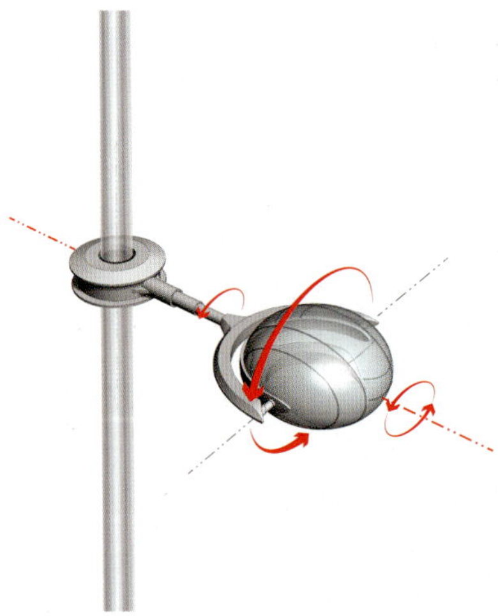

Rotation Axis 2

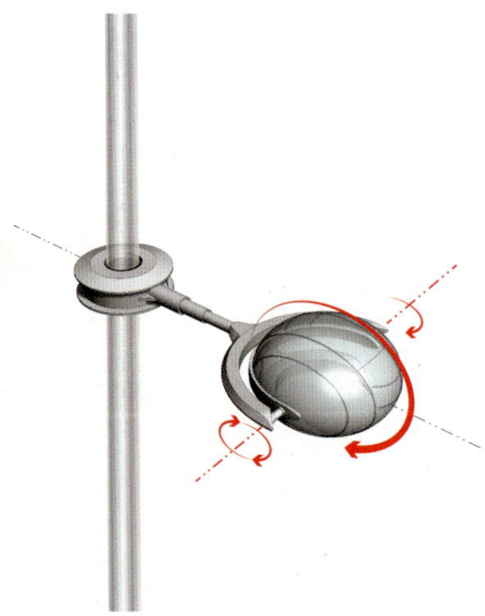

Rotation Axis 3

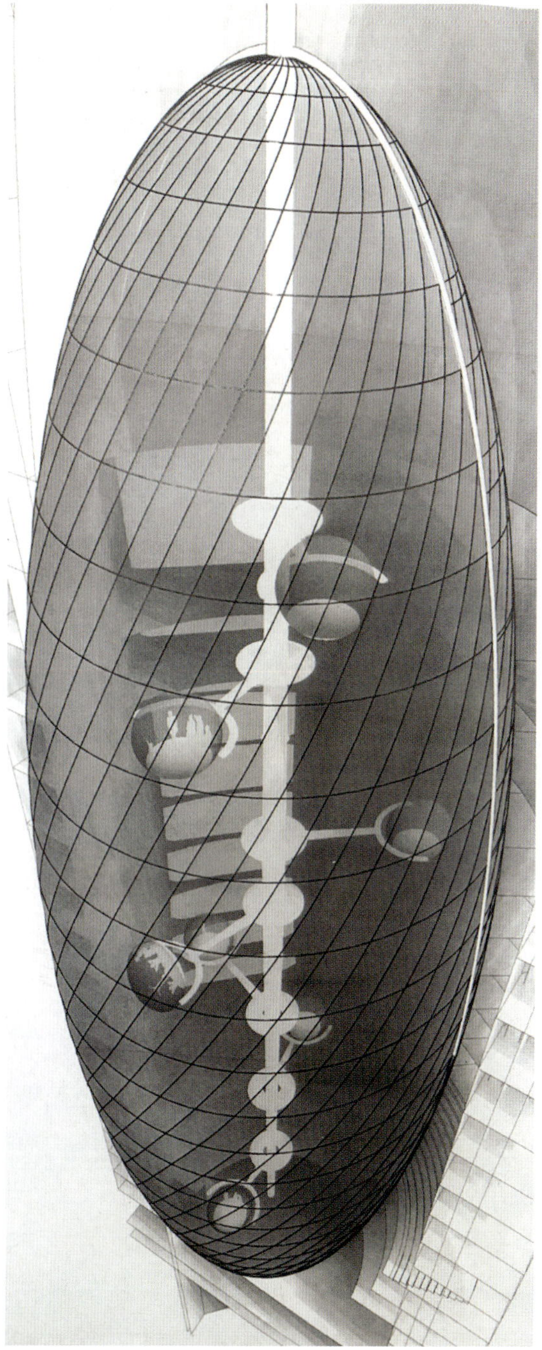

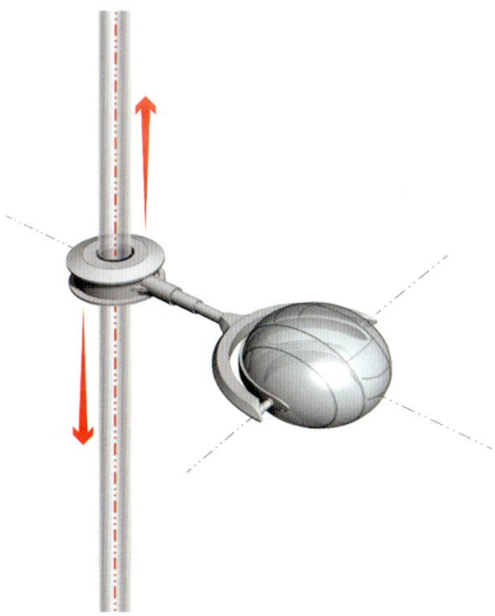

Vertical Movement

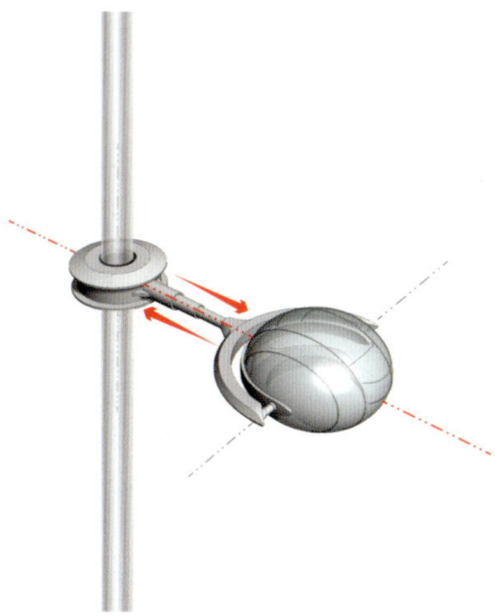

Horizontal Movement

To attain the vision for The Portal, several technologies were considered, which alone were not able to deliver the level of reality that matched the vision. Through consulting, and research and development, it was determined that new technologies needed to be developed to attain the vision.

Systems like the Exterior PixLine 10, a linear LED video fixture for media facades and creative installations, and Flexible LED lighting were analyzed. Exterior LED lighting systems and flexible LEDs can be combined with a wide variety of lenses and diffusers for the right look for every application. For visual effects, sophisticated sounds systems at multiple locations can be installed for the proper depth and sharpness of sounds.

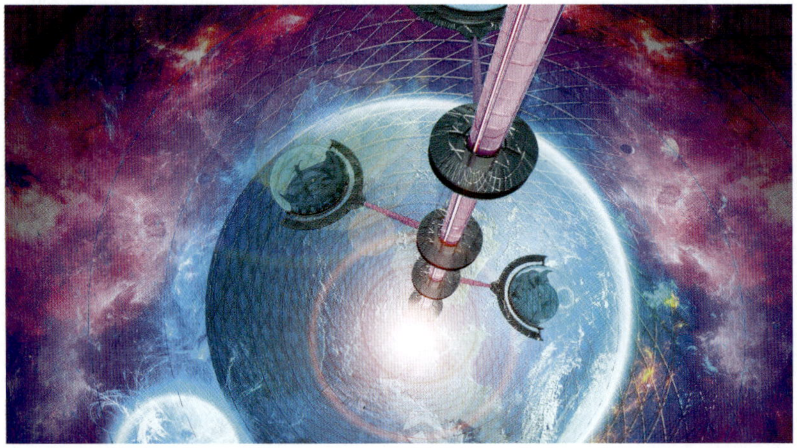

Transporting Pods (Above + Right)

Flexible LED Lighting

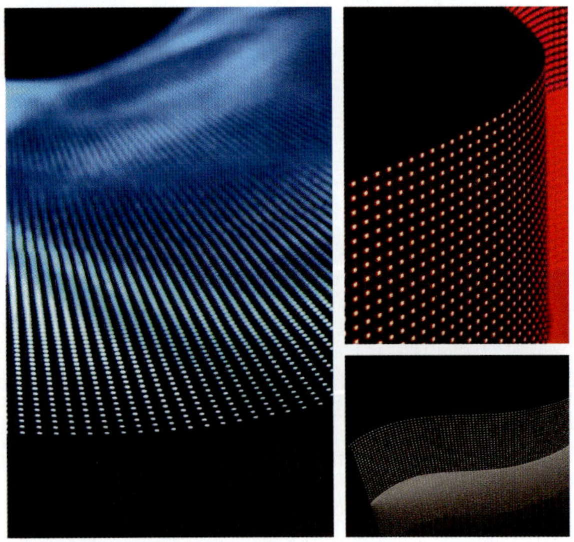

The Portal is shaped to enhance the performance of the tower and help mitigate wind vortices, optimize views, and enhance both the structure and the program. The LEED-Gold design incorporates multiple green spaces that further enhance the sustainability and comfort of experience. Users will experience the tactile sensations of the landscaping elements that are shown to promote a sense of well-being and improve air quality and the local micro-climate.

The tower integrates rainwater harvesting into the sky gardens that targets onsite water management at greater than 100% rainfall. Rainwater is collected using sponge city concepts including sub-soil collection, permeable paving, and recessed green space. Collected water drains to tanks below ground level where it is treated and stored for reuse. A 55% reduction in total indoor water use is predicted.

The building seeks an overall energy reduction through a combination of energy strategies like reducing the cooling load, installation of a high-performance facade, reducing heating loads, reducing lighting loads, and reducing plug loads. A high-performance, Low-E insulated curtain-wall system has carefully designed fins that work with the building's geometry to efficiently reduce solar heat gain and provide the effective protection to the indoor environment, while maintaining access to daylighting and controlling glare.

Wind speed escalates when it comes into contact with a tower of this height. Therefore, cutting openings on the top of tower significantly reduces overall wind loads. Wind loads can also be further reduced through a chamfered, tapering form. The final wind load reduction was estimated to be 41.6%, which will result in significant savings of structural materials and of embodied carbon.

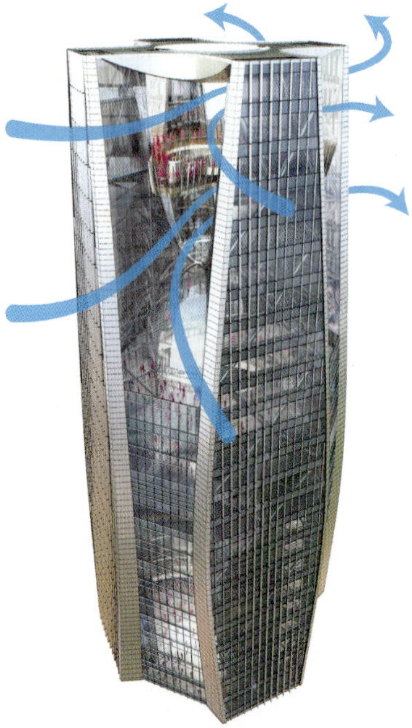

Crown Wind Dynamic Optimization

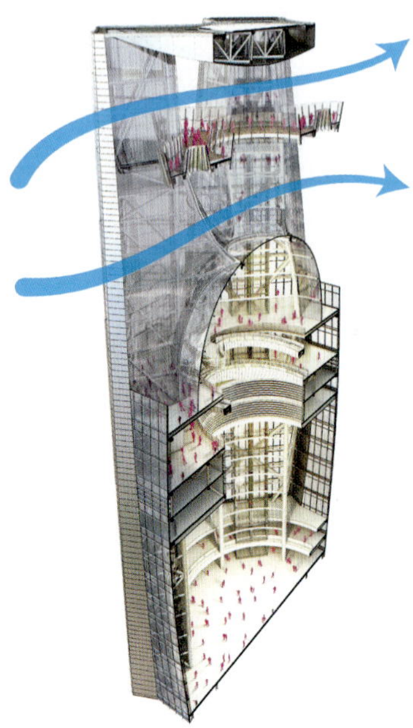

Crown Opening Exterior + Observation

Interior Venting

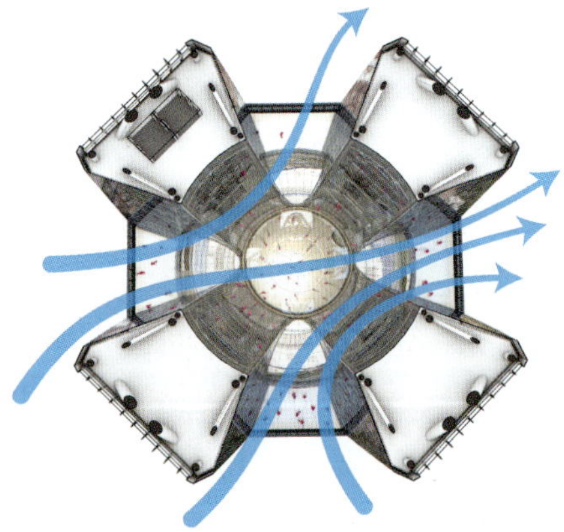

Crown Opening Diagram

SHIMAO TOWER OBSERVATORY

Shenzhen, People's Republic of China

Shimao Tower, known as Shenzhen-Hong Kong International Center, references biomorphic characteristics in an abstract and subtle way, bringing a magnificent sculptural icon to northeast Shenzhen. The tower will be an icon of power and dignity with a dynamic sense of motion once constructed.

At night, the tower transforms into a light sculpture that is animated with the latest high-tech LED systems and programmed displays of kinetic art. At the top is one of the world's highest observation decks, club facilities with restaurants, night clubs, spa facilities, and a spectacular swimming pool, all with breathtaking views of Shenzhen and beyond.

Located in the center of a proposed development, Shimao Tower was designed as a new public realm created to connect the existing Dayun Sport Campus. Set at the center of pristinely landscaped grounds, the master plan connects the existing venues so that the tower becomes the new focal point of activity throughout the entire district. This active connection is a continuation of the current public space system at the center of the existing sports venues to the south.

Function: Assembly + Observation | **Status:** Conceptual, 2018 | **Client:** Shimao Group

DESIGN CONCEPT | SITE

AS+GG developed the Shenzhen Longgang Master Plan, which connects Shimao Tower to the surrounding mixed-use district with beautifully landscaped promenades. The tower is integrated into the dynamic public realm with cultural and retail programs anchored by a cultural center and a main library. Programmed venues have open and enclosed spaces for recreation, leisure, tourism, art, dining, and social gatherings. A major retail facility defines the northeast corner of the site, while a community of apartment towers occupies the northwest section.

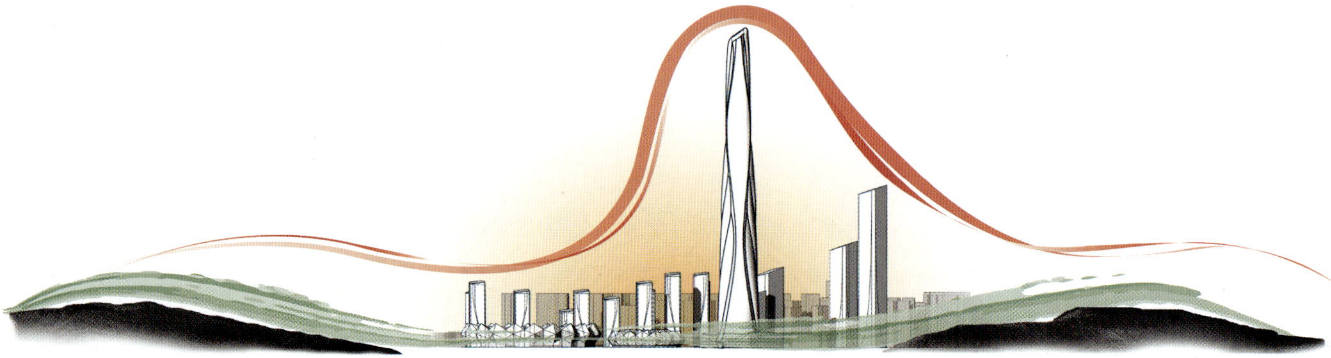

Skyline Diagram

Shimao Tower Centerpiece of Shenzhen Longgang Master Plan | Site Plan (Right)

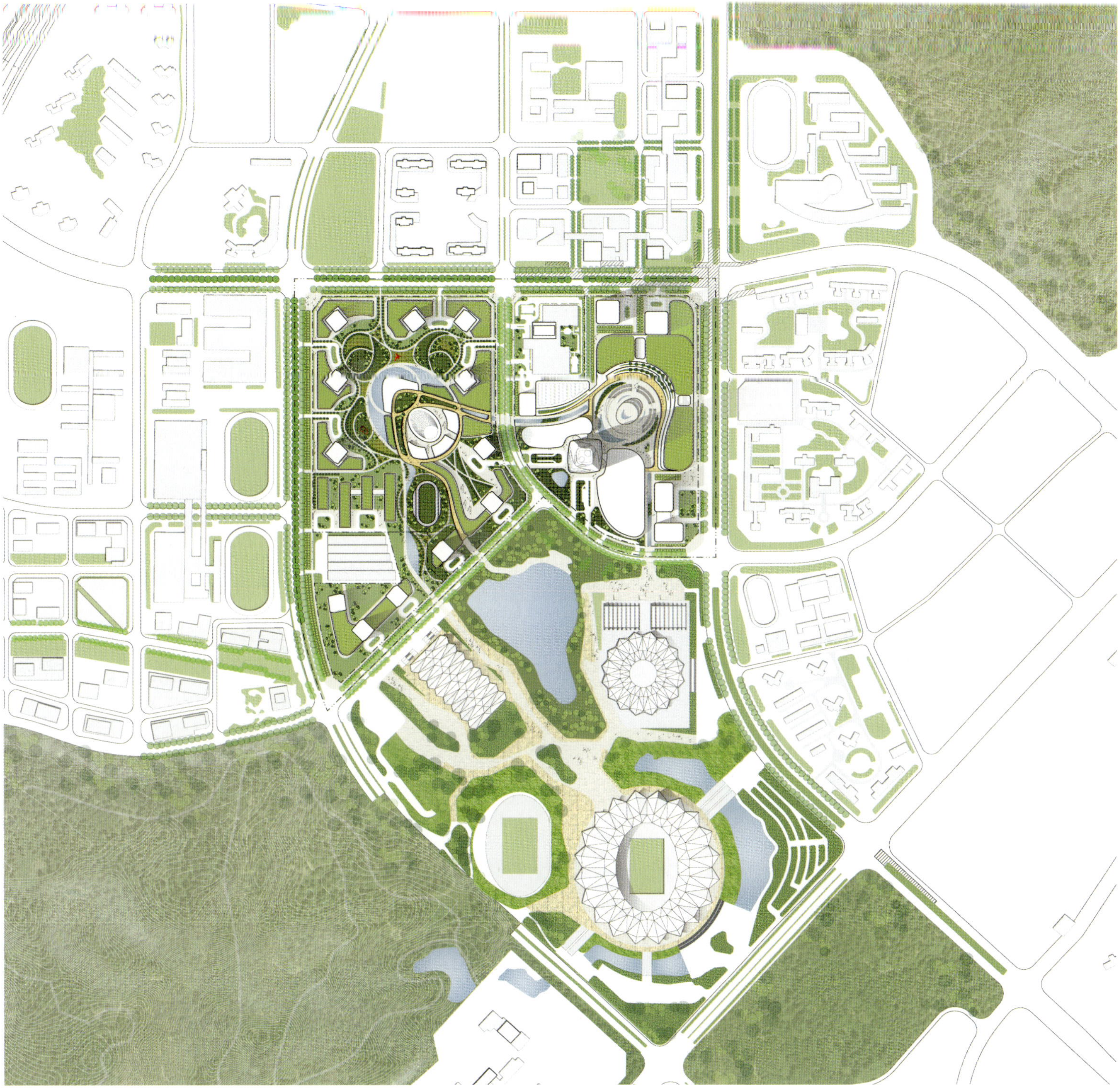

DESIGN CONCEPT | PROGRAM

Shimao Tower has a comprehensive mixed-use program including retail, office, hotel, fitness, and entertainment functions. The tower's top has one of the world's highest observation experiences and additional club facilities with a restaurant, a night club, spa services, and a grand swimming pool. The observation experience has expansive views of Shenzhen and beyond. In the evenings, the tower's visual, sound, and light show reinforces the district's athletic and entertainment purposes.

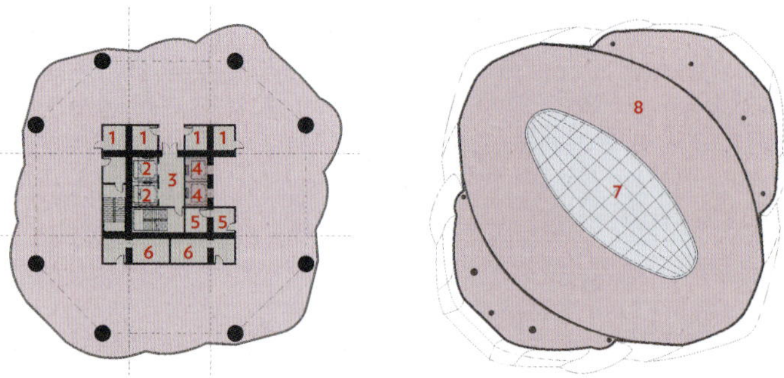

1 MEP
2 FFG
3 Hotel/FF
4 OB
5 Storage
6 Restroom
7 Skylight
8 Observation Deck

Observation Deck Plans

Observation Deck Amenities | Atrium Pool (Right)

DESIGN CONCEPT | FORM

The tower's graceful form references anthropomorphic characteristics, offering a new sculptural icon for northwest Shenzhen's skyline. The tower's top plays a key role in realizing the muscular design expression as it slopes south and tapers to the north, opening views to the Dayun Sport Campus adjacent to the site.

The opening at the top of the tower reduces wind load and creates a space for an outdoor observation area. The articulation of the design is further refined for a fluid and smooth surface. The underside of the opening is envisioned as a colossal projection screen for a visual display program. Retractable vertical seating with multiple levels is stored at the lower portion of the top north wall.

The sports campus and Shenzhen city view are the backdrop of the viewing area, enhanced with the unique sky theater that will attract visitors from around the world. During the day, the wall can be programed with sports coverage of district events or projections of extreme experiences like mountain climbing or hand gliding.

Inspiration

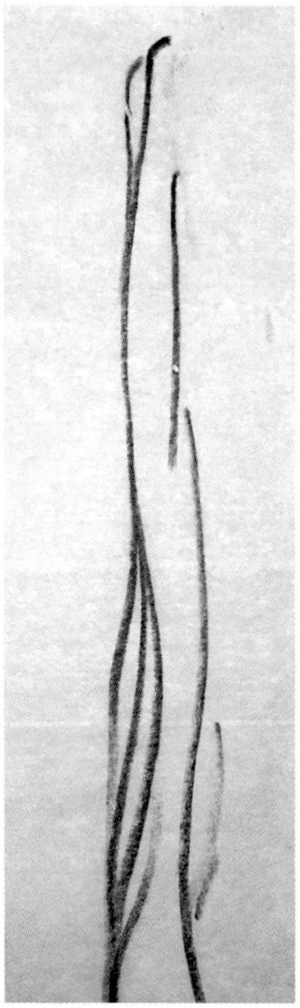

Concept Sketch, 2018

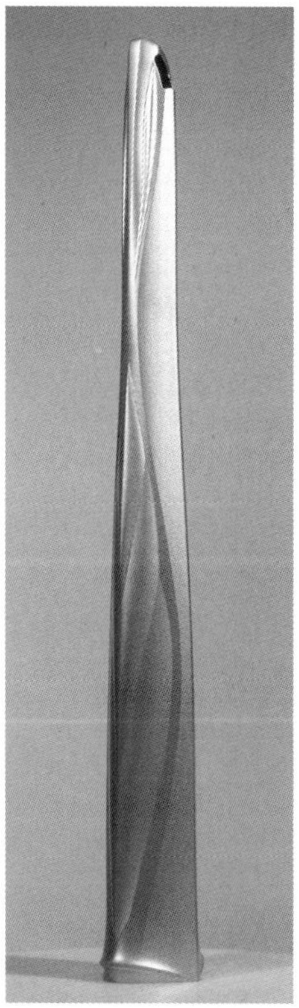

Physical Model

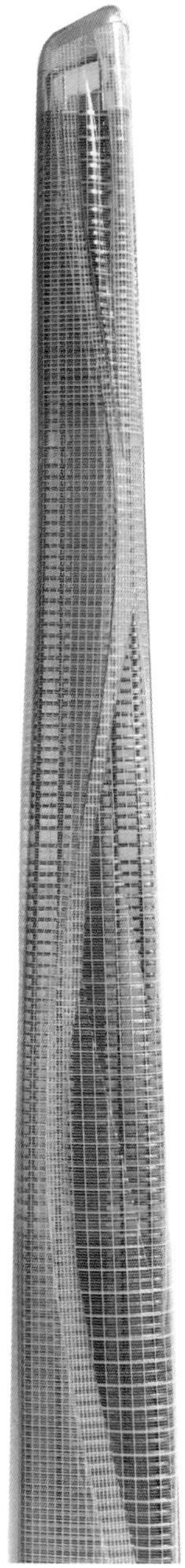

Structural Model

DESIGN CONCEPT | SPACE

Visitors climb a spiral ramp to the rooftop observatory, which is planned to be the premier sky entertainment space in Shenzhen. Inside, guests view an immersive digital club experience where sight, touch, and smell are combined with interactive programs. 3D holograms create a virtual world with depictions of nature, the universe, and other programmable scenes.

Below the immersive experience is an indoor spa, offering activities such as swimming, climbing, and yoga, available to hotel guests and visitors. A hotel club and dining space is located below the spa for a more exclusive experience.

The top experience also allows visitors to observe the advanced technology of the building. The tuned mass damper will be exposed in the main area of the observatory, layered as another dynamic experience for building users.

Observation Deck (Above) | Club Experience (Right + Below)

The environmental goal of the tower is to obtain LEED-Platinum certification; therefore, sustainability is considered in a holistic way. The building is oriented to respond to the existing environmental solar conditions for enhanced passive solar control and high-performance glass further reduces heat gain. Strategic natural lighting in the interior spaces increases human comfort levels.

The observation experience plays a role in the energy efficiency of the tower. The pinnacle is strategically shaped to withstand the winds at the site with a subtly tapering form, rounded corners, and further massing undulation articulation. The top allows wind to pass through without negative effects on the tower. Glass frit options were also studied for shading the exposed observation spaces below.

The project shows the importance of sustaining the culture of the existing site and seeks to become a key activator of the Dayun Sport Campus, by promoting well-being, happiness, efficiency, and comfort with a lifestyle of live-work-play.

> *“Shimao Tower is culturally performance driven, which is often overlooked when discussing the sustainability of a project.*
> *- Gordon Gill, FAIA, Partner,*
> *Adrian Smith + Gordon Gill Architecture”*

Wind Shaping Diagrams | Observation Platform Experience (Right)

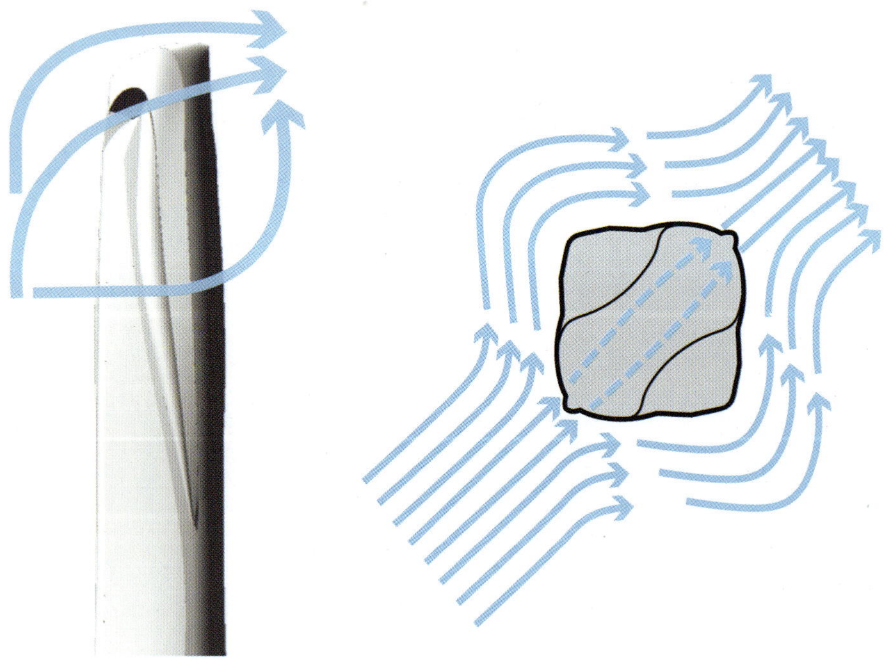

AL WASL PLAZA

Dubai, United Arab Emirates

Framed by five highly sustainable buildings, at 130-meter diameters, Al Wasl Plaza defined the heart of the Expo 2020 Dubai, serving as the central public space during run from October 2021 through March 2022. The lushly landscaped plaza is shaded by a massive trellis that stands 67-meters tall and is veiled in perforated fabric.

The site has transitioned into Expo City Dubai, the post-expo legacy community. The surrounding 500,000 sm of mixed-use buildings now form an urban innovation district that is focused on the intersections between business, technology, and lifestyle. The buildings, streets, and utilities have been repurposed with 1.75 million square-meters available for infill development. Al Wasl Plaza remains the center of activity as a magnet for growth and activity, serving as a dynamic and memorable public space for the district.

Situated in the heart of Dubai, an Emirate within the United Arab Emirates, Expo City Dubai is embarking on a new center at the southern end of the city at the former site of Expo 2020. Positioned to become the next iconic locale, its proximity to the busy Jebel Ali Port, the expanding Al Maktoum Airport, and Dubai Investment Parks ensures its future residents shorter commutes and a model development for the growing Dubai South district.

Function: Performance Space + Public Garden | **Status:** Built, 2021 | **Client:** Expo 2020 Dubai LLC | **Awards:** MIPIM Awards, Best Cultural, Sports & Education Project, Recognition of Excellence, 2023, Architizer A+Awards, Architecture +Joy, Special Mention, 2022; Architecture MasterPrize, Recreational Architecture, Winner, 2022; Dezeen Awards, Cultural Buildings, Longlist, 2022; Re-Thinking the Future Awards, First Award, Cultural Built, 2022; The Chicago Athenaeum, Green Good Design Award, 2022; The Chicago Athenaeum, International Architecture Award, 2021

Strategically located equidistant between Dubai and Abu Dhabi, and directly adjacent to the new Al Maktoum International Airport and Jebel Ali Seaport, Al Wasl Plaza is at the crossroads of global transportation and business. The Dubai Metro connects Expo City Dubai and the new airport to millions of commuters each year. Al Wasl Plaza is the center of activity, acting as a magnet for growth and activity and serving as a dynamic and memorable public space for the district.

Section

Post-Expo Site Rendering | Post-Expo Landscape Diagram (Right)

DESIGN CONCEPT | PROGRAM

As the event space for Expo 2020 Dubai and the current Expo City Dubai, Al Wasl Plaza has the capacity of hosting up to several thousands of people. The program is divided into three rings of activity: the garden, the pedestrian circulation ring, and the cafe zone.

The garden is a sloped "vineyard" configuration featuring landscaped "rooms" for relaxation or activity. During the expo-phase of the project, the garden's central stage hosted the opening and closing ceremonies and daily immersive shows. In the post-expo legacy phase, the space is an open public amenity during the day, offering shade, respite, quiet, and an unparalleled garden experience. At night, the trellis that shades the garden from the sun during the day becomes the ultimate performance space as the world's largest 360-degree immersive projection experience.

The program is complemented with a pedestrian circulation ring that surrounds the garden, acting as a viewing platform for increased attendance during the events. A cafe zone is adjacent to the periphery spaces and is connected to the hotels, food and beverage facilities, and associated administration buildings.

Circulation Ring

Central Stage

Garden

Cafe Zone

Program

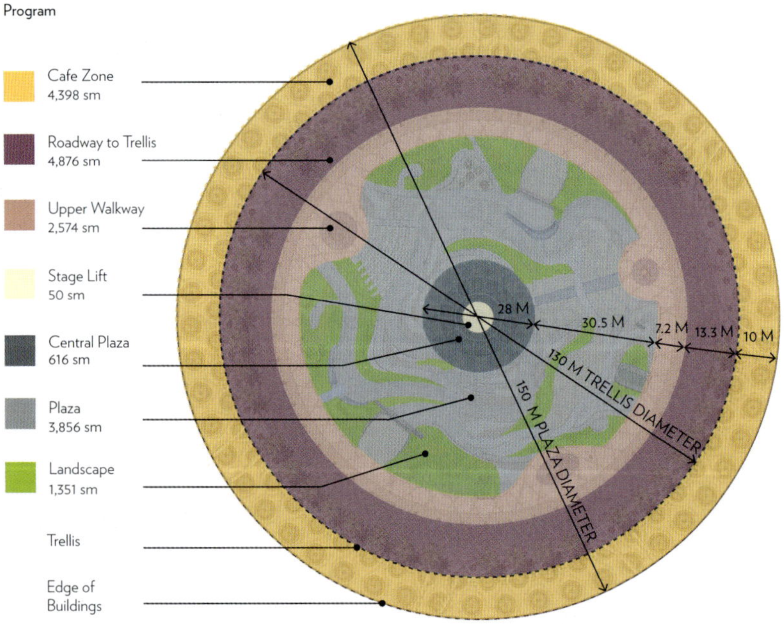

Expo Mode

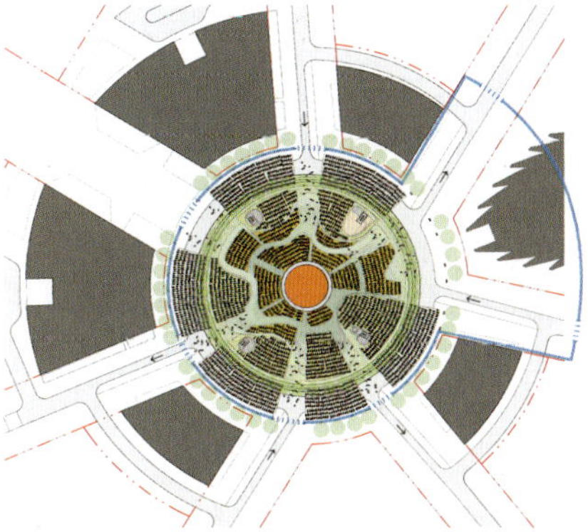

Ceremony Event

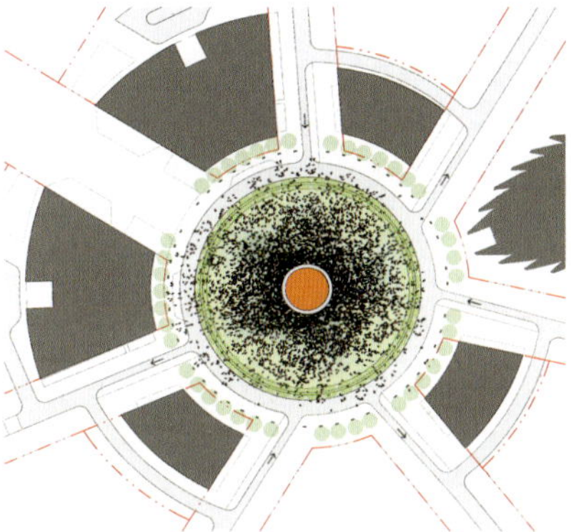

Central Stage Event

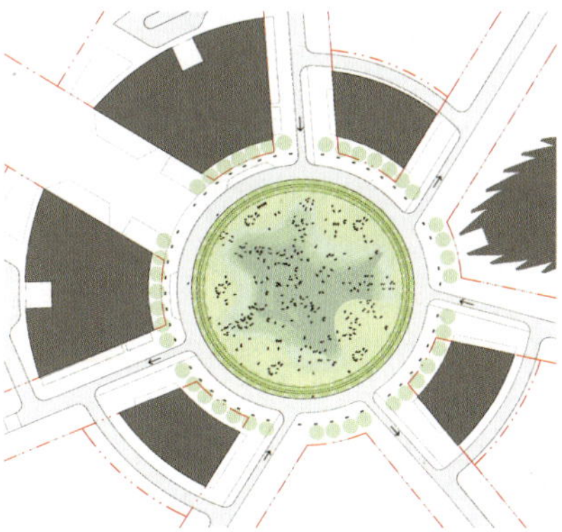

Plaza

Legacy Mode

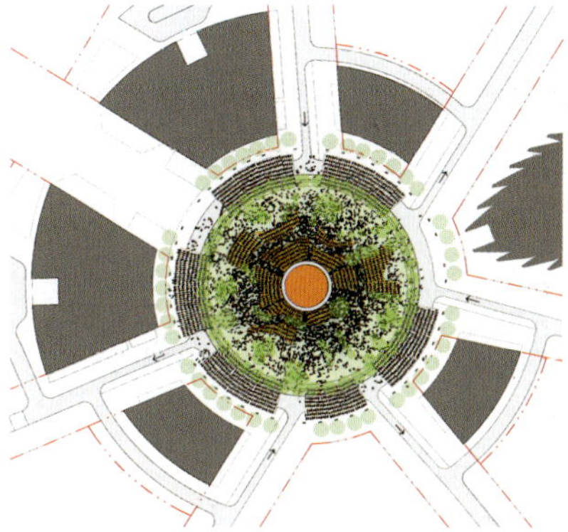

Organized Event

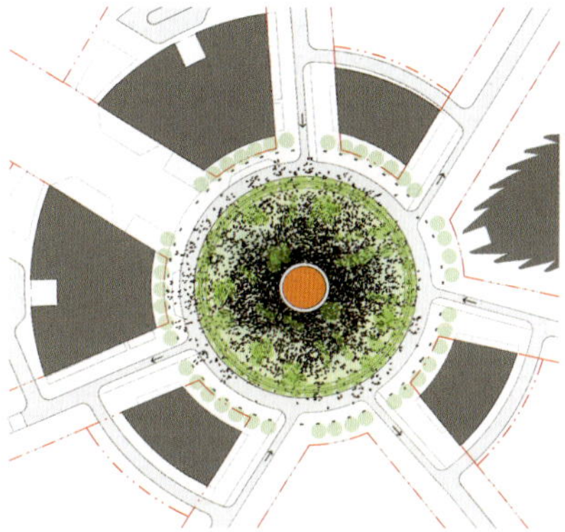

Central Stage Event

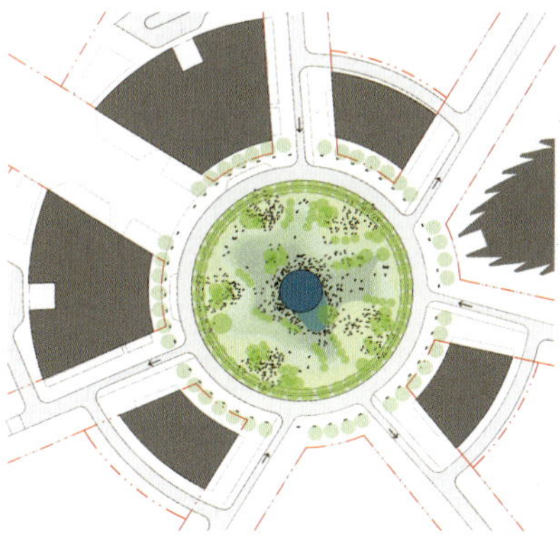

Park

DESIGN CONCEPT | FORM

Al Wasl is the historical name for Dubai, meaning "connection" in Arabic. The name symbolizes Dubai's goal of bringing people together during and after Expo 2020, embodying the plaza's purpose at the center of the site. Al Wasl Plaza is a physical representation of the history, culture, and future of Dubai, sending a strong signal to the future of planning in the region. This ideological shift is a gift to the legacy community and future of those who will work, play, and live in Expo City Dubai for generations.

When designing the form, the goal was to create a formal, yet comfortable space that draws people from all over the world to Dubai. The key design inspiration is based on the translation of the exposition's logo, which was inspired by a recently discovered 4000-year-old Bronze Age ring in the United Arab Emirates. Expo 2020's logo and the pattern of the trellis design inextricably links the history of the expo with Dubai.

Rather than conceiving Al Wasl as a building, it was envisaged as an unparalleled experience, unequaled on a global scale. A place of connection, respite, and interaction of the integrally woven Emirati culture, playfully engaging the visitors' five senses.

> "*Al Wasl is about people. The magnificent showpiece will host the opening, closing and main events along with a variety of other special occasions during the six-month celebration of culture and creativity.*"
> *- Zoe Mutter, Editor, AV Magazine, 2013-2020*

Form Inspiration | Physical Model (Right)

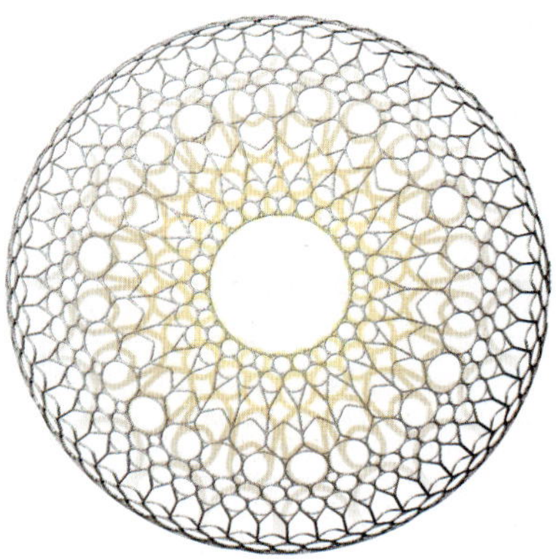

DESIGN CONCEPT | SPACE

These seemingly opposing programs of "respite" and "spectacle" are intentionally merged in the space. The idea for this new typology of civic space is that it is literally an urban room that can offer the unique extremes of reflection and excitement with an invigorating visual concert experience. The technology and scale of the veiled ceiling helps the visitor feel that they are not in an enclosed space. The buildings that frame the plaza are "front row seats" to the venue.

Landscaped with native plants and water features, the abundant garden is as a public gathering space where visitors can engage in the simple aspects of life that are often the most meaningful: enjoying nature, walking with family and friends, or simply gazing up and appreciating the stars in the desert sky. Since transition to Expo City Dubai, Al Wasl Plaza has hosted live including music acts Coldplay and Alicia Keys, iconic composers John Williams and Hans Zimmer, and major events such as the Cop28 Climate Conference and the UAE National Day.

Garden Concept Sketch, 2018

Al Wasl Plaza Garden Rendering (Below + Right)

District
2020
OFFICE
HOTEL

Projection Experience Rendering

Al Wasl Plaza's trellis serves as a surface for shading and air flow regulation and as a massive projection canvas. Clad with 631 PTFE fiberglass mesh panels encompassing an area of 17,500 square-meters, the permeable mesh fabric has a density of 20% open area to provide shade from the intense Middle Eastern sun, while simultaneously allowing diffuse light to penetrate to the garden below and wind to pass through.

The resulting interplay between the fabric and steel superstructure results in a playful and dynamic light and shadow play on the ground surface that is in constant flux. During the evening, the fabric is re-purposed as the projection canvas for the world's largest 360-degree immersive experience. The projected images on the perforated mesh can be viewed from both the interior and exterior of the trellis, acting as a glowing luminous beacon of the district.

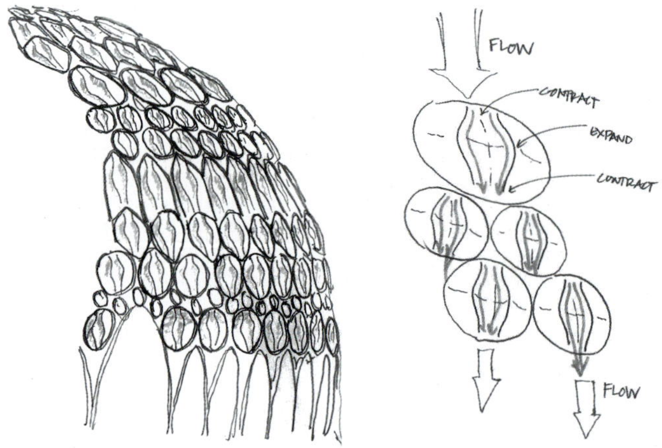

Seaming Sketches, 2018

Trellis + Garden | Light + Shadow Play Physical Model (Below)

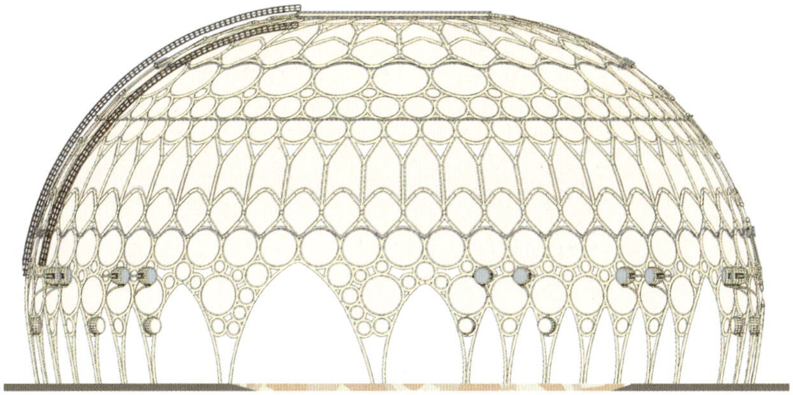

Trellis Elevation

DESIGN CONCEPT | MATERIALS

The immersive experience represents a progressive and iterative approach to realize a world's first. The process involved a collaborative team ranging from projection specialists and fabrication experts in close coordination with the AS+GG design team.

Numerous materials were researched to find the appropriate canvas fabric for the trellis structure. Once chosen, a process of testing for surface saturation, clarity, and visual acuity was undertaken to validate the effectiveness of the projection. A projection setup of 252 state-of-the-art RGB lasers in sets of six are utilized to display a 4K resolution image over 17,000 square-meters of the trellis dome. Each mapping zone receives projection from three projectors for increased brightness, vibrancy, and color saturation.

The projectors and associated MEP are contained in custom housings that were inspired by airplane nacelles. Constructed as monocoque shells entirely from aluminum, the nacelles provide a lightweight design that embraces its form, functionality, structure, and design in one move.

Projector Housing Units

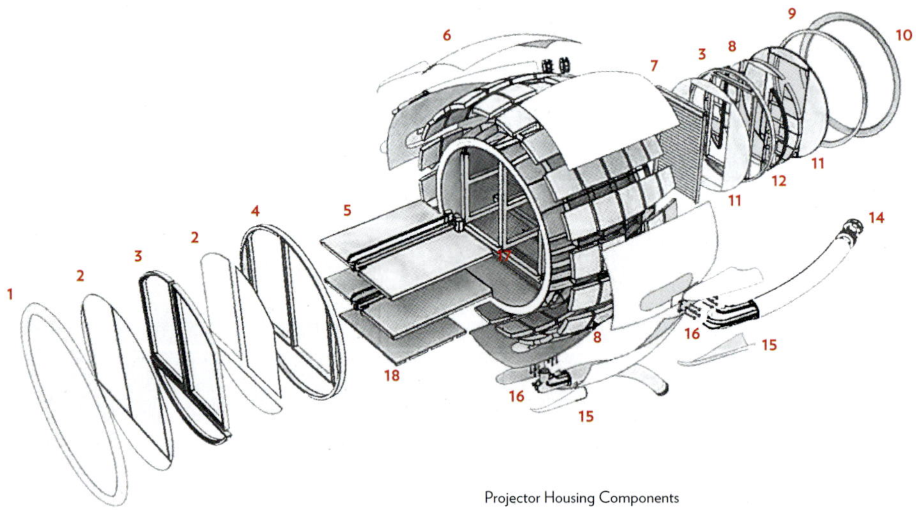

Projector Housing Components

1 Aluminum Ring
2 Glass
3 Aluminum Frame
4 Aluminum Fixed Frame
5 Projector Trays
6 Aluminum Shell
7 Roll-up Door
8 Insulation
9 Aluminum Inner Ring
10 Aluminum Outer Ring
11 Aluminum Panel
12 Aluminum Substructure
13 Aluminum Panel
14 Flange
15 GFRP Arm
16 Structural Arm
17 Tray Structure
18 Chiller Tray

Projection Mapping Zones

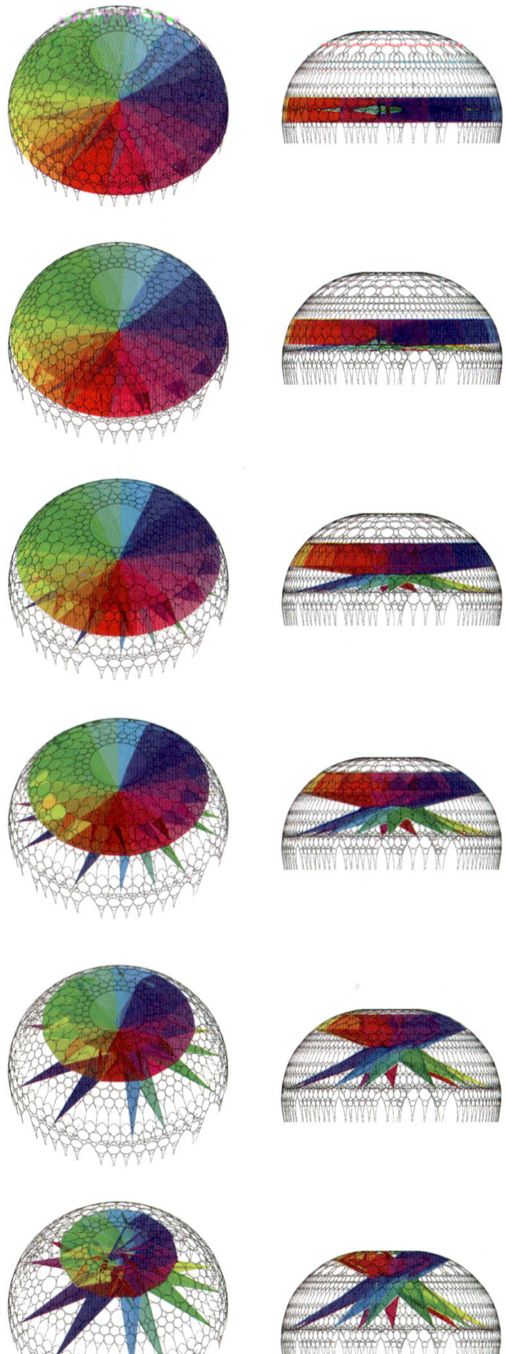

Acoustical design was another critical factor in the Al Wasl experience. Careful analysis and simulations of high and low frequency ranges informed the placement of the speaker and subwoofer arrays around the interior perimeter of the trellis. The sound system is equipped with speaker arrays capable of 10-degree inter-element angles stacks and a usable bandwidth of 35Hz to 20kHz at (-10dB), and high-powered subwoofers with a bandwidth down to 25Hz at (-10dB) and maximum SPL2 of 143dB.

Typically, in exterior applications, speakers are exposed and hung in a utilitarian manner, which can cause acoustic leakage from behind the sound producing elements. Because sound waves are spherical, the outward travels in all dimensions. This was undesirable and required a mitigation strategy. To control this phenomenon, the speakers and subwoofers are housed within acoustically engineered nacelles, similar in construction to the projector nacelles, but fundamentally different in objective and function.

Each nacelle is comprised of acoustically opaque and transparent portions. The top and rear portion of the nacelle are acoustically opaque by means of a 100mm thick ultra-high-performance concrete layer, which reflects the sound waves back toward the intended direction. The front and underneath sides use an acoustically transparent specialized fabric that allows sound waves to pass through while protecting the speaker equipment from the exterior environment. Together, these strategies work holistically to ensure the immersive experience auditory component is projected into the full volume of the trellis.

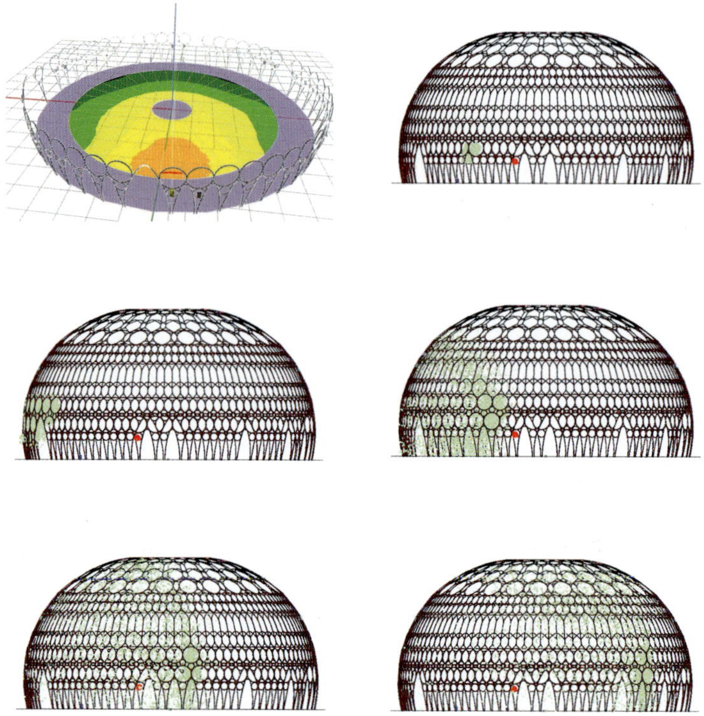

Acoustical Analysis

Speaker Housing Unit | Al Wasl Hosts Coldplay (Right)

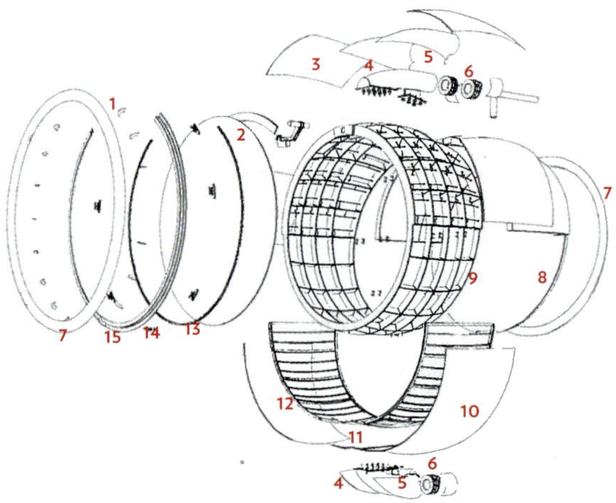

Speaker Housing

1 Ring Ribs
2 Air Mesh
3 Aluminum Shell
4 Structural Arm
5 FRP Arm Shell
6 Flange
7 Aluminum Rings
8 GFRC Shell
9 Aluminum Radial and Axial Ribs
10 Air Mesh
11 Panel
12 Mesh Aluminum Sub-Structure
13 Aluminum Profile 2
14 Magnetic Latches
15 Aluminum Profile 1

Studies related to microclimate formed a foundation for the iterative design process, which provided invaluable insight into aspects of temperature control, wind dynamics, shading, daylighting, and psychrometry. Given the constant intense heat throughout a much of the year in the United Arab Emirates, a primary goal was to create occupiable outdoor spaces that are comfortable for users. This implication requires the design to include aspects of flora in addition to synthetic strategies.

Al Wasl's garden provides an immediate result in controlling the temperature through the introduction of soft surfaces and plantings native to the UAE. The trellis structure adds a secondary layer that enhances the microclimate. Permeable mesh fabric reduces the intensity of direct light, which is diffused to acceptable levels for occupancy while allowing sufficient light to reach the plants below.

A permeable filigree at the base of the trellis works with the oculus 67 meters above, drawing in cooler air from the surrounding ground plane and exhausting hot air through the oculus. Through CFD Analysis, this strategy proved to be a successful passive method for providing cooling, similar in function to the traditional Barjeel wind tower, used in the Middle East for centuries.

Wind Tunnel Model

Wind Tunnel Model

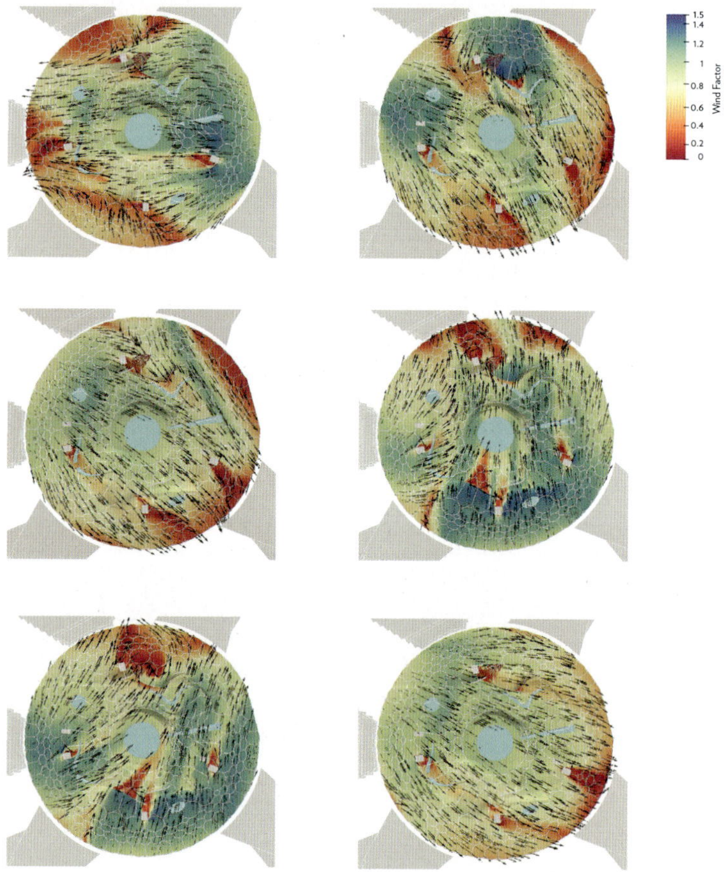

Relative Wind Velocity Analysis

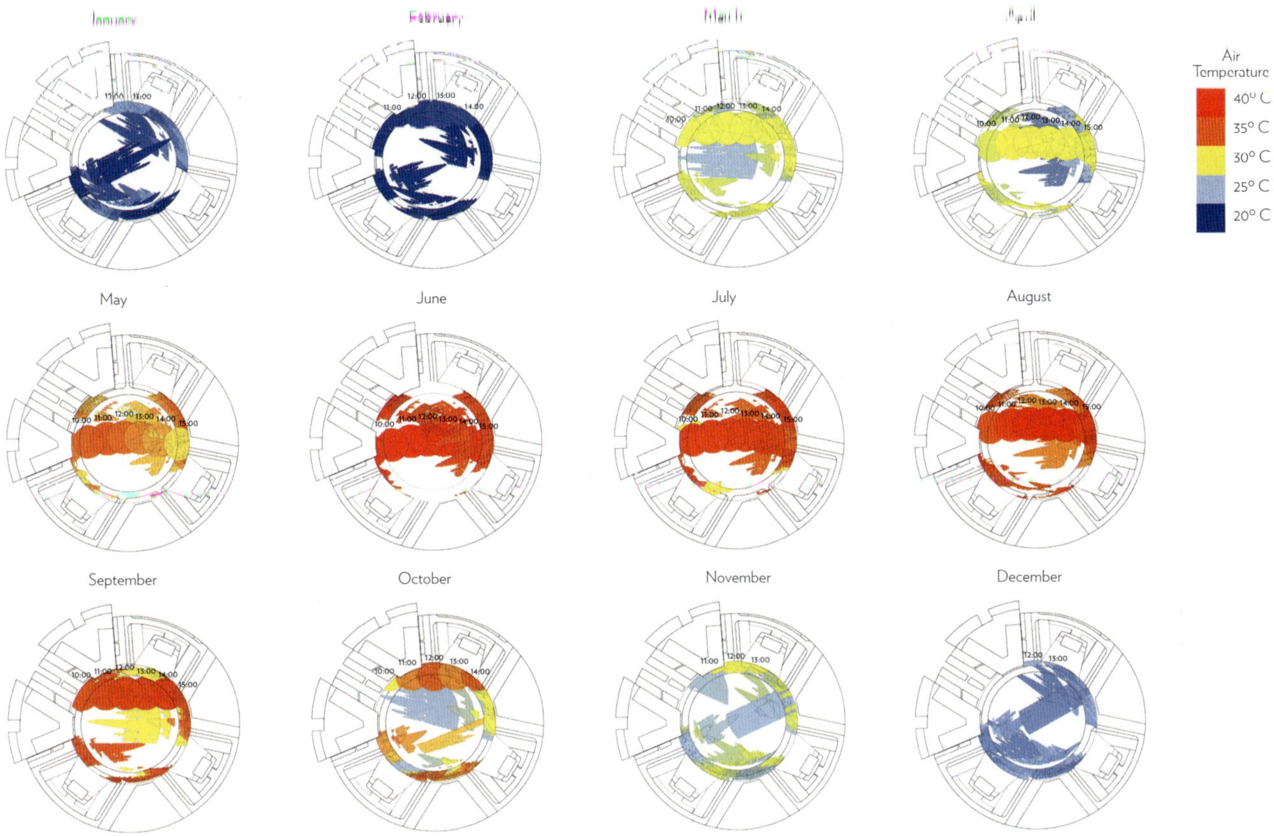

Average Temperatures at Plaza Level over 24 Hours

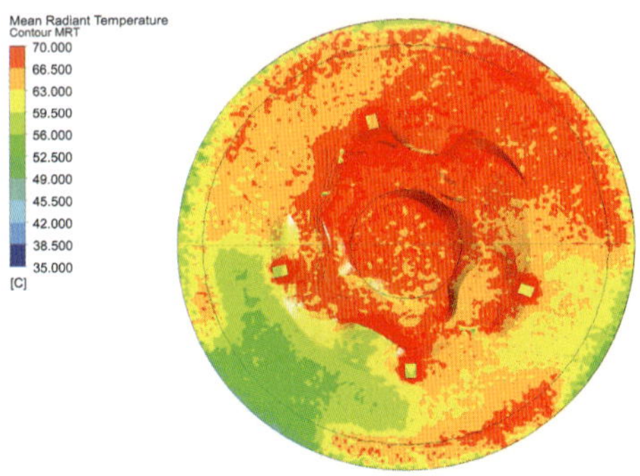

Mean Radiant Temperature Without Trellis
(Summer Solstice)

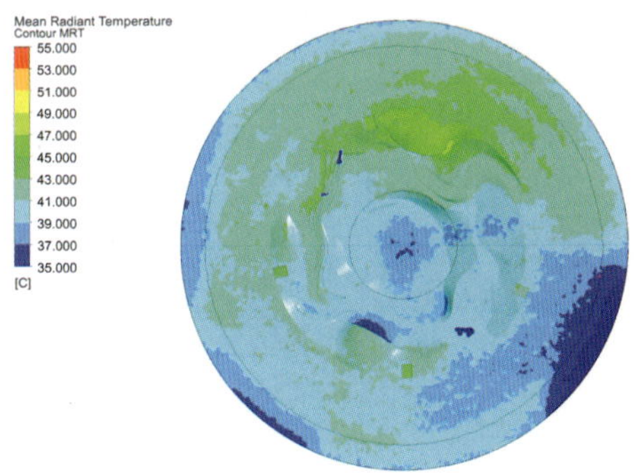

Mean Radiant Temperature With Trellis
(Summer Solstice)

ASTANA DISCOVERY CENTER

Astana, Kazakhstan

The Astana Discovery Center was designed as the final piece of the Expo 2017 Legacy Plan, a roadmap to transform 2017's International Exposition site and associated buildings into a permanent development with technical, cultural, and civic opportunities.

The center's design is a simple, elegant structure for indoor activities that are particularly important for regions like Astana, which have long, cold winters. The new building stretches beyond its footprint, with underground glass cupolas, or "biodomes," that cover pedestrian pathways.

A main feature is the grand botanical garden with a glass facade facing the Nur Alem science museum, the site's main focal point that was discussed in the previous chapter. Behind the transparent facade a multipurpose media surface displays digital information such as educational forums, concerts, arts, and revenue generating advertisements.

The Expo 2017 Master Plan established the vision of a cohesive collection of buildings, programs, and public spaces that worked together to successfully host the Astana 2017 World Expo. In the legacy mode, the master plan has continued to be a business and cultural destination as the Astana International Financial Center (AIFC), which opened in 2019.

Function: Assembly + Observation | **Status:** Conceptual, 2021 | **Client:** Mabetex Group

DESIGN CONCEPT | SITE

The Astana Discovery Center is designed for the site's northwest quadrant, which is currently an under-utilized outdoor plaza. This completes the circular plan and reinforces the position of Nur Alem as the centerpiece of the site, further strengthening the spatial relationship with the Astana Congress Center on the opposite end. The site's concept creates a network of spaces that are linked physically and programmatically, offering a multi-dimensional venue that can be experienced by a wide range of users in multiple ways. The main concept is to convert the Expo Boulevard into a covered street for commercial activities and large exhibitions such as car shows or other large-scale exhibits. This covered street is envisioned as a flexible space that can louver open in the summer and be sealed in the winter.

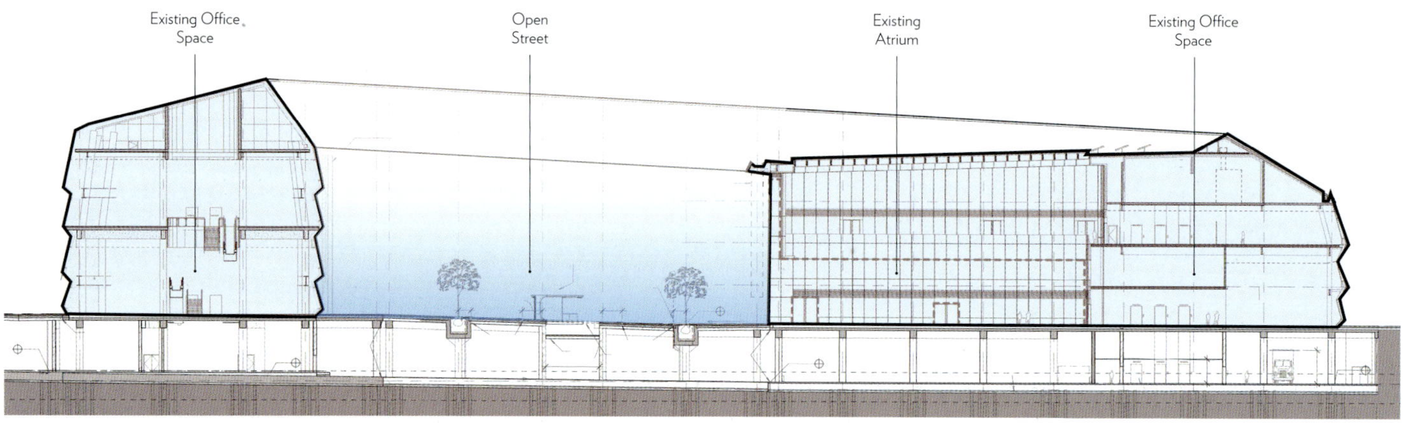

Current Street Section

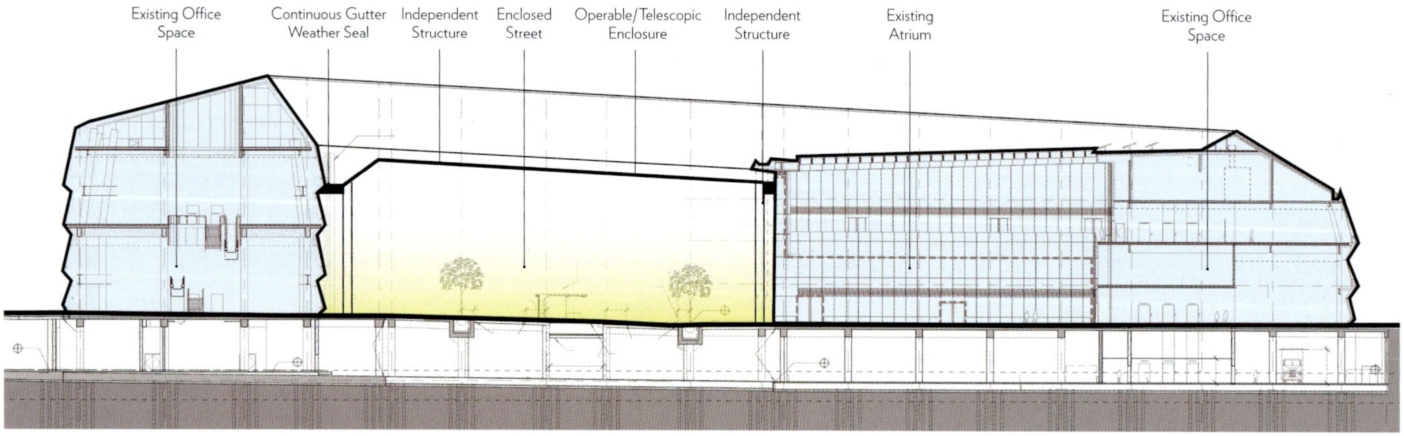

Proposed Street Section

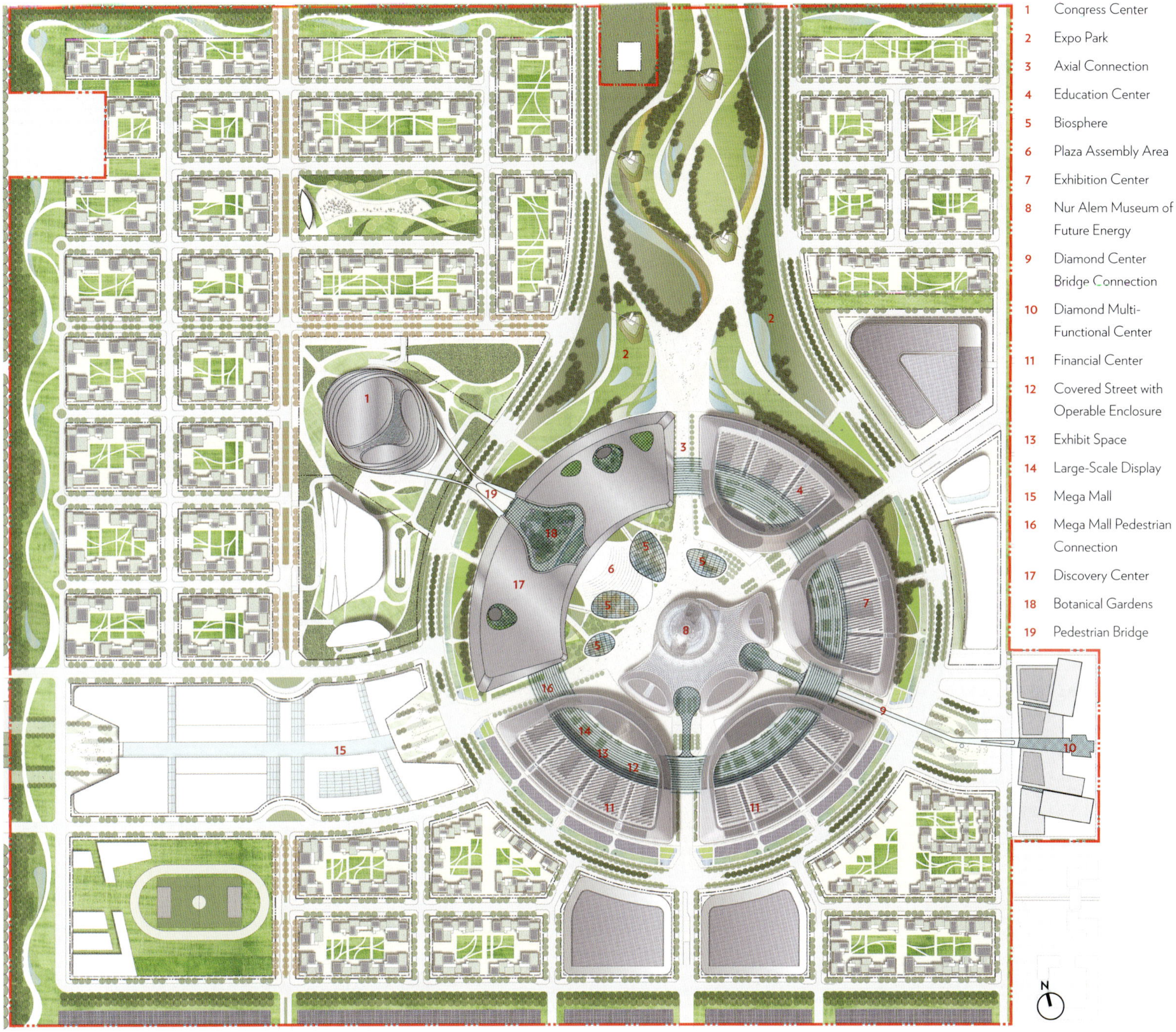
1 Conqress Center
2 Expo Park
3 Axial Connection
4 Education Center
5 Biosphere
6 Plaza Assembly Area
7 Exhibition Center
8 Nur Alem Museum of Future Energy
9 Diamond Center Bridge Connection
10 Diamond Multi-Functional Center
11 Financial Center
12 Covered Street with Operable Enclosure
13 Exhibit Space
14 Large-Scale Display
15 Mega Mall
16 Mega Mall Pedestrian Connection
17 Discovery Center
18 Botanical Gardens
19 Pedestrian Bridge
N

Site Plan

DESIGN CONCEPT | PROGRAM

Programmatically, the Discovery Center provides functions that did not exist in Astana at the time of design. Interior spaces include a grand botanical garden where visitors can enjoy a world-class indoor park. A research facility can provide curated ecology content and work in association with international universities on extended educational projects. The center can also have less conventional programs that can engage the arts, culture, and entertainment of the district such a media center, a boutique hotel, and other retail opportunities.

Gallery Walk | Botanical Garden (Right)

Program Section

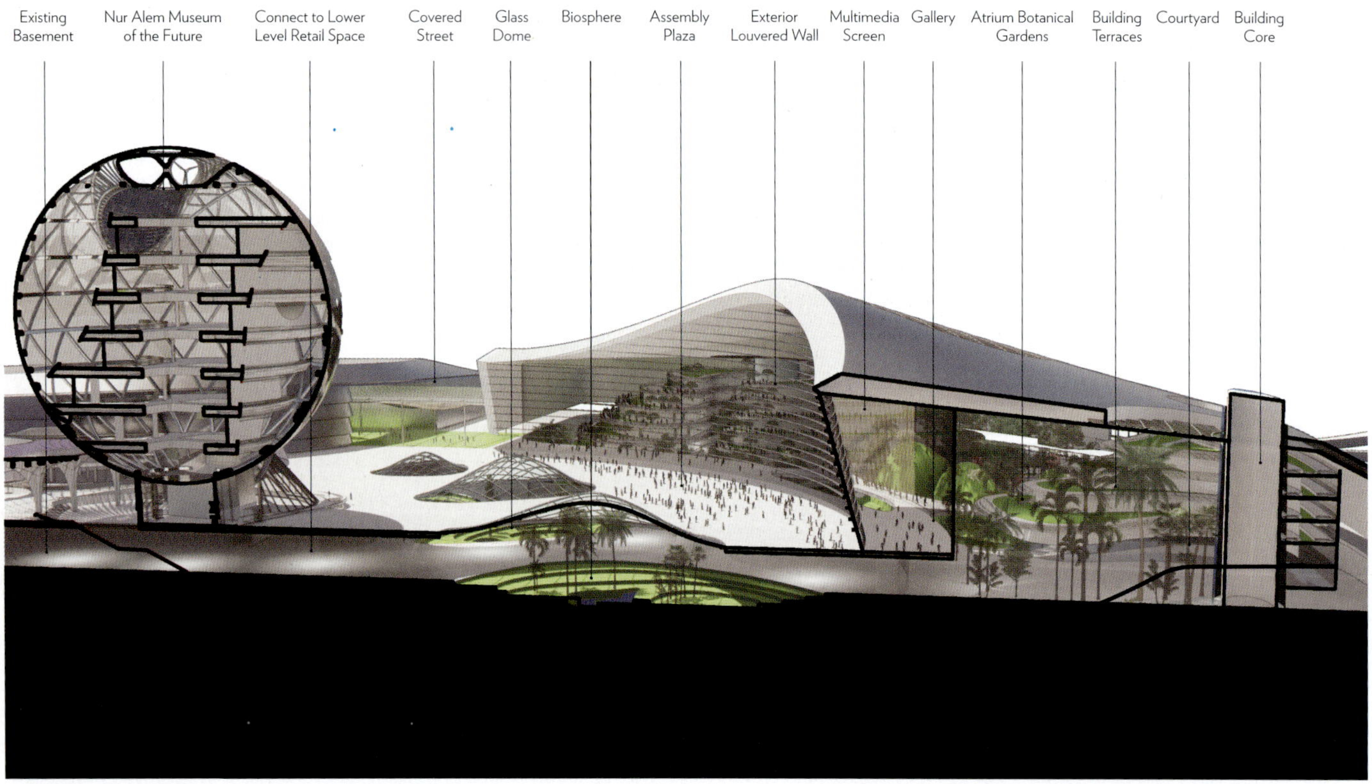

DESIGN CONCEPT | FORM

The catalyst for building the Discovery Center was to improve the functionality of the frequently unused plaza space on the northwest corner of the expo site. During the planning of Expo 2017, AS+GG originally envisioned the Astana Art Center—an art gallery and museum that we explore in the previous chapter—to fill this quadrant in the circular plan. However, the design was not realized, and the space was used as an open public gathering space during the exposition.

The main design approach is one of connectivity and adaptability, therefore a minimal form that slips contextually into the site was designed for the hybrid program. The building frames the plaza in front of the Nur Alem Museum of Future Energy, serving as the roof of a pedestrian connection under the plaza that connects the lower level of the museum to the site's outer ring. This configuration closes the loop to create a fully integrated network of spaces.

Lower Level Retail

EMBRACE THE MASTER PLAN

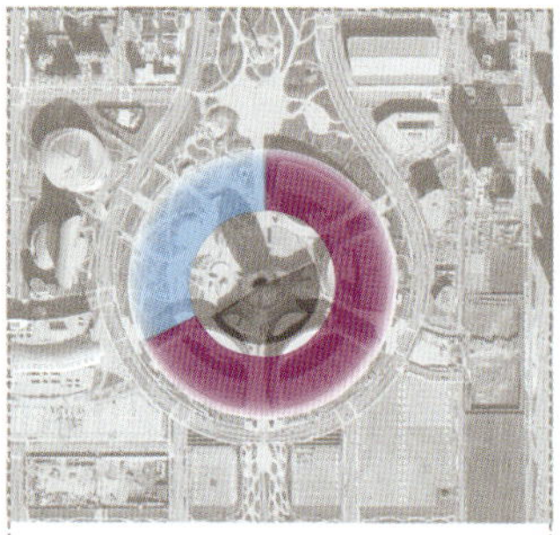

Maintain the character of the master plan and its architecture

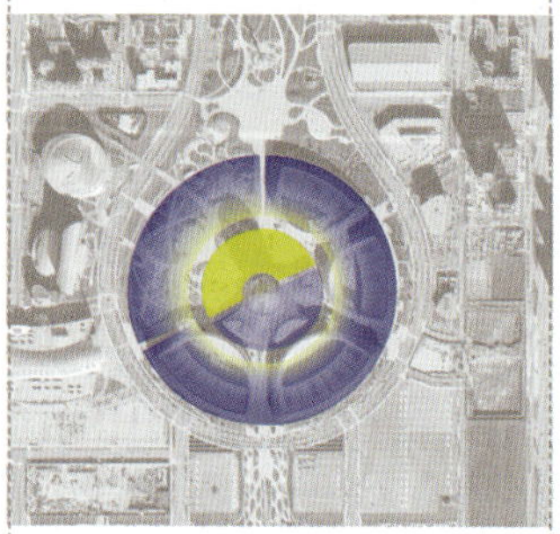

Define a plaza space to serve as an assembly location

OFFER AN EXPERIENCE

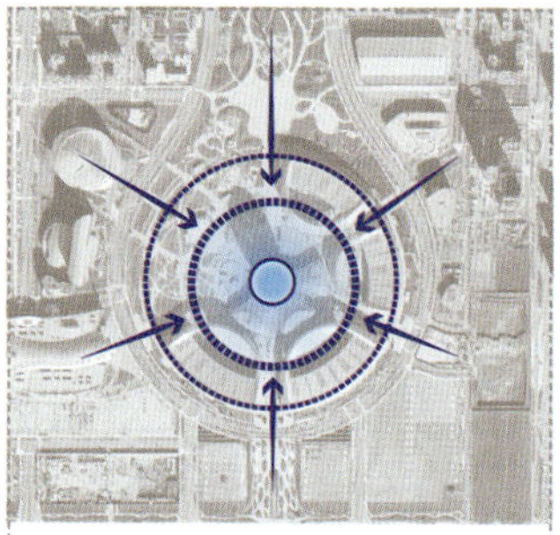

Further establish the Expo 2017 site as an iconic destination

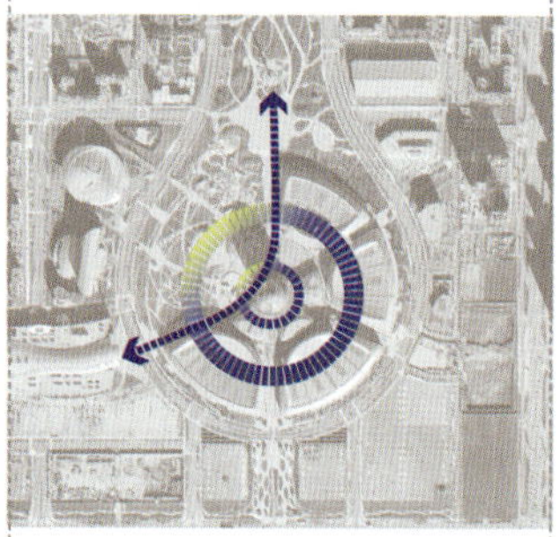

Enhance the public realm experience and relationships

DEFINE A LANDSCAPE

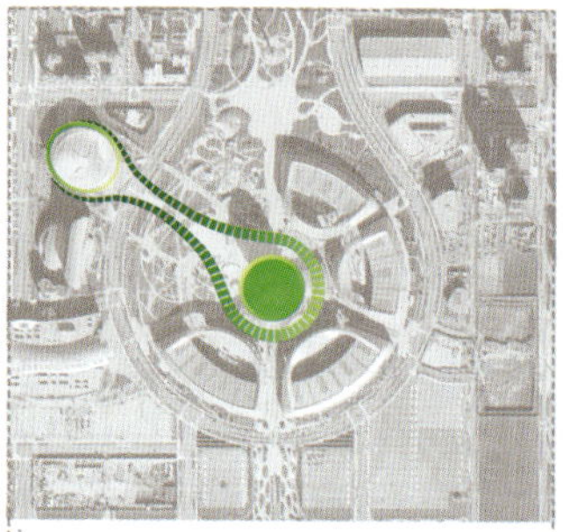

Address the relationship with the Congress Center

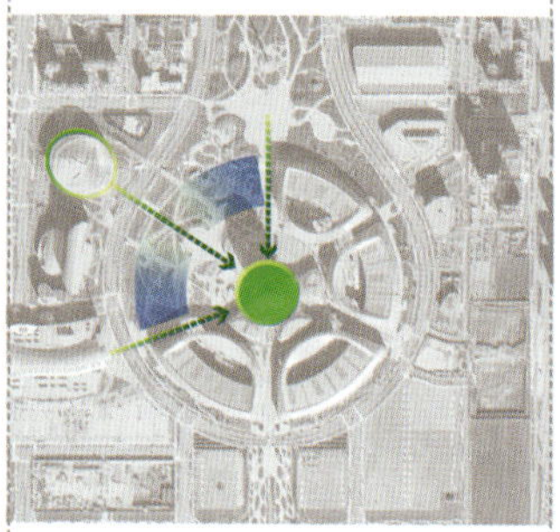

Maintain visual access to Nur Alem

INTERVENTION STRATEGIES

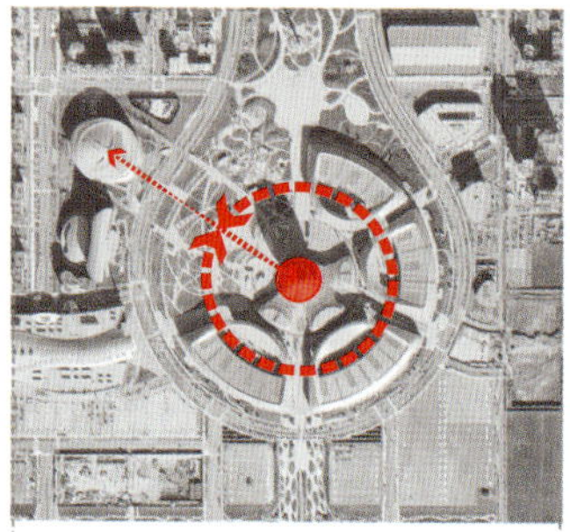

Create a continuous loop for full interconnectivity

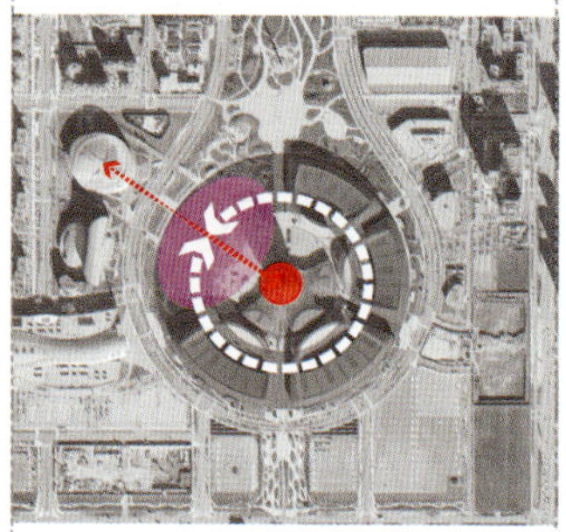

Create an iconic moment/event/program

DESIGN CONCEPT | SPACE

The biodome gardens are indoor, sunken landscapes that are beneath the plaza and span the space between the center and the Nur Alem museum. Covered by domed glass, the space is a retreat from the harsh winters in Astana. The gardens have native tree species such as birch, aspen, and pine, as well as local plants Steppe Dwarf Cherry, Ludwig Iris, and Box Elder. The space can also be used to cultivate rare plantings such as Shrenkii Tulips and Starfruit, both which are designated as vulnerable in the region. Plantings can be used for scientific purposes, including educational and medicinal applications.

Site Plan | Biodome Gardens (Right)

1 Congress Center
2 Pedestrian Bridge
3 Arrival Connection
4 Atrium Garden
5 Hotel
6 Hotel Atrium + Gardens
7 Park Connection
8 Gallery
9 Glass Dome Over Biodome
10 Nur Alem Museum of Future Energy
11 Covered Street
12 Diamond Center Connection
13 Covered Street Connection
14 Assembly Plaza
15 Research Center
16 Green Terraces
17 Media Screen

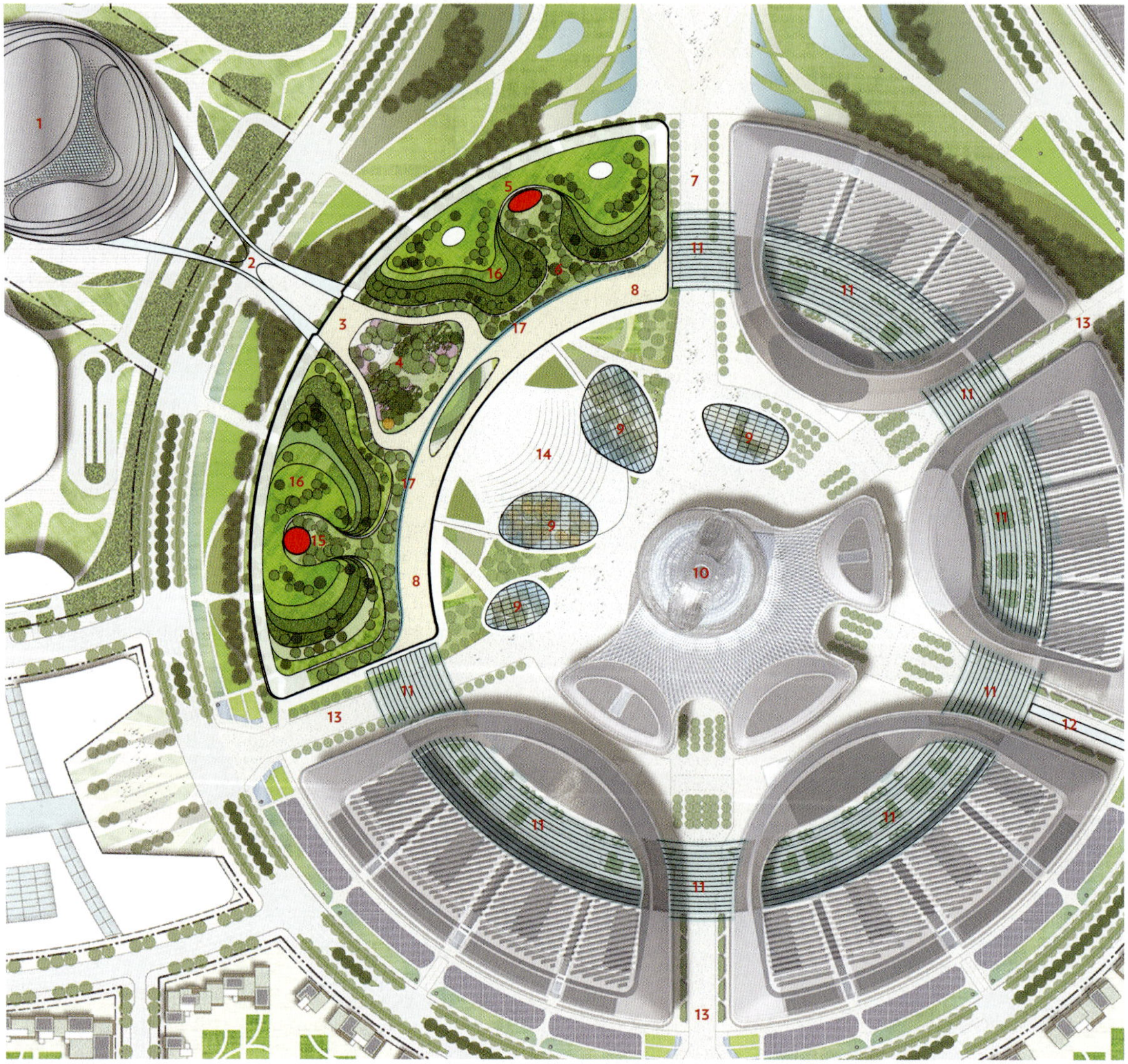

The arching gesture of the Discovery Center's exterior wall has full-height views of the plaza and Nur Alem. The curvature glass may require double-curved glazing. As you enter, the arrival gallery walls are covered with a diaphanous scrim, which is a semi-opaque fabric that we used successfully for the Al Wasl Plaza, the dome centerpiece for Expo 2020 that we discuss in the previous pages of this chapter. This material is proposed to be a mega screen that uses projection mapping technologies.

The screen can serve as a multi-dimensional venue that submerges the visitor in state-of-the-art virtual reality journeys and holographic concerts. The surface can display a variety of information including art displays, educational announcements, and commercial content. Analysis was conducted using the Exterior PixLine 10, a linear LED video fixture used for media facades and creative installations. This active facade can also coordinate with the celebratory lighting already found embedded in the exterior wall of the adjacent the Nur Alem sphere.

Site at Night with Media Wall | Virtual Reality Options (Right)

APPENDIX

TEAM

Contributions

Performance + Assembly: The Experience of Space would not have been possible without the efforts of our talented and dedicated project teams. Please find in the following pages a comprehensive list of Architects, Designers, and Consultants who worked on the projects featured in this book.

For the readers' reference, we have also provided a list of awards and major publications for each project.

We would also like to thank the photographers who have contributed many of the images in the book and are also credited in the following pages.

Project Team - Awards + Publications - Photography + Images

PROJECT TEAM

Istanbul Cultural Center

Design Partners	Adrian Smith and Gordon Gill
Management Partner	Robert Forest
Project Manager	Matthew Dumich
Design Director	Alejandro Stochetti
Senior Designer	Luis Palacio
Sustainability Director	Christopher Drew
Technical Director	Jorge Soler
Designers/Architects	Frederik Berte, Nathan Diestelkamp, Rezvan Farahany, Jennie Matusova, Christopher Miller, Zhaochen Wang, Timothy Winstanley

Astana Energy Hall

Design Partners	Adrian Smith and Gordon Gill
Management Partner	Robert Forest
Project Manager	Brian M. Jack and Matthew Dumich
Design Director	Alejandro Stochetti
Senior Designer	Anthony Viola
Interiors Director	Marc Cerone
Sustainability Director	Christopher Drew
Technical Director	Jorge Soler
Senior Technical	Alyson Hurd Sternquist
Designers/Architects	Iliana Doytcheva, Natalya Ganyukova, Dimitra Gelagoti, Felix Griggs, Kira Ho, Liam Lowry, Jaclyn Marcus, Chris Miller, Miriam Neet, Natalia Quintanilla, Matt Simpson, Zilong Tan, Alex Valverde, Klarke Wang, Kirsten Weismantle
General Contractor	SEMBOL Construction
Design Manager	IT Engineering
Structural Engineer	Werner Sobek
Facade Access	Altitude Facade Access Consulting
Fire Life Safety	AON
Building Information Specialist	CASE
Theater Planning/Acoustics	Charcoalblue
Wind Engineer	RWDI
HVAC/MEP Engineer	PositivEnergy Practice
Civil Engineer	V3 Companies
Vertical Transportation	Fortune Shepler Saling
Geotechnical Engineer	GEI Consultants
Construction Manager	Rider Levett Bucknall

Shattuck St. Mary's Performance Hall

Design Partners	Adrian Smith and Gordon Gill
Management Partner	Robert Forest
Project Manager	Matthew Dumich
Senior Designer	Sobieslaw Fedyk
Interiors Director	Marc Cerone
Sustainability Director	Christopher Drew
Technical Director	Jorge Soler
Designers/Architects	Nicholas Berchtold, Natalia Quintanilla, Matthew Snoap, James Struthers

Congress Center

Design Partners	Adrian Smith and Gordon Gill
Management Partner	Robert Forest
Project Manager	Brian M. Jack, Matthew Dumich
Design Director	Alejandro Stochetti
Senior Designer	Miguel Alvarez
Interiors Director	Marc Cerone
Sustainability Director	Christopher Drew
Technical Director	Jorge Soler
Senior Technical	Chad Smith
Designers/Architects	Ross Battoclette, Frederik Berte, Iliana Doytcheva, Christopher Drew, Natalya Ganyukova, Dimitra Gelagoti, Felix Griggs, Jaclyn Marcus, Jennie Matusova, Chris Miller, Natalia Quintanilla, Thomas Schneider, Alex Semochkin, Matt Simpson, Donald Stark, Zilong Tan, Kirsten Weismantle, Timothy Winstanley
General Contractor	SEMBOL Construction
Design Manager	IT Engineering
Structural Engineer	Werner Sobek
Facade Access	Altitude Facade Access Consulting
Fire & Life Safety	AON
Building Information Specialist	CASE
Theater Planning/Acoustics	Charcoalblue
Wind Engineer	RWDI
HVAC/MEP Engineer	PositivEnergy Practice
Civil Engineer	V3 Companies
Vertical Transportation	Fortune Shepler Saling
Geotechnical Engineer	GEI Consultants
Construction Manager	Rider Levett Bucknall

Willow Creek North Shore

Design Partners	Adrian Smith and Gordon Gill
Management Partner	Robert Forest
Project Manager	Jonathan Orlove
Senior Designer	Sara Beardsley
Interiors Director	John Burcher and Marc Cerone
Sustainability Director	Christopher Drew
Technical Director	Sae Huang Oh
Designers/Architects	George Baciu, Connor Borchardt, John Campbell, Sally Cathcart, Rebecca Cryder, Nathan Diestelkamp, Elliot Eakin, Rezvan Farahany, Kyle Faulkner, Joshua Frank, Gail Goldstead, Felix Griggs, Patrick Keeney, Ryan Kukuraitis, Rebecca LeMaster, Mateusz Nosek, Darcy Osting, Michelle Pak, Natalia Quintanilla, Catherine Rogg, Chris Strasser, Paul Thong, Luis Villafane, Jiajing Xie, Wie Yu
General Contractor	Glenn H Johnson Construction
Structural Engineer	Forefront Structural Engineers
Civil Engineer	Haeger Engineering
MEP Engineer	Sun Mechanical Systems
Acoustics/Audio-Visual	Clark
Fire & Life Safety	Fire Control Inc.
Landscape	The Brickman Group

The Yard at Chicago Shakespeare Theater

Design Partners	Adrian Smith and Gordon Gill
Management Partner	Robert Forest
Project Manager	Ben Johnson
Senior Designer	Juan Betancur
Interiors Director	Marc Cerone
Sustainability Director	Christopher Drew
Technical Director	Jorge Soler
Senior Technical	Chad Smith
Designers/Architects	Nora Ames, Nicholas Berchtold, Rebecca Cryder, Stephen Dinnen, Felix Griggs, Gail Goldstead, Travis Howe, Joel Kerner, Robert Jillson, Rebecca LeMaster, Jennie Matusova, Chris Miller, Katrina Fernandez Nova, Darcy Osting, Andy Park, Natalia Quintanilla, Thomas Schneider, Matthew Snoap, Melissa Marrero, Jeff Snodgrass, Donald Stark, Milica Stojsavljevic, James Struthers, Maria Sturchio, Michelle Swanson, Jennie Tolfa, Alex Valverde, Zhaochen Wang
General Contractor	Bulley & Andrews
Theater Designer	Charcoalblue
Structural Engineer	Thornton Tomasetti
MEP Engineer	Environmental Systems Design
Lighting Designer	Gwen Grossman Lighting Design
Civil Engineer	V3 Companies
Landscape	The Brickman Group
Fire & Life Safety	Jensen Hughes, Inc.
Seating Tower Design	Show Canada
Theatre System	ICL Architects
Digital Survey	Viatechnik

PROJECT TEAM

Steppenwolf Theatre Campus Expansion

Design Partners	Adrian Smith and Gordon Gill
Management Partner	Robert Forest
Project Manager	Jonathan Orlove
Interiors Director	Marc Cerone
Senior Designer	Laura Jimenez
Technical Director	Jorge Soler
Senior Technical	Sara Beardsley
Designers/Architects	Nora Ames, George Baciu, Jade Boudreaux, Allison Conley, Jennifer Cooper, Rebecca Cryder, Kiel Fahnstrom, Kyle Faulkner, Sobieslaw Fedyk, Felix Griggs, Gail Goldstead, Brandon Kroger, Yuchen Liu, Melissa Marrero, Jose Marti, Heidi Nickel, Luis Palacio, Griffin Pemberton, Michael Sandrzyk, Arham Siddiqui, Chad Smith, Donald Stark, Jennie Tolfa, Alyson Velazquez, Timothy Winstanley
General Contractor	Norcon Inc.
Client Representative	CBRE
Theater Designer	Charcoalblue
Structural Engineer	Thornton Tomasetti
MEP Engineer	Environmental Systems Design
Lighting Designer	Morlights
Civil Engineer	Spaceco
Landscape	Oslund and Associates
Fire & Life Safety	Jensen Hughes, Inc.
Signage/Wayfinding	Studio Blue
Bar Designer	FC Studio
Telecommunications	Client First

FKI Tower Conference Podium

Design Partners	Adrian Smith and Gordon Gill
Management Partner	Robert Forest
Project Manager	Brian M. Jack and Ben Johnson
Interiors Director	John Burcher
Senior Designer	Juan Betancur and Anthony Viola
Technical Director	Sae Hwang Oh
Designers/Architects	Elyse Agnello, Miguel Alvarez, Olga Anaya, Sara Beardsley, Rachael Bennett, Alexis Burson, Marc Cerone, April Chen, Colin Craig, Rebecca Cryder, Michelle Dumont, Patrick Fitzpatrick, Danielle Gharst, Brendan Gibbons, Felix Griggs, Ryan Hayes, Gregg Herman, Kira Ho, Jessica Hogue, Brian Hubbard, Jeffrey Knapke, So Young Lee, Soeun Lee, David LeFevre, Michael Newton, Vanessa Newton, Tyler Noblin, Steven Pantazis, David Rariden, Dennis Rehill, Daniel Retzner, Beumhyeung Rhee, Sean Satterfield, Martin Salas, Corey Schnobrich, Daniel Seagraves, Joshua Smith, Eric Snow, Michael Waldo, Brent Watanabe, Peter Weismantle, Bradley Wilkins, Marc Woodcock
General Contractor	Hyundai Engineering & Construction/ STX JV
Architect of Record	Chang-Jo Architects
Structural Engineer	Thornton Tomasetti
Civil Engineer	V3 Companies
Fire & Life Safety	Rolf Jensen & Associates
Acoustics/Audio Visual	Shen, Milsom & Wilke
Wind Engineer	RWDI
Facade Maintenance	Lerch Bates
Cost Estimating	Construction Cost Systems
Landscape Design	SWA Group

Nur Alem Museum of Future Energy

Design Partners	Adrian Smith and Gordon Gill
Management Partner	Robert Forest
Project Manager	Brian M. Jack and Matthew Dumich
Design Director	Alejandro Stochetti
Senior Designer	Anthony Viola
Interiors Director	Marc Cerone
Sustainability Director	Christopher Drew
Technical Director	Jorge Soler and Sae Hwang Oh
Senior Technical	Lin Kim
Designers/Architects	Iliana Doytcheva, Misha Efremov, Peter Eichberger, Rezvan Farahany, Kyle Faulkner, Natalya Ganyukova, Dimitra Gelagoti, Felix Griggs, Jaclyn Marcus, Melissa Marrero, Chris Miller, Natalia Quintanilla, Katherine Seaver, Matt Simpson, Zilong Tan, Kirsten Weismantle
General Contractor	SEMBOL Construction
Design Manager	IT Engineering
Structural Engineer	Werner Sobek
Facade Access	Altitude Facade Access Consulting
Fire & Life Safety	AON
Building Information Specialist	CASE
Theater Planning/Acoustics	Charcoalblue
Wind Engineer	RWDI
HVAC/MEP Engineer	PositivEnergy Practice
Civil Engineer	V3 Companies
Vertical Transportation	Fortune Shepler Saling
Geotechnical Engineer	GEI Consultants
Construction Manager	Rider Levett Bucknall

Mobility Pavilion

Design Partners	Adrian Smith and Gordon Gill
Management Partner	Robert Forest
Project Manager	Matthew Dumich
Design Director	Alejandro Stochetti
Senior Designer	Anthony Viola
Sustainability Director	Christopher Drew
Senior Technical	Jorge Soler
Designers/Architects	Rafi Al-Alim, Laura Jimenez, Jaeho Jin, Patrick Keeney, Joel Kerner, Hyungwoo Kim, Ryan Kukuraitis, Seoun Lee, Luis Palacio, Andy Park, Natalia Quintanilla, Mario Romero, Zilong Tan, Alex Valverde, Jiajing Xie, Shuonan Yang

Astana Arts Center

Design Partners	Adrian Smith and Gordon Gill
Management Partner	Robert Forest
Project Manager	Brian M. Jack and Matthew Dumich
Design Director	Alejandro Stochetti
Senior Designer	Sobieslaw Fedyk
Sustainability Director	Christopher Drew
Designers/Architects	Allison Conley, Nathen Diestelkamp, Richard Gnat, Patrick Keeney, Natalia Quintanilla, Paul Schroeckenstein

Chicago Architecture Center

Design Partners	Adrian Smith and Gordon Gill
Management Partner	Robert Forest
Project Manager	Jonathan Orlove
Interiors Director	Marc Cerone
Senior Technical	Chad Smith
Designers/Architects	Julie Bartocci, Rebecca Cryder, Ryan Dalgaard, Kiel Fahnstrom, Gail Goldstead, Felix Griggs, Griffin Pemberton, Mario Romero, Jeff Snodgrass, Michelle Swanson
General Contractor	Turner Construction
Structural Engineer	WSP
Exhibit Design	Gallagher & Associates
MEP/FP Engineer	Diligent Design Group
AV/ Acoustic Design	ARUP
AV Design/ Installation	Gand Sound Installations
Signage	Forcade Associates
Lighting	Lightswitch

PROJECT TEAM

1 Dubai Space Show

Design Partners	Adrian Smith and Gordon Gill
Management Partner	Robert Forest
Project Manager	Brian M. Jack and Ben Johnson
Senior Designer	Jeff Stafford
Interiors Director	John Burcher
Technical Director	Peter Weismantle
Designers/Architects	Nicholas Addison, Gabriel Ball, Charles Collett, Joshua Cooper, Reinaldo Correa, Thomas Denney, Robert Finigan, Iris Gan, Brendan Gibbons, Christina Halatsis, Christopher Harvey, Gregg Herman, Travis Howe, Brian Hubbard, Boyka Ivanova, Jeffrey Knapke, Phat Nguyen, Andrew Osvalds, Julia Robertson, Karen Rutherford, Kshitij Sawant, Mordecai Scheckter, Daniel Segraves, Siddant Sinha, Eric Snow, Brett Sterly, Rebecca Stewart, Anthony Trifiletti, Brent Watanabe
General Contractor	EDAW /AECOM
Structural Engineer	Halvorson and Partners
MEP Engineer	Environmental Systems Design
MEP Engineer	Syska Hennessy Group
Civil Engineer	V3 Companies
Mobility Consultant	Hyder Consulting
Vertical Transportation	Fortune Elevator Consultants
Facade Maintenance	Lerch Bates
Wind Engineer	RWDI
Fire & Life Safety	Rolf Jensen & Associates
Design Consultant	Scéno Plus

Shimao Tower Observatory

Design Partners	Adrian Smith and Gordon Gill
Management Partner	Robert Forest
Project Manager	Ben Johnson and Weiwei Luo
Senior Designer	Fei Xu
Sustainability Director	Christopher Drew
Technical Director	Iris Gan
City Design Director	Richard Wilson
Designers/Architects	Tyler Austin, Alexander Bahr, Nicholas Berchtold, Bintou Coulbaly, Sobieslaw Fedyk, Liyuan Ge, Yongsan Huang, Joel Kerner, Soeun Lee, Yuchen Liu, Luis Palacio, Natalia Quintanilla, Jonathan Reyes, Jeff Snodgrass, Maria Sturchio, Zilong Tan, Jing Zhang, Yuxin Zheng, Ruoqi Zhong
Structural Engineer	Thornton Tomasetti
Wind Engineer	RWDI

Kingston Leadership Plaza

Design Partners	Adrian Smith and Gordon Gill
Management Partner	Robert Forest
Project Manager	Ben Johnson
Senior Designer	Luis Palacio
Sustainability Director	Christopher Drew
City Design Director	Richard Wilson
Designers/Architects	Tyler Austin, Jennifer Cooper, Ryan Kukuraitis, Joseph Peltier, Natalia Quintanilla, Jeff Snodgrass, Yueming Zhou

The Portal at Runmao Tower

Design Partners	Adrian Smith and Gordon Gill
Management Partner	Robert Forest
Project Manager	Ben Johnson and Weiwei Luo
Senior Designer (Tower)	Fei Xu
Senior Designer (Portal)	Luis Palacio
Sustainability Director	Christopher Drew
Senior Technical	Iris Gan
Designers/Architects	Nora Ames, Tyler Austin, Alexander Bahr, Nicholas Berchtold, Jennifer Cooper, Rebecca Cryder, Caitlin Dashiell, Sobieslaw Fedyk, Iris Gan, Gail Goldstead, Rebecca Greenberg, Wilson Harkhono, Yongsan Huang, Nash Kennedy, Ryan Kukuraitis, Miaoqi Liu, Yuchen Liu, Melissa Marrero, Joseph Peltier, Natalia Quintanilla, Jonathan Reyes, Thomas Schneider, Zilong Tan, Anthony Viola, Perry Wreaks, Tianyu Xu, Dong Yan, Ailing Zhang, Jing Zhang, Meng Zhang, Ruoqi Zhong, Yeuming Zhou
Local Architect	ECADI
Structual Engineer	Thornton Tomasetti
MEP Engineer	WSP Shanghai
Wind Engineer	RWDI
Landscape Architect	SWA Group
Lighting	Office for Visual Interaction, Inc. (OVI)

Al Wasl Plaza

Design Partners	Adrian Smith and Gordon Gill
Management Partner	Robert Forest
Project Manager	Brian M. Jack and Matthew Dumich
Design Director	Alejandro Stochetti
Interiors Director	Marc Cerone
Sustainability Director	Christopher Drew
Technical Director	Peter Weismantle and Sara Beardsley
City Design Director	Richard Wilson
Designers/Architects	Narjes Abbasabadi, Tyler Austin, Alexander Bahr, Gregory Barber, Nicholas Berchtold, Aaron Berman, Allison Conley, Jennifer Cooper, Rebecca Cryder Stephen Dinnen, Tobias Dold, Kiel Fahnstrom, Kyle Faulkner, Sobieslaw Fedyk, Katrina Fernandez Nova, Gail Goldstead, Felix Griggs, Victoriano Hernandez, Theodore Hogan, Lizhi Jiang, Joel Kerner, Changhoon Kim, Sunghak Ko, Ryan Kukuraitis, Inyong Lee, Soeun Lee, Yifei Li, Miaoqi Liu, Yuchen Liu, Yue Liu, Alvaro Luna, Melissa Marrero, Jose Marti, Cory Mollet, Dilip Muralidharan, Christian Newman, Loran Newman, Sae Hwang Oh, Hazem Owais, Luis Palacio, Griffin Pemberton, Jessica Pfeiffer, Natalia Quintanilla, Daniel Ramos, Hiram Rodriguez, Mario Romero, Michael Sandrzyk, Thomas Schneider, Michaela Singson, Jeff Snodgrass, Donald Stark, Alyson Hurd Sternquist, James Struthers, Michelle Swanson, Jennie Tolfa, Eric Tomich, Pablo Velazquez, Ning Wang, Amber Watkins, Timothy Winstanley, Xi Yi, Yuxin Zheng, Ruoqi Zhong

Architect of Record	e.construct/The Fraser Nag Partnership
General Contractor	Laing O'Rourke
Structural Engineer	Thornton Tomasetti
MEP Engineer	Hoare Lea
Civil Engineer	Langan International
Landscape Architecture	SWA Group
Wind Engineer	RWDI
Immersive Experience	Obscura
Acoustics	Threshold Acoustics LLC
Lighting	Office for Visual Interaction, Inc.
MicroClimate	Klimaat
Water Features	Crystal Fountains
Cost Consulting	Rider Levett Bucknall
Facade Access	Altitude
Fire & Life Safety Engineer	Jensen Hughes Associates
Crowd Modeling	Mobility In Chain
Wayfinding	Forcade
Security and ICT	Mediatech
Waste Management	Tricon
Steel Manufacturer	Cimolai
Projection Pod Manufacturer	Kinetica
AV Integrator	Creative Technology
Projector Manufacturer	Christie
Fabric Mesh Manufacture	Taiyo

Astana Discovery Center

Design Partners	Adrian Smith and Gordon Gill
Management Partner	Robert Forest
Project Manager	Ben Johnson
Senior Designer	Luis Palacio
Interiors Director	Marc Cerone
Sustainability Director	Christopher Drew
City Design Director	Richard Wilson
Technical Director	Sara Beardsley
Designers/Architects	Yuxin Zheng, Yueming Zhou

AWARDS + PUBLICATIONS

Istanbul Cultural Center

AIA Chicago, Unbuilt FORWARD Award, 2018

The Chicago Athenaeum, International Architecture Award, 2016

Architizer A+ Awards, Typology Categories, Cultural: Unbuilt Cultural, Special Mention, 2016

Architectural Review, MIPIM Future Project Award, Cultural Regeneration, Commendation, 2016

WAN Awards, Future Projects, Civic Category, Winner, 2015

Hurriyet Daily News, "US company's project aims to revive unused Istanbul Cultural Center," Brice Altay, March 3, 2016

Willow Creek North Shore

The Chicago Athenaeum, American Architecture Awards, 2017

Daily Herald, "Willow Creek to open North Shore campus designed by Adrian Smith + Gordon Gill Architecture," June 9, 2017

Church Design, "Landmark Design," Carolyn Heinze, March 28, 2017

Chicago Tribune, "World renowned architect designs North Shore church," Manya Brachear Pashman, November 28, 2016

Civil Engineering Magazine, "Church Building Design Features Sweeping Curves and Connection to Nature" Robert Reid, November 2016

Patch, "Unveil New Church in Glenview," Tim Moran, November 30, 2016

Daily North Shore, "Willow Creek Opens Glenview Church," Steve Sadin, November 27, 2016

Architect's Newspaper, "Adrian Smith + Gordon Gill Architecture design 72,000-square-foot Church in Glenview, Illinois," Matthew Messner, May 9, 2016

BD+C, "Adrian Smith + Gordon Gill Architecture incorporates Biblical parable into church design," Mike Chamernik, March 24, 2016

The Yard at Chicago Shakespeare Theater

ENR Midwest Awards, Best Projects, Cultural/Worship, 2018

AIA Innovation Award, Stellar Architecture, Honorable Mention, 2017

The American Architecture Prize, Honorable Mention in Architectural Design, Cultural Architecture, 2017

Chicago Tribune, "Best architecture 2017," Blair Kamin, December 15, 2017

Clad Global, "Chicago Shakespeare Theater unveils intimate and innovative new venue on Navy Pier," Kim Megson, October 4, 2017

Chicago Tribune, "Flexible, intimate and innovative, The Yard at Chicago Shakespeare has its opening night," Blair Kamin, September 20, 2017

ENR Midwest, "Chicago's Flexible, Transforming Theater Space," Jeff Yoders, September 19, 2017

Chicago Magazine, "Chicago Shakes' New Venue Will Let People Reshape the Theater Experience," Brian Golden, September 15, 2020

DNA Info, "Chicago Shakespeare's New Theater At Navy Pier Comes As You Like It," David Matthews, September 13, 2017

Crain's Chicago Business, "First look: The Yard, Navy Pier's new mind-blowing theater," Catey Sullivan, September 13, 2017

Chicago Sun-Times, "With The Yard, Chicago Shakespeare sets engineering poetry in motion," Hedy Weiss, September 13, 2017

American Theatre, "The Yard Beyond the Bard," Kerry Reid, June 29, 2017

BuiltWorlds, "Building & Designing the Theater of Tomorrow | Project Innovation: The Yard at Chicago Shakespeare," December 6, 2016

Newcity, "Stage of the Imagination Assessing Adrian Smith + Gordon Gill Architecture's Expansion of Chicago Shakespeare Theater," Phillip Berger, June 23, 2016

Curbed, "A More Detailed Look at the Chicago Shakespeare Theater Expansion," AJ LaTrace, April 13, 2016

BD+C, "Adrian Smith + Gordon Gill Architecture's The Yard at Chicago Shakespeare to begin construction this spring at Navy Pier," David Malone, April 1, 2016

Chicago Tribune, "New Chicago Shakespeare stage will transform Navy Pier," Chris Jones, March 2, 2016

Steppenwolf Theatre Campus Expansion

AIA Chicago, People's Choice Award, Cultural Cateogry, 2023

Architizer A+ Awards, Hall / Theater, Steppenwolf Theatre Campus Expansion, Finalist, 2023

Architect's Newspaper, Best of Design, Editor's Choice, 2022

AIA Illinois, Honor Award, Excellence in Interior Design, 2022

Chicago Building Congress, Commercial Construction under $50M, Merit Award, 2022

The Architect's Newspaper, "Adrian Smith + Gordon Gill Architecture's expansion of the Steppenwolf Theatre brings the backstage to the house," Anjulie Rao, January 12, 2022

World-Architects, "US Building of the Week: Steppenwolf Theatre Campus Expansion," John Hill, January 24, 2022

The Chicago Crusader, "Chicagoland Youth Artists create original works for Steppenwolf," Bonnie DeShong, March 4, 2022

NewCity, "Steppenwolf Debuts Lefkofsky Center," November 3, 2021

Architectural Record, "Smith+Gill Architecture Expands the Steppenwolf Theater Campus in Chicago, James Gauer, November 4, 2021

Lincoln Park Chamber, "A New Season, A New Building, A New Era at Steppenwolf," March 6, 2020

American Theatre, "Steppenwolf Breaks Ground on New Home," March 8, 2019

Chicago Tribune, "Steppenwolf Theatre, known for bold moves, plans a new $54M theater-in-the-round project," Chris Jones, March 5, 2019

WBEZ, "Steppenwolf Theatre Plans $54 Million Expansion," Carrie Shepherd, March 5, 2019

Chicago Now, "Steppenwolf Theatre to add new building to its campus," Carole Kuhrt Brewer, March 5, 2019

Curbed Chicago, "Steppenwolf expands theater with dramatic, geometric design from Smith + Gill," Jay Koziarz, March 5, 2019

Contract Magazine, "AS+GG Designs Steppenwolf Theatre Expansion," Mallory Szczepanski, October 8, 2014

FKI Tower Conference Podium

The Architecture Master Prize, Architectural Design, Tall Buildings, Winner, 2017

Re-Thinking the Future, Sustainability, First Award, Commercial, 2016

AIA Chicago, Divine Detail Award, FKI Tower BIPV, 2016

The Chicago Athenaeum, International Architecture Award, FKI Tower

The Chicago Athenaeum, Green Good Design Award, Green Architecture, FKI Tower, 2015

Civic Trust Awards, Civic Trust Award, FKI Tower, 2015

Korean Architecture Award, Excellence Award, FKI Tower, 2014

Korea Presidential Commission on Architecture Policy, Korea Green Building Award, FKI Tower, 2014

AIA Chicago, Distinguished Building Award, Citation of Merit, FKI Tower, 2014

CTBUH, Best Tall Building Asia and Australasia, Finalist, FKI Tower, 2014

SEAOI, Excellence in Structural Engineering Award, Best Project $150 million and over, Winner, 2014

Architizer A+ Award, Office Building High Rise, Finalist, 2014

Design Diffusion, "Playing with Angles," Manuela Di Mari, May 2016

American-Architects Magazine, "Building of the Week: FKI Tower," John Hill, January 2015

Civil Engineering, "Angled Facade Boosts Energy Efficiency," Kevin Wilcox, February 25, 2014

Architect Magazine, "Adrian Smith + Gordon Gill Architecture Open New Headquarters for FKI," Caroline Massie, January 28, 2014

World Architecture News, "Unique facade for FKI headquarters," January 24, 2014

BD+C, "Adrian Smith + Gordon Gill-designed Federation of Korean Industries tower opens in Seoul," January 23, 2014

Inhabitat, "Korean Tower Boasts One of World's Most Efficient Solar Facades," Andrew Michler, October 29, 2010

Concept Magazine, "New Head Office of the Federation of Korean Industries," May 2010

Architect's Newspaper, "Unveiled: Federation of Korean Industries Tower," Alan G. Brake, February 11, 2010

AWARDS + PUBLICATIONS

Nur Alem Museum of Future Energy

The Chicago Athenaeum, American Architecture Award, 2019

Global Architecture & Design Awards, Cultural Projects, Built, Second Award, 2018

AIA Tap Innovation Awards, Stellar Design, Astana Expo City, 2016

Dezeen, "Nine examples of spherical architecture from around the globe," Tom Ravenscroft, August 29, 2020

ArchDaily, "Expo 2017 Legacy: World's Largest Sphere," October 12, 2017

New York Times, "Can a Giant Science Fair Transform Kazakhstan's Economy?" David Segal, September 9, 2017

Dezeen, "Architects unveil energy-themed pavilions at Astana Expo 2017," Jessica Mairs, June 20, 2017

Architect's Newspaper, "Adrian Smith + Gordon Gill's ambitious glass sphere pavilion," Heather Corcoran, August 11, 2017

Departures Magazine, "Expo 2017: Astana Unveiled," Nathan Turner, April 20, 2017

Architectural Record, "Adrian Smith + Gordon Gill's Massive Astana Expo City Nears Completion," Anna Fixen, March 1, 2017

Building Design + Construction, "How to make a 'pure' glass sphere," Robert Cassidy, February 18, 2016

Dezeen, "Adrian Smith + Gordon Gill Architecture to design Astana Expo 2017," October 23, 2013

Astana Arts Center

The Chicago Athenaeum, International Architecture Awards, 2019

Rethinking the Future, Global Architecture & Design Awards, Cultural Category, First Award, 2019

AIA Chicago, Unbuilt FORWARD Award, 2018

Chicago Architecture Center

AIA National, Interior Architecture Award, 2021

AIA Chicago, Interior Architecture Award, 2020

The Magnificent Mile Association, Business Impact of the Year, 2019

Friends of Downtown, Best New Attraction, 2019

Chicago Commercial Real Estate Awards, Special Achievement of the Year, 2019

USA Today, 10 Best Readers' Choice, Top Five Best New Attractions, 2019

Offsite, "Chicago's Architecture Center Shines," Geneva Vest, February 19, 2019

Architect's Newspaper, "The new Chicago Architecture Center offers informative, tangible experiences," Elisabeth Blasius, September 6, 2018

Architect Magazine, "Look Inside the New Chicago Architecture Center," Sara Johnson, August 31, 2018

Curbed, "Chicago Architecture Center debuts new riverfront location to the public," Jay Koziarz, August 31, 2018

WBEZ, "What's That Building? The Chicago Architecture Center," Dennis Rodkin, August 30, 2018

Chicago Magazine, "The Chicago Architecture Center Opens Tomorrow. Here's What to See," AJ LaTrace, August 30, 2018

Chicago Tribune, "The Chicago Architecture Foundation has a new name and a new home," Blair Kamin, August 29, 2018

Chicago Sun-Times, "Chicago Architecture Center takes its place as 'must-see' cultural destination," Fran Spielman, August 29, 2018

Chicago Reader, "The Chicago Architecture Foundation is now the Chicago Architecture Center, Deanna Isaacs, August 29, 2018

Chicago Business Journal, "Chicago Architecture Center opens," Lewis Lazare, August 29, 2018

1 Dubai Space Show

L'espresso, "The new design is born," J. Caracciolo Falck, January 15, 2009

Identity Magazine, "The future is now," Dorothy Waldman, November 2008

Cityscape Magazine, "New look for old," Clair Malcolm, November 2008

Building, "The tallest building in the world: the contenders," Dan Stewart, October 14, 2008

World Architecture News, "Meraas Development taps Adrian Smith + Gordon Gill for megaproject," Sharon McHugh

Chicago Sun-Times, "Looking Up..." David Roeder, October 8, 2008

Chicago Tribune, "Chicago architects plan more towers in Dubai," Blair Kamin, October 7, 2008

The National, "Dubai sees no reason to stop scraping skies," Bradley Hope, October 6, 2008

The Portal at Runmao Tower

Architectural Record, "On the Boards: a Museum, Towers, and New Urban Waterfronts," Josephine Minutillo, January 27, 2020

Architect Magazine, "South HeXi Yuzui Financial District and Tower,", November 6, 2019

The Nanjnger, "500 Metres High! Tallest Building in Nanjing Set for Change," Frank Hossack, April 1, 2020

World Architecture News, "500 meter tower to achieve LEED-Gold," Katie Henry, November 26, 2019

New Atlas, "Sculpted supertall skyscraper will boast energy-efficient design," Adam Williams, November 13, 2019

Building Construction + Design, "AS+GG releases design scheme for the South HeXi Yuzui Financial District and Tower," David Malone, November 6, 2019

Shimao Tower Observatory

Architect's Newspaper, "Adrian Smith + Gordon Gill designs tallest building in China," January 16, 2019

Dezeen, "Adrian Smith + Gordon Gill reveals design for China's tallest skyscraper," Lizzie Cook, January 14, 2019

Building Design + Construction, "AS+GG-designed tower will be the tallest in China," David Malone, January 14, 2019

Arch Daily, "Adrian Smith + Gordon Gill to Design China's Tallest Skyscraper," Eric Baldwin, January 11, 2019

Al Wasl Plaza

MIPIM Awards, Best Cultural, Sports & Education Project, Recognition of Excellence, Finalist, 2023

Rethinking the Future, Cultural Category, First Award, 2022

The Chicago Athenaeum, International Architecture Award, 2021

The Chicago Athenaeum, Green Good Design Award, 2021

Prestige, "These Are Expo 2020 Dubai's Most Breathtaking Pavilions," January 28, 2022

Clairn, "Un Jardin urbano y un domo traslucido, el corazon de Dubai," Graciela Baduel, February 22, 2022

The National, "Ten attractions to continue at Expo 2020 Dubai, from UAE pavilion to famous water illusion," Ramola Talwar Badam, March 1, 2022

The New York Times, "A World-Class World Expo," October 24, 2021

Architect's Newspaper, "Expo 2020 Dubai teases blossoming pavilions ahead of rescheduled festival," Matt Hickman, October 14, 2020

Designboom, "Expo 2020 Dubai Reveals Pavilions," October 6, 2020

Arch Daily, "One Year to Go: Expo 2020 Reveals Latest Pavilions as the Event Moves Forward," Christele Harrouk, October 5, 2020

Dezeen, "Dubai Expo reveals main pavilions ahead of rescheduled event," Tom Ravenscroft, October 1, 2020

Dezeen, "Nine examples of spherical architecture from around the globe," Tom Ravenscroft, August 29, 2020

*Wallpaper**, "Exploring The Dubai Expo's architecture in progress," Harriet Thorpe, May 28, 2020

Construction Week Online, "Expo 2020 Dubai video features HE Reem Al Hashimy praising Al Wasl Plaza," Neha Bhatia, September 19, 2019

Construction Business News, "Expo 2020 Dubai lifts final piece of Al Wasl Plaza's dome into place," Kasun Illankoon, September 9, 2019

MEED, "Al-Wasl Plaza dome adorned with steel crown," September 18, 2019

Gulf News, "Al Wasl Plaza at Expo 2020 site to offer a variety of experiences," April 17, 2017

Forbes Middle East, "A New Breathtaking Hall Is In The Making For Expo 2020 Dubai," Amro Elserty, April 5, 2017

PHOTOGRAPHY + IMAGES

Istanbul Cultural Center pp. 10-35

All images and drawings © Adrian Smith + Gordon Gill Architecture

Shattuck St. Mary's Performance Hall pp. 36-49

All images and drawings © Adrian Smith + Gordon Gill Architecture

Astana Energy Hall pp. 50-67

Photographs by Leyla Kabdi pp. 50-51, 59, 60-61

Photograph by Paul Raftery p. 55

All other photographs and drawings © Adrian Smith + Gordon Gill Architecture

Congress Center pp. 68-89

Photographs by Leyla Kabdi pp. 68-69, 73, 80-81

All other photographs and drawings © Adrian Smith + Gordon Gill Architecture

Willow Creek North Shore pp. 90-113

Photographs by Tom Rossiter pp. 90-91, 93, 99, 102, 103, 104, 105, 106-107, 111, 113

All other photographs and drawings © Adrian Smith + Gordon Gill Architecture

The Yard at Chicago Shakespeare Theater pp. 114-131

Photographs by James Steinkamp pp. 114-115, 116, 118, 119, 124-125

Photograph by Hannah Kennedy p. 120

Photograph Joe Mazza p. 120

Photograph by Michael Litchfield p. 120

Photographs by Chuck Osgood pp. 122, 123

Photographs by Vito Palmisano pp. 127, 131

Drawings by Charcoalblue pp. 121, 127

Rendering by Chicago Shakespeare Theater p. 127

All other photographs and drawings © Adrian Smith + Gordon Gill Architecture

Steppenwolf Theatre Campus Expansion pp. 132-153

Photographs by James Steinkamp pp. 132-133, 135, 137, 139, 143, 145, 146, 147, 148-149, 151, 152, 153

All other images and drawings © Adrian Smith + Gordon Gill Architecture

FKI Tower Conference Podium pp. 156-171

Photographs by Namgoong Sun pp. 156-157, 159, 161, 162, 163, 164, 165, 166-167, 168, 169

All other photographs and drawings by © Adrian Smith + Gordon Gill Architecture

Nur Alem Museum of Future Energy pp. 172-191

Photograph by Parilov at Shutterstock p. 174

Photograph by Boris Stroujko at Shutterstock p. 175

Photograph by Ilyas Mukhambetzhanov pp. 184-185

Photograph by National Company Astana Expo 2017 p. 187

Photograph by Nick Melnichenko p. 191

All other photographs and drawings © Adrian Smith + Gordon Gill Architecture

Astana Arts Center pp. 192-207

All images and drawings © Adrian Smith + Gordon Gill Architecture

Chicago Architecture Center pp. 208-229

Photographs by Anthony Tahlier p. 154-155 (Ch. 2 Intro), 216

Photographs by James Steinkamp pp. 208-209, 211, 2012, 213, 214, 215, 217, 218, 219, 220, 221, 222-223, 224, 225, 226, 227, 228-229

All other photographs and drawings © Adrian Smith + Gordon Gill Architecture

Mobility Pavilion pp. 230-245

All images and drawings by © Adrian Smith + Gordon Gill Architecture

1 Dubai Space Show pp. 248-263

Images by Scéno Plus pages 258, 259

All other images and drawings © Adrian Smith + Gordon Gill Architecture

Kingston Leadership Plaza pp. 264-275

All images and drawings © Adrian Smith + Gordon Gill Architecture

The Portal at Runmao Tower pp. 276-293

All images and drawings © Adrian Smith + Gordon Gill Architecture

Shinmao Tower Observatory pp. 294-305

All images and drawings © Adrian Smith + Gordon Gill Architecture

Al Wasl Plaza pp. 306-329

Photograph by David Lloyd © SWA Group, pp. 306-307

Photographs by Expo 2020 Dubai LLC pp. 310, 320-321, 323, 325

Photograph by Sandeep Revadigar page 319

Photograph by Junell Cornejo pp. 312-313

Photograph by RAW-films at Shutterstock pp. 328-329

All other images and drawings © Adrian Smith + Gordon Gill Architecture

Astana Discovery Center pp. 330-343

All images and drawings by © Adrian Smith + Gordon Gill Architecture